# The Young John Muir

*Frontispiece.* John Muir, Madison, Wisconsin, 1863. Photographer unknown. (Courtesy John Muir Papers, Holt-Atherton Department of Special Collections, University of the Pacific Libraries. Copyright © 1984 Muir-Hanna Trust)

# The Young John Muir

AN ENVIRONMENTAL BIOGRAPHY

*Steven J. Holmes*

THE UNIVERSITY OF WISCONSIN PRESS

The University of Wisconsin Press
2537 Daniels Street
Madison, Wisconsin 53718

3 Henrietta Street
London WC2E 8LU, England

1     3     5     4     2

Printed in the United States of America

Library of Congress Cataloging-in-Publication Data
Holmes, Steven J. (Steven Jon), 1960–
The young John Muir : an environmental biography / Steven J.
Holmes.
326 pp.     cm.
Includes bibliographical references (p. 289) and index.
ISBN 0-299-16150-1 (cloth : alk. paper).
ISBN 0-299-16154-4 (pbk. : alk. paper).
1. Muir, John, 1838–1914.   2. Naturalists—United States—
Biography.   3. Conservationists—United States—Biography.
I. Title.
QH31.M9H65—1999
333.7'2'092—dc21
[B]                                                    98-44888

To my mother,
Anne Marie Oderkirk

The potential space between baby and mother, between child and family, between individual and society or the world, depends on experience which leads to trust. It can be looked upon as sacred to the individual in that it is here that the individual experiences creative living.

D. W. Winnicott

There was a child went forth every day,
And the first object he looked upon and received
   with wonder or pity or love or dread,
   that object he became,
And that object became part of him for the day or
   a certain part of the day . . .
   or for many years or stretching cycles of years.

Walt Whitman

# Contents

# Illustrations

# Acknowledgments

*O love*
*that fires the sun*
*keep me burning*

To all who have made this book what it is, and have made me what I am, thanks.

Lawrence Buell of Harvard University has provided steady guidance, insightful critique, and cheerful support for this project, from its beginnings as a dissertation to the present form. Additional ideas and encouragement have come from David D. Hall and William R. Hutchison of Harvard Divinity School, John Elder of Middlebury College, John Tallmadge of the Union Institute, John McDargh of Boston College, Robert Orsi of Indiana University, and Dennis Williams of Southern Nazarene University, as well as from the anonymous readers of an aborted article for *Environmental History*. The style and color of my thinking owe much to my earlier study with Werner Sollors and Stephan Thernstrom at Harvard University; Richard Niebuhr and Sharon Welch at Harvard Divinity School; John S. Dunne at the University of Notre Dame; and Larry Alderink and especially Tom Christenson at Concordia College.

I am indebted also to all of the various colleagues, administrators, and libraries—too numerous to name—who have helped me over my academic career. In particular, Harvard Divinity School and Harvard University's programs in American Civilization and in History and Literature have been invigorating and supportive communities of scholars and friends. Thanks to Kay Shanahan, Christine McFadden, Cynthia Fabiano, Marcia Dambry, Alan Heimert, and Janice Thaddeus for their administrative and support work, i.e., for making things happen. Thanks also to Daryl Morrison and the staff at the Holt-Atherton Department of Special Collections at the University of the Pacific, for facilitating use of the John Muir papers and microfilm. Mary Elizabeth Braun and others at the University of Wisconsin Press have been helpful, insightful, encouraging, and fun to work with during the long process from book proposal to publication. I have also learned much about bookmaking and the book business—among other less professional things—from my friends and former coworkers at Syracuse University Press, the Harvard Divinity School Bookstore, and the Andover-Harvard Theological Library.

Special thanks to my students, for all you have taught me.

### Some kind of ecstasy got a hold on me

Music has done much to shape and empower my thought, my heart, and my life. Particular thanks to the Grateful Dead, Peter Gabriel, The Pentangle/John Renbourn Group, R.E.M., and Beethoven for beauty, energy, and a creative melding of musical styles that has nourished my own interdisciplinary ideals; to Bob Dylan, Jackson Browne, and the Indigo Girls (Amy Ray and Emily Saliers) for passion, political commitment, guts, and human insight; and most especially to Bruce Cockburn, for all of these gifts and more—for the lines from his songs I have chosen to grace these pages and for the music and visions that flow through my body, heart, and mind.

Thanks also to artists such as Chagall, Botticelli, and the nameless medieval fashioners of stained glass in England and France, for the gifts of elemental color, shape, and living light.

### There's love in the world but it's hard to find

My deepest gratitude and love to all of my friends, for companionship, ideas, joy, challenges, and fun. For support, style, substance, and sanity during my time working on this project, I would especially like to thank Gillian Andrews, Cynthia Baker, Lundy Bancroft, Pleun Bouricius, Ken Del Po, Barry Fink, Rachel Freudenburg, Becky Gould, Soren Hauge, Barbara Haugen, Cheryl Henderson, Leon Jackson, Christopher Kowalski, Molly McMillan, Michael McNally, Seth Mirsky, John O'Keefe, Katy Payne, Rachel C. Rasmussen, Kathleen Skerret, Libby Smith, Sue Smith, Mike Yarrow, and the Ithaca Friends Meeting. And the kids: Alice, Fabi, and Liam.

My partner, Carlene Pavlos—your heart, smile, will, and mind have multiplied my life by the power of two (to adapt a phrase from the Indigo Girls). Thanks, Dearie.

I thank my family, with gratitude, respect, and happiness: my mother, Anne Oderkirk, to whom this book is dedicated; my father, Fred Holmes; my stepmother, Ann Newton Holmes; my late stepfather, Dean Oderkirk;

and my brothers, Brian and Keith Holmes. To quote Muir: "I still feel you all as the chief wealth of my inmost soul and the most necessary element of my life."

*All the diamonds in this world*
*that mean anything to me*

Finally: Waterdog Pond, Conn Creek, Golden Gate Park, the mountains and woods and coastline of northern California; Maple Lake, Carlos State Park, Itasca, the Red River of the North, the sweet rancid incense of cows and the crispness of growing corn, the back roads and farms and waters and woods of Minnesota and the upper Midwest; Niagara Falls and Chimney Bluffs; Buttermilk Falls in autumn, Taughannock Falls in winter, Ithaca Falls in spring, the rhododendrons in the Cornell Arboretum, the sweet wonders and fields of Fall Creek; little purple flowers everywhere; a sunsparkling drop of water held gently by a flower's petals in a crack in a rock high in the Rockies; jade waves pounding, diamond foam caressing the rocks of Star Island and the Cliffs of Moher; rain dripping from a flaming young maple in New Hampshire; the apple blossoms and dancing bees, the happy crocuses and sudden purple fire of early azaleas in Cambridge; Arnold Arboretum, the flowing cherry trees, the gift-bearing dogwoods and magnolias and lindens, Hemlock Hill, the spreading beds and blankets of scilla all in bloom, in bloom—my heart in bloom.

To all who have made this book what it is, and have made me what I am, thanks.

*Quelqu'un danse comme une flamme!*

*The Young John Muir*

# Introduction

# Reimagining Muir,
# Remapping Biography

For scholars and the general public alike, John Muir (1838–1914) has come to stand as one of the patron saints of twentieth-century American environmental activity, both political and recreational. Perhaps uniquely, Muir's presence is felt on all levels of culture: his writings are regularly discussed in academic books and journals, his legacy is powerfully invoked in concrete political debate and activism, and his sayings and visage appear on countless Sierra Club calendars, greeting cards, picture books, and so on. On a deeper level, Muir has profoundly shaped the very categories through which Americans understand and envision their relationships with the natural world. More than any other comparable figure, Muir's cultural influence has been expressed in a series of vivid images of his personal relationships with particular natural places. This is not by accident; indeed, one of his own primary literary tactics—as well as a recurring rhetorical strategy within the environmental movement—was to offer his life story as the embodiment of a more generalizable model of a certain sort of personal experience of the natural world. Clearly, the tactic has worked, as Muir's presence—as ecological thinker, as political spokesman, as religious prophet, and most of all as a personal guide into nature—has become almost ubiquitous in late-twentieth-century environmental consciousness. It may not be too much to say that Muir constitutes contemporary America's preeminent image of the "Green Man," an enduring mythic figure in Western culture that (in William Anderson's words) exemplifies "the archetype of our oneness with the earth."

A detailed study of cultural images of Muir could constitute a mini-history of modern American romantic attitudes toward nature. Here, however, I will only briefly outline three of the most influential of these motifs: the young Muir as "wild child"; the dramatic story of his "ecstatic conversion" in Yosemite Valley, as the focal point of a religiously inflected relationship to the natural world; and an equally pervasive domestic language of the natural world as his own "true home."

The image of Muir as wild child forms the core of his autobiographical reminiscence *The Story of My Boyhood and Youth* (1913), which was originally intended as a moral tale for children but has come to be regarded as an environmental classic by adults as well. Reflecting standard romantic associations between childhood and the natural world, the first paragraph locates the roots of his lifelong affinity with nature in an "inherited wildness": "When I was a boy in Scotland I was fond of everything that was wild, and all my life I've been growing fonder and fonder of wild places and wild creatures. Fortunately around my native town of Dunbar, by the stormy North Sea, there was no lack of wildness, though most of the land lay in smooth cultivation. . . . after I was five or six years old I ran away to the seashore or the fields almost every Saturday, and every day in the school vacations except Sundays." Mentioning the attempts of his father to discipline and control this wildness by confining the young boy to the backyard—and foreshadowing the familial conflict that would be one of the main themes of the book—Muir asserts the overriding power of his inner call: "In spite of the sure sore punishments that followed like shadows, the natural inherited wildness in our blood ran true on its glorious course as invincible and unstoppable as the stars" (1–2). The formative power of this primal energy flows through all the twists and turns of Muir's coming-of-age story, culminating in his graduation from college and into a life of immersion in nature: "There with streaming eyes I bade my blessed Alma Mater farewell. But I was only leaving one University for another, the Wisconsin University for the University of the Wilderness" (286–87). The maternal imagery implies that this was a sort of rebirth, a second childhood, allowing Muir to continue to be a wild child even as an adult. Indeed, although as a public figure he often is referred to as the "father of American environmentalism," as a private individual he is probably more often understood as a "son of the wilderness" (the title of Linnie Marsh Wolfe's influential biography).

Underlying this wild child motif is a religious dimension that comes into full bloom in the language with which he commonly describes his adult experiences of nature, perhaps epitomized in the story of his initial encounter with Yosemite in 1869, at age thirty-one. As presented in *My First Summer in the Sierra* (1911), this story (in John Tallmadge's words) "embodies his mature beliefs about how human beings can achieve and sustain a healthy relationship with the land" (62). According to biographer Frederick Turner, the entry for June 6 "blazes from the page with the authentic force of a conversion experience" (172).

We are now in the mountains and they are in us, kindling enthusiasm, making every nerve quiver, filling every pore and cell of us. Our flesh-and-bone tabernacle seems transparent as glass to the beauty about us, as if truly an inseparable part of it, thrilling with the air and trees, streams and rocks, in the waves of the sun,—a part of all nature, neither old nor young, sick nor well, but immortal. Just now I can hardly conceive of any bodily condition dependant on food or breath any more than the ground or the sky. How glorious a conversion, so complete and wholesome it is, scarce memory enough of old bondage days left as a standpoint to view it from! In this newness of life we seem to have been so always. (*First Summer*, 20–21)

Such ecstatic experiences would recur throughout his career in the mountains, leading to a keen and intimate awareness of—and personal dependence on—the presence of the divine in nature; an 1890 comment (in Alaska) was just as applicable to himself as to the natural world: "Every particle of rock or water or air has God by its side leading it the way it should go. How else would it know where to go and what to do?" (*John of the Mountains*, 319). Other of his aphorisms—"The clearest way into the Universe is through a forest wilderness"; "In God's wildness is the hope of the world" (adapted from Thoreau)—have gained wide currency in popular environmental culture. Thus, in various forms, a religious dimension characterized both his experiences of the natural world and the political and literary activities resulting from such experiences; in Catherine Albanese's words, "To go to the mountains and the sequoia forests, for Muir, was to engage in religious worship of utter seriousness and dedication; to come down from the mountains and preach the gospel of preservation was to live out his life according to the ethic that his religion compelled" (101).

Somewhat more subtly but no less pervasively, at crucial points Muir uses the metaphor of "home" in explicating his relationship with nature—and even in describing the natural world itself. His keen, scientifically trained observations were often couched in domestic language, as he constantly saw nature providing a home for its inhabitants; for example, remembering a tiny flower in a storm on the coast of Cuba, he wrote that "the little purple plant, tended by its Maker, closed its petals, crouched low in its crevice of a home, and enjoyed the storm in safety" (*John of the Mountains*, 57). Moreover, nature provided a home for Muir as well, most powerfully in Yosemite, which in letters to friends he would refer to as "God's mountain mansion"; eventually, he imagined his bonds with Yosemite in more intimate, familial terms: "The very stones seem talkative, sympathetic, brotherly. No wonder when we consider that we all have the same Father and Mother" (*First Summer,* 319). Accordingly, such language provided the basis for many of his most politically influential essays: "Thousands of tired, nerve-shaken, over-civilized people are beginning to find out that going to the mountains is going home; that wilderness is a necessity; and that mountain parks and reservations are useful not only as fountains of timber and irrigating rivers, but as fountains of life" (*Our National Parks,* 1). Indeed, his assertion that "going to the mountains is going home" expresses both one of his major rhetorical tactics in promoting wilderness preservation and one of the underlying personal dynamics of his own life. Thus, Frederick Garber's characterization of Thoreau may be equally applicable to Muir: "Getting the self to be at home in the world became the main business of [his] life, the single and central vocation to which all other forms were subsidiary" ("Henry David Thoreau," 399–400). For Muir (as for Thoreau), however, this "central vocation" at times involved a deep tension with his actual home and family; as he told a visitor to his Martinez, California, farm in 1903, "'This is a good place to be housed in during stormy weather, . . . to write in, and to raise children in, but it is not my home. Up there,' pointing towards the Sierra Nevada, 'is my home'" (quoted in Fox, 74).

Whether diffused through published texts, popular images, or oral history and legend, these images of Muir's patterns of relationship with the natural world have enjoyed great popularity. Countless environmentalists, backpackers, general readers, and academics have felt a personal relationship with Muir, and with nature through Muir; scholar Michael P. Cohen writes that his book about Muir "is also a book about my own thinking; and not only my own thinking, but the thinking of a whole community, of my generation. Muir has always had a special place in our hearts, and we have often thought of him while we sat around campfires, walked through the woods, or climbed the walls of Yosemite" (xiii). Despite this great interest, however, the core images of Muir's life have come under relatively little critical analysis. Or rather: it is perhaps *because of* the sway that they have held over the minds and hearts of many of those concerned about the environment that such images of Muir have become in a sense sacrosanct, and thus have escaped scholarly scrutiny or public critique. However, it is clearly time for a reevaluation of these images and of Muir's life as a whole, both on scholarly and on conceptual—even moral—grounds.

In the scholarly realm, most students of Muir have uncritically accepted and repeated the basic narratives and themes of his earliest biographers, William Frederic Badè and Linnie Marsh Wolfe—and behind them, of Muir's own self-presentation in his autobiographical books. However, these traditional interpretations are suspect in a variety of ways.

For example, at the level of textual criticism, while it has long been known among scholars that the influential *My First Summer in the Sierra* was based upon a revised version of the original journal, it usually has been presumed that the published book follows the original journal fairly closely. The situation is much more complex than this, however. No original journal exists; the handwritten notebooks upon which the book was based actually date from 1887. Moreover, a close analysis suggests that these notebooks include extensive revisions and additions made to the original journal between 1869 and 1887, in part undertaken for the specific purpose of *creating* an ideal model of a dramatic, transformative encounter with wilderness (see appendix A). Thus, we cannot take these 1887 notebooks (and even less, the published *First Summer*) as biographically accurate; in particular, many of the most characteristic elements that have long been associated with Muir's 1869 entry into Yosemite—including his language and experience of becoming "a part of all nature" through a dramatic, ecstatic "conversion" and total reorientation of his life—must be understood not as his immediate, intuitive responses to Yosemite but rather as the self-conscious results of his later literary and philosophical development. Thus, on sheer textual grounds, we must reopen the questions of what Muir experienced when he first entered Yosemite, what it meant to him, and what it might mean for us. (A somewhat different—and less extensive—textual analysis and conceptual reconsideration are required for the journal that is the basis of another of Muir's most influential works, *A Thousand-Mile Walk to the Gulf;* see appendix B.)

Other problems lie more in interpretation than in materials. For example, the broader religious dimension of Muir's relationship with nature has been a favorite subject of speculative analysis, with a startling—even baffling—array of results. To mention just a few major scholars, Michael P. Cohen uses Buddhist and Taoist concepts to interpret Muir's life and religious thought; Catherine Albanese argues that Muir lived out the transcendentalist worldview that Emerson and others had developed earlier in the century; Dennis Williams concludes that "Muir was neither a Buddhist nor a Taoist nor even a transcendentalist" but rather a Protestant mystic, whose God "was a unique, personal being, the creator and loving father of the world, both immanently still creating and managing it, and transcendentally separate from it" (96); and Max Oelschlaeger, strongly influenced by Charles Hartshorne's process thought as well as by deep ecology, sees Muir as regaining a biocentric evolutionary pantheism that Western culture had lost since the Neolithic age. Which is the real Muir? Obviously, within present scholarship Muir's religiousness itself has become a multivalent symbol, capable of being filled with a wide variety of meanings and contents.

By contrast, Muir's childhood autobiography has been read fairly monochromatically, through the lens of a romantic wild child image that in fact leads us to ignore many of the actual events of the narrative: the young boy's fascination with hunting and with viciously competitive childhood games, his wholesale commitment to environmentally destructive farming practices, and his evocative descriptions of pain and death in nature. When such negative images are acknowledged, they usually are discussed solely with reference to Muir's relationship with an oppressive father, thus defusing any troubling implications for an idealized childhood harmony with nature (see for example the introduction to the Sierra Club edition of *The Story of My Boyhood and Youth*). Similarly above— or beneath—scholarly critique has been Muir's use of domestic language, the cultural influence of which is evident in the omnipresent "nature as home" slogans of late-twentieth-century environmental consciousness. In one of the few scholarly discussions of Muir in terms of domesticity, Michael Smith (96–98) focuses only on Muir's adult political rhetoric and literary and scientific imagery, not on his personal biography or emotional life. More commonly, many commentators—both popular and scholarly—simply repeat Muir's own language of "coming home to the mountains" with no reflection or analysis. Indeed, Muir's language presents a seldom-acknowledged difficulty: despite the consistency of his usage of the term "home," he often does *not* employ specific domestic imagery in describing the natural landscape, giving a somewhat barren or schematic language that resists further interpretation in terms of the usual cultural motifs. In the absence of more definite imagery or references, the simple invocation of "nature as home" leaves scholars with few openings for a detailed historical analysis—at the same time as it invites each reader to fill the gap with their own set of personal memories and associations. Here as in the case of the wild child motif, our prevailing romantic assumptions have allowed us to accept Muir's language at face value, without confronting the inconsistencies or probing the dynamics of the life story contained within it.

Moreover, such scholarly problems reflect deeper conceptual and moral issues. How is it possible for such a diverse array of images or models of relationship with nature to coexist in a single, integrated life? Indeed, on the surface, some of these images seem contradictory: If Muir only grew in "inherited wildness" from childhood on, what need could he have had of a specific conversion experience? How could a solitary, ecstatic conversion experience fit into the rhythms and relationships of a "domestic" relationship with nature? Whether for Muir's life or our own, are these patterns—individually or together—really liveable? Do they really work as ways of orienting ourselves to our natural surroundings and of relating to the particular environments of our lives with depth, power, feeling, flexibility? Is the Muir myth—or, rather, myths—adequate for conceiving, grounding, and expanding our own relationships with the natural world?

Clearly, the patterns embodied in the traditional accounts of Muir's life have been attractive, inspiring, and empowering for many persons over the past century. If I question the scholarly accuracy and conceptual adequacy of such patterns, I do so with a keen sense of the moral urgency of these issues; my goal in reinterpreting Muir is not to debunk him but to reexamine the Muir myth in a way that I believe may touch our lives even more deeply.

But if we cannot trust the traditional stories, how *can* we understand the processes by which the natural world came to hold such meaning and power in Muir's inner life and in his subsequent cultural legacy? For those interested in more general questions, what can Muir's life—as opposed to his own self-presentation or the resulting cultural mythology—teach us about (in Tallmadge's words) "how human beings can achieve and sustain a healthy relationship with the land"? In addressing these questions, it is essential that we strive to see the human being behind the myth, and strive to see him whole—from all sides, not only those that accord with our political or cultural goals or assumptions. In particular, we must place the traditional images of Muir in the full context of what I have come to call his *environmental biography,* a richly textured account of the development of his patterns of relationship with the specific environments—natural, domestic, and built—in which he lived and moved and had his being over the course of his lifetime. Such a consideration must include the ways in which his relationships with particular places were shaped and given meaning through personal psychological dynamics, through specific ideas and feelings, through interpersonal relationships, through cultural influences and social structures, through the memories and images of the loved (or feared) places of his past, and through his apprehensions of the larger forces and powers of the universe. At the same time, we must be sensitive to the individual's power to see, feel, imagine, and act in new ways, to respond creatively and spontaneously to each encounter with a new environment. Finally, we must acknowledge and explore the power of the environment itself in requiring or evoking new patterns of imagery, feeling, and behavior on the part of humans, thus constituting an independent actor in an individual's life. In the case of Muir, of course, it was the *natural* environment in particular that held most power in his life (or, at least, holds most interest for us now), and so his environmental biography affords an opportunity to focus primarily (though by no means exclusively) upon one individual's life-in-nature.

But how shall we write environmental biography? What insights and images can help us understand the development of Muir's—or anyone's—lifelong relationship with their surroundings, particularly the natural world? To my knowledge, no one has proposed a coherent framework for understanding the personal, psychological, and spiritual dimensions of a concrete individual's experience of specific environments over time. To be sure, a number of scholars have seen the need for such a framework; in one early instance, Gaston Bachelard proposes an "auxiliary of psychoanalysis" that he calls "topoanalysis," "the systematic psychological study of the sites of our intimate lives." For Bachelard, it is through the memory of the places of solitude that we know ourselves and discover our creativity: "And all the spaces of our past moments of solitude, the spaces in which we have suffered from solitude, enjoyed, desired and compromised solitude, remain indelible within us, and precisely because the human being wants them to remain so." Correlatively, we must attend to a more exterior dimension as well, those places that have "invited us to come out of ourselves," those roads, paths, and fields that have drawn us outward into action and adventure in the world (8, 10, 11). More generally, in the introduction to a pioneering application of psychological categories to the nonhuman environment, Harold Searles writes:

> The thesis of this volume is that the nonhuman environment, far from being of little or no account to human personality development, constitutes one of the most basically important ingredients of human psychological existence. It is my conviction that there is within the human individual a sense, whether at a conscious or unconscious level, of *relatedness to his nonhuman environment*, that this relatedness is one of the transcendentally important facts of human living, that—as with other very important circumstances in human existence—it is a source of ambivalent feelings to him, and that, finally, if he tries to ignore its importance to himself, he does so at peril to his psychological well-being. (5–6)

Although neither Bachelard nor Searles—nor any of their successors in environmental philosophy or psychology or in humanistic geography—gives a full account of individual environmental development, their approaches and insights provide fertile soil from which further reflections may emerge.

In a similar vein, my historical reconstruction of one person's life-in-nature—that of John Muir—stresses the inner dimension, as I look for the psychological and spiritual dynamics of self-construction and of meaning-making, for the spark that is struck when cultural symbols, environmental realities, and historical circumstances scrape against a living, breathing, growing human being. As theorists at least since Freud and

William James have realized, the symbolic ideas, images, and actions that on their "external" side are the stuff of religion and culture are, on their "internal" side, the stuff of psychological and emotional development. Of course, traditional Freudianism has been the major approach in the exploration of the affective and symbolic dimensions of interactions with the physical environment, particularly the natural landscape (in the field of American cultural history, see, e.g., Annette Kolodny and Richard Slotkin). However, in striving to speak both about the historical-cultural and about the individual, my explorations of Muir's life and world have been informed by a more recent formulation of psychoanalysis, the object relations approach.

Traditional psychoanalysis focuses most attention on the emergence of distinct psychic patterns and energies within the mind and body, regarding the external world (especially other persons) mainly as a stimulus or setting for internal development. However, if one chooses to pay equal attention to the interpersonal dimension of human existence, the whole course and character of human development become saturated with the presence and power of those with whom one is in relationship. It is the longing for relationship with other persons—not the sheer expression of drives or the fulfillment of needs—that object relations theorists see as the core of human psychic life. Drives, pleasures, needs, repression, and so on—all the stuff of Freudianism—make sense not as autonomous or independent inner forces but as players in the drama of interpersonal relationships; indeed, these psychological dynamics are merely tools in the ongoing project of establishing and maintaining relationship with others.

With respect to the two central notions of traditional Freudianism, the Oedipus complex and libido as sexuality and as aggression, I find the object relations interpretations to be sensitive and compelling—and directly relevant for environmental biography. Instead of presuming a standard inner conflict regarding mother, father, and child—the Oedipus complex—as the basis of lifelong patterns of psychological life, an object relations approach takes the time to discern *which* relationships in fact are most important in an individual's childhood, and how these relationships set up long-term patterns that both shape and are shaped by the experiences of one's later life. In particular, in asserting the formative power of the pre-oedipal years, object relations theorists have explored the importance of the child's earliest relationship with the mother—but have also acknowledged that the mother's influence is mediated, shaped, and augmented by a whole range of relationships with other persons, symbols, and objects such as toys, each with its own special place and meaning in the child's (and, later, the adult's) psychic world. In understanding environmental experience, however, the scope of object relations theory must be expanded to include relationships with one's total environment—with natural beings and processes, with the built environment, and even with the beings and forces of the supernatural or religious realms—as well as with other human persons and creations. In contrast to a narrow focus on the human world, *all* of these types of beings and presences must be regarded as possible proper participants in fundamentally important relationships, images, and desires. (For the details of my expansion of object relations theory—among other theoretical issues— see appendix C.) Might Muir's childhood love for—or fear of—a particular *place* have had as powerful a psychological influence and meaning as his love or fear of another person? Might his experiences with particular plants or animals have formed his inner life and longing? What were the dynamics of such environmental love and fear, and how did they shape his subsequent memories of particular natural or domestic places? How did these emotions, attachments, and memories intersect with the feelings and images of his relationships with humans—or with the powers and beings not of this world, ghosts or spirits or God? What were the legacies, continuations, and re-creations of these processes and dynamics as the child grew into the adult?

Similarly, rather than presuming (as does traditional Freudianism) the primacy of sexual and aggressive drives as the force behind a person's interpersonal and symbolic patterns, an object relations approach opens up a wider array of possible "primal" (sometimes also "mature") motivations and meanings—most important a fundamental longing for supportive, nurturing, and mutual relationships. According to Anna Freud, "a baby wants to love its mother with all its bodily powers" (quoted in Milner, *Hands*, xx); I would go further and say that a mature person may want to love other persons, home, the natural world, and the divine with all of his or her bodily, emotional, intellectual, and cultural powers. Such love is perhaps best understood as *eros*, which Audre Lorde defines as "those physical, emotional, and psychic expressions of what is deepest and strongest and richest within each of us, shared; the passions of love, in its deepest meanings" (56); and such rich and deep passions may characterize our relationships with home, with the divine, and—perhaps most important for understanding Muir—with the natural world as well as with other persons.

The range of ways of loving—the breadth of eros—involves an implicit vision of human motivation, indeed of the fundamental realities of human being. On my view, these involve such traditional psychological concerns as the quests for security and relationship, for trust and autonomy, and for engagement and control, as well as the acknowledged powers of sexuality and aggression—but also such nonpsychological dimensions as sheer curiosity, friendship, communal identity, truth, beauty, hope, justice, moral value, a visceral and energized aliveness in one's own body, an openness to the world, contact with the rhythms and patterns of nature, religious centeredness, and ecstatic experience. This is a multilayered and intricate life we lead, and a rich array of possible meanings, motivations, and energies is needed to capture the depth and poignancy of each twist, turn, and glance of such a life.

Finally, in striving to understand the relationships and motivations that shape and express the environmental biography of a concrete individual, we must attend to the developmental and historically conditioned character of all dimensions of inner and outer life. On the one hand, the individual's psychological structures and meanings are constantly in developmental and biographical motion; on the other hand, both culture and society move constantly along their own trajectories of historical change. In each life, biographical development and historical conditions merge and mingle to create one complex, multifaceted reality. We make ourselves in social context—or, our society perpetuates itself through us—on a number of deep levels: gender identity, roles, privileges, and oppressions; sexual patterns and energies; racial and class structure and consciousness; ethnic or national identity, allegiance, and indoctrination; aesthetic sense and spirituality; visions and concrete realities of body and family, birth and death; the shape and texture of eros itself; and more, much more. Along with the specific gravity that each of these dimensions of human being brings to a particular heart, mind, and flesh over the course of a life, they each contribute—to varying degrees—to the texture and structure of that person's images of and relationships with his or her natural and built environments.

Moreover, the places and beings of the nonhuman world are not a static setting for these human developments but themselves undergo constant change and growth according to both internal and external dynamics. The literal shape and the ecological character of each particular environment within which life is lived evolve under natural and human forces, and the symbolic meanings of those environments are further transformed through other levels of cultural, social, and physical change. At the intersection of all this change stands the person, actively forging a world and selfhood through interpretation, meaning, choice, and bodily presence. This triple-conditionedness—developmental, historical, and environmental—runs through all of the dimensions of human life, forcing me to constantly ground my assertions and interpretations in the available material on Muir's life, times, and places.

Thus, in searching out an appropriate conceptual perspective for environmental biography, I find myself undertaking cultural biography, religious biography, and psychosocial biography as well. As I pursue the hints and shadows of Muir's life-in-nature, the object relations approach allows me to weave together insights from a variety of fields—environmental psychology and ethics, humanistic geography, social and cultural history, gender and ethnic studies, literary criticism, and religious studies—in analyzing the inner dimensions of an individual's relationship with particular environments over the course of a life, and in relating those environmental experiences to broader issues of self, society, and cultural context. Interestingly, despite the suspicion with which I have come to regard the Muir myth, I am drawn back to some of its basic images as starting points for developing a more nuanced understanding of environmental experience and development: the wild child theme (reinterpreted more broadly as the developmental origins of relationship with nature), religiousness, and domesticity. As noted above, there is much truth in these motifs, both for an understanding of Muir and for an understanding of our own lives and experiences of the natural world; as with most myths, the historical power of these images arises because they do touch something deep within us. Given this power, I have no intention of wholly excising them from our story of Muir but rather mean to reinterpret them, seeing and feeling them afresh.

In the end, however, significant aspects of Muir's experience are doubtless irreducible to psychological or historical analysis, no matter how broadly conceived. Despite my obvious attraction to various theoretical perspectives, I do not present them as giving a complete description of the inner forces and dynamics—much less the meanings—of Muir's life. Rather, we must give appropriate (and appreciative) attention and value to the unique and spontaneous aspects of Muir's being, his capacities for wonder, courage, choice, and creativity in his encounters with the human and natural worlds. In doing so, I am looking for what the existentialists would call "freedom," Muir's fundamental human power to *do something,* and perhaps do something *new,* with the developmental patterns and the actual relationships that he has been given. In an intricate and astonishing dance, Muir (like all of us) simultaneously was shaped by his patterns and circumstances and possessed the power to shape them, was chosen by and chose the elements of his life and world. In Whitman's phrases, "Apart from the pulling and hauling stands what I am . . . / Both in and out of the game and watching and wondering at it" ("Song of Myself," section 4). Ultimately, at the core of all the cultural, historical, environmental, and psychostructural conditionings, all the bright and textured facets of what we call life—meaning, color, feeling, thought, word, story, memory, hope—are made real in the fire of one's own action of body, mind, and heart. This process is perhaps ineffable (in the mystical sense), or fundamental in a way that reaches beneath psychological or disciplinary categories and into those depths of life that can only be understood wordlessly, through living, and sometimes not understood at all. I want most of all to respect and honor these depths, writing not only to analyze but to express my own wonder and hope that human life includes such moments of encounter, strength, and creativity. Even with respect to those aspects of his life and being that *can* be fruitfully analyzed in conceptual terms, I do not intend my explorations of these themes to explain them away; the personal and cultural achievements embodied in Muir's experience of the natural world as a religious home for humans are in no way invalidated (and in fact are strengthened and reaffirmed) by glimpsing the concrete dynamics and challenges—as well as the mysteries and gaps—that provided the materials and motivation for those achievements. It may well be not through theory or analysis that we come to our deepest understandings but through the felt companionship of another person's life story, as a spur and guide to reflection upon our own.

In this book, I give a detailed environmental biography of Muir's early years, up to and including his initial encounter with Yosemite, with a special focus on the dynamics and meanings of his relationship with the natural world. Given the importance of the young Muir in recent environmental rhetoric and consciousness, such a reevaluation is important in itself; it also provides the basis for a continuing reconfiguration of our understandings of his later life, though I do not attempt that in this work. Moreover, the process of developing a theoretical framework useful for environmental biography may help us to reimagine the patterns and meanings of our own interactions with the natural world; given the lack of an accepted interpretive framework for environmental biography, I engage in more theoretical discussion than is usual in a regular biography. Rather than attempting to develop a comprehensive synthesis of all of my interpretive disciplines—a monumental task—I shall introduce specific theoretical insights as they help me to understand concrete issues in Muir's life and development. (I should explain that much of my scholarly discussion takes place in the notes, leaving the main text as a relatively straightforward narrative; I encourage the general reader to explore the interpretive issues further by consulting the notes at any points of particular interest. Again, a more sustained and abstract presentation of the theoretical underpinnings that guide my analysis is found in appendix C.) At the same time, with my own historicist and humanist bent, I suspect that any single theoretical approach would have to be refigured and perhaps wholly recast for each different historical period and cultural context—and perhaps even for each natural setting or individual subject. Thus, I tackle the conceptual issues not in order to propose a full-scale theory but rather as an occasion for exploring an individual's life with a certain sort of depth and sensitivity, the details of which may or may not be applicable to anyone but Muir himself. (Of course, as will become obvious, I do believe that at least some of the major themes in fact *are* more widely relevant.) The core of this book is not theoretical analysis but biography, reflecting my conviction that the best way of apprehending the power and dynamics of relationship with nature—or of any aspect of human living—is through immersion in the concrete details and narrative shape of a particular life.

My goal, then, is to reconstruct Muir's early life from the ground up, as part of a wider project of reimagining the inner dynamics of human interactions with the natural world. In particular, Muir's own languages of childhood wildness, of religion, and of domesticity can be richly refracted both through historical and through theoretical lenses; in this way, his mythic images can be more closely tied to his concrete experience and being, to his encounters with particular natural and domestic environments, human relationships, and religious realities over the course of his life. Muir's relationship with nature was a much more complex, ambiguous, and shifting affair than has been previously recognized, involving the full range of human emotions—anger as well as love, fear as well as ecstacy, dependence as well as self-assertion. Triangulating between historical and biographical evidence, theoretical frameworks, and my own insights and sensitivities, I offer a story in which we can see Muir—and perhaps ourselves—through new eyes.

# One

## *Fostered Alike by Beauty and by Fear*
### Scotland and Wisconsin, 1838–1856

John Muir was born on April 21, 1838, as the third child and first son of
a middle-class family in Dunbar, on the east coast of Scotland. His father,
Daniel Muir, had come to Dunbar in 1829 (at age twenty-five) as a military recruiting agent, but soon married a woman who had inherited a
grain-and-feed store; Daniel took over the business and continued it after his first wife's early death. His second wife, Ann Gilrye, was the
daughter of a meat merchant who had himself migrated to Dunbar from
Northumberland, thirty-five years before. A religious seeker—perhaps
zealot—for much of his life, Daniel prohibited pictures, music, and other
adornments from his house, forcing Ann to pour her attention and creative energy into the couple's beautiful walled-in backyard garden, an occupation in which Daniel delighted as well. Soon, however, Ann's life was
taken up with children: Margaret in 1834, Sarah two years later, then
John, David, Dan, and the twins Mary and Anna; a final daughter, Jo-
anna, would be born later in America. The family (with servants) lived
upstairs from the store, in a large stone house in the High Street business district.[1]

The first reported event of Muir's life occurred at age two, at his infant
brother David's vaccination (*Boyhood*, 11). John, apprehensive about the
tall black-coated doctor hovering over the newborn, was initially reassured by his mother's compliance. When he saw blood being drawn from

---

1. The basic facts of Muir's life can be found in any of the previous biographies, the
most complete of which are Turner and L. Wolfe, from which the material for this paragraph
is drawn. Our primary material on Muir's childhood comes from his own adult reports: the
original draft of his autobiography, dictated to a stenographer in 1908 (often referred to as
the Pelican Bay manuscript); a 1910 revision; and the further revised version published in
1913 as *The Story of My Boyhood and Youth*. The three versions are substantially similar,
while differing in a number of details and occasionally in style; I shall quote from the published version for convenience, with reference to the earlier forms when appropriate.

David's arm, however, he could restrain himself no longer, and he jumped up and bit the doctor's own arm—only to be astonished when both doctor and mother responded by laughing at him! Mundane and amusing as this little vignette is, it captures several crucial psychological dynamics. Muir's initial turn to his mother for guidance and reassurance suggests that this was the usual relationship between the two—a common but nevertheless monumental achievement in the development of a young child. An infant's task in the first months (and perhaps years) of life is to negotiate the fundamental challenges of order/chaos and pleasure/pain in such a way as to come to a felt sense of confidence that the world is responsive to and supportive of his or her existence, that the world is fundamentally *for* rather than *against* him or her. Because the first world of the infant is most importantly his or her mother (in those cultures where the mother is the primary caregiver, that is), it is in the mother/infant relationship that this felt sense of confidence or basic trust initially develops (or fails to develop). Indeed, at the earliest stages, the infant cannot distinguish his or her own body and will from those of the primary caregiver; through appropriate physical presence and loving attention, the caregiver constitutes what D. W. Winnicott calls the infant's *holding environment,* the felt reality of physical and emotional support that evokes, strengthens, and guides the emergence of the child's own capacities for self-awareness and assertion. Out of the primal unity, the process of separation (or individuation) paradoxically depends on the successful maintenance—and internalization—of the powerful bonds and emotional patterns of the initial relationship. By age two, Muir had come to feel himself as a separate being in some ways but not in others, with both separation and connection grounded in the sense of confidence and basic trust exemplified in his turn toward his mother.[2]

---

2. Erik Erikson describes basic trust as "a sense of being 'all right'" and "a deep, almost somatic conviction that there is a meaning in what [one is] doing" (103); his insight into the bodily basis of this trust accords with the object relations notion of a simultaneously physical and emotional holding environment. Moreover, in asserting that the achievement of such trust depends on "the quality of the maternal relationship," Erikson recognizes the importance of what D. W. Winnicott calls "good-enough mothering": "The mother's adaptation to the infant's needs, when good enough, gives the infant the illusion that there is an external reality that corresponds to the infant's own capacity to create" (Winnicott, *Playing and Reality,* 12). It is only when the infant experiences the mother/world as responding to his or her needs and wants that those needs and wants—and thus the baby's body and being—seem worthwhile, meaningful, and real. Thus, the "illusion" of correspondence, i.e., the experienced continuity between infant and mother/world, is the basis for an initial sense of expectation, trust, meaning, and creative energy. For further discussion of the holding environment and of other object relations concepts (given in italics in the text), see appendix C.

Moreover, this relationship was the basis for Muir's ability to act on his own, even in a way that went against his mother's actions. In yelling and biting the doctor, he expressed both his anxiety in the face of the threatening figure and his own growing ability to assert control over external situation and internal anxiety. Significantly, he was rebuffed by laughter—not in a way that would fatally undercut his confidence in self and world, but nevertheless signaling the need for its transformation. What did his "astonishment" feel like, and mean, to the two-year-old? On the one hand, it probably contained a strong element of gratification at once again being the center of attention, and so Muir experienced his mother's laughter as a slyly comforting affirmation of her concern for him. On the other hand, like it or not, even this regained attention placed the mother/child relationship on a different footing, in the context of Ann Muir's need to turn away from her first son to answer the appropriate needs of a succession of further children. In fact, her ambiguous laughter created (or, rather, continued and echoed an earlier process of the creation of) a *potential space* between mother and child, an emotionally charged relationship within which Muir was free—or, was forced—to assert a more independent will, body, and mind, while still being held by (and himself actively maintaining his connection with) the most important being in his world. Not incidentally, his response to the situation included the creation of a new self-role within which the maternal qualities of attending, caring, and protecting could be internalized and thus perpetuated in his own relationship with his brother. Perhaps it was this felt need for the creation of a new role and relationship—in answer to the increased ambiguity arising in his relationship with his mother—that branded this early incident onto Muir's memory, to be remembered in all its clarity some seventy years later.[3]

Along with their effects on his human relationships, these early psychological dynamics and challenges also shaped and saturated Muir's ex-

3. According to Erikson, "The general state of trust . . . implies not only that one has learned to rely on the sameness and continuity of the outer providers but also that one may trust oneself and the capacity of one's own organs to cope with urges" (102). In more traditionally Freudian terms, this sort of trust involves libidinal object constancy, attained through "an integrated maternal representation that can function to provide comfort and support in mother's absence," based in increasing trust that she (even if absent) will respond to the child's distress with comfort, and further in the child's internalization of this expectation into a capacity to comfort him or herself (Tyson and Tyson, 106). At the same time, as Winnicott stresses, it is the appropriate "failure" of the mother to protect or serve the child in all situations that forces the child to become real to him/herself, and external objects to become real (as capable of being the cause of frustration and hatred as well as of satisfaction and love). That is, a disruption in primal confidence is necessary as a stimulus and window toward the development of the capacity to relate to self and to others.

periences of the physical environment, including the natural world. Indeed, the larger environment is a psychic presence from the beginning; at the earliest stages, the human and the nonhuman worlds are not distinct but intertwined, forming a continuous realm in which the developing capacities both for subjectivity and for relationship can flourish. In particular, the infant's nonhuman surroundings are part of the entire holding environment; thus, the fundamental experience of maternal holding and basic trust has its counterpart in the child's sense of confidence in relation to the physical world—as a result of a similarly complex and fragile process. Just as the newborn's body and will are not yet differentiated from those of the primary caregiver, so too does the infant's being blend with that of the nonhuman world, in all its chaos *and* harmony, all its threat *and* its comfort. As the developing human pulls together a sense of individual body and selfhood out of the "blooming, buzzing confusion" (in William James's phrase), he or she must both encounter and create experiences of a physical world that is *for* rather than *against* that body and selfhood—experiences that are dependent equally upon the primary caregiver's presence and guidance, the infant's own powers of imagination and assertion, and the warmth, support, and aliveness of the world itself.[4]

As one element in this process, an increased sense of the nonhuman world as welcoming is evoked—paradoxically—by the redirection of the emotions of an originally successful maternal relationship. Against the backdrop of the development of trust and confidence in the earliest mother-child relationship, an experience of the mother's unavailability (for whatever reason) moves the child to turn to other objects—from a teddy bear or blanket to pets, the grass upon which one lies, or (when just a little older) significant experiences of special places or scenes—for support, warmth, confidence, holding. The ability of such objects to provide support depends both upon the child's previous experiences of the larger environment *and* on his or her imaginative ability to invest these objects with some of the feelings and meanings previously experienced in relation to the mother. By the latter process, such objects serve as what

4. Discussing the legacy of this process in adult life, Searles observes: "Not only do we have unconscious memory traces of infantile experiences in which we were surrounded by a chaotically uncontrollable nonhuman environment that was sensed as being part of us; in addition, we presumably have unconscious memory traces of our experience of losing a nonhuman environment which had been sensed, heretofore, as a harmonious extension of our world-embracing self" (39). (For a discussion of the child's immersion in the world that emphasizes the harmonious and positive elements, see Barrows.) In general, Searles gives what is still the most sustained and detailed formulation of the role and meaning of the nonhuman environment in human emotional development; his provocative ideas and materials augment and extend many of the dynamics I discern in one particular life, that of Muir.

Winnicott calls *transitional phenomena,* allowing the sense of basic trust and confidence that was developed in the earliest relationship with the mother to spill over into the other beings of the world, compensating for any loss in the felt presence of the mother—and adding to the child's trust and confidence in the physical environment itself. The process can take place even in the full presence of the mother, when the infant's attention is directed—or merely wanders—away from the mother to the larger world; in Wordsworth's description,

> Is there a flower, to which he points with hand
> Too weak to gather it, already love
> Drawn from love's purest earthly fount for him
> Hath beautified that flower. . . .
>
> *(Prelude* II:245–48)[5]

Thus, on one level, the emotions of the young child's experiences of nature reflect both the fullness of the mother-infant relationship and its ambiguity, both the felt reality of the mother's crucial contributions to a past holding environment and the powerful, even desperate, need to reconstitute such an environment in the face of change. At the same time, the child's relationship with the natural world itself carries its own load of emotion and challenge, shaped by and shaping his or her inner life in ways parallel to human relationships. From their origins in earliest infancy, these dynamics and goals run through the whole of childhood development—indeed, through the twists and turns of an entire life.

Although no incidents illustrate the direct presence of Ann Muir in John's childhood introduction to his natural surroundings, his maternal grandfather (who lived just across the street) was particularly important to him: "My earliest recollections of the country were gained on short walks with my grandfather when I was perhaps not over three years old. On one of these walks grandfather took me to Lord Lauderdale's gardens, where I saw figs growing against a sunny wall and tasted some of them, and got as many apples to eat as I wished" *(Boyhood,* 2–3). Especially for a child, such experiences of place are deeply associated with people, as self, other persons, and world are confronted, negotiated, and reconstructed, each in the intimate presence of other. In this incident, Muir still

---

5. This whole section of *The Prelude* (II:233–65) parallels Winnicott. The flower serves as a transitional object, created by the "Poetic spirit," which—"creator and receiver both, / Working but in alliance with the works / Which it beholds"—exists and works in the potential spaces between mother and infant and between infant and the natural world. I should perhaps stress that in this context, I am considering Wordsworth as a theoretician, as himself a sort of proto–object relations environmental psychologist, rather than as a historical cultural influence on Muir (though he *was* the latter as well).

responded to situations largely through his mouth, biting and incorporating with more pleasant results than in the vaccination episode, but also
used sight and movement in exploring and claiming an expanding human, natural, and built environment. On another walk with his grandfather, John heard a sharp sound in a haycock, and discovered a tiny field
mouse with even tinier babies; aside from being particularly accessible,
attractive, and delightful to the boy's developing senses, these warm,
small, struggling, protected animals provided a way for Muir to see himself and his own place in the world. (Additionally, the meaning of the
incident may have been shaped in part by Burns's poem "To a Mouse,"
either in childhood experience or in adult memory; see Cohen, 343.) The
fact that the child's companion in these experiences was his mother's father suggests that the gardens, apples, and field mice were actors in a dual
process of maintaining a relationship with his mother and of negotiating
his increased separation from her—as well as being the subjects of new,
open-ended relationships in their own right.

However, just as the human world held threats, mysteries, and challenges, so too did the natural world, and again the two realms were
closely related.

> I well remember among the awful experiences of childhood being taken
> by the servant to the seashore when I was between two and three years
> old, stripped at the side of a deep pool in the rocks, plunged into it among
> crawling crawfish and slippery wriggling snake-like eels, and drawn up
> gasping and shrieking only to be plunged down again and again. As the
> time approached for this terrible bathing, I used to hide in the darkest cor-
> ners of the house, and oftentimes a long search was required to find me.
> (*Boyhood*, 16–17)

While Muir's visceral terror at the pools and eels was undoubtably real,
such experiences also served as symbolic expressions of a whole range
of anxieties, fears, and opportunities that beset a growing two-year-old.
Moving through these situations with more or less success—through actively mastering things himself, having someone else do so, or perhaps
most often finding that the threat wasn't as bad as he had feared and
could be endured—helped Muir to maintain and extend a sense of basic
trust in other persons and in an increasingly differentiated environment.
At the same time, his adventures in the world called forth or strengthened
new capacities of heart and body, including the ability to hold within
himself an increasingly complex range of emotions and energies. Thus,
his psychic life spread itself—and was dragged—through the places and
pathways of his childhood geography, which at this point encompassed

home, garden, neighborhood, and limited areas of seashore and countryside.

This childhood world expanded significantly at age three, when Muir entered primary school, where he would stay until about seven or eight. The short march up the street to the Davel Brae schoolhouse, located on a hill overlooking the sea, would have far-reaching implications—psychological, social, and imaginative as well as intellectual. Perhaps significantly, it was under the guidance of Grandfather Gilrye that Muir had already learned his letters and numbers from street signs and the big town clock, and so his grandfather's paternal/maternal presence may have accompanied Muir as he entered school, easing the shock of transition and guiding his physical, mental, and emotional journey into his new self and world.

Perhaps most profoundly, going to school marked the passage from a primarily female-associated domestic world to the male-dominated (and, as we shall see, increasingly masculine) official world of the classroom and unofficial world of the schoolyard, providing a geographical and social location for the young boy's developing senses of male identity and of male privilege.[6] To be sure, Muir's initial male identity and privilege were grounded in and shaped by his earlier experiences of women, girls, and home. Many of the psychological dynamics described above in relation to his mother probably operated (to a lesser degree) in Muir's relationships with his sisters as well, especially given the Scots tradition of the elder daughters as "mothering" the younger sons (L. M. Wolfe, 12); further, he clearly felt attended to and held by the family's servant girls, despite the negative associations of the seaside bathings and other incidents. On the one hand, then, the preschool boy's place at the center of a household of attentive and caring women itself constituted powerful forms of male identity and privilege; on the other hand, the passage out

6. By male privilege I mean the array of powers, benefits, freedoms, and expectations—of self and of world—that are systematically accorded males in a male-centered society. Although the two dimensions are importantly related, male privilege is distinct from male identity: the latter refers to who a person *is* as a male, the former to what he can *do* as a male, both constructs operating on both internal/psychological and external/sociopolitical levels. Conceptually at least, it is possible to have a male identity without claiming male privilege, or to assert male privilege without a strong inner sense of male identity; moreover, privilege and oppression also work themselves out in other contexts—social and economic class, race, education, and so on—each of which can intersect with specifically male privilege in various corroborative or conflicting ways. I am indebted to Gillian Andrews, Lundy Bancroft, and Carlene Pavlos (working primarily in the realm of domestic violence) for helping and pushing me to see male privilege as a powerful interpretive category—and more important, as a reality in the world.

of that domestic world in a socially regulated manner taught new lessons of what he as a male could be in the world and what he could expect to do in and to receive from that world. Indeed, the adult Muir's description of his first day at school captures the female support behind the young boy's entry into a new world: "I remember the servant washing my face and getting soap in my eyes, and mother hanging a little green bag with my first book in it around my neck, and its blowing back in the sea-wind like a flag" (*Boyhood,* 3–4). Strikingly, although girls in this region of Scotland attended school at up to 80 percent of the rate for boys (R. D. Anderson, 109–13), Muir's adult reminiscences mention only boys as schoolmates; gender segregation within the classroom—and even more out on the schoolyard—would have made Muir's social experience of school highly gender-specific, with the power of maleness if anything increased by the immediate presence of girls as explicitly second-class persons.

With respect to the academic side of his experience in primary school, the adult Muir recalled the feelings of pride that the schoolboy came to feel in the "grand triumphal advancement" (*Boyhood,* 4) from one spelling-book to the next. Of course, such emotional motivations for success at word manipulation probably far outstripped any real intellectual engagement with the content of education, given the young boy's limited capacities for abstract thought and the focus on rote memorization of language skills that characterized his early school years; this was probably also true of his father's demands that he memorize hymns and Bible verses, for which the reward was a penny and paternal approval (until at some point his father reversed his tactics and utilized punishment by whipping to motivate young John). In any case, the tendency of children to completely miss or ignore the intended content of religious language is perfectly captured in the adult Muir's description of singing in school: "[T]he best of all was 'Lord, dismiss us with Thy blessing,' though at that time the most significant part I fear was the first three words" (*Boyhood,* 10).

In time, however, the words began to mean something—intellectually, emotionally, and morally—to the boy, as revealed by his reactions to the stories that he read in (or, probably, was read from) schoolbooks, most memorably "Llewellyn's Dog" and "The Inchcape Bell." In the former, a hunter kills his favorite dog under the mistaken impression that the dog has killed his infant son, only to find that the dog had in fact saved the son from a huge wolf; in the latter, a wicked pirate destroys a warning bell that a good-hearted priest had placed upon a dangerous rock, only to meet his death in a storm on that same rock. The original draft of Muir's autobiography stresses the official moral lessons of the stories, the hasty and irrational judgments of Llewellyn and of Ralph the Rover leading to disastrous outcomes for both of them.[7] However, it is hard to see these interpretations as the source of the extreme emotional effects on Muir and his young classmates—constant rereading and crying for hours— reported by the adult. The explanation given in the published *Story of My Boyhood and Youth,* a child's natural sympathy with animals, seems somewhat closer to the mark but is dictated by the political and cultural goals of the adult (as part of a moral argument against the inhumane treatment of animals). Perhaps the real point of connection to the schoolchildren's lives came through a more primal identification with the dog, whose fate dramatized their own experiences of unjust punishment, and with the infant son, whose seemingly miraculous delivery from violence may also have been reassuring to the little children amid their own real and imagined dangers. Even the official lessons of the stories, justice and fateful retribution, may have been understood by the children not so much on a moral plane as in terms of their basic trust in the ways of the human and of the natural worlds.

Alongside this early exposure to (and appropriation of) the official educational, moral, and religious culture—and probably more important in the inner life of the young Muir—was his increased contact with the unofficial culture of childhood stories, folk customs, and supernatural beliefs. Some of these he undoubtedly encountered in song, for according to a late autobiographical fragment, "[m]y first conscious memory is the singing of ballads, and I doubt not they will be ringing in my ears when I am dying" (Turner, 16), but more specific sources and materials can also be discerned. For example, continuing his story of the awful seashore bathings, Muir reports that a few years later he had come to enjoy swimming with other boys in the deep pools; the earlier danger and revulsion had receded and coalesced into a specific supernatural entity, "an invisible boy-devouring monster" at the bottom of the pools, called by tradition "sookin-in-goats" and easily avoidable through carefully testing the waters (*Boyhood,* 17). Not only did the older boy possess more physical prowess and self-control than previously, he also had a means of exter-

7. The various versions of Muir's autobiography contain conflicting information as to the published sources of these stories. One possible source, Chambers's *Moral Class-Book* (mentioned in the 1910 revision of the autobiography), in a later (1856) version is arranged as a series of moral lessons, complete with appropriate biblical quotations at the end of each chapter. "Llewellyn's Dog" is included under the category "Moderation in anger— forbearance and forgiveness," while "The Inchcape Bell" is presented as an encouragement to "Conscientiousness in the avoidance of wanton mischief." Whatever the source, Muir probably received these or similar moral and biblical teachings in the same breath as the story itself.

nalizing any lingering anxiety (as well as remembered fears) in a justifiable, localized, and socially understood manner, through the name and symbolic reality supplied by folk tradition.

In particular, the family's servant girls strongly shaped young John's expanding experience of the world through their images, actions, and stories. Muir and his siblings were "instructed by the servants in the nature, looks, and habits of the various black and white ghosts, boowuzzies, and witches" (*Boyhood*, 19) and heard common tales concerning them; the story of Tam O'Shanter (whether in Burns's version or another is unclear) suggested to the impressionable children that such supernatural beings could be escaped by simply outrunning them. In another instance, the servants and children took a more active role in cultural creation, inspired by a historical incident in which an Edinburgh innkeeper sold the bodies of the homeless dead (some of whom he had killed) to the medical school for autopsies. Muir and his child community brought together their perceptions of the external world, inner childhood fears, and supernatural imagery to create the Dandy Doctors, whose "business method, as the servants explained it, was with lightning quickness to clap a sticking-plaster on the face of a scholar [i.e. schoolboy], covering mouth and nose, preventing breathing or crying for help, then pop us under his long black cloak and carry us to Edinburgh to be sold and sliced into small pieces for folk to learn how we were made" (7). The Dandy Doctors terrorized the children of the town for months, fulfilling at least some of the myriad psychological and social needs that such figures are created to fulfill, which for Muir probably included the need to concretize present and past fears in a form that could be dealt with simply by running away from it.

Interestingly, Muir also chose to confront these and other fears more directly, through another servant-generated doctor figure—the ghost of a previous inhabitant of the house into which the Muir family had recently moved, who (according to the servants) haunted a second-floor room containing old laboratory equipment. One of John and David's early "scootchers" (games of daring) was seeing how far they could each go into the haunted room at night, before fear drove them back out. In the original version of his autobiography, Muir revealingly relates that "we took pleasure in seeing how far we could frighten ourselves without getting caught with the ghosts" (46:11636).[8] The sense of an almost physical pleasure at learning to control both body and emotion suggests that Muir

---

8. As explained in the Works Cited, parenthetical references are to the microfilm edition of the collected papers of John Muir, by reel and frame numbers (e.g., this reference is to reel 46, frame 11636).

was struggling to familiarize himself with his own growing body as well as with the strange new house. The same motives are evident in the Muir boys' most famous "scootcher," hanging (by two hands, then one hand, then one finger) out of their third-floor window, then climbing out onto the slippery roof in the face of a strong wind.[9]

This new home was the setting for more innocent experiences as well. The very fact of John and David's having their own room, away from adults, allowed and encouraged increased senses of privacy and of self-assertion; however, the fact that it was a shared room meant that their privacy itself was also shared, their selfhood was not as individuals but as a pair.[10] In particular, this sense of shared identity was developed and expressed in new forms of play; as one instance, it was at this time that the boys began in their bedtime play to imaginatively explore the distant countries about which they had heard in school.

> After mother had carefully covered us, bade us goodnight and gone down-stairs, we set out on our travels. Burrowing like moles, we visited France, India, America, Australia, New Zealand, and all the places we had ever heard of; our travels never ending until we fell asleep. When mother came to take a last look at us, before she went to bed, to see that we were covered, we were oftentimes covered so well that she had difficulty in finding us, for we were hidden in all sorts of positions where sleep happened to overtake us, but in the morning we always found ourselves in good order, lying straight like gude bairns, she said. (*Boyhood*, 22–23)

Thus, the boys' first playful encounters with the lands of the Scottish diaspora included both a spirit of independence and adventure and the in-

9. Exploring the ways in which, "[s]tarting with childhood, our explorations in and around home allow us to develop a sense of self as individuals," Clare Cooper Marcus writes: "While many childhood memories relate to places found or built—homes-away-from-home—most of us also recall some environments that scared us, a setting we returned to, and dared ourselves to enter, to overcome our fears. It might have been the neighborhood 'haunted house,' a spooky place in the basement, a dark alley, or part of the schoolyard where a bully might confront us" (12, 30). Throughout Muir's childhood, such places of fear—from the terrible seaside pools to these experiences in the new house and on to Dunbar castle and the school grounds (discussed below)—served as occasions for physical as well as emotional testing and growth.

10. According to Maxine Wolfe, the creation of a sense of selfhood through privacy occurs both through increased control of social interactions and through the growing ability to manage or to withhold information or to make up stories and pranks. Similarly, Proshansky and Fabian (27–29) stress the importance of the child's own room in the development of a sense of separate self-identity, but they also point out the ways in which the larger home provides an arena for learning cooperation with others. In the case of a shared bedroom, it seems most correct to speak of an aspect of cooperative or shared privacy and identity developing within the bedroom itself.

timate (though unconscious) presence, guidance, and holding of their mother.

Moreover, it was in the backyard garden of the new house, which Muir's father (and probably his mother as well) tried to make "as much like Eden as possible" (*Boyhood*, 12), that young John first discovered the delights of flowers. As with the field mice, flowers provided the boy with attractive, accessible objects in which to pour some of his emotions of wonder, care, curiosity, and joy, intertwined with supportive and prized familial associations. The reverence and awe with which he regarded his aunt's "sacred" lilies, beautiful and untouchable in her corner of the garden, contrasts with the active, tactile curiosity shown as the children dug up their own little plots of beans and peas every day, to see how far they had grown. A memorable flower show at the schoolhouse, and (presumably) continued walks in town and in country with his grandfather and with others, gave further opportunity for enjoying flowers and other plants.

In the context of this pattern of expanding relationships with persons, places, and natural objects, a significant qualitative change in the young Muir's feelings and behavior took place in the middle of his primary school years (see *Boyhood*, 1–2, 23–29). Though the chronology of much of his autobiographical reflections on this time is somewhat vague, the adult Muir points specifically to age five as the time when he started to spend as much time as possible—mainly Saturdays and school vacations, but not Sunday—away from home and family, exploring the coast and countryside with companions. (Interestingly, Wordsworth as well pinpoints age five as the time that he "Had run abroad in wantonness, to sport / A naked savage, in the thunder shower" [*Prelude*, I:299–300].) At this same time, Daniel Muir intensified his use of punishment and disciplinary action to try to keep young John at home, focused on school and Bible studies, and away from exposure to danger as well as to "bad thoughts and bad words." In a striking image, the previously Edenic backyard garden now became a prison for John and David, with the boys' inevitable escapes from that prison (by climbing the walls) followed by equally inevitable punishment by whipping upon their return home. In school as well, the level of punishment at the hands of the teacher increased, and a new element emerged as Muir began to engage in constant individual and group combat with his schoolmates. The group battles often took the form of the imaginative reenactment of events of Scottish history, from the wars against England (epitomized in the figures of William Wallace and Robert the Bruce) to more recent military action on behalf of the British Empire (in places such as India); the nearby ruins of Dunbar Castle provided inspiration and settings for much of this fighting.

Finally, Muir and companions found a new pleasure in such activities as torturing cats (by throwing rocks at them, dropping them out of the third-story window to see if they would land feetfirst, etc.), encouraging dog-fights, and observing the "horrid red work" of pigs being killed in a nearby slaughterhouse. In general, beginning around age five, the young Muir's increased energies of self-assertion, aggressiveness, and curiosity, fanned by the pain and the loss of control brought on by physical punishment, poured themselves out into the spaces and bodies (including his own) available to him.

On one level, we can understand this explosion of energy and activity in the context of changing familial circumstances. Daniel Muir regarded his eldest son as a challenge and test for his faith, and so he responded to the boy's growing capacities for willful independence with ever more exacting demands for moral rectitude and ever more harsh punishments for failure. At the same time, as part of his own lifelong pattern of willful independence, Daniel's extreme religious views and actions—which at this period included pulling the family out of local kirk attendance and almost becoming Episcopalian—brought him into overt opposition and conflict with his father-in-law; in the original draft of the autobiography, Muir specifically mentions that his father seldom visited Grandfather Gil-rye, which—given that they were next-door neighbors—hints at a high level of tension within the family (46:11646). In addition, a fifth child, Daniel junior, was born at this time, adding to a sense of crowding on the parts both of John and of his father; in particular, both of them probably felt frustration or anger at having less contact with wife/mother Ann. In response to these household tensions, John was able to oppose his father and to strengthen his bonds with his mother through actions previously associated with his maternal grandfather, namely, flight to the country-side. In important ways (though more ambivalently than in the adult re-port), the tactic worked: "Kings may be blessed; we were glorious, we were free,—school cares and scoldings, heart thrashings and flesh thrash-ings alike, were forgotten in the fullness of Nature's glad wildness" (*Boy-hood*, 50).

At the same time, the familial origins of this ambiguous age-five wild-ness included a deeper psychological dimension as well, related to those inner dynamics referred to through the psychoanalytic notion of the Oed-ipus complex. In the traditional understanding, the resolution of the Oed-ipus complex marks a new stage in the child's sexual development and relationship with family members (especially parents), a lessening of sex-ual intensity and confusion accompanied by an opening-out into wider social relationships. However, if childhood sexuality is a strong enough power to shape the development of interfamilial relationships before age five, there is no reason to think that it completely disappears or becomes latent between the resolution of the Oedipus complex and the onset of adolescent sexuality; rather, whatever urges, feelings, and images constitute childhood sexuality propel the child out into new social and natural worlds that are themselves saturated by multiple layers of sensuousness, emotion, and meaning. Indeed, in this context it is more correct to speak not of childhood sexuality but of childhood eros, not a particular genitally oriented pattern of activity, relationship, and drive but a more fluid and flowing reality of powers, energies, longings, challenges, joys, and gifts, all appropriate to the body, heart, and mind of that period of life. To be sure, genital and distinctively psychosexual developments are important sources that flow into the pool (or whirlpool) that is childhood eros—but there are many other wells, springs, and underground streams as well.

Mutually arising out of the interplay between body, psyche, relationship, culture, and environment, erotic feeling (in childhood as at all ages) may take a variety of forms, from tender care to selfish dominance; in children around age five, this process is accentuated and shaped—indeed, perhaps it is created—by a heightened level of socialization into gender roles. For Muir, reaching the "manly" age of five constituted a deepened internal break from his domestic world of mother, sisters, aunts, and servant girls, furthering the transition begun when he first entered school. Following social and cultural patterns, the young boy's psychic and interpersonal life came increasingly to be dominated by the company of almost exclusively male playmates and heroic figures, met and (literally and figuratively) wrestled with in the larger geographical spaces that it was the privilege of males to enter and to conquer. Thus, whatever the innate shape and character of the young boy's erotic energy, it could not help but emerge in the aggressive forms dictated by his social and cultural context. At the same time, his poignant private pain at the loss of the female (and "feminine") domestic world of which he was once so deeply a part—and his active struggle to maintain glimpses and stolen moments of connection to that world—further sharpened the knife edge of the young boy's emerging maleness and added a cunning urgency to its violent expression.

Moreover, the common postoedipal pattern of active engagement with the natural environment may constitute an independent developmental project of its own. The psychological and familial developments occurring around age five serve as incentive and opportunity for the child to come into more intense contact with the world outside the home, increasing the importance of natural objects as actors in the child's life; thus, according to Edith Cobb, at the core of childhood experience is "a direct organic participation of the perceiving nervous system in systems of nature, a sheer unbounded psychophysical experience of nature as cosmos, evoking a passionate response which, despite Freudian interpretations of the origins of passion, is not erotic" (by which she means "sexual"). Rather, the source of this passion is the child's (indeed, the human) need to give creative form to experience: "The child's ecological sense of continuity with nature is not what is generally known as mystical. It is, I believe, basically aesthetic and infused with joy in the power to know and to be. These equal, for the child, a sense of the power to make. . . . In childhood, the cognitive process is essentially poetic because it is lyrical, rhythmic, and formative in a generative sense; it is a sensory integration of self and environment, awaiting verbal expression" (33, 23, 89). Although the real ferocity and savagery of Muir's actions suggest that we temper her suspicion of Freudian explanations, Cobb's insights into the developmental meanings of environmental experience in shaping childhood creativity, curiosity, and cognitive abilities give an added dimension to our picture of the five-year-old Muir. Indeed, utilizing a less traditionally Freudian definition of eros, it may be that the child's creative engagement with the natural world is the primary arena in which the erotic occurs (or is created), as the bodily and psychic energy that directs the child toward the establishment of new and deeper relationships with nature, grounded in but expanding beyond previous layers of emotional and psychological attachment and meaning. In any case, we must understand all of these challenges and dynamics—familial restructuring, psychosexual developments, gender identity, and new capacities for sensuous imagination—as swirling in and around the young boy, evoking and requiring new energies and assertions in the face of the loss, uncertainty, and gift of change.[11]

11. Yet another aspect of the psychological meanings of Muir's transformation at age five is suggested by an insight of Winnicott's. In discussing "the positive value of destructiveness" in infant development, Winnicott suggests that a child's acts of destructiveness initially do not involve negative emotions ("anger" or "hatred") toward the object, but are more a creative act of reality testing. In fact, it is only when the object does not "survive" that the sense of deprivation and loss leads to real anger—when, for example, after an aggressive outburst, the mother does not return to the baby, thus shattering the baby's experience of the mother as a dependable nurturing presence. On the other hand, when the object is seen to survive, the infant feels security and even joy. In the process, the object becomes real (and thus capable of being related to): "The destructiveness, plus the object's survival of the destruction, places the object outside the area of objects set up by the subject's projective mental mechanisms. In this way a world of shared reality is created which the subject can use and which can then feed back other-than-me substance into the subject" (*Playing and Reality,* 94). Of course, such understanding of an infant's reality cannot be used as a direct description of what is going on in the five-year-old Muir with respect to his natural surroundings. Rather, the insight may be helpful in a number of more subtle ways: (a) as a suggestion of a structurally similar process that is repeated, according to slightly different

Thus, with some such array of energies, pains, and longings, the five-year-old boy ventured out into the larger world around Dunbar. Alongside the savagery and wildness, Muir (like most children) reached out to natural beings with curiosity and even empathy. In particular, his fascination and emotional connection with birds were probably infused by the freedom and spontaneity that they exhibited, which he desired in his own life and circumstances. Birds also filled the same role as flowers had previously, as soft, bright, attractive, accessible beings, thus providing him access to the emotional associations of his earlier childhood (perhaps especially his early relationships with women, including his mother). Additionally, alongside the practical needs of a hungry boy, it may not have been psychologically neutral that the outcome of most of his countryside explorations was to steal food—apples, carrots, turnips, "anything eatable"—from local farmers. As in his first countryside walks with his grandfather, Muir explored and assimilated his surroundings in part through his mouth, actively sustaining a lived experience of the natural world as "mother earth"—at an age when the psychosexual legacy of the oral urge for the breast is not (as for us adults) an abstracted presumption but a felt reality, a force, a focus, and a power that regularly rises above the surface to guide and fix one's heart and life at moments of need, urgency, or real play.

Again, the inner energies and patterns that young John brought to the countryside were further shaped by the specific cultural and social phenomena that he encountered there. Although he in part went to field, moor, and coast to get away from the relationships of home and of town, the landscape that he encountered was fully populated by humans and reflective of their structures and values. The agricultural land of the Lothians was the most productive and highly developed in all Scotland; in the 1730s, John Cockburn had established Ormiston (in East Lothian) as a model agricultural village, displaying the "improved" and intensive farming practices that would soon transform the entire region (see Saunders).

---

dynamics, at various points along a person's developmental trajectory; (b) as a description of an act of regression and/or the reemergence of a situation that actually occurred in the infant Muir; or (c) as a metaphor that helps us to understand a completely different pattern operating at this later period in his life. At this point, I am content to settle for the last interpretation as sufficient for my purposes (though this case may in the long run provide support for a more developed theoretical formulation of the first or second options). That is, it may be that at least some aspects of Muir's aggressiveness toward animals and toward his natural surroundings helped him in establishing a positive emotional relationship with them, and even in establishing their reality as independent objects capable of relationship and worthy of trust. We will see another possible example of this dynamic in the case of Muir's teenage hunting, discussed below.

As Muir himself admits, "most of the land lay in smooth cultivation" (*Boyhood*, 1), and the fields through which he and his friends ran embodied not wildness but rather traditional eighteenth-century values of order and harmony, along with an emphasis on efficiency and productivity related to a more modern, industrial ethos. Although Muir in his adult reminiscences focuses on those remnants of wilderness that he was able to find in the countryside (mainly in birds and the seacoast), the clean, ordered, understandable fields and roads were equally attractive and compelling to the young child; reassuring objects of investigation in themselves, they also provided negotiable pathways for exploration and accessible settings for human relationships.

In these culturally shaped surroundings, Muir found not solitude but a full range of human presence. Significantly, the boy was constantly in the company of schoolmates or siblings: every reference to the countryside is phrased in terms of "we," implying both a lack (or possibly an avoidance) of individual privacy and the enduring power of his familial relationships in mediating his experiences of the natural world. In particular, the sense of shared privacy that John had previously experienced in the bedroom with David expanded to include other young boys as well, with the bonds uniting them further shaped and inflamed by the erotic energies and cultural patterns of the period. This deeply communal experience of the environment contrasts sharply to the strong emphasis on solitude found in many—perhaps most—other influential American environmental texts from Thoreau onward, and even to the alternating use of "I" and "we" in Wordsworth's *Prelude;* similarly, *The Story of My Boyhood and Youth* completely lacks the emphasis on privacy and solitude that Richard Coe sees as characteristic of most childhood reminiscences. As we shall see, Muir's relationships with his male playmates—tempered and transformed by his past and future female relationships—shaped a mode of companionate experience of and with the natural world that would remain throughout his life.

In addition, Muir shared the Scottish coast and countryside with adults as well as with other children. All the boys were well acquainted with the townsfolk whose livelihood was made by braving the gales, depths, and rocks of the sea, and the fishermen's stories and instruction in wooden-ship whittling must have been a rich part of the fabric of the boy's growing awareness of his surroundings. Similarly, numerous passages contain reference to the farmers living there; many of the peasants were probably fairly prosperous as a result of the agricultural improvements of the age (including "peasant democracy," giving the peasants more leeway and security on their use of and residency on the land, with the payback for the laird being increased yields). At the same time, the people who were displaced and left unemployed by those "improvements" gravitated to the towns, where they presented a grim contrast to the more successful country folk, as Muir's memories of the poor of Dunbar suggest (L. M. Wolfe, 7).

This human presence in the landscape was deeply infused with supernatural, moral, and religious dimensions as well. In one of Muir's earliest remembered adventures in the countryside with a schoolmate, the Dandy Doctors pop up again, leading the boys to crawl on hands and knees for the miles back home (46:11597). In later years, the Doctors' role was taken over by an actual figure, the gamekeeper: invoked as the one who will catch the boys and hang them for thievery, the gamekeeper was endowed by threatening country folk with powers and fearful intentions in a way that added elements of supernatural malevolence and of mystery to an ordinary human person. More mundanely, the autobiography often comments on the farmers' hostility to the thieving town boys; Muir must have known some of those farmers through Daniel Muir's grain business and probably experienced them as agents of his father, extending to the countryside the latter's moral discipline and threats of punishment.

This extension of power and authority to the countryside is more dramatically evident in the passage where, having "first heard of hell from a servant-girl," Muir envisions it as "only a sooty pit with stone walls like those of [Dunbar] castle," out of which he was confident he could climb (*Boyhood*, 18). Muir's embodiment of moral authority in the landscape once again finds an interesting parallel in Wordsworth, in the well-known incident where the young poet steals a boat at night and rows out into the silent lake; already "troubled," he sees a huge black mountain peak rising up "like a living thing" to pass moral judgment and to instill guilt (*Prelude*, I:357–400). For Muir, however, it was not a natural object that carried moral power but rather a human construction, the castle (albeit somewhat naturalized by being in ruins), as interpreted through a specifically religious image. Moreover, what is curious about this story is that it could *not* have been the first time that Muir had heard of hell: the incident presumably occurred after age five, when he began to explore the countryside extensively, but he would surely have heard of hell in teacher's lessons or father's prayers and hymns before that time, perhaps described in monstrous, violent, and disturbing ways. Rather, this incident was memorable and powerful for being the first time that the young boy was able to associate the frightening word "hell" with an understandable meaning, envisioned in terms of a concrete, experienced reality that evoked the fears and anxieties of his own experience of life—including those arising as part of his adventures in nature and castle and his awareness of his father's proscription and punishment of those adventures. For the young boy, hell literally *was* being stuck in a dark pit (of the castle), with his (actual) father's judgment hanging over him. Significantly, the image allowed Muir to control his threatening surroundings and to triumph over his fears and difficulties by imaginatively exercising and celebrating his own skill and prowess at climbing, much as earlier he could simply run away from the Dandy Doctors or other threatening figures; interestingly, then, his deliverance from his childhood woes came about through successful execution of the very activities that brought them about in the first place (climbing adventures in the castle). In this way, official religious imagery began to hold meaning for him by taking over the emotional and cognitive roles of folk supernatural figures, while the setting, occasion, and content of this religiousness remained intimately connected with the natural and human landscapes.

Soon, however, Muir began to locate the source of moral discipline—in particular, the regulation of his own behavior within the natural world—within his immediate relationships with actual people, as one aspect of yet another qualitative shift occurring at around age seven. Significantly, this is the age at which the child develops new capacities for reflection, for objective thinking, and for taking another person's perspective as equally as valid as one's own (perhaps more so).[12] It was also at this age that Muir moved up to the grammar school, where the fighting was both more communal and more competitive and the teacher's whippings more severe than in the primary school. As the adult Muir relates, schoolyard battles could begin from nothing more significant than a "saucy stare" (*Boyhood,* 35); the anger, shame, and sense of objectification in the face of the aggressive gaze (see, e.g., Evernden, 88–94) arise in part from the child's extreme sensitivity to the possibility of being judged by another person, when such judgment defines one's very identity. In

12. For one interpretation of the social, cognitive, and affective changes that occur around age seven, see Piaget (38–60). Fundamentally, "the child becomes capable of cooperation because he no longer confuses his own point of view with that of others. He is able both to dissociate his point of view from that of others and to coordinate these different points of view" (39). Thus, for example, games become more structured, with participants' behavior controlled by an agreed-upon set of laws, allowing a mutual understanding of what it means for one individual to be the "winner." In a parallel way, the child becomes capable of "reflection," which is "nothing other than internal deliberation, that is to say, a discussion which is conducted with oneself just as it might be conducted with real interlocutors or opponents," i.e, "internalized social discussion" (40). This leads, among other things, to a sense of morality based on shared respect for the other—and for oneself—as an autonomous individual, subject to an objective set of ethical standards or laws; significantly, the character of this morality and "mutual respect" is grounded in (and again, an internalization of) the character of the earlier phase of unilateral subservience to the authority of the parent. (See also Tyson and Tyson, 183–87.)

another new form of violent schoolyard interaction, the children would take turns whipping each other for as long as they could, the first one showing any emotion or pain being the loser (*Boyhood*, 34–35). This "game" shows the boys communally identifying with the patterns of discipline and punishment that had previously been applied by external authority figures, and aligning this with the admired male values of fortitude and endurance that they saw in their traditional cultural warrior-heroes (Wallace, Bruce, etc.). The competition has less to do with strength, more to do with individual self-control in a context of group solidarity. Similarly, an everyday countryside exploration (44–45) shows the boys engaged in a competition over who knows the most birds' nests, of what type, relative scarcity, song quality, etc. The meaning of their interaction with nature is primarily in terms not of physical contact or sensuous appreciation but rather of mental understanding and control, for purposes of competition (and thus increased social standing, peer respect, etc.).[13]

Moreover, the adult reminiscences stress over and over again Muir's awareness of the intimate connection between his flights to the countryside and the subsequent punishment at the hands of his father (see, e.g., *Boyhood*, 1–2, 43–44). Indeed, the two must have become inseparable in the young boy's consciousness, so that the positive meaning of the natural world for him depended (in part) upon contrast with the negative experience of punishment. On a more foundational psychological level, the very reality of the natural world came to be infused with the presence of his father, "flight to nature" functioning not so much as an escape but as another mode of relationship, even a desired and chosen one.

The different layers of this unexpected—and disturbing—dynamic can be disentangled only with care and with caution. One layer represents sheer self-preservation: In his struggle to defend himself and his delicate happiness and vulnerable delight from the threat of his father's power and authority, the young Muir ended up integrating that authority into his very selfhood, internalizing it and turning it against himself as his only means of regulating it. In a sense, he turned his own saucy stare inward, objectifying his own body in order to be able to bear the punishment and condemnation that were inextricably linked with contact with the natural world. At the same time, he most likely felt both guilt and exhilaration,

---

13. Stephen Trimble claims that both for adults and for children, "the land releases us from competition. Such acceptance restores us for the social fight" (Nabhan and Trimble, 23). For Muir as a child, however, the land was both the setting for and the object of very literal fights, which were simultaneously social and environmental. Interestingly, Trimble directly follows his statement with a discussion of the value of a sense of individual possession in the exploration of the environment, but fails to acknowledge the competitiveness that often flows from such claims of possession.

both fear and vitality, for behavior so directly contrary to his father's commands, as well as for those actions that his newfound aggressiveness and independence allowed him to imagine or desire but that he did not actually carry out; thus, on some levels his father's authority served both as an occasion for increased (and increasingly lively) self-assertion and as a way to protect himself from the confusing and threatening dimensions of his own inner desires and energies.[14] Finally, this pattern of escape and punishment provided an arena for continued contact with one of the most important beings in Muir's life—painful contact, to be sure, at times excruciating contact, but contact nevertheless, and therefore on some level attractive and meaningful to the young boy. This is of course not to say that Muir in any sense "wanted" the pain of punishment, but rather that he wanted the *relationship*—however distorted—that was offered him, and indeed the maintenance of that relationship may have been possible only because of the presence of nature as a salve for that pain.[15] In these

14. These aspects of the presence of prohibition and punishment at the core of the "wild child" can be further understood by again drawing a parallel to Winnicott's observations of infants. According to Winnicott, for an infant to feel hated by the mother is a precursor to the ability to be loved: "If he is not hated, if what is unacceptable about him is not acknowledged, then his love and lovableness will not feel fully real to him" (Phillips, 89). Disapproval by the mother allows the child to distinguish a sense of a good and "lovable" self from whatever "bad" or confusing dimensions may be appearing as part of the normal process of separation and individuation. At the same time, the emotional experience of disapproval serves as an incentive to "hate" the mother, and hence to separate from her even more. Transposing these dynamics to a later stage of development, we can see Muir's experience of his father's prohibitions as allowing and encouraging a greater sense of a separate selfhood, which selfhood had to be contained and controlled in order to be protected from threats both from within and from without. This is not to say that prohibition, pain, and harsh moral authority are the *only* ways for such developments to take place, but to suggest that they were what was available to the young Muir at the time for his own creative use. However, the child's powers of imaginative transformation are not unlimited, indeed are tenuous and fragile, and in many cases parental disapproval and hatred do not serve the inner growth of the child but rather distort or destroy it.

15. Discussing Fairbairn's emphasis on "object seeking" rather than on Freudian pleasure seeking as the core psychological dynamic, Stephen A. Mitchell writes: "The superordinate need of the child is not for pleasure or need gratification, but for an intense relationship with another person. If the caretakers provide opportunities for pleasurable experiences, pleasure is sought, not as an end in itself, but as a vehicle for interaction with others. If only painful experiences are provided, the child does not give up and look for pleasurable experiences elsewhere, but seeks the pain as a vehicle for interaction with the significant other. It is the contact, not the pleasure, which is primary" (27). However, such a perspective must be used only with *extreme* caution in interpreting childhood experience and love, for it runs the real danger of blaming the victim—the child—for participation in inappropriate or destructive behavior. In such situations—physical punishment, sexual abuse, extreme psychological control, and others—the *cause of* and the *responsibility for* inappropriate behavior and relationship lie always with the adult, not with the child. What the object

and perhaps other ways, "wildness"—whether in the natural world or in himself—came to be equated with "what father prohibits," and the felt power of that prohibition and presence contributed much to the reality and to the meaning both of the inner and of the outer forms of wildness.

From another perspective, however, the child's experience of wildness surely had something to do with a different emotional reality within himself, and even with a clear and close looking into the heart of the natural world. Despite—or, perhaps, with the help of—all of the psychological, cultural, and familial conditioning that grounded, limited, and shaped his being, the young Muir (like all of us, at all stages of life) discovered or created points of freedom and insight within himself and within his relationships with other persons and with the world. From the evidence of his adult reminiscences, this process occurred most powerfully in his encounters with the sea.

> With red-blooded playmates, wild as myself, I loved to wander in the
> fields to hear the birds sing, and along the seashore to gaze and wonder at
> the shells and seaweeds, eels and crabs in the pools among the rocks when
> the tide was low; and best of all to watch the waves in awful storms thun-
> dering on the black headlands and craggy ruins of the old Dunbar Castle
> when the sea and sky, the waves and the clouds, were mingled together as
> one. (*Boyhood*, 1–2)

To be sure, multiple psychological dynamics must have entered into his experience of the sea: the meanings of these scenes were informed by earlier experiences such as his terror at and eventual triumph over the seaside bathings and the sookin-in-goats, or his exploits, adventures, and associations regarding the castle; equally, his gazing and wondering at eels and at the pounding of the waves and storms harnessed and set free some of the varied erotic wants and energies that were both a legacy of his earlier bodies and a present power flowing within him, firing and guiding and coloring his mind, mouth, eye, and muscles. At the same time, it is just as certain that an unexplainable, irreducible something happened between Muir and the surging waves, between Muir and the mingled oneness, between the young boy and the sea, a something within which the child—the person—tasted power, compassion, and wholeness.

---

relations perspective allows is not a new explanation of causality or motivation but rather a new way of understanding the meaning of such patterns and predicaments in the inner life of the child, and even the ways in which the child is able to creatively transform and use unhealthy, destructive, even horrific circumstances as means of pursuing and protecting his or her love and selfhood. In many situations, of course, such creative use is not possible, and the child's love and selfhood—and even his or her very life—are tragically and criminally destroyed.

Thus, buffeted by internal need and external authority and yet moved forward by energy, wonder, and joy, Muir created within himself and between himself and his environment a space that sustained the power and meaning of many of his most important past and present personal experiences, developmental achievements, and human and natural relationships. The process by which the places and scenes of his childhood landscape shaped his inner life was no doubt similar to that described by Wordsworth (and true of us all):

> . . . and thus
> By the impressive discipline of fear,
> By pleasure and repeated happiness,
> So frequently repeated, and by force
> Of obscure feelings representative
> Of things forgotten, these same scenes so bright,
> So beautiful, so majestic in themselves,
> Though yet the day was distant, did become
> Habitually dear, and all their forms
> And changeful colors by invisible links
> Were fastened to the affections.
>
> (*Prelude*, I:602–12)

At age eleven, this whole world of a growing boy's joy and pain, love and fear, challenge and achievement, relationship and selfhood, was completely and irrevocably swept away.

Daniel Muir's abrupt decision to emigrate to America in February 1849 was not out of character. An orphan from Manchester, Muir had moved with his sister to Lanarkshire (just outside of Glasgow) when young, then left home for the city as a teenager, eventually enlisting in the army and going to Dunbar as a recruiting agent. As we have seen, his life in Dunbar was marked by increasing tension with established church and community, culminating in his zealous adherence to the new Campbellite movement; thus, a desire for "religious freedom" as well as a sense of missionary responsibility was part of his decision to leave the country. However, a deeper motive arose out of the intersection of his religious trajectory and his personal needs, specifically a desire for a more self-contained family of which he was the absolute and undisputed head. In Dunbar, his authority was constrained and diluted by the presence of grandparents, teachers, servants, church, social mores, and even the subtle presence of historical figures as alternative role models, as well as by business demands that took him away from home for much of each day. By contrast, the American social and physical landscape would place him at the center of familial authority, fear, and love. Interestingly, he enacted this authority in the very process by which he undertook the move, announcing it to the family capriciously the day before they were to leave and deciding on their final destination only after reaching Buffalo. Only John, David, and Sarah accompanied their father to the New World; Ann and the rest of the children stayed behind, to join them later that summer after land had been cleared and a home built.[16]

Muir's autobiography portrays the children as feeling "utterly, blindly glorious" and "care-free as thistle seeds" upon hearing of their imminent departure for the "wild, happy land" of America (*Boyhood*, 54, 55)— but their responses were surely more complex than that. For young John, the move must have constituted a huge challenge and threat. Like all children at age eleven, he was already faced with the difficult task of incorporating within himself both his emerging sexuality and new age- and gender-specific social roles. Moreover, as we have seen, the same aspects of life in Dunbar that had constrained his father's authority—grandfather, servants, the very structure of the landscape—had provided Muir with the means of negotiating his world, protecting himself both physically and emotionally and creating a space for self-expression and for relationship. With the move to America, all of this was stripped away. Perhaps most important, even his relationship with his mother was profoundly transformed: after the shock of their unprecedented (if temporary) separation, she was preoccupied with her new responsibilities and tasks as frontier mother and homemaker, while he spent much of his time outside the domestic sphere, working in the fields. The elements of ambiguity and distance already present in their relationship were intensified manyfold, along with the child's corresponding need to look elsewhere

---

16. The family pattern that Daniel Muir created is similar to that which Philip Greven has described as the "evangelical family": "Ideally, evangelical families consisted only of parents and children. Parents needed exclusive influence and control over their children in order to accomplish their goals. The distance they maintained between their households and the surrounding community and the distance that characterized their relationships with other adults who might be present at various times within their households—servants and occasionally grandparents—served to intensify the relationship binding parents to their children and children to their parents. Within relatively isolated and self-contained households, the focus of authority and the source of love was united in the parents, who dominated the household and determined the principles and practices that were to shape the temperaments of their offspring. Within the confines of the nuclear family, children found no alternatives, no defenses, no mitigation, no escape from the assertion of power and the rigorous repressiveness of their parents" (*Protestant Temperament*, 25). A detailed analysis would be needed to outline the many layers of similarities and differences between the eighteenth-century New England Calvinist families that are the subjects of Greven's study and the nineteenth-century Scottish immigrant Kirk-turned-Campbellite Muirs; the general parallels, however, are instructive.

for support and holding. Strikingly, although Muir's reminiscences of his childhood in Scotland include his mother as an important presence, she is almost never mentioned in the account of the Wisconsin years. Thus, along with the standard developmental issues of approaching adolescence, Muir was confronted with the additional challenge of literally reconstructing almost his entire social and physical world from the ground up, in the increasingly intimate presence of a harsh and domineering father.

How did he respond? What can a boy do to survive, and hopefully to retain and to develop a sense of selfhood and worth, in such circumstances? As children (indeed, most people) usually do, Muir initially tried to fit his new situation into the past life with which he was familiar, recreating both his past environment and his patterns of relating to it. In contrast to adult immigrants' full awareness of the culture and identity that they were leaving behind, "[c]hildren's alarm came from the immediate physical experience of leaving, not from its long-term implications" (West, 29); thus, for Muir it was not initially a self-conscious Scottish culture or identity that he sought to restore at the center of his life, but rather his immediate patterns of familial relationship as well as the immediate social and physical landscape in which that family was embedded. Interestingly, his parents were able to do this in a literal way, building a large, sturdy, middle-class house that replicated the one that they had left behind in Dunbar. Alongside the house, Daniel and Ann Muir carefully planted plots with the flower seeds that they had brought over from Scotland, transplanting the family's beloved Dunbar flower gardens to the New World—a practice common in the Scottish diaspora (Bentley, 16). However, as a child, John had few means of such literal re-creation of his lost home, and so he turned to memory, imagination, and patterns of action as tools for negotiating and shaping the psychological meanings of his new environment.

As one element of this imaginative re-creation of his past world, Muir's adult reminiscences continue to describe his experiences and identity in communal rather than in individual terms ("we" rather than "I"), especially including David: "We were just old enough, David and I, to regard all these creatures as wonders, the strange inhabitants of our new world" (*Boyhood*, 78). Interestingly, the boys were introduced to the landscape surrounding the homestead by an "all-knowing" Yankee hired hand, who seems also to have acted as a source of local folklore (thereby faintly replacing both Grandfather Gilrye and the servants in Dunbar). Still children, the brothers explored their new environment with a curiosity, energy, openness, and attention to details that would establish deeper psychological bonds with the land than would ever be possible for their parents (see West, 101–4). When they first arrived at the new homestead, "we ran along the brow of the hill that the shanty stood on and down to the meadow, searching for trees and grass tufts and bushes, and soon discovered a bluebird's and a woodpecker's nest, and began an acquaintance with the frogs and snakes and turtles in the creeks and springs" (*Boyhood*, 63). In particular, as during their last years in Scotland, John and David's major fascination in exploring nature centered in birds.[17] That this continuing avian interest served to ease the shock of transition is suggested by the children's admiration of the kingbird: "[I]n Scotland our great ambition was to be good fighters, and we admired this quality in the handsome little chattering flycatcher that whips all the other birds" (66). At the same time, they were almost equally interested in the flowers, grasses, and animal life found in the meadow in front of the lake and along the lake shore, perhaps as a parallel to their beloved Dunbar seacoast; interestingly, the adult Muir also reports the children's fascination at Wisconsin thunderstorms, which perhaps evoked some of the same feelings as the North Sea storms and waves. Yet another passage, although heavily influenced by later perspectives and language, hints at how Muir imaginatively constructed his new surroundings through both contrasts and continuities with his earlier life, specifically school:

> This sudden plash into pure wildness—baptism in Nature's warm heart—how utterly happy it made us! Nature streaming into us, wooingly teaching her wonderful glowing lessons, so unlike the dismal grammar ashes and cinders so long thrashed into us. Here without knowing it we were still in school; every wild lesson a love lesson, not whipped but charmed into us. . . . Young hearts, young leaves, flowers, animals, the winds and the streams and the sparkling lake, all wildly, gladly rejoicing together! (63–64)[18]

17. Discussing the process of readjusting to life immediately after the Holocaust, Elie Wiesel states, "One doesn't start over—one continues." In his own case, trying to reestablish a "normal" life in Paris after his experiences in the concentration camps, Weisel found himself drawn back to the very same tractate of the Talmud he had been studying before being taken away to Auschwitz (*Fresh Air* interview, Nov. 14, 1995).

18. At the same time as such language reveals the ways in which the young Muir interpreted Wisconsin through the lens of Scotland, it may also suggest ways in which the adult Muir came to interpret Scotland through the lens of Wisconsin. An experience of a new environment may transform one's memories of an older one, by emphasizing those aspects of the old environment that provide either strong continuities or strong contrasts with the new (see, e.g., Wapner et al., 46, 222). Thus, the young Muir's intense experiences of the "wildness" and of the "freedom" of the Wisconsin frontier may have fixed in his memory images of Dunbar both as wilder (continuity) and as more of a place of bondage (contrast) than he had actually experienced it as a younger child. Of course, such considerations force us to be even more cautious in using personal reminiscences as biographical evidence—without foreclosing the richness of the attempt.

Despite such initial responses, the primitive Wisconsin frontier was a completely different environment from the ordered, gentle, socially infused Scottish countryside—to say nothing of the even more modern, clock-regulated townscape of Dunbar—and so must have seemed foreign and even overwhelming to the young boy. The adult Muir recalls that "[e]verything about us was so novel and wonderful that we could hardly believe our senses except when hungry or while father was thrashing us" (*Boyhood*, 71); intended to reinforce the theme of joy in and wonder at nature, this passage suggests a subtle dissociation of his mind and emotions from his body and from his natural surroundings, as a result of sheer sensory and emotional overload. Suggestively, the reminiscences stop centering on personally experienced activities and events, focusing instead on external description of a world from which his self and body seem distanced. This sense of dissociation in response to the trauma of environmental dislocation was increased by the continued physical punishment that Muir endured at the hands of his father. Muir himself notes a similar parallel between the experience of the new landscape and the experience of violence; illustrating the last quotation above with a story of his first encounter with a meadow full of fireflies, he comments: "I thought that the whole wonderful fairy show must be in my eyes; for only in fighting, when my eyes were struck, had I ever seen anything in the least like it."[19]

Environmental dislocation and paternal discipline were further merged in one of the biggest contrasts between Muir's Dunbar and his Wisconsin lives, namely, the arduous farm work that he was soon impelled to undertake at the Fountain Lake homestead. As his family backyard in Dunbar had gone from paradise to prison, so in Wisconsin the natural world quickly was transformed from a place of escape and freedom to an arena of work and bondage; Linnie Marsh Wolfe (34) notes the long-term damage that the strain of work inflicted upon the growth, health, and stature

19. This phenomenon of psychological dissociation as a response to physical punishment and pain follows a pattern described by Greven in *Spare the Child:* "The ability to disconnect feelings from their contexts and to disconnect one's sense of self from the external world are at the heart of the process of dissociation that underlies so many psychological phenomena. Dissociation is one of the most basic means of survival for many children, who learn early in life to distance themselves, or parts of themselves, from experiences too painful or frightening to bear" (148). Although Greven focuses on the child's dissociation from emotions, I see a pattern of dissociation of "self" from body as well, as a result of parental punishment; in addition, I am proposing that a similar sort of dissociation may result from traumatic or troubling experiences of one's physical environment. Finally, we should consider distancing from one's environment as itself a psychologically powerful form of dissociation, especially for a child (such as Muir) whose emotions, body, and interpersonal world are so deeply embedded in the physical environment.

of Margaret, Sarah, David, and John.[20] For the former town children, this new relationship with the land involved unfamiliar and harsh demands, as food and shelter depended upon hard work and struggle against vegetation, soil, and weather. The ambivalent feelings toward his surroundings that must have arisen in young John—confusion, fear, dependence, joy, freedom, anger, frustration, sense of loss—were both intensified and channeled by his father's actions. Comparing the huge bonfires of brush from the newly cleared land to the much hotter fires of hell into which bad boys (and all who disobey God) would be cast, Daniel Muir let it be known early that religious discipline and paternal authority would again be embodied both in the familial and in the physical landscape of Wisconsin. Unlike the Dunbar servant girl's image of hell as a "sooty pit" that a good climber such as John could conquer, this new hell would allow no such imaginative—or actual—escape. Although the published autobiography concludes this story by discounting the terror and lasting impact of this experience, the original draft reinforces the harsh message by following it immediately with another story of a whipping.

Thus, in the isolated, self-contained family, bereft of protection or alternative authorities, and in the face of the insistent demands of farming, Muir had no practical choice but to obey his father's/Father's commandments. At the same time, on the psychological level, Muir aligned himself with his father for reasons associated not only with fear but with need and even love. Barely a teenager, he had not yet successfully forged an independent identity; with self and world increasingly centered in his father, too much conflict or disruption would have been too much to bear. Given his particular circumstances, Muir needed—or, perhaps, chose to need—his father to give stability and direction to his life, and he did whatever was required in order to maintain this relationship. Such a process cannot be generalized (e.g., in the slogan "every boy needs a father"), but rather depends on the specific needs, circumstances, and goals of each child—as well as on the particular capacities, strengths, and weaknesses of each father. Keep in mind also that identification with a father does not imply loss of love for the mother; indeed, one of the primary motives of such identification, from the oedipal stage on, is as a *means* of loving the mother—and of feeling oneself as the sort of person that the mother would love—in one of the few ways allowed by familial and cultural patterns.[21]

20. West (chapter 4) stresses the importance of children's work in the economic development—and hence the environmental transformation—of the western frontier.

21. Other aspects of Muir's psychological identification with his father—and of the father's counteridentification with his son—are discussed by Stoll (72–79). Although Stoll emphasizes Muir's eventual rejection of this identification, I believe that the ways in which he embraced it are equally if not more important in understanding his inner life and experiences, both at this time and in the future.

The depth of Muir's bond with his father is evident in two stories. In the first, a few years after coming to Wisconsin, Daniel angrily ordered John to shoot a favorite horse who was "misbehaving." Despite the deep affection that he felt toward the animal, Muir unhesitatingly moved to carry out the order: "I went to the house and brought the gun, suffering most horrible mental anguish, such as I suppose unhappy Abraham felt when commanded to slay Isaac" (*Boyhood*, 102). Whether or not he conceived the Abrahamic parallel at the time, Muir probably did experience and accept divine/paternal authority as overwhelming any personal wishes he might have had, without foreclosing the subsequent emotional suffering. Eight years later, told by his father to dig a well through solid rock at a new homestead, Muir almost died from carbonic acid that had accumulated in the well overnight—only to be told to get back into the well a day or two later to finish the job. In the published account, which most commentators have used to emphasize the harshness of Daniel Muir's tyranny, John allows himself to express some anger toward his father along with pride in his own work: "Father never spent an hour in that well. He trusted me to sink it straight and plumb, and I did" (234). In the original telling, however, while Muir puts forth the same bitter accusation against his father, he implicitly retracts it with the statement that "[s]ome would say we never would get water, but father kept me at it until we did, and we did" (46:11772). Repeatedly using the "we" that previously had referred almost exclusively to siblings and playmates, Muir here locates his own achievement, pride, and identity in a shared relationship with his father, not in opposition to him.

As both of these stories suggest, one aspect of this alignment with his father was a strengthening of Muir's orientation *against* his natural environment, or important parts of it at least. Excelling at all the farm tasks that confronted him (plowing, stump digging, rail-splitting, woodcutting, hoeing, harvesting, and so on), Muir was as guilty as anyone of the "fierce over-industriousness" and "foolish ambition" for which he chides the early settlers in his autobiography (see, e.g., *Boyhood*, 222–23). Again, this intensity was probably motivated by a complex constellation of inner feelings—the desire to provide for and to protect his siblings and mother, sadness at leaving his Dunbar life, love for and fear of his father, pride in achievement, and sheer determination that his selfhood (and body) not be destroyed by the ordeal. Many of these factors were probably also present in the sense of pleasure that he found in hunting. Clearly an economic necessity and a cultural expectation, in Muir's case hunting operated on emotional levels as well, bringing out some of the same feelings that had led the boy in Dunbar to stone cats, intensified by the adolescent's physical and psychological development (perhaps including sexuality). Although the published autobiography is somewhat embarrassed and forgiving with respect to his childhood hunting, the original draft is more straightforward in admitting that one of his prime ambitions as a child was to kill a loon (46:11682); both versions contain adequate testament to the young boy's fascination with the violence he observed in—and inflicted on—the wild animals he encountered.

At the same time, the texts make clear at a number of points that Muir was ambivalent about shooting birds, as he continued to delight in their beauty and to derive inspiration and psychological sustenance from them. Indeed, intertwined with its violent and aggressive aspects, one of the attractions of hunting must have been the chance to spend time alone in intense engagement with the natural world; it is for precisely this reason that Thoreau extols the virtues for the young of hunting, saying that he owed to his own childhood hunting experiences his "closest acquaintance with Nature" (*Walden*, 141). Similarly, while the grueling farm work engendered in Muir a negative stance toward his physical environment, it also laid the basis for a more positive identification with the farm animals: "We used to notice the humanity in [the oxen] by their being so tired, and calling for their food, and their patiently plodding and pulling the wagon in hot weather, when we would stop to let them rest, their tongues out lolling. Then they would have such a real look in their eye, just like a person. And then they would draw a long sighing breath, just exactly like an exhausted person, and yet they were so patient and never resented a whipping" (46:11705). Not only did the oxen help with the work, they also reflected Muir back to himself, and thus served as companions in his own experiences of work, exhaustion, patience, and punishment.

His conflicting feelings toward his familial and natural environments are perhaps best expressed in his descriptions of animal families. In the midst of admiration for the humanness, love, and beauty present in the families and homes of birds and of farm and wild animals, Muir relates a series of domestic tragedies: a squirrel frozen in its nest, a beehive robbed and destroyed by the hired men, a whole family of gophers driven out of their burrow by a shrike, "all of then crying and running in all directions as if at this dreadful time home, sweet home, was the most dangerous and least desirable of any place in the wide world" (*Boyhood*, 197). At other dreadful times, Muir's own sometimes-sweet home was equally dangerous and undesired. As if to express Muir's unstated feelings, each of the five central chapters of the published autobiography ends with a story of an animal killed and a home broken, by human hunters or by natural dangers.[22]

22. This pattern of dying animals and ruined homes in *Boyhood* is particularly striking given Lisa Mighetto's observation that "there is little animal suffering ... described in Muir's writing" (xxiii). To be sure, one of the motives behind the eventual publication of *Boyhood* was as a polemic against the inhumane treatment of animals, thus requiring some

Eventually, in creating a new self to negotiate his ambivalent familial and natural environments, Muir came to internalize his father's authority to a greater extent than ever before. This dynamic is best illustrated in an incident that occurred when he was around fourteen (see *Boyhood*, 124–29). Earlier that summer, at his father's instigation, John and David had learned to swim, guided only by the elder Muir's hurried instructions and suggestion to watch the frogs for more complete lessons. While swimming in Fountain Lake, John became frightened and unnerved after accidentally brushing against the bottom of a boat, and sank toward the bottom, helpless and out of control. Almost drowned, his mind suddenly cleared and he was able to remember how to swim, successfully making his way to the shore, safe but humiliated. (His feelings of humiliation and helplessness may have been partly based in reawakened memories of his "terrible bathings" in seaside pools, and his later fear of the "sookin-ingoats," from his childhood in Dunbar.) Luckily, his father did not hear the commotion, and so no punishment was forthcoming from that source. The following day, however, Muir concluded that because he had lost control of himself, he should be punished—more precisely, his body should be punished, "as if my body was one thing and my mind another thing" (46:11742). Rowing again to the middle of the lake, Muir dove back into the water again and again, facing his fear and mastering the threat of the water. The original draft of the autobiography continues: "As I dove I said, 'Now, take that, and that, and that'—as if getting even with myself for behaving so badly before. Getting even with my body for behaving itself so badly before, and telling my body to obey my mind" (46:11743). The importance with which he regards the incident is stressed as he goes on to illustrate the same theme with a number of stories not involving himself, and (in the original telling) a long story about a dangerous situation in the Sierra that he overcame through similar willpower—suggesting too that this need for body control would be a lasting aspect of his personality and of his experiences in the natural world.

In his adult reminiscences, Muir interprets this lake incident in various ways: as a "victory over self," as a victory of "mind" over body, emotions, and environment, and as a facet of Scottish character ("they must keep their bodies subject to the principles they are taught" [46:11745]).[23]

---

illustration of animal suffering; however, at least some of the emotional meaning of these images must have been grounded in the thoughts, feelings, and perceptions of Muir's childhood.

23. Greven again provides a suggestive parallel pattern: the evangelical family's "policy of unrelenting repression . . . shaped [their children's] personalities and provided the foundations in experience in early life of the denial of self and self-will that formed the innermost core of evangelical religious experience and belief" (*Protestant Temperament,* 35). Further, "At the very core of evangelical experience, the foundation upon which piety was based,

However, more fundamental than religious values, mind, or Scottish character is the overarching presence of his father. As noted above, although Daniel Muir initiated the project of swimming, he provided little actual guidance or support, and in fact the boys learned on their own. In the emergency, however, Muir interpreted his ability to swim—and thus to save his life—in terms of his ability to carry out his father's "instructions." This is much more evident in the original version of the autobiography than in the published form: in the case of his initial near drowning, the later version portrays Muir as remembering that *he* could swim underwater, but the earlier text describes him as remembering and obeying *his father's* instructions. In recounting the following day's events, the original draft emphasizes that Muir had never dived before, but did "what my father had told me" in diving, and then repeats the phrase (and the reliance on the instructions and on the felt presence of his father) in describing how he successfully swam back up to the surface. (The second of these references makes it into the published *Boyhood*.)[24]

Psychologically, these passages provide an almost textbook description of the inner development that psychoanalysis has termed "superego," as the parent's internalized voice is expressed as will and as conscience. Strikingly, however, it was obviously not his father's own voice that directed Muir's actions, but rather a "father's voice" that the son helped to *create* in this particular situation: John and David were the ones who taught themselves how to swim, and it was thus their own "instruction" that John actually remembered in the emergency. From this perspective, the incident illustrates not the development of superego but the continued elaboration of the "ego," the individual's own "voice" as a valid and powerful reality. Interestingly, despite David's presence at the beginning, John seems to have returned to the lake the next day alone, and thus this incident constitutes the first extended description phrased in terms of "I" rather than "we"—suggesting the development of a more individual selfhood in contrast to the shared world and identity that had previously

---

there existed a profound alienation of individuals from their own bodies and an intense hostility towards their own innermost natures" (65). Extending Greven, the religious and familial roots of alienation from self and from body can be seen to provoke alienation from the natural environment as well.

24. Interestingly, Stanley (37) reports that a few years later, after they had moved to a new homestead a few miles away, Daniel Muir decided to rebaptize the entire family—by immersion—in nearby Knights Lake. If John in fact was baptized on that occasion, it may have reinforced the Fountain Lake incident in establishing an association between lakes and his father's religiously based authority. On a more Gothic note, *Boyhood* (214–17) includes the story of a feebleminded neighbor for whom Muir cared deeply—also a victim of evangelical violence, at the hands of his brother—who tried to drown himself in Fountain Lake.

characterized his childhood. However, for specific psychological reasons, Muir chose or needed to identify his own emerging inner voice with his father's authority, power, and position in his psychic world, thus coloring that voice as simultaneously ego *and* superego. Clearly, interpreting this experience in terms of both superego and ego at the same time requires a shift in how we think about those psychological constructs: not as the straightforward internalization of an externally experienced pattern (superego) that opposes a preexisting and internally grounded structure (ego), but rather as the creation and re-creation of a unified though complex new psychological and cultural reality by the young person him or herself, drawing on a wide range of relevant materials clustered around a centrally important parental figure.[25]

Moreover, the Fountain Lake incident contains many elements of the wilderness romance/coming-of-age tradition, from James Fenimore Cooper's Leatherstocking tales to Leslie Marmon Silko's *Ceremony*: a life or death struggle in nature; the presence (in Muir's case, imagined) of a male "guide"; the discovery of new resources of strength and self-discipline; an unexpected resolution; and subsequent identification with cultural norms of adulthood.[26] In particular, such stories often emphasize the crucial role of a mentor in helping the young boy to a right understanding of his place in the natural world. A classic instance of this motif is found in William Faulkner's "The Bear." As an eleven-year-old boy learning to hunt, Ike McCaslin has come to feel his future inextricably linked with that of the huge, ancient, clubfooted bear that has roamed the familial hunting

25. In his early development of an object relations perspective, Fairbairn similarly reinterpreted the superego and the id as structures *within* and *supporting* the ego. Understanding the psyche as "composed of a multiplicity of dynamic structures falling into two classes: viz. (1) ego-structures, and (2) internal objects," he viewed the superego as the union of the "antilibidinal ego" and the "rejecting object" (1:112, 137). The superego "originates in an essentially empathic relationship towards frustrating figures, who are at the same time the most vital individuals in the environment of the child" (2:101–2). As a primitive and childish "organisation of sentiment" that functions negatively (frustrating the object-seeking behavior of the libido), the superego is dissociated from consciousness and so gains a certain sort of independence from the ego (2:100, 113–14); however, it still comes into being and is maintained *in the service of* the vitality and strength of the developing selfhood, not in opposition to it.

26. This cultural tradition has reappeared in the 1990s in the current interest in "initiation rituals," popularized by the "men's movement" and Robert Bly's *Iron John*. Gary Nabhan ("Going Truant," in Nabhan and Trimble) stresses that such initiation into adulthood can also constitute an initiation into a heightened environmental awareness. Curiously, however, Nabhan's description of his own coming-to-be-a-naturalist does *not* involve the presence of a mentor of any sort. Perhaps Muir's fundamentally self-guided or self-mentored initiation experience is more relevant for—or at least more characteristic of—the modern world than are primitive tribal rituals.

grounds for years, eluding all other hunters' attempts to capture or even sight him. The old bachelor Indian Sam Fathers, aware of the mysterious connection between Ike and the bear, trains the boy in the special ways needed to undertake the task of tracking him. This involves "relinquishing" all the trappings of civilization and hunting, including gun, watch, and compass. When he does so, Ike "enters it"—the primeval forest.

> When he realized he was lost, he did as Sam had coached and drilled him: made a cast to cross his backtrack. . . . But there was no bush beneath it, no compass nor watch, so he did next as Sam had coached and drilled him: made this next circle in the opposite direction and much larger . . . and now he was going faster though still not panicked, his heart beating a little more rapidly but strong and steady enough . . . and he did what Sam had coached and drilled him as the next and the last, seeing as he sat down on the log the crooked print, the warped indentation in the wet ground. (199–200)

Ultimately, Ike's moral, physical, intellectual, and emotional acquiescence to (and repeated conscious invocation of) Sam Fathers' guidance leads to the desired goal, the "victory," a sight of the bear's paw print and then of the bear himself.

The dynamics illustrated in Faulkner's story parallel Muir's relationship with his father, or rather with his internal image of his father: Muir experienced/constructed his father's presence in a positive, nurturing way, as instructor and as role model for his own emerging strength and identity. Ironically, however, in Muir's case this largely self-generated "mentoring" involved the imposition of a harsh and judgmental authority upon his natural surroundings rather than any sense of relinquishing personal control over the environment; moreover, that authority extended to his own body and emotions as well. The real utility and power of these psychological constructions are clear: Faced with harsh discipline and a chaotic, demanding environment, the young boy responded creatively to defuse the threat of the discipline by bringing it within himself, a tactic that allowed him to negotiate natural hardships, to respect and to assert his own body and abilities, and to avoid actual punishment and instead experience approval and companionship in his relationship with his father. At the same time, however, this process fostered a dependent sense of identity, a pattern of dissociation of body and emotion from self/mind, and an aggressive, controlling attitude toward his own body and toward the natural world.

Around the age of fifteen or sixteen, the adult Muir recalls, he "began to grow hungry for real knowledge," a hunger that marked the beginnings of a new flowering of his intellectual and imaginative life (*Boyhood*, 240, 245). As with the changes that occurred at age five, the fact that Muir can pinpoint a precise age for an important qualitative shift suggests a psychological basis in the development of specific cognitive and emotional capacities.[27] Of course, this shift also had a social and cultural context: in mid-nineteenth-century America, fifteen or sixteen was the usual age both of puberty and of full participation in economic activities; apprenticeships normally began a year or two before this (see Kett, chapter 1). Interestingly, Muir mentions mathematics and grammar as his first subjects of study, suggesting a need for sheer exercise and training of mental functions and pointing to one of the ways that he was able to fulfill the educational functions of an apprenticeship while still at home. His success at persuading his father to buy him books on these subjects foreshadowed the transformation of family relationships to which these cognitive developments would lead.

After relenting on the math and grammar, Daniel Muir clamped down and would let none but religious books into his household. John smuggled in literature and philosophy anyway, reading them by candlelight for a few stolen moments before being ordered to bed. As Muir later remembered, "Father failed perhaps two or three times in a whole winter to notice my light for nearly ten minutes, magnificent golden blocks of time, long to be remembered like holidays or geological periods" (*Boyhood*, 246). As his similes suggest, the struggle for access to books as well as the act of reading itself served as an escape from his father's authority. A huge victory in this process came when Daniel, impatiently ordering his oldest son to bed once again, unsuspectingly gave him permission to awaken as early as he wished for purposes of reading—permission that

27. Piaget (60–64) summarizes the emergence of "formal operational thinking" as the capacity for abstract thought, the use of hypotheses and theories, the construction of general laws and systems; according to Tyson and Tyson (187–90), the latest research suggests that the process is usually completed sometime between fourteen and seventeen. To be sure, certain aspects of formal operational thinking may have developed as early as Muir's first years in Wisconsin, and are perhaps reflected in his more distanced and ordered descriptions of the natural world at that point in the autobiography. However, the fulfillment of these new potentials depends both upon the maturation of the nervous system and upon the presence of an appropriately challenging and supportive social and educational environment. Thus, by fourteen or fifteen, Muir's neurological development may have been ahead of his social context, motivating him to reach out for (or to create) whatever opportunities for intellectual exercise he could find.

Muir immediately exercised by waking up at one in the morning, seemingly every day! Drawing on the intense body control and willpower exhibited in the lake incident, Muir remained within the letter of his father's discipline while carving out a space and time in which his own interests and identity could emerge.

However, his intellectual and emotional growth was fueled not only by reading and books. Knowing that his father would not allow him the firewood that would be needed for reading light, Muir instead used his hard-won early morning free time for building wooden models of the ingenious inventions that he had conceived while walking behind the plow. The very process of making the models held various layers of meaning: his father had whittled various objects (including a prized violin) while a youth in Lanarkshire, and John himself had carved model boats with his friends and fishermen in Dunbar. The Wisconsin inventions were much more ambitious affairs, however, requiring the skill with tools that Muir had developed over the long years of farm work. Like work on the farm (but more enjoyable), the activity of carving was both a clear source of pride and an occasion for intimate contact with natural materials.

More important, the inventions gave symbolic expression to Muir's continuing private struggle with self, body, father, and environment. As pure products of his imagination, not intended for actual use, these inventions can be read as material texts that reveal his inner life and concerns. Most were labor saving devices (a self-setting sawmill, waterwheels, automatic animal feeders, fire lighters, etc.) or measuring instruments (thermometers, barometers). Many of these were hooked up to ingenious clocks, which would start or stop them at any desired time. The themes of regulation and measurement both of work and of environment run through most of his inventions; the fact that he did not put them to practical use does not mean that they were not psychologically useful to him. Describing the completion of his first model, the sawmill, Muir says it was "discharged" from his mind, suggesting that the invention held a psychological weight or meaning for him; similarly, his statement that "somehow it seemed impossible to stop" points to inner forces compelling the activities of inventing and building (*Boyhood*, 251, 256).

His next invention was an "early-rising machine," a clock-regulated bed that would tip up and rouse the sleeper at a preset hour. Given his own ability to rise early, this invention was unnecessary in practical terms, but it perhaps functioned as a monument to Muir's own machinelike control of his body—and thus as both an embodiment and a repudiation of his father's wishes. Similarly, while Muir reports that his father was pleased by a seemingly Gothic-inspired clock bearing the inscription "All flesh is grass" and "shaped like a scythe to symbolize the scythe of Father

Time," the implicit message is that father Muir is not the highest authority over his son's activities. Taking this theme further, Muir next conceived and began to build a huge clock like the town clock in Dunbar, hoping to place it on the roof of the barn. Symbolically, this may have been an attempt on Muir's part to bring the work activities of the farm under some sort of structure or regulation other than that imposed by his father, thus re-creating the farm in the image of his beloved Dunbar (and of the ordered, rationalized countryside that surrounded it). Perhaps sensing these meanings, his father forbade him from completing the project. The way in which Muir describes his acceptance of this decision conveys some sort of emotional, almost nostalgic attachment to the image of the clock: "So I had to lay aside its big wheels and cams and rest content with the pleasure of inventing it, and looking at it in my mind and listening to the deep solemn throbbing of its long two-second pendulum with its two old axes back to back for the bob" (*Boyhood*, 258).

Alongside of and intertwined with his solitary activities of reading and inventing, Muir's teenage intellectual growth both allowed and was nourished by a parallel flowering of community and cultural life. By this time, the Muir farm at Fountain Lake had been surrounded by several other homesteads, mostly fellow Scots immigrants, and this sense of community was bolstered when Daniel—again somewhat capriciously—chose to establish a new farm, Hickory Hill, a few miles away from the original one. Although this move again saddled Muir with onerous tasks, it also brought him closer to the neighbors from whom he could borrow books and to peers with whom he talked, discussed books, shared poetry, played practical jokes, went to occasional school and spelling bees, and so on. The practical needs of the growing rural community provided other occasions for social contact: "Corduroying the swamps formed the principal part of road-making among the early settlers for many a day. At these annual road-making gatherings opportunity was offered for discussion of the news, politics, religion, war, the state of the crops, comparative advantages of the new country over the old, and so forth" (*Boyhood*, 209). Of course, Muir's move out into this frontier community life both was grounded in and helped to extend his senses of male identity and of male privilege, the inner and outer patterns of what he could expect to be and to do as a man in the larger world outside the home and farm.

In particular, a neighboring Scotsman, William Duncan, gave Muir a much-needed glimpse of an alternative father figure and of an alternative dimension of the Scots cultural tradition. Duncan chided Daniel Muir for the latter's negligence and harshness in the well-digging incident, and soon after, John turned to him to borrow books—significantly, Scott's *Waverley* novels, among others. Duncan embodied for his younger fellow immigrant the Scots tradition of "the intelligent, intellectually curious workingman," a tradition that included Muir's future hero Hugh Miller and that served to validate and to encourage his present intellectual interests (Turner, 64). In particular, Duncan gave Muir needed encouragement and companionship in the latter's inventing, as the older man "was wont to come along about chore time in the evening; then he and the boy would duck down cellar to inspect some new contrivance. There they would talk in whispers so as not to disturb Daniel studying in the room above. Duncan was so proud of John he couldn't keep from telling folks about the latest clock that would 'work like a man with a brain'" (L. M. Wolfe, 55). Another recent arrival in the neighborhood, Philip Gray of Edinburgh, set up a lending library in his home, featuring standard literature as well as current periodicals, including abolitionist material; Gray's sons David and John, along with David Taylor, became good friends of John and David Muir. Such human and cultural relationships opened up Muir's growing literary life to the important influences of classical authors (Plutarch and Josephus), literary classics (Shakespeare, Milton, British poets), religious philosophers (Thomas Dick), scientists (Hugh Miller), and explorers (Humboldt and Mungo Park).

Although most scholars have stressed the purely intellectual aspects of this broadening of Muir's mental horizons, equally important to the young man was the expansion of his imaginative and emotional worlds. His exposure to English romanticism (and the romantic orientation toward nature) had an undeniable impact on him (see, e.g., Turner, 61–71); on an emotional level, however, it was Scottish authors and culture that held particular significance for his personal growth. Scotland was deeply present in his life, not only in the form of the memories and feelings of his childhood but also in the enduring family and neighborhood culture of folklore, religion, song, language, and customs (see L. M. Wolfe, 35–44). Thus, for example, Muir felt a special affinity with the cultural and physical landscape of Scott's novels, which were read widely by Scots throughout the world and functioned as an important means of establishing Scottish identity in the diaspora (Gittings, 142). One of Muir's earliest discoveries was *The Bride of Lammermoor;* set in the hills and along the coastline of his own childhood, the novel probably both evoked and extended his awareness of the Scottishness of his being. Of course, the romance, mystery, and excitement of such texts, along with their construction of masculinity in terms of loyalty, physicality, freedom, willfulness, and emotional expressiveness, accord well with what we now have come to interpret as the expected affective world and developmental tasks of males during the teenage years; however, it is more precise to think of

Muir as participating in the wide-ranging nineteenth-century cultural *creation* of such a pattern of teenage male psychology, of which our present-day perspectives are the inheritors.

Other aspects of a peculiarly Scottish sensibility spoke directly to Muir's own condition on the Wisconsin frontier. The atmosphere of loss, longing, melancholy, fate, and defiance characteristic of much of Scottish culture helped him make sense of his personal experiences of home, family, and world, as well as contributing to a growing awareness of his own particular place in the historical saga of the Scottish diaspora. Further, Scots tradition (especially as reconstructed by eighteenth- and nineteenth-century authors such as Scott) is strongly grounded in a historical sense, in which individual identity is constructed through identification with family, lineage, location, and physical surroundings; thus the term "house" (as in "the House of Ravenswood" of *Lammermoor*) signifies simultaneously an actual building, the surrounding estate and landscape, a family, and a historical legacy, with the male head of the household the embodiment of them all. Social relationships are an extension of the familial model, stressing hierarchy, face-to-face relations, and reciprocal obligations between all members of society. According to Alice Chandler, the use of Scots tradition by "the medievalizing imagination" of the nineteenth century was grounded in "a single, central desire—to feel at home in an ordered yet organically vital universe" (1).[28] It was this very desire that lived in the heart of the young immigrant on the American frontier.

In these and other ways, Scots writings and culture, conveyed to Muir by a community of transplanted Scots, allowed him to reconstruct his own personal heritage in terms of an overarching symbol, "Scotland," which was at once wider and shallower than his childhood experience of Dunbar had been. Quite simply, he learned to be Scottish not in Scotland but in Wisconsin. This model of a personal reconstruction of a cultural tradition is both parallel to and distinct from the public processes described by Eric Hobsbawm as the "invention of tradition" and by Werner Sollors as the "invention of ethnicity," as modes of the construction and assertion of group identity in the modern world. Muir was clearly in contact with and affected by both of these types of public processes—for example, Sir Walter Scott himself represents an invented image of Scottish

28. With respect to the American cultural context, T. J. Jackson Lears discusses the important place of Scott in the development of "antimodernism," especially the "medievalizing" tendencies and the "martial ideal" (99–107). Although Lears's analysis begins in the 1880s, I suspect that personal experiences such as Muir's were the sources out of which the later cultural movement would emerge.

tradition and identity. However, the specific "invention of Scotland" I am analyzing in Muir is a very private, individual phenomenon, taking form within his own experience and life course, fueled by individual motivations and situations and fleshed out with unique images and associations. This personal invention began as an almost instinctive affair: as we have seen, as soon as he immigrated to America, the adolescent Muir began to interpret his new home in terms of his own memories and knowledge of the old, as a spontaneous creative response to a new and difficult situation. It was not until his later teenage years, however, that this immediate, visceral allegiance to "home" was expanded and reinterpreted—in part through the use of public cultural materials, including "invented" ones—into a powerful image of Scotland and a deeply felt sense of Scottish heritage and identity. Thus, his strong lifelong identity as a Scot reflects the importance not only of his childhood in Dunbar but also—and perhaps even more—of this cultural reconstruction while a teenager in the Wisconsin woods.[29]

One dimension of this constellation of values and images was embodied in the figure of the Scots explorer Mungo Park. To be sure, Muir is reported to have also read Humboldt at the time, but the writings of the German naturalist were too abstract and scientifically sophisticated for Muir to fully grasp at this point: in contrast, the adventures of his countryman carried directly accessible emotional and cultural appeal as well as intellectual challenge. In *Boyhood* (259–60), Muir recounts a memorable incident in which he read passages of Park's *Travels in the Interior Regions of Africa* to his mother, evoking interest and encouragement from her but only scorn from his father.

What values and visions would Muir have encountered in Park? Discussing the motives that led him to Africa, the explorer states:

> I had a passionate desire to examine into the productions of a country so
> little known and to become experimentally acquainted with the modes

---

29. Describing the public process, Hobsbawm writes: "'Traditions' which appear or claim to be old are often quite recent in origin and sometimes invented. . . . [T]he peculiarity of 'invented traditions' is that the continuity with [the historic past] is largely factitious. In short, they are responses to novel situations which take the form of references to old situations, or which establish their own past by quasi-obligatory repetition. It is the contrast between the constant change and innovation of the modern world and the attempt to structure at least some part of social life within it as unchanging and invariant, that makes the 'invention of tradition' so interesting to historians of the past two centuries" (Hobsbawm and Ranger, 1–2). Interestingly, the private phenomenon of an "invention of tradition" that I discern in the teenage Muir seems to proceed by some of the same mechanisms (reference to the past, repetition) and to fulfill the same functions (creation of stability in the face of change) as does the public process.

and life and character of the natives . . . and if I should succeed in render-
ing the geography of Africa more familiar to my countrymen, and in opening to their ambition and industry new sources of wealth, I knew that I
was in the hands of men of honour, who would not fail to bestow that re-
muneration which my successful services should appear to them to merit.
(Park, 2)

With exploration, economic imperialism, and personal gain his primary
concerns, Park's narrative is dominated by adventure stories and by accounts of the natural resources, products, and trade patterns of the country. Both the picaresque and the economic dimensions would have
touched important chords in Muir: as a child he had been fascinated by
stories of Scottish sailors, soldiers, and pirates; more recently, the practical young farmer and pioneer in another "primitive wilderness" may have
been particularly interested in the descriptions of the agriculture and technology of the distant land. Discussing the human inhabitants, Park gives
a relatively positive view of the level of "civilization" of the Negroes, in
large part because of his estimation that "the belief of one God, and of
a future state of reward and punishment, is entire and universal among
them" (250). These "pagans" rank higher than the cruel, savage, barbaric
Muslims, while the occasional invocation of providential support for
British endeavors signals the explorer's perception of Britain's own most-
divinely-favored-nation status. Thus, the familiar moral hierarchy sus-
tains Park's cultural, national, and economic goals.

With respect to his actual experiences of the landscape, Park often interpreted Africa as Muir did Wisconsin: through the lens of Britain. This
is hinted in one of his first descriptions, in which economic concerns are
again evident: "The country itself, being an immense level, and very generally covered with woods, presents a tiresome and gloomy uniformity to
the eye; but although nature has denied to the inhabitants the beauties of
romantic landscapes, she has bestowed on them, with a liberal hand, the
more important blessings of fertility and abundance" (8). Perhaps not
surprisingly, most of his few attributions of beauty or emotional value to
the landscape come in terms of the familiar "romantic landscapes" for
which he longed. Thus, at one of the dramatic high points of his narrative,
Park writes: "I saw with infinite pleasure the great object of my mission—
the long sought for majestic Niger, glittering to the morning sun, as broad
as the Thames at Westminster, and slowly flowing *to the eastward*" (176–
77). Similarly, on the way to Timbuctoo, his other primary destination,
"we passed a large town called Kabba, situated in the midst of a beautiful
and highly-cultivated country; bearing a greater resemblance to the centre
of England than to what I should have supposed had been the middle of
Africa" (184). Thus, one of the major themes of the whole work is that

of the physical, cultural, economic, and imaginative domination of a new environment by a powerful male—an image that, more than any specific intellectual content, spoke directly to Muir's own situation and needs. As we have seen, Muir's immigration to Wisconsin posed threats to which he responded through intense control both of the external world and of his own body and feelings, and in this Park provided him with useful instruction for how to be a Scot in a strange land.

The impact of this reappropriated Scottish cultural legacy was nowhere more evident than in Muir's religious life, which constituted yet another arena in which the teenager's newly developed intellectual and cultural abilities allowed him to renegotiate his relationships with his family and with his environment. Having had the Bible literally whipped into him as a child, he now began to use scriptural arguments to successfully confront his father. In at least one early case, he was initially encouraged by William Duncan, who publicly accused Daniel of neglecting his family's health by adopting a strict vegetarian diet. His father did not back down on that occasion, but soon afterward Muir himself (taking on the role of his mentor) was able to cite Scripture to convince Daniel of the biblical basis of meat eating. Other arguments followed, Muir's quick mind often allowing him to gain the advantage.

However, we should not too quickly assume that these and other incidents signal the emergence of long-simmering rebellion on the part of the teenage Muir. Most commentators emphasize Muir's outright opposition to his father during this period; such a view presumes that a person can—indeed, must—"break away" from family in order to become an "independent" self. Although I do not deny the depth and importance of such opposition, it seems equally true that Muir's continuing, measured *accommodation with* his father contributed in crucial and powerful ways to his process of self-creation, as well as allowing him to keep other important family relationships. The ability to *maintain* emotional bonds, even in times of opposition, is as much (if not more) essential to emotional maturity as the ability to break such bonds.

With respect to religious belief itself, it is important to realize that Muir was exposed to many shades of opinion other than his father's zealous views. In Scotland, he had close contact with the established Kirk, favored by his mother and grandparents, among others. In America, the family's religious community, the Campbellites—originally a transatlantic Scottish American movement, which in the New World had merged with other groups to form the Disciples of Christ—was much more wide-open and varied than Daniel Muir's idiosyncratic stance. Although many commentators (including Albanese and Nash) have vaguely characterized the Muir family religiousness as Calvinist—Turner (69) and Wilkins (61) both using the odd term "crypto-Calvinist"—one of the defining characteristics of the Campbellites was an explicit rejection of certain major Calvinist doctrines. Alexander Campbell of Glasgow took as his goal the restoration of the primitive Christian church through strict obedience to the divine law as laid down in the New Testament. At the same time, "he was also a fervent exponent of eighteenth-century rationalism, a disciple of John Locke and the Scottish philosophers" (Ahlstrom, 1:544). Thus, his movement had no fixed creed, but trusted in the individual's ability to rationally discern the "plain sense of the Bible" to resolve disputes— which, consequently, often went unresolved, despite Campbell's authoritarian attempts to assert his own interpretations. Ultimately, the various movements that came together in the Disciples of Christ shared many of the values and visions of popular evangelicalism—individualism, democracy, biblicalism, moralism, lay ministry, personal responsibility for public betterment, the millennial role of America, the perception of the American West as the new Eden—as well as a rationalistic and antisectarian stance that in fact aligned them with some of the more liberal trends within American Protestantism. Indeed, Donald Worster takes Muir's Campbellite background as representative of the broader Protestant roots of the American conservation movement, distilled into the four qualities of "moral activism, ascetic discipline, egalitarian individualism, and aesthetic spirituality" (196).[30]

Despite—in some cases, because of—his father's religious zeal, Muir was exposed to these varied currents and influences through fellow Disciples and through the denomination's extensive publishing efforts, including numerous tracts and the newspaper *Millennial Harbinger* (which, as various letters attest, his parents continued to send to him and he continued to read long after he moved away from home). Further, the Disciples' instincts for evangelizing and for theological discussion brought them in contact with Christians from all of the other denominations present on the frontier. Henry Howe, a Disciples circuit rider in southern Wisconsin from 1864 to 1868, mentions preaching, listening, and discussing with Methodists, Baptists, Presbyterians, Episcopalians, United Brethren, German Reformed, and others throughout the region; similarly, Daniel Muir, himself an ardent preacher and evangelist, publicly engaged the religious life of his adopted country, and perhaps often brought his eldest son along as well. Indeed, continuing his account of the possibilities for social interaction at road making and other community gatherings, Muir recalled that "the principal opportunities, recurring every week, were the hours after Sunday church service," where Muir and his neighbors discussed

30. For detailed discussion of popular Protestant evangelicalism and of the Campbellite/ Disciples of Christ movement, see Hatch; Hensley; and Hughes and Allen. On the Muir family religiousness, see Stoll; Williams; and Worster.

spirit rappers and other religious matters (as well as various public issues of the day) (*Boyhood*, 209–11). John's youthful poem "The Old Log Schoolhouse" (1860) shows his close acquaintance with preaching of various doctrines, as he satirizes the pride, exclusiveness, and narrowness of itinerants of all stripes—in a manner that accords well with the Disciples' fundamental antisectarianism.

As one example of how his inherited religious culture ended up *supporting* Muir's recent expansion of his intellectual horizons, consider one of Muir's prized books of this period, Thomas Dick's *Christian Philosopher*. The learned Scotsman states his purpose in the preface to the second edition (1824):

> The following pages were written under the impression that the visible manifestation of the attributes of the Deity are too frequently overlooked by Christians in their views of the great objects of religion, and in the worship they offer to the Father of their spirits. . . . It is presumed, that no Christian reader will for once imagine, that the views illustrated in this work are intended to be *substituted* in place of the peculiar revelations of the Bible. The object of this volume is to illustrate the harmony which subsists between the system of nature and the system of revelation; and to show that the manifestations of God, in the material universe, ought to be blended with our views of the facts and doctrines recorded in the volume of inspiration. (vii)

The bulk of the book is taken up with enthusiastic description and theological interpretation of the discoveries of modern science; in a representative example of his style, Dick invites his readers to "attend to the *atmosphere*, in the constitution of which the wisdom of God is no less conspicuous than in the other departments of nature" (72). To be sure, even such theologically liberal sentiments leave room for the possibility that the human and natural conditions of the earth are still in the process of being molded by the Divine and have not yet attained the perfection of temporally or metaphysically distant future states: "If, then, the eye of man (who is a depraved inhabitant of a world partly in ruins) is an organ so admirably fitted for extending our prospects of the visible creation— we may reasonably conclude, that organized beings of superior intelligence and moral purity, possess the sense of vision in a much greater degree of perfection than man in his present state of degradation" (103). Ultimately, however, the universe as it is must be regarded as an expression of God's will:

> A third conclusion is, that *the successive changes, to which our globe has been subjected, have been improvements in its condition as a habitable world,* that there has been a correspondent advance towards perfection in

the natures of the animals and plants which have been placed upon its surface; and that *the Deity, during this long period of successive changes, was gradually fitting up this world for the ultimate residence of moral and intellectual beings,* such as the human species that now inhabit it. (187)

Although the book's wealth of scientific knowledge surely was fascinating and inspiring to Muir, the liberal theological ideas were not as new to him as most scholars have presumed. Anglo-American science—and theological interpretations of science such as that of Dick—were strongly influenced by Baconianism and Scottish common sense philosophy, leading to an inductive approach that strove to get rid of theory and hypothesis in favor of the observation and classification of empirical facts. But this is precisely what the Disciples (influenced by some of the same historical movements) tried to do with respect to biblical interpretation, in their rejection of creeds and other "mere human opinions and inventions" and in their insistence on the plain, self-evident meaning that (they believed) any open-minded reader would find in Scripture. For example, James S. Lamar, whose *Organon of Scripture* (1859) was the culmination of early Disciples philosophy, claimed that the inductive method applies equally to the "Book of Revelation" and to the "Book of Nature." Both contain empirically observable facts, which can be classified, the common elements drawn out, and the essential truths seen, to be agreed upon by all—thus helping to bring about the movement's defining goals of mutual understanding, elimination of sectarianism, and the restoration of the primitive, unified church. Such language and ideals are strikingly similar to those of Dick. Although there is little concrete evidence as to the specific aspects of the Disciples intellectual tradition with which Muir had contact, the fact that the tradition could result in a thinker such as Lamar suggests that it also prepared Muir quite well for his encounter with Dick.[31]

Thus, despite the pressure of his father's authority, Muir had some latitude in matters of belief, and so we can assume that he actively chose his beliefs (and his manner of expressing them) for reasons of his own. Of course, at this stage in a young person's life, "choice" in the sense of a totally autonomous, free, conscious, rational decision is virtually impossible, even in a nurturing and supportive environment—and Muir's was far from that. The sense of "choice" that seems more appropriate here would be the ability to assent with (most of) one's whole being, to do what is right for oneself, what fundamentally fits who one is; past the stage of sheer emulation, in the process of freeing himself from (and at the

---

31. On the common sense influence on Anglo-American science, see Hovenkamp; on Lamar and the Disciples, see Allen.

same time creating himself out of) his father's more explicit persuasion, control, and coercion, Muir was at a place where his religious beliefs (and other dimensions of his inner life) could come out of "who he was" at that time. This is not to deny that he still was decisively shaped by (and even needed) his father's influence, by his childhood legacy, by unconscious desires and conflicts, and so on, or that on many levels whatever definition of self he had achieved was provisional or temporary. Rather, my point is that all these elements were part of a definite human being, in large part self-grounded, responsibly creating an immediately lived identity and path in the world.[32]

At this point, we can turn to the only concrete evidence that we have concerning his beliefs at the time—an evangelical letter to a teenage friend—and place it in the wider context of the concerns, images, and dynamics that mark this period of his life. Sometime in 1856, at the age of eighteen, Muir wrote a long letter to his friend A. Bradley Brown in which he attempted to dramatize the emotional and spiritual transformations that he thought should follow from belief in Jesus Christ as one's savior (see 1:20–25). Comparing the Christian believer to a tired, hungry, homeless, outcast orphan wandering through a desolate landscape on a wild, stormy night, Muir evoked the joy and hope that such a wanderer would feel upon seeing the lights of a warm, cozy, happy mansion. Further, Muir stressed the resulting feelings of gratitude and love toward the "lord" of the mansion, who leaves his company to let in the wanderer, feeds and clothes him, and watches over him "as tenderly as the fond mother over her sick child." Just as such a wanderer would never forget that man, but rather hold him forever "in the best place in the warmest end of your heart," so too should the Christian believer remember Jesus, who "came far from his home, and out into the storm," enduring the worst insults and pain, to find and to save us. Muir concluded: "O dear friend let us give our hearts to Christ our Saviour and love him and follow in his footsteps forever, then however far we may be separated while we

---

32. Adapting Erikson's notion of "fidelity" as a "capacity 'to set one's heart,'" Sharon Parks proposes that "the threshold of young adulthood is marked by the capacity to take self-aware responsibility for choosing the path of one's own fidelity" (77). To be sure, this process (or a similar one) takes place at *all* ages, not just late adolescence/young adulthood; everyone is constantly forming and reforming a sense of identity in the context of the particular constraints and resources of one's cognitive and emotional development, important relationships, cultural images and expectations, environmental demands and opportunities, and so on. Thus, the distinctive "achievement" of late adolescence is not so much a wholly new structure (à la the Eriksonian understanding of "identity") but rather a changed quality to a constantly evolving dynamic of life—a new breadth of self-awareness, an increased depth of responsibility, a heightened heaviness and lightness of the weights that one's heart can bear.

each follow our destiny here, we shall meet again above the region of storms in that bright mansion of the blessed, the home of our Saviour and Father, to part again no more forever."

As Turner (67) suggests, Muir was going through a period of religious struggle, testing his familial faith against his own emerging emotional, intellectual, and ethical standards; however, to a greater extent than most commentators (including Turner) have realized, that struggle was taking place *within* the religious world inherited from his family. For example, Daniel Muir would write to his eldest son (after the latter left home) of the centrality of "remembering Jesus in one's heart" at the same time as he stressed the outward expression of this faith in proper action, often judged from a narrow and legalistic standpoint ("Be sure and please your Heavenly Father by believing his every word and keeping his commandments" [1:126]). For his part, John chose to emphasize the personal dimension; in writing to Bradley, he evoked the believer's relationship with Jesus as friend and companion as well as savior and lord, a relationship based in love as a response to the love that Jesus has given. In this, of course, Muir stood squarely in the midst of much of mid-nineteenth-century evangelicalism (before the split into opposing conservative and liberal camps), which encompassed a personal "religion of the heart" with some of the same sense of hope and optimism with which it tried to incorporate modern scientific discoveries. Thus, Muir portrayed belief as the act of giving Jesus "the best place in the warmest end of your heart" and remembering him "with steady deep love while memory lasts." Perhaps as a result of the young immigrant's own struggle to preserve in his thought and feeling the legacy of his distant childhood, for Muir it was remembering itself—in particular, the memory of the heart—that bore the weight of faith.

Moreover, the imaginative passages of the letter suggest ways in which this theological stance was reformulated in the light of other cultural images—including specifically Scottish ones—so as to hold special meanings for the young Muir. The scene with which the letter opens—a homeless orphan slogging wearily through a rough, stormy wilderness—has various possible literary antecedents, from *The Pilgrim's Progress* to one of Muir's old favorites, Burns's "Tam O'Shanter":

> The wind blew as't wad blawn its last;
> The rattling showers rose on the blast;
> The speedy gleams the darkness swallow'd;
> Loud, deep and lang the thunder bellow'd;
> That night, a child might understand,
> The Deil had business on his hand.
>
> (Burns, 47)

Interestingly, Muir's letter contains many elements of the tradition that Colin Manlove has termed "Scottish fantasy": a solitary protagonist, a Manichaeanism expressed in absolute contrasts (especially of light and dark), the importance of houses, and an ethic and aesthetic of barrenness and self-denial. Although it does not end in suicide (as in many instances of Scottish fantasy), Muir's earthly journey does end in death, which (as a Christian evangelist) he resolves into an image of a bright otherworldly home.[33] More concretely, Muir's "princely mansion," filled with "comforts and cordials" and a "gay warm company" with a "lord" at the head, resembles nothing so much as a Scottish estate à la Sir Walter Scott's novels. The "lord" of the mansion embodies a public, male persona grounded in specifically Scottish ideals of nobility and of kinship, as he undertakes the civic responsibilities of leadership of his own "company" and support for the orphaned and homeless; Muir's sketch suggests Scott's frequent descriptions of the feudal feast, "the bountiful meal at which all classes come together to share in their leader's generosity" (A. Chandler, 44–45). Interestingly, the lord was thus a theologically appropriate figure for Jesus, as Muir's portrayal implies; at the same time, the figure expresses a more gentle, private, female dimension (also often attributed to Jesus) as he watches over the weary traveler "as tenderly as the fond mother over her sick child."

Muir's attraction to such imagery must have gone deeper than cultural allusion, expressing both his own childhood legacy and his present experiences and aspirations. The evocation of a Scottish estate suggests the enduring power that Scotland held for the young immigrant, and especially the feelings of permanence, stability, and community that he associ-

---

33. In one example of Scottish fantasy, "For [Alasdair] Gray's Duncan Thaw the world is a place of bleakness and rejection where the only answer is the self-rejection of death" (Manlove, 22). Perhaps more intriguingly, *The Story of My Boyhood and Youth*—especially the initial chapters—can also be read as a Scottish fantasy, incorporating other of Manlove's characteristic elements: groundedness in the Scottish land, the special power accorded underground places (the seaside pools and castle of Dunbar), a "violent, even gleefully savage" strain (Manlove, 20), an attraction to the wildness beneath civilized society, and an assertion of egalitarian equality. In his adult writings, of course, Muir finds redemption not in heaven but in the natural world close at hand; thus, nature takes the place of (or is the site of) what Manlove refers to as "the fantastic": "In Scottish fantasy the fantastic experience and the world from which it emanates are very close to ours—into which they can come at any time. . . . there is much more the sense of exploring and transforming the familiar, rather than investigating the strange" (27, 29). Like Muir, many of the major writers of Scottish fantasy—George MacDonald, Robert Louis Stevenson, Andrew Lang, J. M. Barrie, and others—lived as adults outside of Scotland; thus, these authors' emphasis on the familiar as fantastic may have something to do with the quest to reconnect with or to reconstitute a lost childhood home.

ated with the old stone buildings of Dunbar. More personally, the description of the lord contains some of Muir's still-powerful feelings for his grandfather, whose welcoming hand and house had often proved a haven from his father's harshness. In the New World, the weariness and confusion Muir felt while clearing the Wisconsin forest found expression in the traveler's "toilsome way" through "rough thorny places"; though not literally orphaned, he must have often felt distanced or alienated from his harsh father and his overworked mother (especially during the throes of teenage-hood). Most recently, throughout 1856, Muir had been trudging daily the six miles between the original homestead and the site of the new farm, and some lonely, stormy evening may have been the original inspiration for the scene; as he passed by the homes of other Scots immigrants, some of them surely opened their doors to him in a more warm and responsive way than he could expect from his father. At the same time, Muir's own home probably contributed to the idealized mansion of the Bradley letter; according to Linnie Marsh Wolfe, "With two and a half stories, [the Muir house] had eight rooms, a wide front hallway, and a dignified entrance facing the road" (29), the house being set back from the road on a hill. (For a description of the new Hickory Hill home, seemingly similar to the first, see Wolfe [42–43]). His brothers and sisters formed a "gay warm company" of their own, while the shifting presence and absence of his mother—associated both with a past fullness and with a present lack and longing—signified at least the possibility of a nurturing and caring maternal presence. Finally, we must remember that on many levels the son continued to love and to idealize the father, and to need him as authority and as role model for his own emerging manhood; thus, the aura of leadership, responsibility, attention, love, and justice attributed to the lord reflect both John's appreciation of and his continuing hopes for his relationship with Muir senior.

Thus, a whole array of specific, positively charged persons and places stood behind the culturally shaped lord/mansion imagery, infusing the ultimate Jesus/heaven symbolism with a particularly personal level of emotional power and depth.[34] Further, in the process of fulfilling these religious and psychological functions, such motifs require their opposites: night, storm, wilderness. Of particular importance for my concerns,

---

34. As I hope should be apparent by now, this entire process can be described in object relations terms as the reconstruction of a range of internal object representations and their use both in mediating primary relationships and as transitional phenomena. Grounded in the legacy of earliest youth, the process is also open to the power and presence of newer persons, places, cultural influences, and psychological dynamics from later life; thus, my analysis is intended not as a reduction of adulthood to the experiences of infancy but as a rich description of the varied sources and shapes of a growing maturity.

Muir's use of these images conveys a certain devaluation of "this world" both in its social *and in its natural* aspects. In contrast to the interconnection of the domestic and the natural that is characteristic of Gothic architecture and novels (see A. Chandler, 7–9; McDannell, 34–37), Muir's mansion is sharply separate from the howling, stormy wilderness that surrounds it; the "big lighted front" of the mansion, marked by "long rows of windows, tier upon tier" that make it "forbiddingly grand," sets it apart both from the landscape and from the human traveler. Similarly, heaven, "that bright mansion of the blessed," lies "above the region of storms," beyond the present world. Parallel to the fourteen-year-old's dissociation of mind from body in the face of threats from father and from environment, we here see Muir escaping similar threats by dissociating his attachments, feelings, and hopes from his present world, orienting them instead toward an "otherworldly home."[35]

On my reading, he experienced this otherworldly home as a rich, multilayered reality that simultaneously represented the lost home of childhood Scotland, appropriated various elements of his cultural heritage, pointed to the more attractive and supportive elements of his present situation, constituted an active and powerful religious belief, and expressed his continuing hopes for family and home in the future. Thus, for the teenage Muir, religiousness was centrally a matter of trusting and reaching out to emotionally charged persons—rather, an emotionally charged Person. Holding such a Person in one's heart helps one to negotiate the pain, loss, and forsakenness that characterize this world (both natural and social/familial) and to reach one's true home in a better world, "the home of our Saviour and Father," where friends and loved ones shall meet again forever. As an aspect of his inner life, this multilayered construction of religiousness complemented the focus on control—of self, world, and family relations—expressed in his activity of inventing: both allowed escape to a place in which he could express the intense feelings of loss, love, longing, and hope that had been his blessing and his curse since childhood. Similarly, his religiousness paralleled—and often incorporated—his active appropriation of cultural symbols (an idealized "Scotland," literary images and scientific texts, traditional religious values) and experiences from his personal history and surroundings (grandfather, Dunbar, immigrant neighbors). Finally, his religious perspective, his inventing,

---

35. According to Bachelard, the image of a mansion or house is uniquely suited to serve as a means of psychological protection, for "the house is one of the greatest powers of integration for the thoughts, memories and dreams of mankind. . . . It maintains [a person] through the storms of the heavens and through those of life. It is body and soul. It is the human being's first world" (6, 7).

and his cultural life were all strongly shaped by his direct experience of his natural surroundings themselves—demanding, dangerous, and confusing.

For Muir as a young child, engagement with his natural environment served as an arena within which to respond creatively to the pains and demands of home and school; by the time he was a teenager, however, a vision of a heavenly home was required to help him to imaginatively negotiate the pains and demands both of his human home and of the natural world. To be sure, this devaluation of nature was juxtaposed with an array of more positive ideas, images, and associations. At other times and in other situations, Muir surely regarded his natural surroundings with wonder, joy, and trust, bringing forth into his teenage years both the primal relationships with nature he had established as a child and the associations with loved persons and happy times of the past and present; such experiences may have found expression in the blissful descriptions of nature that he read in his favorite romantic poets (or in theological perspectives such as that of Thomas Dick). Even the depth of pain of his experiences in the Scottish and Wisconsin landscapes—and the corresponding negative emotions, symbolic devaluation, and physical aggressiveness with which Muir responded to that pain—had the positive effect of allowing the natural world to be more real to him than would have been the case in an easy, uneventful childhood. As with Wordsworth, Muir's youthful relationship with his surroundings was "[f]ostered alike by beauty and by fear" (*Prelude,* I:302); in both pain and delight, harmony and opposition, the natural world was one of the defining presences of his experience and identity from an early age. As for the weary, homeless traveler in the letter, so too for the young Muir "life is sweet," and so he dared to confront the pains and difficulties facing him by reaching out to loved people, to powerful ideas and images, and to deeply felt patterns of relationship with his natural surroundings. Here as at various other points in his youth, Muir drew upon the various, somewhat fragmented resources that he found on the Wisconsin frontier to create a path through the world, guided not primarily by the wisdom of any particular cultural or social system but by his own instincts for emotional, psychological, and physical survival.

# Two

# Adrift on This Big Sinny World
## Wisconsin, 1856–1863

By his early twenties, Muir was in the ambiguous social and economic position that Joseph Kett has characterized as "semi-dependence." He participated fully in the work-life of family and community, thus fulfilling essential economic functions, but he was not a property owner or family head, nor was he socially recognized as a full adult. Kett has identified a number of rites of passage through which a nineteenth-century American male might achieve a more independent status and thus "become a man": church membership, marriage, acquiring a farm, going to the city for work, entering a profession, or leaving home for further training or education. Such institutions often combined cultural, social, and economic dimensions; for the New England Puritans, for example, a culturally shaped inner experience of conversion, publicly witnessed and validated, led the individual to social standing and economic and political power. In frontier Wisconsin, with a religious landscape shaped by revivalism and disestablishment, membership in a particular church did not necessarily open up avenues of more general public power, though this occurred to some extent; rather, the lack of integration of sacred and secular intensified the importance of personal religious experience and allegiance in structuring the identities both of the individual and of a smaller social grouping (a specific church, sect, etc.).

In the Muirs' own tradition, the Campbellites/Disciples, it was not conversion that conferred religious and social status but rather the rational choice to undergo baptism and, subsequently, to shape one's life around Christ through individual rectitude, participation in the community, and in particular through the support of the group's evangelical efforts.[1] Daniel Muir's allegiance to the latter cause was one of the reasons that he

1. Hughes and Allen (112–16) interpret the early Disciples' focus on baptism as a rejection of the emotional uncertainty and psychological dependence engendered by the Calvin-

came to America in the first place, and it was (partly) to raise more money to contribute to the worldwide Disciples missionary efforts that he had bought the new farm at Hickory Hill; by then he was spending most of his time not in farming but in reading the Bible and himself evangelizing throughout Wisconsin. Thus, the elder Muir embodied the personal and public role of the farmer-evangelist, and this would have been the dominant model of religious and social identity presented to his oldest son.

Muir's ultimate inability or refusal to enter into this role reveals much about both his personal condition and his social context. He clearly tried on the role of evangelist, and did so with much intensity and according to characteristically Disciples tenets; the letter to Bradley Brown was not a call to emotional conversion but an impassioned yet rational discourse on the proper place of Jesus in one's heart and life, arguing by analogy for the concrete decisions that logically follow from Christian belief. Alongside this evangelizing impulse, he obviously felt some degree of pride in his skill and achievements as a farmer, and he had become known in the community for his work; thus, he could easily have stepped into— and probably bettered—his father's career. By his early twenties, however, he was simply tired of farmwork, and inventing had become the locus of his energy, talent, and neighborhood fame. Moreover, he was reaching a point of being able to express his dissatisfactions with the ways in which his father had structured the family's life, in terms both of the farming regime and of Daniel's activities as itinerant. Perhaps most important, Muir was never really "offered" the role of farmer-evangelist in an encouraging, supportive way to begin with; that is, although Daniel Muir *embodied* a possible adult role, he did not actively *initiate* or *sponsor* his son into that role. He did not offer to help set John up in farming, give or loan land or equipment, or even encourage him to do it on his own,

---

ists' reliance on conversion as the sign of God's election. Recoiling from the anxiety and distress they had suffered while "under conviction" and awaiting an experience of conversion, the founders of the movement came to believe that such a process could not be God's way of drawing sinners to Himself. Rather, Christians "can and must reconcile themselves to God through rational belief of scriptural testimony and through righteous behavior. Christ did not die . . . to atone God to human beings but human beings to God, and his life and death in part provided an example that we should follow in his steps" (113). Thus, Alexander Campbell's insistence on immersion as the proper mode of baptism contained within it a message of "immediate certainty of salvation and an end to waiting and mourning. No longer would a sinner anxiously wait for months or even years, seeking an experience that might ratify his or her election. Instead, the sinner simply would hear the gospel and submit to immersion for the forgiveness of sins" (115). As we shall see, it was these motifs of rational choice and of baptism—not that of conversion—that would guide Muir's self-understanding for years to come.

nor does he seem to have actively helped or encouraged his son to take up the calling of itinerant preacher. Instead, Daniel continued to use John as a laborer on his own farm, keeping him in the subservient position that he had occupied during his teenage years.

Daniel's failure to acknowledge his son's changing position and needs was grounded in his own life history (as well as in his awareness that the farm depended heavily upon John's work). Himself an orphan, he had not received paternal or familial guidance and sponsorship when he stood on the threshold of adulthood (or at any other point in his life, for that matter); his own "coming of age" occurred haphazardly, when he first went to Glasgow to find work, eventually entering the army. The latter gave him a surface direction, but it was probably not until he married and had a family that he achieved a deeper psychological and social identity. Interestingly, his fervent (and changing) religious commitments played a dual role here, providing important social standing and sanction but also allowing him to keep his distance from the "established" religious and social matrix, and thus to maintain a sense of personal uniqueness as an individualist and/or outsider. As noted above, both in Scotland and even more in Wisconsin, Daniel needed a clear role as undisputed master of the family; again, his experience as an orphan may have led to his attaching intense importance to stable family relationships. Finally, the ideals of adulthood that Disciples culture put forth emphasized one's spiritual state and role in the strictly religious community, and so would not have encouraged the elder Muir to concern himself very much with his son's "worldly" career. Whatever the reasons, all of Daniel's paternal energies were directed toward structuring the family in a certain static way, with little attention paid to the process of helping his children to move out of that structure in an appropriate manner.

Thus, Muir's turning away from the role of farmer-evangelist involved both an active decision on his part and a breakdown of familial and cultural processes. At the same time, it is important to realize that this rejection/failure of one particular religious role did not imply any lessening of his Christian fervor. The central evidence we have for his religiousness at this time, the "Old Log Schoolhouse" poem, satirizes (and even excoriates) fire-and-brimstone preachers not as a rejection of Christianity but indeed in the name of a purer, truer Christianity, rational and anti-sectarian—a characteristic Disciples critique of other sects. Muir continued to evangelize for years after leaving home, but he did not want to become an evangelist, in large part because he did not want—or, was not allowed—to become like his father in such an explicit way. Thus, the fact that he did not take on the primary religious and social role available to him was shaped not by any significant changes in his own beliefs but rather by the specific dynamics of the young man's relationship with his father.

However, few other options were available to help Muir move out of his state of emotional and socioeconomic semidependence. True, he saw his sister Sarah marry a fellow Scots immigrant, David Galloway, who subsequently bought the old Fountain Lake farm and homestead from Daniel; Sarah's experience reminds us that the avenues through which a woman could enter adulthood on the Wisconsin frontier were much more limited than those open to men, and that the very fact of having a variety of possible ways of leaving home constituted one of the privileges held out by society to young males. For his part, Muir's younger brother and constant companion David soon claimed this male privilege, as he fell in love with a neighborhood girl and, hoping to make marriage possible, left home to work. However, there is little indication of any romantic interests on Muir's part during this time, and neither marriage nor sheer money-making work seems to have appealed to him. He had some thought of becoming a physician, but no immediate way to work toward this dream. Perhaps most important, he was not yet emotionally ready to leave his family; as he reflects in his autobiography, he was "loath to leave home" and "was naturally extremely shy and had been taught to have a poor opinion of myself, as of no account" (*Boyhood*, 260).

As is well known, this sense of hesitancy and confusion—even stagnation—regarding his adult identity and career path would dog Muir for years; indeed, even after he eventually left home, he would not "establish himself" or "settle down" through work and family until his early forties. It is tempting to interpret this extended period of uncertainty—covering the whole of the rest of this book—in terms of Erik Erikson's concept of a "moratorium," a sort of holding pattern that is structurally understood as a continuation of adolescence, characterized by a distinct refusal or failure to enter adult identity, maturity, and stability. However, there are problems in understanding Muir's youthful wanderings and uncertainties as a moratorium: on the one hand, the whole concept and cultural reality of "adolescence" was still in the process of being created in the mid-nineteenth century, and much of Muir's earlier experience does not fit into that category; on the other hand, throughout his twenties and thirties Muir would move forward both on personal and on public levels in definite and important ways that go beyond a mere holding pattern. In a more helpful formulation—one that attributes more depth and definition to the active commitments and creations of this period—Daniel Levinson views "early adulthood" as the time during which an initial adult male identity is first formulated but then immediately subject to adaptation, compromise, and reformulation; the continual change and renegotiation of identity during this period does not signify any essential inadequacy in a young man's sense of self or way of being in the world but rather is an essential aspect of the long and difficult process of relating self to world. Such a perspective, grounded in the historical and biographical details of his life and cultural context, helps us to view Muir's young adult decisions, actions, and dreams both as expressions of a coherent identity that was real to him at the time and as definite steps—however tenuous—in the creation of a future selfhood and personal and career path.[2]

In his early twenties, on the threshold of young adulthood and manhood, Muir struggled to draw upon both inner insight and external support in taking his first steps out into a larger world. His most attractive option was to capitalize on his skills and interest in inventing and to try to get a job in a machine shop or factory, with a future goal of education in medicine. However, the encouragement of his sisters could not offset emotional hesitancy, lack of guidance, and the uncertainty and vagueness of the plan. The latter two problems were significantly addressed in August 1860 when William Duncan, in his culminating act as Muir's first mentor and alternative father figure, suggested that John show his inventions at the upcoming state fair in Madison. Duncan felt sure that this would attract attention to Muir and would land him a job in a machine

---

2. As formulated by Erikson, the moratorium is a "period of delay"—created both by the needs and decision of individual youth and by the sanction and wisdom of society—that may appear to constitute "a combination of prolonged immaturity and provoked precocity" but also serves as an opportunity for "experimentation with identity images" before the final entry into adulthood (156, 158). By contrast, in his study of the male life cycle Levinson emphasizes the idea of a definite—even expected—process of transition, possessing more structure and weight than a mere "period of delay" or experimentation. According to Levinson, the "early adult transition" (ages 17–22 in his study) is a time when "the growing male is a boy-man; he is terminating his pre-adult self and his place in the pre-adult world, and at the same time starting to form his first adult self and to make the choices through which he establishes his initial membership in the adult world" (21). The twenties are the "novice" phase, in which a first adult life is actually established and tested, allowing the lifelong process of negotiation and reformulation to concretely begin. Again, however, the specific tasks, images, and normative ages—and even the very existence—of this particular "life stage" are historically and culturally conditioned (a fact of which Levinson himself seems unaware), and so cannot be applied blindly to Muir; but as with Erikson's insights into the interactions between subjective experience and cultural/social context, I find Levinson's general concepts and structures to be helpful guides in exploring my materials on Muir.

Interestingly, I suspect that some of the differences between Erikson and Levinson stem from their own cultural and historical contexts. Working primarily in the 1940s and 1950s, Erikson could see (and expect to see) a "normative" adult identity, ideally achieved once and for all; while acknowledging the struggle involved in attaining that identity, he does not view that struggle as part of adulthood but primarily as a prelude to it. Levinson, in the late 1960s and 1970s, would be more likely to admit flexibility and fluidity in the process and to allow tentative or provisional identity to be valorized as "adult."

shop. Still pushed and pulled internally, Muir finally made the decision to leave home in September. To the end, Daniel Muir refused to recognize John's independence, offered no material support or emotional encouragement, and withheld all words of blessing or even goodbye. His only acknowledgment of the event was a grim warning that leaving home would be a mistake, for strangers would not care for him as had his family.

Happily for Muir, this prediction proved wrong—or perhaps right— as frontier society welcomed and supported him in a number of ways that spoke both to his vocational and to his emotional needs. As Kett describes it, semidependence in the nineteenth century did not end when one left home but rather was extended through a number of cultural institutions, economic structures, and social relationships, all functioning on a continuum with the family (and, for men, further shaping and extending male identity and privilege). From all accounts, the people with whom Muir came in contact on his way to the fair—from the engineer who gave him an exhilarating ride on the cowcatcher of the train to Madison to the officials who quickly made a place for him at the fair—were uniformly interested in, impressed by, and encouraging of the young inventor from the backwoods. His inventions (the early-rising bed and a few clocks) were the hit of the fair, garnering him favorable notice in area papers and an unexpected cash prize from fair officials, the latter presented with the statement that "[t]he Committee regard [Muir] as a genius in the best sense, and think the state should feel a pride in encouraging him" (L. M. Wolfe, 61). Equally encouraging was his discovery that he could present himself well in public, giving entertaining explanations to his viewers (especially the children). Summing up his experiences, Muir wrote home that "all seem to wish me well" (1:64). Such support and publicity led to a number of job offers, and thus Muir fulfilled his ultimate goal by making an arrangement to work in the machine shop of a Mr. Wiard of Prairie du Chien, Wisconsin, inventor of a much-heralded iceboat for winter travel on the upper Mississippi.

Despite these initial successes, Muir's entry into the larger world was soon beset by difficulties, some of them based again in familial and in cultural failures. As Kett notes, while the usual age for an apprentice was in the teenage years, later entry was by no means uncommon. However, Muir's position was still anomalous; during his extended stay on the farm, he had fulfilled on his own many of the functions of an apprenticeship (learning basic mathematics, becoming familiar with tools and technology, and so on), and was clearly more talented and skilled than most— probably including his "master," Wiard. What his farm experience had not given him was the essential dimension of exposure to and sponsorship into a wider social and economic world, and this was in part what he hoped for in an apprenticeship. It is important to remember that Muir had to make this decision alone, with no guidance and minimal experience. Thus, on the one hand he seems to have chosen Wiard partly because he reminded him of his father (emphasizing the mid-nineteenth-century continuity of family and work as institutions of semidependence), as suggested by his strangely affectionate description of him as "stern looking Mr. Wirad [*sic*]" in a letter to Sarah; on the other hand, he feared lest his new master turn out to be a Catholic. In the same letter, saying that he felt himself "at the mercy of so many chances and influences," Muir revealed that he planned to try the arrangement for only a few months before heading eastward—much less than the usual time for a full-fledged apprenticeship. The actual agreement between the two was something between an apprenticeship and a mere job: Muir was to receive neither money nor the sense of intimacy, responsibility, and personal investment of a traditional apprenticeship, but rather be recompensed for his work only in the form of access to Wiard's tools and books. As it turned out, Muir did not get even that much out of the relationship. Wiard used Muir for his own purposes, giving his "apprentice" almost no training nor even any time for the promised use of books and tools for self-education. Thus, Muir's achievement of gaining an apprenticeship was a hollow one, both because of his own mistakes and uncertainties and because the institution itself was collapsing as a means of education and socialization; in the end, Muir—like many youths of his day—ended up merely "tending machines" (Kett, 145).

Unfortunately, these vocational difficulties would not be quickly resolved. By January 1861, Wiard's iceboat had proved a failure and Muir's dissatisfaction with his "apprenticeship" had led him to leave Prairie du Chien and to move back to Madison. Still determined to make it on his own, he spent some difficult weeks working at odd jobs—addressing circulars, running errands, doing household chores, and so on. In time, a chance encounter with a student led him to enroll in the freshman class of the new Wisconsin State University (now the University of Wisconsin), where he would remain for the next two and a half years—without, however, coming any closer to a resolution of his questions regarding career and life path.

Beneath these vocational changes and uncertainties, the move away from home confronted Muir with enormous emotional and psychological challenges. Given the intensity of his bonds with his family—expressed in his deep allegiance to the communal "we" as the basis of his identity—and of his complex attachment to the farm and landscape, the separation from home must sometimes have felt like literally losing a part of his body.[3] The loss and pain of the experience underlay a bizarre and harsh letter to his sisters Mary and Anna, written soon after he arrived in Prairie du Chien. Reminiscing briefly upon his childhood, Muir's letter seems to arise out of a distant, confused dream:

> one morning when I was half awake and half asleep long ago when I was in my bed Pa told me I had got *twin sisters*. I don't know whether I was glad or not but I rather guess if he had come a minute afterwards and told me that the twin sisters had gone away up to the skies among the clouds I don't think I would have asked for the place where they went up or cried a bit. I got on my clothes and had to go and see them & am sure I would rather have gone to school and got whipped on both hands, but I had to go and had to kiss them too. (1:70)

Missing his sisters deeply and unsure of how to live without them, Muir found it easier to imagine them dead, the bonds of love abruptly sundered.

Moreover, the isolation and rigidity of his life on the farm, which had helped forge such strong familial bonds, had also kept him from any extensive exposure to the people and ways of the world; though he was fortunate in finding initial contacts, they were fragile and unfamiliar, affording less emotional support than had family and friends at home. For the first time in his life, he was on his own in creating an uncertain future. Thus, he experienced both exhilaration and disorientation upon leaving home for the state fair; everything was unfamiliar, and the sometimes light tone of a letter to Sarah expressed real confusion and apprehension.

> I am not bound but Sarah I am now adrift on this big sinny world and I don't know how I feel. Jumping out of the woods I was at once led and pushed and whirled and tossed about by new everythings everywhere. For three or four days my eyes at least were pleased and teased and wearied with pictures and sewing machines and squashes and reapers and quilts and cheeses and apples and flowers and soldiers and firemen and thousands of all kinds of faces, all of them strange but two. (1:64)

Although he was apprenticed, Muir still did not feel "bound" in either the social-vocational or the personal sense, with deep psychological and even perceptual implications. In his move "out of the woods" to Madison and Prairie du Chien—as in his immigration from Scotland at age

---

3. Discussing certain schizophrenic patients—whose conditions he sees as expressing in exaggerated form many of the same dynamics as in normal pychological development—Searles observes that "the loss of various elements of the nonhuman environment, elements which have become a part of the person's body image, may be experienced as a mutilation of the physical body itself, entirely similar to the reaction which may be felt upon the loss of another *person*" (153–54).

eleven—Muir's senses and perceptions were overwhelmed by new surroundings and threatening experiences, resulting in a dissociation of self from body, environment, and feelings. Thus, in this letter to Sarah he could only describe his body as an object buffeted about by other objects (and itself fragmented into its component pieces, "my eyes at least") and his surroundings as a disparate list of objects seen. Similarly, in the letter to Mary and Anna, Muir described his experiences through another fragmented list of objects: hills, hollows, marshes, sand creeks, bridges, and rivers, "and they all whirled and I came to Madison and then I got to Pr. du Chien and this is Tuesday evening" (1:70). His sense of distancing from his own body—and confusion at its seeming helplessness—is conveyed in an earlier letter to Sarah: "A body has an extraordinary amount of longfaced sober scheming and thought to get bread and butter for their body" (1:48).

Muir's sense of dislocation, uncertainty, and dissociation was even stronger in his first letter to Sarah from Prairie du Chien.

> I am in the world now and I don't think I know how I like it. I guess it has used me better than I could expect but most of its love is very hollow I believe. Since I left I have never been able to mark the flight of time. It seems like seven or eight days since I left home and seems like seven or eight years and it seems like a dream. I hardly ever know what day it is or what year, I don't often think where I am and I don't think I care much. I don't think I can tell you what I am doing or not doing. And I hardly know how I feel. I am not unhappy, I generally whistle when I do my chores. I guess I am happy. (1:72)

Hardly aware of time or space, confused by and mistrustful of his surroundings, Muir only knew what he was feeling by clinically observing what his body was doing. Although in some ways such a response may have emerged passively as a result of his experiences of dislocation, it also constituted an active way for Muir to protect his sense of identity from threatening disruptions; very likely, the emotional and psychological changes were just too much for him to handle all at once, given his uncertain inner resources and lack of guidance and support from trusted others, and so his dissociation was a defensive, protective maneuver. Other responses were more direct: when he found that he was no longer waking up on his regular, controlled pattern, but sometimes at two or three, sometimes at seven, he addressed this loss of bodily control (of which he was always so proud) by actually using one of his early-rising machines, which "mercilessly" threw him on the floor at a clock-regulated hour.

This image of the early-rising bed gives an initial clue to the tactics that Muir used in dealing with the difficulties—public and private, professional and psychological, practical and emotional—that confronted him: It was in large part through the use of familiar resources from his past—as well as their extension through the creation of new images, interpretations, and relationships—that Muir once again would attempt to reconstitute self and world in the face of change. Initially, his most important response was the reassertion of the meaning and strength of family bonds. Over the next few years, the family was able to maintain actual contact relatively often: Muir went home to work on the farm every summer he was a student, family members made occasional visits to Madison, and brother David joined him at the university for a few months in the autumn of 1862. At the same time, Muir created ways—through exchange of letters, objects, and prayers—to feel the presence of his family despite the distance.

Significantly, his sister Sarah (and her husband David Galloway) received the most, and the most expressive, of Muir's early letters. Sarah and John, only two years apart in age (second and third children, respectively), had long been close confidantes. After Sarah had married and moved back to the old Fountain Lake homestead, John had turned to the oldest sister, Margaret, for companionship, but when he was free to choose which of his family relationships to reconstitute in letters, he most often chose Sarah. This may have been partly in order to keep his deepest thoughts and feelings away from their father, who might have read any letters sent home to the whole family (with whom Margaret still lived); however, it was also because John could communicate more freely with Sarah than with his other siblings. Margaret's letters, while genuinely warm and affectionate, are often somewhat preachy and unimaginative; John, for his own part, felt the need to act parentally toward his younger siblings, and often sounds stilted and didactic in writing to them (even David, to begin with at least). With Sarah, however, John from the start seemed able to express what was important to him and to feel her emotional presence supporting him in the new directions in which he was developing.

From her perspective, Sarah's letter relationship with John opened a new world for her as well, giving a mode of imaginative access to larger social and intellectual worlds that were otherwise denied to girls and women. Significantly, even though Sarah had accompanied Daniel, John, and David during the first summer in Wisconsin, Muir's adult reminiscences refer exclusively to him and David, suggesting that from an early age she was excluded from the explorations of nature and of culture in which the young boys were engaged. Indeed, it may not have been until this exchange of letters with her younger brother that Sarah was able to move beyond the Muir and Galloway family spheres, in imaginative and intellectual ways at least, and to participate in some of the opportunities and worlds open to Muir as a male; thus, their letter relationship served her desires for expanded contact with the larger world at the same time as it served Muir's longings for continued contact with home and family. In addition, Sarah's husband David, nine years Muir's senior, was a friend and sometime mentor, a liked and respected alternative male role model to Daniel Muir; thus, on some levels Sarah and David constituted a family that accorded better with John's hopes and longings than did his own, giving his letter relationship with them an added depth and power. At the same time, we must keep in mind that Muir did exchange letters with all the members of his family, and that a stilted or perfunctory tone might in itself reveal a powerful psychological dynamic or a meaningful aspect of an important relationship.

However, letters did not enable Muir to re-create the presence of family in any straightforward way. Clearly, a letter does not simply re-present a person, and a letter relationship is not merely an attenuated or time-delayed relationship. Rather, both the kind of relationship and the people who are striving to relate through letters are new, creations of the medium and of both persons' usage of the medium. As noted, Muir was free to write in certain ways to Sarah and not to other family members, either because of shared temperament or because of the fact of her living away from parental authority. Partly because of this, Sarah became a new person for him, conditioned not only by their past relationship but also by the particular present circumstances, needs, and desires that motivated and shaped each letter, and by the ways in which she was able to respond (and even the ways in which Muir *imagined* that she responded). At the same time, letter writing itself became a new kind of activity for him, one which could hold and convey the feelings, needs, and patterns of relationship he had experienced—and was experiencing—with Sarah. Finally, through letter writing Muir became a new person to himself as well as to his readers; the act of writing brings about both the relationship and the person put forth in the letter. As we shall see, these varied workings of letter writing would prove crucial in the development of many of Muir's most important relationships—familial, romantic, religious, and intellectual—throughout his life.[4]

4. In a different yet parallel arena, that of romantic relationships, Karen Lystra has explored the ways in which nineteenth-century lovers used letters to evoke or to convey the presence of the beloved: "Though never an adequate substitute, correspondents experienced letter writing as symbolically akin to personal presence" (25). Letters also served as an arena for the re-creation of self: "[T]he self was brought into clearer focus through the communication process required by the conventions of romantic love," and letter writing was "a process of strengthening, and sometimes even creating, a role best called the 'romantic self'" (26–27).

Another important aspect of letters, and one that supports their function of representing the presence of loved ones, is their materiality. Letters are physical objects that can become saturated with meaning, both as occasions for the experience of an absent person's affection and as shapers of one's image of that person. Thus, those meanings, experiences, and images can be affected by the physicality of the letter itself and by the physical conditions of reading and writing, as well as by what a person chooses to actually do with the letter—save it, reread it, burn it, change it, kiss it, and so on. Further, letter writing was paralleled by other, more overtly material means of making contact with distant people, namely exchanging various sorts of tokens—drawings, portrait photographs, cards, and botanical specimens such as flowers, leaves, or moss (see, e.g., 1:49). Such material objects appear in Muir's letters as a powerful means of solidifying his sense of the presence, love, and care of distant family members, thus augmenting one of the functions of the letters themselves. Indeed, according to Millie Stanley, through the "family practice of enclosing flowers and bits of greenery in their letters," Muir "shared the heart of his world with his family and they shared their world with him" (73).[5]

Within these reformulated familial relationships, the affirmation of the family's religious culture served as a particularly important means for finding comfort and stability in the face of separation and changing circumstances. Rather than trying to leave it behind as soon as possible, Muir actively hung onto his familial religiousness as a means of giving stability to his inner life and instruction for his outer behavior—and, not incidentally, because he believed it to be *true*. All of the family's letters from this period are full of requests for prayer, exhortations to piety, cautions about the dangers of the world and of personal sin, and hopes for the future life; even the agonized letter to Mary and Anna from Prairie du Chien ends with the promise of reunion.

> But all the Marys and Annas will die someday. You are young my dear twins and perhaps you will live a long time. O how very blessed you will be if you live all the time with Jesus who died on a cross long ago for you.

5. Clearly, these tokens and letters served the psychological function of transitional objects, as emotionally charged everyday objects that make possible a person's separation from primary relationships without loss of the selfhood or vitality that those relationships have nurtured into existence. Similarly, Lewis Hyde writes of the "erotic life" of gifts: "It is the cardinal difference between gift and commodity exchange that a gift establishes a feeling-bond between two people, while the sale of a commodity leaves no necessary connection. . . . The bonds that gifts establish are not simply social, they may be spiritual and psychological as well. There are interior economies and invisible economies. Gift exchanges may join figures and forces within the drama of our inner lives. . . . Our gifts may connect us to the gods as well" (56–58).

O how much he loves you, surely you will love him all your days. Be patient and suffer all things for that dear Jesus' sake and soon you will be
with him in "The Happy Land far away." Goodbye my dear sisters God
bless you and all the rest. (1:70)

In a somewhat less morbid vein, Muir continued his first letter to Sarah
with the hopeful observation that "[t]he whole affair will soon be wound
up. May we shew ourselves faithful servants whatever be our job, that
when these trial days are past we get the eternal reward through the merit
of our Saviour Jesus Christ. How apt we are to forget him amid this exciting life game. God bless you all" (1:48). Whatever became of him in Madison, Muir believed, he had somewhere to turn for hope and sustenance,
and this belief in itself provided hope and sustenance. To be sure, the
penultimate line suggests guilt over his own neglect of some religious
thought or practices that he had come to regard as duties, but his religious
conscience was still a powerful presence and an active guide in his life. For
example, as in the Fountain Lake incident, Muir anticipated his father's/
Father's judgments by refusing to read any of the newspaper stories of his
success, for fear it would lead to sinful pride. In a similarly cautious response to his general experiences, he wrote: "There is, Sarah, a flood of
praise poured on me from nearly everybody here. You know how dangerous it is for a body that likes it as well as me. I know you pray for me
Sarah and it is a comforting piece of knowledge" (1:48). Happily, Daniel
Muir seems to have mellowed somewhat over time, sending John some
money, clothing, and blessings along with more positive religious encouragement than previously: "I am glad to know you are attending upon the
means of grace regularly. Keep your mind upon God's business, and never
cease to walk in his ways, and he will bless you in time and eternity. I am
glad to hear from you always. A wise son makes a glad father. I remain,
your affectionate father, Daniel Muir" (1:89). Throughout Muir's years
at the university, the whole family continued to use Christian language
and imagery to express personal affection and concern, and most letters
ended with expressions of thankfulness for the love of Jesus and exhortations to continue in the path of Christian righteousness.[6]

Along with reaffirming and re-creating his familial relationships and
religiousness, Muir responded to his move away from home by establishing wholly new relationships as well, especially with the families with
whom he boarded. For his first month in Madison Muir found a homey

6. Indeed, intertwined with the processes by which Muir reformulated his familial relationships, the reverse was true as well: Stanley (55–61) suggests the ways in which family
members reformulated their image of John and created ways to continue to feel his presence
in their lives, as part of their own responses to his departure.

welcome with the Varnells, "a very good and respectable family"; in a letter to Sarah, Muir reported that when he left Madison for Prairie du Chien, "[a]s I bade Mrs. Varnell goodbye she took my hand and looked as she might cry and said 'I hope you shall succeed and have good health, Goodbye and God bless you'" (1:64). In Prairie du Chien, he lodged in the "cheery and comfortable" boardinghouse of the Pelton family, paying for it partly by taking care of fires, wood, and other chores and immediately making himself both indispensable and well liked. However, the transition was not without difficulties: his religious sensibilities were somewhat offended (and his shy, uncertain self-image threatened) by the "dandy society" of the Pelton household, where the "mannerly and educated" people kissed, had parties, and played games. When invited to play "fox and geese," Muir responded with the words of Solomon, "My son, if sinners entice thee consent thou not." Not surprisingly, Muir had "a great character here for sobriety" (1:73).

The Peltons would continue to be an important emotional presence in Muir's life throughout his university years—and beyond. Soon after leaving Prairie du Chien, Muir wrote a long letter to the Peltons in which he described his feelings upon returning to "Madison's icy mountains": "For a week or two after leaving you all I often felt rather lonely perhaps gloomy though I am always happy in the center. I was plunged through the ice but those first shocks are gone and now I almost feel first rate" (1:152–53). In contrast to the prolonged tone of confusion and uncertainty that marked his letters during his initial move away from home, this passage shows a relatively centered young man, one somewhat better able than before to respond on his own to change and to disruptions; this centeredness reflects both the continued strength of his familial relationships and an increased confidence in a personal world outside of the family sphere. Interestingly, the Muir family's letters to him suggest that he did not tell them exactly what he was studying over his first two years at the university, as he probably needed to maintain a sharp separation between his own family connections and his new intellectual life. Moreover, his letters to family from the university period exhibit a somewhat more reserved tone than those written during his first few months away from home. This is even more striking in comparison to the intimacy, intensity, and playfulness that mark his letters to the Peltons—or, more precisely, the women of that family: mother Frances, niece Emily (about Muir's age), and the "baby," Fannie (under two when Muir left for Madison). His relationships with the Peltons not only were comparable to his family relationships in supporting his inner life but also extended it in ways that his family relationships could not.

In fact, Muir's letters suggest a subtle blurring of the boundaries of his

emotional relationships with each member of the Pelton family, suggesting that he initially related to them as a group rather than as individuals.
(As suggested in chapter 1, given Scots child-rearing practices, Muir's
stance toward his own mother and sisters may have been somewhat ambiguous and overlapping, providing a similar lens through which to relate
to the Peltons.) In the long letter quoted above, Muir directly addressed
himself both to Mrs. Pelton and to Emily at various points, in addition
to inserting hypothetical conversations with Fannie; thus, all of the Peltons were his companions on a nostalgic imaginative tour of the Hickory
Hill farmstead.

> In this great field is where I've sweated and played, worked and rejoiced.
> There is the garden where Maggie and I have lavished away many joyful
> hours. And away down this slope and over the level prairie is where we
> have taken hundreds of long walks and talked of earth and heaven. Now
> if you are not too tired I'll take you to two places more. Just by that great
> oak is where in the moonlight evenings I used to spend hours with my
> head up in the sky. I soared among the planets and thought. One place
> more that "best place" I spoke of, that is across this ravine and up the
> opposite hill a little bit in that thick little grove is where I used to *pray*.
> (1:151–52)

Walking them through the landscape of his own and his family's past life,
Muir placed the Peltons themselves within the familiar/familial relationship that he had previously shared with his sister; the emphasis on the
physicality of setting and of activity (including playful concern for their
tiredness) adds an intimate, even sensual tone to the emotional aspects of
their companionship. (Interestingly, Muir had also begun exchanging bits
of moss, pictures, etc., with the Peltons as well as with his family.) He
then moved beyond these familial patterns into a matched pair of more
private experiences, solitary thought and prayer, the former open, expansive, and ambitious, the latter enclosed and protected; thus, Muir implicitly invited the Peltons into an individual experience that he had deliber-
ately held apart from his family relationships.

   Moreover, in writing to the Peltons, Muir was not only reconstructing
his relationships with them but also reconstructing his own past. In this
letter, his descriptions of the farm—often taken by scholars as evidence
of a positive, even ecstatic relationship with the natural world that Muir
enjoyed while a teenager—are at least selective and at most constitute a
literal rewriting of his life on the farm in terms of what he thought the
Peltons wanted to hear (which was probably close to what he wished it
had been). As argued in chapter 1, any such idealized view must be balanced by an equal emphasis on the ambiguities and conflicts of his teenage experiences of his environment. At the same time, I would not deny

the reality, depth, and power of the positive experiences about which he was writing; some deeply felt memories must have been stored in Muir's heart, to be presented as token and as gift to the Peltons. Indeed, it is likely that some level of joyous and energized relationship with the natural environment while young is an important source and ground of a later ability to establish joyous and energized relationships with other places *and with people,* for Muir and for all of us.[7]

Later in the letter, a poem (seemingly written in the course of writing the letter itself) further suggests the ways in which the Peltons "held" the new Muir who was emerging out of the constraints of his family and of his childhood.

> There is a tree of goodly form, and tall
> . . .
>        . . . o'er all
> Upon the *hills,* she *shouts* her songs of *worth*
> To small eyed trees, and brambles far below
> Twas thus *I* heard her sing when long ago
> I sought an hour of rest beneath her shade
> "O god of trees, Ye vines and brambles all
> I pray you listen, list I beseech you.
> O listen, listen, listen lend your ears
> I do implore you listen, listen, listen
> And now, ye God of trees, brambles and vines
> Give heed, I King of Trees I'm good
> Ye brambles I am good. I'm good
> Ye vines and God of trees.
> I'm loathe to speak my praise I'm good
> Fruits of all hues are on me, and around
> I bless forever always, and every fruit
> Is on me, to help mankind, and brute."
>                       (1:156)

---

7. Searles, presuming a generally positive relationship with nature during adolescence, proposes that "it may be not so much that the adolescent's predominant emotional orientation shifts *from* the nonhuman environment *toward* the world of human beings, but rather that from his loving relatedness to nature and to other elements of his nonhuman environment there *emerges* a loving relatedness, now the primary focus of his emotional life, to other human beings" (94). Thus, although traditional object relations theory stresses the ways in which nonhuman objects gain meaning through association with humans, the reverse process is true as well: relationships with humans may be shaped and energized by primary relationships with natural or other physical objects. Incorporating this insight into a general object relations framework allows us to apply it to any age, not just adolescence (although that may be a particularly fruitful time for such processes to occur). However, we may want to question Searles's presumption that orientation toward humans is the "primary focus" of the "healthy individual's" emotional life, or his corollary that to maintain an identification with nature is to stay in adolescence (99).

Significantly, the repeated cries of "listen" and "I'm good" seem to apply not only to the tree but to Muir himself. Just as the young boy Muir had used his natural surroundings in Scotland as an arena in which to escape from the physical control of his father, the young adult—newly freed from the shackles and pains of farmwork—was beginning to forge ways of identifying with a personified nature as part of his escape from the psychological legacy of his father. Perhaps especially revealing is the line "I'm loathe to speak my praise I'm good"—a clear expression that Muir was beginning to overcome the lack of confidence and self-assertion instilled in him by his father.

In addition to these images of the natural world, in this case it was the poem itself that provided the psychological "space" for Muir's development, a space conditioned by his religious imagery and literary interests. The mood and setting ("Twas thus I heard her sing when long ago") echoes "Tintern Abbey," and one can only wonder whether Muir was especially attracted to that poem because it expresses the importance of Wordsworth's relationship with his sister as a crucial element of his emotional and religious experience of nature. At the same time, the description of the tree itself may have been partly inspired by *Paradise Lost,* where the snake describes the Tree of Knowledge as "A goodly Tree . . . / Loaden with fruit of fairest colours mixt, / Ruddy and Gold" (IX:576–78); such a referent suggests a deeper ambivalence about his own self-assertion. Further, yet another space—that between the poem and the audience, the Peltons—served Muir as another setting of self-affirmation and a reconstructed worldview. Although Muir may have made similar religious and personal affirmations while he was still living at home (e.g., in the "best place" mentioned above), the act of writing out his experience in a stylized poem to the appreciative, admiring, and admired Pelton women helped to solidify and to deepen the reality of those inner changes.[8]

8. Clearly, the various spaces embodied in this letter—between Muir and the natural world, between Muir and the poem (and its literary antecedents), and especially between Muir and the Peltons—function as new sorts of Winnicottian potential spaces, within which new transitional objects (representations and relationships) can emerge. Where for the infant, the potential space depends primarily upon the appropriate presence and support of the mother, in this case it depends upon a wider range of "others"—nature, culture, friends—who were "there for" Muir in supportive and creative ways. In particular, the felt attention and concern of the Peltons seem to have called forth a new Muir in a way parallel to that which Nelle Morton has described as "hearing one another to speech," through a mode of "hearing engaged in by the whole body that evokes speech—a new speech—a new creation" (55, 128); in the Peltons' case, such "hearing" was actually "reading" Muir to a new form of self-creation through writing. At the same time, the factor (or, one of the factors) that allows such new potential spaces to operate is the original experience of being successfully "held" by the mother.

The importance of the Peltons in Muir's life—and his importance in theirs—was not limited to his first weeks or months in Madison, but extended throughout his time at the university (and beyond). For example, he expressed the depth of his feeling for Fannie in an 1861 letter addressed explicitly to her, during one of her recurring bouts of sickness.

> Fannie you are a dear precious thing, and frail. . . . Will the woes that have so loved to cluster on your soft little body go all away, will skippy gleeful life be given fragile Fannie[?] Her Father and her Mother held her life, will she sweeten their age? Ah Fannie, did you know that gush of fear, and hope, and love, you would be crystal gratitude, and affection, throughout and throughout forever[.] . . . How fondly then do I trust that you will remember your creator in the days of your youth and serve him in the beauty of holiness all your days. And though all shall not be sunniness all shall be blessings. And when your body lies hushed down in the buried coffin your spirit made holy shall be in heaven. (1:148–49)

The letter strongly echoes the one written to his younger twin sisters Mary and Anna a few months earlier, but with a more positive emotional tone. At the same time, since Fannie was only two years old at the time, Muir must have known that the letter would be read by Mrs. Pelton or by Emily, allowing some of these emotions and ideals to be shared in his relationships with them as well. It is not surprising that Fannie's death in the spring of 1862 prompted Muir's most emotionally troubled letter of this period: "Fannie is dead O God what can I say, or what can I do." His letter of condolence to Mr. and Mrs. Pelton ends with a restatement of his orientation toward an otherworldly home: "Jesus loves the little dear, and all is well and you'll go to her in just a little while though she cannot come to you" (1:252).

Later that year, Mrs. Pelton's own sickness also evoked strong feelings in Muir: "Dear Mrs. Pelton, I often think I feel your fevered brow, and wish myself near to bathe it. I still hear your difficult breathing, and read the distress you cannot speak, and though your dearest friends long accustomed to soothe the pain of sickness are at hand with all the care of their love and natural affection, I nevertheless long and ache to be near you with an intensity which I cannot describe" (1:200). Characterizing his relationship with Mrs. Pelton in terms of her "motherly advice," Muir expressed his "gratitude for your genuine kindness to me when timid and inexperienced I first felt the chill countenances of so many strangers" (1:201). What the "mother" image meant to him is further revealed in a letter to Mrs. Pelton the following autumn, after she had returned to her childhood home in Massachusetts to finish recovering from her illness and from Fannie's death: "I think I can realize your anxiety to be with your mother; no earthly being can fill the place of our own selfdenying affectionate mothers. And such a mother is yours from the few words she addressed to myself when so homesick. I fondly trust, Dear Mrs. Pelton, that a mother's attention and your New England air will under God's blessing restore you to full health" (1:222). As the last sentence implies, the nineteenth-century ideology of domesticity linked motherhood, health, and religiousness with an actual physical place, "home"—itself a many-layered concept (akin to the "house" of Scottish romance) involving building, family, and geographical location.[9]

Paradoxically, even as he insisted that no one could "fill the place of" his own mother, Muir nevertheless allowed Mrs. Pelton to partly do so, by invoking motherliness as a general category characterized by self-denial, kindliness, attention, affection, and presumably other of the standard mid-Victorian ideals. Unfortunately, little in his letters or other biographical material expresses Muir's adult relationship with his mother, beyond a positive picture of mutual warmth, support, love, and interest that actually accords well with many of the cultural ideals. On the one hand, it is clear that his relationship with her did not involve anywhere near as much conflict as the one with his father, and so upon leaving home he did not need to create alternative mother figures to address the gaps and differences; his actual mother was just what he wanted. On the other hand, at least since the move to Wisconsin (and probably at various points before that), Muir had felt a loss of his mother as an available presence in his life, and an important—perhaps major—theme of his emotional life throughout his youth was the continuing struggle to revivify that presence and his connections to it through various emotional and personal tactics. Thus, his positive image of motherhood reflected neither an adequate present reality nor a sheer idealization (cultural or psychological), but rather the paradoxical presence/absence of a powerful childhood relationship now lost and for which he still deeply longed. Moreover, the strength of this relationship allowed a culturally influenced category of motherliness to shape his interactions with nonfamily such as Mrs. Pelton.

Despite these connections, it would be both too much and too little to say that the Peltons constituted a "substitute family" for Muir away from home—Mrs. Pelton as mother, Emily as same-age sister, Fannie as younger sister. Too much, because he still had full relationships with each

---

9. Such images crop up everywhere; as one random example, J. G. Hoyt, discussing "Educated Labor" in an 1859 article in the *North American Review,* stated: "Someone has said that the three most beautiful words in the English language are Mother, Home, and Heaven. They naturally go together, either of them implying the other" (380). Further, "A fine-looking house, like a fine-looking woman, cannot but exert a cheerful and elevating influence upon the community" (381); this "renovating power" of home affected the physical health as well as the moral and spiritual character of its inhabitants.

of the members of his own family, and the character of his feelings toward them did not seem to change even if their level of expression tapered off; too little, because his relationships with the Peltons involved important new dimensions as well. The character of his stance toward the Peltons can best be understood through Muir's own description of Mrs. Pelton (echoing phrases in his letters to all of the Pelton family) as "a friend in Christian love" (1:222).

Indeed, the language of Christian love shaped his relationships with a wide range of friends (and with his own family as well), each with a different emotional inflection. In his teenage evangelical letter to Bradley Brown, concern for a friend's salvation stood at the very core of his motivation in writing, and the letter thus took on a more dramatic, intense, self-conscious, and even "romantic" tone. In that instance, his challenging, exhorting, somewhat impersonal stance was closely related to his familial (especially paternal) religious culture, but may also have expressed something of his patterns for relating to male friends in particular. During his years at the university, Christian friendship continued to shape his relationships with men, and in fact surviving letters to other male friends during this period reflect the same challenging, somewhat argumentative tone (see, e.g., his theological debate with Duncan Paton, 1: 282). Such a pattern of relationship with other men was culturally institutionalized in such forms as college debating societies, and Muir in fact participated in the Athenaean Society, especially in his final year (L. M. Wolfe, 81). By contrast, his Christian friendships with women—especially the Peltons—were much more emotionally open and expressive, encompassing sadness, joy, hope, support, playfulness, affection, longing, and even an element of physicality and sensuality (in references to bodily conditions and health, and in the evocation of shared experiences of nature). Grounded in an underlying dramatic sense akin to that overtly expressed in the letter to Brown, Muir's letters to the Peltons show him experimenting with a new self-in-relationship, and thus free to "play"— and, on some levels at least, to become—that self with more intensity and breadth than were possible in the predetermined arena of family relations.

However, as in the case of Muir's letter relationship with his sister Sarah, his and the Peltons' friendships in Christian love held widely different meanings for each side at the same time as they represented a shared emotional and spiritual world. Clearly, given the gender roles and patterns of the day, Muir had access to powers and worlds that the Pelton women did not, and it was his exercise of those powers—for example in the move back to Madison for work and school—that provided much of the content of their letter relationship. Within those roles and patterns, each of the friends gave what they could to the other: on the one hand, a continued relationship with Muir gave the Pelton women a chance—perhaps a rare one—to expand their worlds on important imaginative and intellectual levels (if not on the bodily, social, and geographical levels that were open to him); on the other hand, relationship with them gave him an ability to maintain and even to expand his connections to an emotional and symbolic female and domestic world that was not included in a socially given or expected male identity. Significantly, however, the two sides' experiences of the relationship were not only different but unequal, as it was Muir who had the most power to move in and out of the relationship as he wished, as was most convenient for his emotional state and life path. Thus, another aspect of Muir's male privilege and identity was his very ability to maintain connection with the female and domestic realms *on his own terms,* through the mediated relationship—his friendship in Christian love—with the Pelton women.

As one element of this power, the role of Christian friendship also allowed Muir to pointedly *avoid* certain types of relationships with women. Muir was strongly attracted to Emily, and (as later letters show) the two became quite close; the relationship surely involved some element that we would describe as erotic. However, had Muir channeled that erotic energy into the standard construction of a "romantic" male-female relationship, he would have had to confront the issue of marriage. Marriage was all around him: his sister Margaret had by this time joined Sarah in the wedded state, and brother David was busy courting and planning; letters from his brother-in-law David Galloway often described the pleasures and contentment of family life (while mercifully admitting that it might not be fitted for everyone); other letters from same-age male friends raised the topic regularly. After visiting Muir, David Galloway went so far as to describe Emily to the rest of the family as "John's girl" (L. M. Wolfe, 63). Muir, however, clearly wanted a different (though as yet unknown) sort of life, and so to have felt his attraction to Emily as sexual—i.e., to have been "sexually attracted" to her—would have led him into a realm that he was not psychologically prepared to enter.

At the same time, we should not too quickly interpret Christian love as a substitution for or an avoidance of romance, or as powered primarily by repressed sexual desire; rather, Christian love constituted a distinct form of relationship with its own dynamics and sensitivities, one more common, accepted, and socially supported in the nineteenth century than in the later twentieth. A friendship in Christian love was not an incomplete or unhealthy distortion of the "real" energies and desires of John and Emily's relationship, but was exactly the relationship that they—or, at least, he—wanted; the fact that this relationship was shaped at its core by historical and cultural forces does not invalidate this statement, for the same is true of sexual and romantic relationships as well, in our day as in the past. Thus, the stance of Christian friendship, while not changing the felt reality of the eroticism central to Muir's relationship with Emily, embodied (or, perhaps, created) that eroticism in a way that fit in with the other dimensions of his life at the time (though it is not as clear how this construction of their relationship fit in with *her* goals and desires). This congruence in turn allowed those erotic aspects to continue as an important source of emotional energy for Muir, alongside the legacy of familial relationships and the very real bonds of friendship and of shared concern that gave depth and meaning to his Christian love with the Peltons.

These changing constructions of emotion, of identity, of symbolic meaning, and of relationship with family and friends conditioned—and even saturated—Muir's encounter with the religious, scientific, and cultural patterns of the Wisconsin State University. Most scholars, following Muir's own later interpretation, have straightforwardly viewed his university years as an intellectually liberating influence on him, opening his mind to new possibilities and encouraging him away from the rigid religious world of his youth. However, although there are certain elements of his experience that fit this description—most notably, as we shall see, his exposure to the specific scientific disciplines of botany, chemistry, and geology—these intellectual developments were psychologically possible for Muir only because of their *continuities* with his previous intellectual, religious, and interpersonal life. As with any college student, Muir could make creative use of new intellectual ideas and options only when he could fit them into his enduring senses of self and of world, grounded in past experiences and supported by present human relationships—all of which in turn strongly shaped the specific character and content of those ideas and options, as well as of the university culture in general. Thus, his time at the university did not so much give Muir a wholly new way of thinking as provide a powerful refiguration of his cultural, social, and psychological context, within which both old and new intellectual perspectives could take on new and deeper meanings.[10]

10. My understanding of Muir in Madison has been strongly influenced by Sharon Parks's study of the role of higher education in the growth of personal identity and religious faith. Working from a developmental-psychological perspective, Parks views educational institutions as (potentially, at least) helping young adults to build or to rebuild a unique, self-chosen world and inner life after the break with family traditions. Specifically, the college experience can (to a greater or lesser extent) nurture cognitive structures, forms of community, and forms of emotional bonds or dependance that are familiar and supportive enough to evoke loyalty and security, yet "loose" enough to permit individual exploration and decision. Utilizing such a lens gives a fuller, more nuanced picture than does an overemphasis on purely intellectual aspects, and is particularly useful in illumining the personal and psychological meanings of Muir's intellectual development during this period of his life.

Given the personal and practical uncertainties that marked his initial forays away from home, the seeming inevitability of Muir's move into the realm of higher education can be deceiving. To be sure, comments in letters of the time corroborate Muir's retrospective claim that after arriving in Madison the second time, entering the university "was my ambition, and it never wavered no matter what I was doing" (*Boyhood*, 274). However, there is no mention of this desire in any of the letters written *before* this period, and it seems probable that his attitudes toward the university were somewhat more conflicted. Muir's near-total lack of contact with any official cultural or social institutions (including education) during his farm years made the university seem intimidating and distant; his unkempt beard and lack of social polish set him apart from the normal college student of the day—even in frontier Wisconsin, where the young university (located in the state capitol city) still catered mainly to the children of legislators and businessmen. Though he was clearly interested in literature, philosophy, science, and technology, neither he nor his society would necessarily have associated these arenas with higher education any more than with independent explorers, writers, inventers, or artisans (such as fellow Scot Hugh Miller); significantly, it was only after the failure of his attempt at an apprenticeship that Muir turned toward formal education. Thus, we should not underestimate the depth of confusion and ambivalence, the "fear and trembling" (*Boyhood*, 275), nor the courage and vision, with which Muir entered the university.

Faced with the challenges of adapting to yet another new situation, Muir again actively created concrete continuities between his old life and his new one by bringing forward specific personal experiences and relationships from his past—which, significantly, the university culture was able to receive and even to embrace. This dynamic occurred on the most intimate and everyday levels, such as his living arrangements. For financial reasons, he found himself "batching it" in a dorm room instead of sharing in the family life of a boardinghouse, thus living outside of an explicit family setting for the first time in his life (despite his mother's surprise and implied worry [1:109]). In a letter to his younger sisters during his first semester, Muir imagined their presence: "I know you would like to come to our pretty grounds to gather flowers, lots and lots of happy girls are scattered over the hill and along the lake bank all the summer days getting the beautiful flowers that grow here" (1:117–18). Charging his present environment with some of the emotional energies of his family relationships, Muir went further and brought the natural world inside, filling his room with flowers, plants, and brambles, reminding him of his sisters and of home. Some of this domestic vegetation consisted of the tokens he had exchanged with family and friends (especially the Peltons), and these, along with letters, drawings, and portrait photographs, again helped him to recreate the emotions of their presence in his new surroundings. Further, Muir filled his room with inventions, both old and new: his early-rising bed, various new clocks, an easy chair fitted with a blank shotgun to energize the unwary lounger, a fairly extensive set of scientific instruments, instruments for measuring the growth of plants, and so on. As a result, his room became something of a museum for the university and Muir a well-known character, bringing him a dimension of communal life to reinvigorate the constant familial and social "we" of his boyhood and youth.[11]

As during his farm years, these inventions tell us much about the values and ideals both of Muir and of his admiring companions at the university, among them discipline, social usefulness, and the religious character of work. Muir's crowning creation, a study desk (still on display at the Wisconsin Historical Society), involves a rotating mechanism attached to a clock, which lifts a textbook from a stack, deposits it (opened to the proper page) on the desk, leaves it there for a preset time, and then whisks it away to the bottom of the stack, to be replaced by the next book. In whittling this out of wood, Muir again chose to embody these functional values in a symbol-laden form: the back legs of the desk are books, while the front legs are compasses, representing classical learning and the sciences; these foundations support a desk made of gears (some necessary for the mechanism, some not), signifying useful work; all this supports and is incorporated into a bell and steeple, transforming the whole into a literal temple of learning and giving a religious goal and meaning to education, science, and work. Such values accorded well with the "modern" leanings of the university in general during this period; if anything, it was Muir who was the modern, putting these values into practice with an intensity few others at the university (faculty included) could match. Paradoxically, in bringing forth his own legacies of Scotland and of farm life,

11. Muir's dormitory room illustrates what Marcus calls "the personalization of space": "[I]t is the movable objects in the home, rather than the physical fabric itself, that are the symbols of self. Even the prisoner . . . is permitted to bring into prison certain effects that are personally meaningful (posters, pinups, family pictures). Even when stripped of all symbols of self-hood, all possibilities of choice, we do concede that the personalization of space is an inalienable right. . . . In adolescence, posters fixed to the bedroom wall, photos displayed, clothes left in disarray—all may make a statement to parents: This is who *I* am! I am my own person, even if I'm not quite sure yet what that is" (11, 12). As in the case of Muir's shared childhood bedroom, however, the personalization of space can support the emergence of a communal or shared selfhood as well as an individual one. Indeed, Marcus goes on to acknowledge the role of personalized space in embodying relationships: "Objects, pictures, furniture, posters, ornaments—all remind us of significant people, places, phases, experiences, and values in our lives" (74).

Muir in these instances anticipated certain cultural and technological values—such as regularity, control, and efficiency—that would become dominant in later nineteenth-century industrial America, but that were not yet fully established in the somewhat parochial, classically inclined university of 1860.

Muir even went so far as to propose regulating the life of the entire university in the same ways that he had come to regulate himself. According to a later reminiscence by classmate Milton Griswold, soon after he entered the university Muir suggested to chancellor John W. Sterling that he could make enough early-rising beds for the whole university community! Perhaps fortunately for the Wisconsinites, I have found no evidence that this proposal was ever put into action. Similarly, a 1917 reminiscence by Bradley Brown (see 53:23–25) relates that Muir asked Sterling for permission to place a huge clock on top of one of the buildings of the university—just as, as a teenager, he had attempted to rebuild the Dunbar town clock on the family's barn. Unlike Daniel Muir, Sterling agreed and gave the inventor the privilege of choosing where the clock should be placed; again, however, there is no evidence that the plan was actually carried through. Interestingly, an 1862 drawing contains the kernel of the same idea, in a fanciful "sundial" that towers over the landscape and transforms the sun's motion into a cosmic clockwork; the few houses in the drawing stand isolated on a barren landscape, surrounded mainly by the stumps of trees (see figure 1). Encountering new spaces of potential freedom and affirmation, the young man could only take advantage of them by first structuring and controlling them—and, implicitly, himself—by importing values, patterns, and even actual objects from his past life. In doing so, he helped to co-create the young university, and indeed frontier culture itself.

For its part, the university in which Muir found himself—like frontier society in general—did not embody a unified, complete cultural whole, but was rather the scene of (and in fact was constituted by) a complex array of conflicts and compromises. As a state institution, the Wisconsin State University was from the beginning explicitly nonsectarian, and the founding charter declared that no particular religious belief or form of worship would be required of any student or faculty member (see Butterfield, 21). At the same time, it is clear that this rejection of sectarianism did not amount to an exclusion of religion, and some sort of religious presence and allegiance was in fact a foundational presumption both of the university and of the culture that supported it. The association of state-supported education with religion is embodied in the famous clause of the Ordinance of 1787: "Religion, morality, and knowledge being necessary to good government and the happiness of mankind, schools

Figure 1. "Sundial" of Muir's invention, Madison, Wisconsin; originally drawn ca. 1862 and later finished for publication. (Reprinted from *The Story of My Boyhood and Youth*, plate facing p. 132)

and the means of education shall forever be encouraged" (quoted in Pyre, 31).[12]

The precise character of this religiousness, however, is less clear. On the one hand, the limited but real diversity within the university's constituency required that whatever dimensions of religiousness were found therein be so deeply rooted in the local culture as to be above controversy even in contentious times, some type of common-denominator frontier Protestantism. On the other hand, the form that this Protestantism took was shaped by the presence of a northeastern-based civil religiousness (itself fraught with conflicts between conservative and liberal impulses)

12. Indeed, when land grants emerged as the major means of federal "encouragement" of higher education, it was by no means self-evident that denominational colleges could not receive such support. Through the 1860s in Wisconsin, church-run schools such as Lawrence, Beloit, and Carroll were larger and better equipped than the fledgling state university; in the years 1855–58, these colleges mounted serious legislative challenges to the university's claim to land-grant income. Even when the university won full rights to land-grant support (in part by claiming that it would provide the scientific, technical, and practical education that the religiously supported schools lacked), this represented a compromise victory for the denominational schools, by protecting their appeal to their own constituencies and by assuring each that its rivals would not gain control of state institutions or funding. For the early history of the Wisconsin State University, see Butterfield; Curti and Carstensen; and Pyre.

that was attempting to define the national culture; this national civil religiousness was still in the process of being established (and, of course, transformed) in and through the new governmental, cultural, social, and economic institutions of the frontier. The fluid situation allowed for the creation of what was in effect a *state* civil religiousness, a de facto—but not necessarily stable or consistent—synthesis between national structures and local conditions.

The state university was one of the major embodiments of this public religiousness and culture, as made clear in the 1850 inaugural address of the first chancellor, John Lathrop. A preliminary address by A. Hyatt Smith, representing the Board of Regents, introduced basic imagery of the national and state civil religions: America, with Wisconsin in the vanguard as "the youngest descendent of the Old Thirteen" (especially of New England), has a divinely appointed mission to establish prosperity, happiness, and political and religious liberty. If the nation and states fail, "they may look for the righteous indignation of the Ruler above, who will hold them to a stern and fearful accountability" (Lathrop, 10), but success would give America leadership among the nations of the world. Such success would depend in large part upon the success of the state's public education, both in the university and in the common schools.

Lathrop himself echoed these ideas in more elaborate form, through a scientific, historical, and theological discourse on progress as the distinctive responsibility and destiny of mankind. Since "it is by the educational process, that each successive generation, the pupil of the past, the instructor of the future, shall constitute itself in its turn a co-worker with God" (38), the Wisconsin State University must take care that its institutional structures, curriculum, and faculty advance these goals. Classical education is essential to preserve and convey the fund of cultural and intellectual achievements bequeathed by the ages, but scientific research is also required to add original contributions to that fund. As the person most responsible for carrying out these ideals, a Wisconsin professor must possess excellent qualities of mind, character, and body, and "as a subject of God's moral government, his life should be regulated by the Christian ethics, he should be unshaken in the Christian faith, should drink deep of the Christian spirit, and be animated by the Christian hope" (49). Subtly reinterpreting the legal prohibition against a political or religious test for faculty, Lathrop stated that "it is enough for us as the appointing power, that in his high vocation, [the Wisconsin professor] is too profoundly Christian to be sectarian—that he is too intensely American, to be partizan" (50). Such Christian Americans—as faculty, students, and general public—would through education lead the way in the growth of "the progressive civilization of mankind," whose racial cast was made explicit in the claim that "the life blood of that higher and still higher civilization is to be the blood of the Anglo-Saxon—enriched, it may be, from the veins of Celt, Teuton, and Scandinavian" (52). This last clause tailored Lathrop's message to local demographic conditions in the upper Midwest, and indeed his political focus was not primarily the United States in general but rather his adopted state in particular: "And where, I ask, on the surface of our globe, is the civilization of this leading race to find an opening to a more glorious development than *here*, on the genial soil of Wisconsin?" (29). The state university, then, as "the chosen instrumentality by which Wisconsin shall discharge her duty to man," has the opportunity to "accomplish a glorious destiny, by ministering, in no humble degrees, to the advancement of the cause of God in this world, which is none other than the cause of human intelligence and virtue—the great cause of an ever progressive civilization" (53). However, such high ideals did not entirely convince Lathrop's local constituency: in 1859, charges of corruption, mismanagement, Madison elitism, and "godlessness" forced his resignation, the latter term probably referring both to the institution's nonsectarianism and to the unfamiliar emphases on science and on national progress described above.

Moreover, these images and ideals were more than mere rhetoric; rather, the official religious and cultural values were reflected in and extended by the daily social life and by the concrete institutional structure of the university. Anecdotal evidence suggests that most students were actively religious out of personal choice: in their diaries, Harvey Reid (who would become a friend of Muir) and Burr Jones describe themselves and other students as regularly attending Sunday services and Bible studies in local churches, sometimes twice in one day; Samuel Fallows attended church and camp meetings (mainly Methodist) with various friends, many of whom were "student preachers" in smaller churches, and he eventually convinced the daughter of a prominent local Unitarian family both to convert and to marry him. (Fallows ended up a Methodist bishop.) Similarly, the absence of religious requirements for faculty could not change the fact that most qualified candidates were trained in seminaries or in religiously affiliated colleges. Reid's Bible studies were conducted by O. M. Conover, graduate of Princeton Theological Seminary and professor of ancient languages at Madison from 1852 to 1858, while Reid's favorite preacher seems to have been Conover's successor, James D. Butler of Vermont, graduate of Middlebury College and of Andover Seminary and past pastor at a Congregational church in Cincinnati. John W. Sterling—professor of mathematics, de facto dean of students, and acting chancellor from 1860 through 1866—graduated from Hamilton College and from Princeton Seminary before serving as a missionary in

Pennsylvania, after which he taught a few years at Carroll College, a Presbyterian school outside Milwaukee. Respected by students, colleagues, and public for his principled character and gentlemanly conduct, Sterling adhered to a liberal Protestantism whose ethical focus was suggested in his 1871 baccalaureate sermon: "Whether we accept the doctrine of the Christian faith or not, the fact cannot be controverted that there are evil tendencies and influences to be resisted; that there are contests to be made, which demand the utmost vigilance, patient endurance, systematic and vigorous exertion" (Butterfield, 76).

In addition, the university structure included explicitly Christian religious exercises that were indeed nondenominational (as the charter required) but none the less central to the life of the community. Daily chapel, required of all males, was an elaborate and serious affair (according to Jones): the faculty sat on a platform behind the podium, while seniors "in all their dignity" sat in the front of the student body, with the other classes in rows behind; the actual service included Bible reading and prayer, followed by a student declamation. The 1858 catalogue notes the existence of a student-organized Bible study group, led by Butler, in which several other faculty members and their families participated; around the same time, a choir was formed to praise the Creator and for enjoyment and personal growth. Although Butler was recognized as unofficial university chaplain, he himself named Daniel Read, the professor of "Mental Philosophy" who taught the required senior course on "Christian Evidences," as the person who "taught the students to pray" (Curti and Carstensen, 182); interestingly, Read was one of the few faculty members who were *not* seminary trained, suggesting that Christian apologetics and prayer were disciplines expected of or exercised by any well-educated person of the day. Students' personal conduct, deportment, and morals were observed and regulated by the faculty with as much seriousness as was their scholarship. Symbolic expressions of religion were more muted, but still real: the university seal represents the light of knowledge emanating from God; academic ceremonies included religious presence, from the opening prayers and closing benediction that surrounded Lathrop's inaugural address to baccalaureate sermons such as Sterling's.

Clearly, important parts of the university's religious worldview—both as explicitly expressed in word and image and as conveyed through social context and institutional structure—would have been familiar, welcoming, and attractive to Muir. His Disciples heritage stressed both nonsectarianism and human responsibility for perfection, in ways having much in common with the liberal Protestantism expressed by Lathrop. (Regent Smith's image of God as a righteous judge, a Calvinist remnant seemingly out of step with Lathrop's more positive tone, was of course a strong part of Muir's paternal heritage, one that was becoming more in tension with the thrust of Muir's own development as well as that of the university.) The noninstitutional character of worship, preaching, and belief that was characteristic of the Disciples (and other evangelicals) in the days of the circuit rider would have prepared Muir for a form of religiousness that found ritual expression in public forums other than church, and indeed Muir participated regularly in all of the religious activities of the university as part of his wholesale social, emotional, and intellectual immersion in the community. Other elements of this university culture, such as the millennial roles of Wisconsin and of America, would have been familiar to Muir even if they held little or no personal import. Thus, although some aspects of this general orientation were new to him—for example, an image of humans as "co-creators with God" may have gone beyond anything he had encountered before—the strong cultural and religious continuities were crucial for Muir's future. Though he probably did not make explicit intellectual connections between his scientific interests, his social context, and his religious beliefs, the "surface" connections were quite important on a personal level: the continuing symbolism and ritual of Protestant culture, community, and science enabled Muir to retain some sense of loyalty to religious beliefs and institutions, providing both the emotional support and the intellectual insights that would allow him to plunge wholeheartedly forward into the creative work that held his future.

At the same time, certain elements of the university and of frontier culture forced Muir into a position of opposition and even alienation. As Chancellor Lathrop's address makes clear, there was a dimension of the life of the university that pointed beyond the classroom and the school grounds to a self-conscious "Wisconsan" and "American" identity (provisional and contested as those cultural images were). For Muir, however, as we have seen, Scottish culture and pride, embodied in a continually reformulated image of Scotland itself, were a living presence in his life and self-image; in Lathrop's racialist language, Muir had not yet emptied his Celtic veins to enrich the lifeblood of the dominant Anglo-Saxon America, and in fact resisted any such process of Americanization. The truly bloody event that brought these issues to the forefront, and in fact pervaded Muir's whole experience of the university, was the Civil War.

The months in 1860 and 1861 during which Muir left home for Madison and Prairie du Chien were times of change and uncertainty not only in his personal life but in the life of state and nation as well, as political and cultural tensions between North and South burst into open secession and warfare. Given the energy with which the new states of the upper Midwest threw themselves into the Union cause, it is not surprising that by early July the presence of the war was felt in Wisconsin. (It is important to remember that at this time public allegiance was conceived in relation to the individual states as much as to the federal government, as Lathrop's address suggests and as was institutionalized in the state-identified regiments that actually fought the war—see, e. g., D. E. Sutherland, chapter 1.) A series of letters to Muir from new school chum Harvey Reid noted with distaste the militaristic mood of an honor guard at a local Independence Day celebration, and expressed outright revulsion at news of some (pre–Bull Run) battle in the South: "This is called by some a *holy war* but to my mind there is little of *holiness* in sending thousands of unprepared sons to eternity through the bloody gates of a *Sabbath-fought* battle" (1:124).

Muir's responses are unpreserved, but other letters make it clear that he shared Reid's religiously inflected disgust both with the war and with the prevailing Northern—in particular, Wisconsin—enthusiasm for it. Observing the activities of the Seventh Wisconsin regiment at nearby Fort Randall (the training camp outside Madison) sometime in 1861, Muir wrote to Sarah that "their appearance is very imposing but how can all the great and showy coverings of war hide its real hideousness" (1:147). References to the "war demon," the "unsettled state of the country," and so on appear throughout his letters from these years, and by late 1862 Muir was weary of the news and the culture of conflict: "This war seems further from a close than ever. How strange that a country with so many schools and churches should be desolated by so unsightly a monster" (1:251). Seemingly lacking any sense that the carnage might be justified as a battle against the horrors of slavery (never mentioned in the surviving letters), Muir did not demonize the Southerners as the enemy but rather saw all participants as condemned by the Prince of Peace for the sin of war.

> Should not the secessionist who maybe is Christian and who if we were acquainted with him would be a bosom friend through life—should he not be shot solemnly, when the Judge sheds tears on pronouncing the doom of the atrocious murderer? How strangely it seems to me I should feel if in heaven one praising with the white robe should for a little cease his praise and tell me that I had beheaded him that sunshiney day at Bull Run. (1:170)

Unlike Whitman, Muir was led by his religious attitudes and by his lack of any sense of American identity to feel no connection with the national or political issues involved. Indeed, the war served only to lower his opinion of American politics and culture; according to Stanley (101), in his college debating society he vehemently argued the affirmative on the topic "the American people are incapable of self government." As a result, his active response to the war was directed only toward that which immediately affected him, in the general mood of the community and in the concrete presence of the training camp. However (and again in contrast to Whitman the "Wound Dresser"), Muir primarily felt drawn to confront the vice, immorality, and confusion he found in the camp, which sometimes seem to have been more horrific to him than the actual violence on the battlefield. Accordingly, Muir's major actions in response to the crisis involved evangelical work in the camp and through personal contacts and letters, as he tried to look after the moral and spiritual lives of the young men thrown into the dreadful experience of the soldier. This response was parallel to those of the Christian Commission and the YMCA, and for a brief period in 1863 Muir was the president of the local university chapter of the latter organization.

Beneath this religious language and activity, itself deeply felt, one can discern a more visceral psychological and emotional rejection of the violence and confusion of the war, as unwanted threats to his own tenuous sense of personal identity. In a letter to Mrs. Pelton in 1861, discussing his meeting with some Prairie du Chien acquaintances in Fort Randall, Muir dealt with these personal stresses by taking strongly parental stances toward men who were probably only a few years younger than himself. After hearing their "abominable" conversation and "camp language," Muir "lectur[ed] them a few minutes upon the necessity of having the Character formed and being possessed of tightly clenched principles before being put to such a trial as a three year soaking in so horrible a mixture." Later, fearing that such a fatherly approach might not succeed, he appealed to Mrs. Pelton's motherly influences.

> Now don't for any sake let Byron's and Dwight's Mothers know what I have written for this would only make them sorrowful and the boys angry, but I do anxiously wish you would tell them to write often to them all the time, for O it is good to get letters from home, and then to think that scarce one good influence reaches the poor boys. How much they need the holy influence of home, as they unfold the pages folded by a Mother's or Sister's hand they will forget where they are and as they anxiously read the pure thoughts and advices in the tent corner and those not half expressed sympathies which sisters and Mothers only have, tears will flow and when he next joins his companions vice will not seem as before. Now won't you be sure and tell them. (1:168–69)

At the same time as these culturally shaped paternal and maternal patterns gave Muir a way to respond to the war itself, they also served to address his own emotional needs, as he re-created familiar and reassuring presences within himself. Significantly, however, in his interactions with the soldiers he was able to express only the fatherly persona; thus, his experience of the war helped maintain his patterns of relating to men in a somewhat moralistic and rigid (if heartfelt) way, explaining in part why new emotional patterns were so often worked out in his relationships—especially his Christian friendships—with women such as the Peltons.

Further, Muir's emotional rejection of the war and of American identity intensified his allegiance to Scotland as the center of his cultural or ethnic identity if not his formal political loyalty. Interestingly, an early letter from his arrival in Prairie du Chien hints at the importance of his personal image of Scotland in dealing with the disorientation of his initial move away from home. Dismissing the town of Prairie du Chien itself as a "miserable place," Muir first focused his attention on the surrounding prairie, "walled in" by the steep limestone bluffs on the east side and bounded by the Mississippi on the west. It is important to remember that this would have been the most rugged and striking scenery he had seen for eleven years; fortunately for him, this new and dramatic landscape was one that could be understood through a visual parallel to more familiar and loved environments, namely, the rocky coast of Dunbar and/or the walled castles of Scott's novels. Muir added a Gothic touch by noting the local legend that "on the very top of the ridge a notionable Catholic was buried according to his dying injunctions." His own imaginative response to the bluffs around the prairie reenacted his childhood patterns: the ridge "is so steep and high you can hardly scramble to the top, but I mean to try it some day," just as the boy dared the walls of Dunbar castle and even the sooty pit of hell. Shifting his attention to a single home and family, Muir described the "dandy (or 'polite') society" of the Peltons' boardinghouse in an intriguing way: "It was worthwhile to see their ladyships and lordships eating turkey and playing blind man's buff on Thanksgiving evening in the great hall" (1:73). Having no other experiences of town society on the frontier, Muir subtly interpreted it in the only terms he knew, in which memories of Dunbar perhaps combined with images from Scott. Although the attractive aspects of this construction were in tension with the moralistic judgments of his religious perspective, both approaches served to make familiar a strange environment and to connect it with some of the deep sources of identity and of vitality within the young man.

Similarly, during his university years in Madison, Muir again transformed his image of Scotland to fashion a usable national identity, this time drawing upon his new academic life and skills. A surviving university-era notebook on Scottish geology, geography, and history (probably not lecture notes, but rather gleaned from some unknown text or texts) provides a window on this process. The "Scotland" presented here is a collection of facts and images, unified mainly through a logical, impersonal arrangement based in academic methodology: geographical regions are described south to north and east to west, then geology presented in terms of mountain ranges, rock strata, and mineral resources, followed by an alphabetical listing of landmarks and towns ("Abbey Craig," "Abbotsford," "Abbotshall," etc.) with accompanying historical notes. (Muir only got as far as "Gilmeston.") As would be expected, the longest entry is the one for Dunbar, but even this shows no personal additions; Muir seems to have been striving to envision Scotland as an "objective" whole, through the lens of impartial science.

At the same time, a culturally approved romanticism appeared again even in scientific contexts: "The western coast is so torn and lacerated by the sea as to defy description, abounding in rocky promontories and presenting the most sublime and savage scenery" (31:83). Further, it was clearly the dramatic contrast between geographical regions—the increasing emotional impact as one moves from south to north and east to west—that acted as the fundamental structuring device in the supposedly objective presentation of the essay. Interestingly, the most dramatic descriptions are those of regions far from Muir's native Dunbar—the north and west, especially the Highlands and the coast. In fact, it was precisely these regions that had come to stand in the popular mind as cultural symbols or archetypes of the whole of Scotland, as part of a larger public invention of a "traditional" Scottish identity that began earlier in the century but was still in the process of development in the 1860s, springing from sources and motives far removed from Muir's personal experience (see Trevor-Roper). Whether or not this popular identification of Scotland with the Highlands and with the northern and western coasts shaped the text that Muir was reading, it probably shaped *his reading of it,* having come to the young immigrant through other cultural sources such as Scott.

At other levels, more personal dynamics allowed the wider cultural "invention" to hold particular power for Muir. To the eyes and body of Muir as a small child, even the relatively tame agricultural landscape and coast of Dunbar would have seemed—rather, *been*—rugged, dramatic, and massive. Later, when he was trying to recapture the feeling and power of these childhood perceptions as an adult, the images of a wild, rocky, mountainous Scotland would have seemed—again, been—more true to his own experience and emotions than an objective survey. Thus, the text's descriptions of the north and west appealed more strongly to his felt imagination than did those of the area around Dunbar, and probably supplied new language and images to express his childhood memories (which find ultimate expression in his own descriptions of Scotland in *Boyhood*).

Further, it seems probable that his recent revulsion against the realities of American warfare made his earlier enthusiasm for the mythic militarism of Scottish heroes less palatable. In the absence of this more local, Dunbar-centered, orally transmitted history of war and heroes, the written chronicle of architecture and landscapes (culturally slanted to the north and west) represented for Muir a more acceptable version of Scotland's mythic past and power. Perhaps most strikingly, Muir's notes on Scotland contain very little reference to agriculture, which would have been the dominant influence on the landscape around Dunbar. Although this omission was partly grounded in the relative weight of his childhood impressions, it also probably reflected his own impatience with and rejection of the farming life he had experienced in Wisconsin. Scotland could function as a powerful symbol and ideal for Muir only if it were not associated with the pains and struggles of the present—but it still had to carry the power and emotion of the past. Thus, his continuing reinvention of his own personal Scotland was aided by a simultaneously scientific and cultural inventory of stereotypic Scottish landscape scenes and local identities, most of which he had never seen but which mingled with his ever more distant memories of Dunbar and so gained an aura of emotional connection and personal reality.

Further evidence of the meaning for Muir of this transformed Scotland appears in an exchange of letters with Mrs. Pelton in 1862. After Fanny's death, and herself suffering from a lung disease, Mrs. Pelton had returned to her parents and childhood home in Massachusetts to recover. From there, she wrote to Muir of the joys of her native countryside (and of the soothing presence of her mother), wishing he were with her and suggesting that her Berkshires might serve as "a substitute for your 'Scottish Highlands'" (1:216). (Was it she, or Muir himself, who envisioned Scotland in terms of the Highlands?) In his response, Muir agreed—even identified—with her estimation of the emotional impact of the natural environment of childhood: "I am sure that your feelings are of no common kind, while you gaze upon the scenes of your happy youth; each object, hill stream or tree, will crowd numberless pleasing thoughts and associations upon you. Under such circumstances I think I should almost run wild with delight" (1:222). For him, however, that landscape could be no substitute for Scotland: "*Scotland* alone will ever be Scotland to me. My love for my own Scottish land seems to grow with every pulse so that I cannot see the name or hear it but a thrill goes to every fibre of all my body. One of the more prominent of my future hopes is that I should one day visit SCOTLAND" (1:223).[13] As a parallel to his and Pelton's focus on the natural characteristics of her Massachusetts, Muir's love of Scotland

13. Discussing Scottish writers not living in the homeland, Manlove comments that "for many Scots their native land comes more clearly into being the further and longer they are from it" (17).

was by this point conceived primarily in terms of the natural environment, indicating a subtle shift from the mythic, literary, and historical imagery of previous references. His evocation of the Scottish landscape incorporated a whole range of simultaneously personal and cultural meanings, including childhood, home, physicality, and motherhood, viewed through lenses both of nostalgia and of hope. Such imagery served to transform childhood memories into useful material to address present emotional needs, including both his strong relationships with the Peltons and his revulsion against the prevailing militarism of his immediate social context.

Alongside this reinvigoration of his Scottish identity, Muir expressed his rejection of the war and of the wider American culture by immersing himself even more fully in his academic studies, particularly science. Interestingly, Muir's stance reversed Emerson's response to the war as a welcome expression of the spontaneous instincts of the people. Before the war, according to Emerson, "we valued ourselves as cool calculators; we were very fine with our learning and culture, with our science that was of no country, and our religion of peace;—and now a sentiment mightier than logic, wide as light, strong as gravity, reaches into the college, the bank, the farm-house, and the church. It is the day of the populace" (quoted in Fredrickson, 66). Muir, alienated from "the populace," would have none of this, and in fact remained in the college and in the farm-house, finding increased meaning and safety in the "religion of peace" and especially in the "science that was of no country."

In this context, the university's major contribution to Muir's development came in the form of exposure to specific scientific disciplines. According to the original version of his autobiographical reminiscences, "I didn't take the entire curriculum—picked out what I thought would be most useful to me, particularly chemistry, which opened a new world to me, and a little Greek and Latin and Botany and Geology, and when I got apparently all I could get from the University, I quietly walked off without saying anything about a diploma—without graduating" (46:11812). Although the facts seem accurate, the tone of intellectual and emotional autonomy that this passage conveys—the "coolness" of Muir's self-presentation—is contradicted by contemporaneous evidence that his engagement with intellectual disciplines was strongly mediated and charged by the same patterns of emotion, interpersonal relationship, and religious understanding that had shaped the rest of his life up to that point. People, dreams, and images—not pure ideas—guided and gave meaning to the young man's exploration of science at the university. The dynamics of this process are perhaps most obvious in Muir's study of chemistry and geology under Professor Ezra Carr.

Ezra Slocum Carr had arrived in Madison in 1856, bringing with him the new ideas and orientations that were changing the face both of theology and of the geological sciences in early-nineteenth-century Europe and America. A native New Yorker, he had studied and practiced medicine in the Northeast before turning to geology, in which field he soon made important contributions through his work in the New York and Wisconsin geological surveys. Culturally, Carr embodied the combination of idealism and pragmatism characteristic of that strain of transcendentalism centered in Vermont, birthplace of his wife Jeanne and his "adopted home state" (see Schofield). On the one hand, his intellectual work helped discredit the attempted reconciliation of geology and religious orthodoxy proposed by Edward Hitchcock and others, paving the way for the somewhat more liberal (but still religiously grounded) ideas of his hero Agassiz. On the other hand, a strong sense of social obligation, from his leadership of the Vermont temperance society in the 1840s to his later involvement in the California Grange in the 1870s, gave a moral and practical tone to his teaching and scientific work. In his address upon entering the Wisconsin State University, Carr asserted that "Earth knowledge has more spiritual value for the youth of America than erudition concerning the amours of Jupiter and Venus. . . . When I walk with students in green fields and forests, and show them Nature's basement rooms, how the foundations of the earth were laid, I see in them tokens of mental animation which are the strongest stimulants to my own exertions" (L. M. Wolfe, 76). Thus, Carr possessed the intellectual, social, and religious qualities that would make him an ideal Wisconsin professor as described by Chancellor Lathrop—and, not coincidentally, a powerful role model for Muir, both as scientist and as adult male. Despite his charisma as a teacher, however, Carr could be somewhat rigid, stern, and distant in personal relationships, and this perhaps foreclosed overt emotional intimacy in his relationship with Muir; at the same time, this very distance may have evoked memories of Muir's father and thus reinforced Carr's adequacy as a role model for the young man.

Appropriately, Muir understood the core of his personal relationship with Carr in simultaneously scientific and religious terms. Writing to Ezra's wife Jeanne in 1865, Muir stated that "[w]e remember in a peculiar way those who first gave us the story of Redeeming Love from the great book of Revelation, and I shall not forget the Doctor, who first laid before me the great book of Nature, and though I have taken so little from his hand he has at least shown me where those mines of priceless knowledge lie and how to reach them" (1:378). The metaphor of the "book of Nature" was one that would guide Muir throughout his life, and Carr was not the one who introduced the metaphor itself to Muir; Thomas Dick used essentially the same language, and Muir would surely have encountered it in other scientific and theological writings before he arrived in

Madison. Rather, Carr's importance was in actually laying the book before him, in making the metaphor (and the associated ideas) meaningful
to Muir in a new and powerful way. More than anyone in Muir's life to
that point, Carr embodied both religious and scientific values in a person
with whom Muir could be in a respectful, affective, and collegial relationship, and supplied specific forms of scientific activity in which Muir could
labor. At the same time, the familiarity and continuing importance of the
religious imagery were part of what allowed the personal relationship and
the intellectual activity to be so powerful to Muir, as relationships, religion, and science mutually conditioned each other against the background of his previous experiences and patterns.

Although most commentators have stressed the long-term importance
for Muir of Carr's geology lessons, we have seen that Muir himself regarded chemistry as the discipline that "opened a new world" to him.
According to roommate Charles E. Vroman, Muir "was acknowledged
by common consent to be the most proficient chemical student in college.
There were no laboratory facilities in the University at that time so Muir
built a chemical laboratory in the room. With the multitude of things
already there, the chemical laboratory capped the climax" (quoted in
Stanley, 86–87). His handwritten notebook on "Principles of Physics or
Natural Philosophy," devoted to foundational concepts of physical chemistry—one of the "mines of priceless knowledge" to which Carr introduced him—contains hints of Muir's personal attraction to his teacher,
such as a few jokes and striking turns of phrase written down verbatim
from Carr's lectures. Aided by such emotional incentives, Muir gained a
language with which to describe the structure and relationships of the
physical world through the concepts of atoms, states, pores, attractive and
repulsive forces (electricity, magnetism, etc.), equilibrium, and so on. For
example, "A solid is matter in which cohesive attraction is not so far overcome by repulsion as to make it indifferent to form" (31:44), and "Pores
of a body are that part of the apparent which are not occupied by atoms"
(31:52). These in-between spaces are filled by the "subtle fluid," which is
"the agent of heat, light, and electricity" and which "is considered as
pervading all space" (31:53). The relative strengths of the attractive and
the repulsive forces determine a substance's porosity, which in turn deter-
mines the apparent qualities of hardness, brittleness, etc.

Significantly, these fundamental chemical concepts stressed the dynamic relationships to be found within matter; as Muir recalled in his
later autobiographical reflections, the essence of what he got from his
scientific studies in Madison was insight into "the attraction and repulsion of the atoms composing the globe, marching and retreating—the
harmony, the oneness, of all the life of the world, etcetera—the methods

by which nature builds and pulls down in sculpting the globe; one form of beauty after another in endless variety" (46:11823). A passage from his scientific notebook reflects the enthusiasm and sheer delight with which the young Muir absorbed his chemistry lessons and made them a part of his entire worldview.

> Some animaliculi are said by those who have measured the same to be of such a size that thousands can go hop skip and jump side by side through a needle's eye. Now it may be proved by mathematics which cannot lie that when one of these chaps draws aside his tail, he draws ourselves and all the earth aside, and of course the mischief does not stop here but the glorious sun is moved and then other suns and others through all immensity. (31:65)

Eventually, this exposure to chemistry would strongly shape his thought and language throughout his life; as one example, we see in this passage the core insight formulated later as one of the adult Muir's best-known aphorisms: "When we try to pick out anything by itself, we find it hitched to everything else in the universe."

As such language suggests, these scientific studies contained a religious element as well. Muir's early assimilation of a religious interpretation of science, as expressed by Thomas Dick and others, was shared by many at the university: regent Alonzo Wing claimed that through geology one can "study the handiwork of the Builder of Worlds" (Curti and Carstensen, 86), while the chemistry professor before Carr, Stephen Pearl Lathrop, had posed the rhetorical question "What more worthy employment, then, can man find for his faculties than the investigation of these hidden forces that tell in so plain a language of the Mighty Power which called them into action?" (Butterfield, 29). A similar worldview is found in Muir's notebook: "Nature is, in its most extended sense, all that is created; or, according to the poet 'a name for an effect whose cause is God'" (31:37). Thus, Muir was attracted to chemistry not only as an interesting, useful, and exciting way of investigating and describing natural phenomena but also as a worldview harmonious with his evolving religious perspectives, most importantly the sense of the presence of God in the physical world— a perspective fully supported by the structure and content of his social experience at the university as well.

These personal, social, and religious meanings of science were by no means limited to chemistry and Professor Carr; equally if not more powerful were the ways in which his study of botany came to be infused with a wide range of emotions, images, and relationships. Muir's autobiography locates his introduction to botany in a chance meeting with another student, Milton Griswold, and Griswold himself provides corroboration for the story (*Boyhood*, 280–83; for Griswold's reminiscence, see 51:17–22).

Even more than those "mines of priceless knowledge" to which he was introduced by Carr, Muir was attracted to botany as a disciplined activity that gave order, focus, and direction to his ways of experiencing the natural world. Far different from the somewhat abstract, mathematical, and hypothetical principles of the other sciences (even given Carr's attempts at an engaged, interactive pedagogy), botany was active and energetic, incorporating all dimensions of his physical being—sight, taste, smell, touch, bodily movement—along with his intellectual, emotional, and spiritual dimensions. While as a science it gave Muir another vision of an ordered—sometimes even mechanistic—system of nature, as an *activity* it constituted a new form of play.[14] Even on the level of sheer perception, the discipline of botany seems to have provided him with a new way of seeing, of focusing on the world and of attending to specific things within it, which helped make the world more accessible, understandable, and safe. In a later (1863) letter to his brother Dan, Muir described himself on a botanizing expedition as "gazing at all times intently on either side for new plants" (1:323); the very intensity of his gaze suggests that Muir at this point psychologically needed some sort of structured activity in order to relate himself to the natural world.[15] During his initial years in Wisconsin, Muir had used bird-watching and hunting as activities—indeed, as cultural practices—that brought him into meaningful relationship with his environment; now, in college in his mid-twenties, botany—more precisely, the activity of botanizing—provided a different and more adequate environmental practice.

14. According to Stephen Fox, the disciplined, comparative analysis of the relationships between plant species "appealed to Muir as a mechanical operation: treating a plant like a machine of separate parts with known functions, which meshed together in an orderly, purposeful whole" (40). (Remember also that among Muir's Madison-era inventions were devices for precisely measuring the daily growth of plants, suggesting a somewhat mechanistic interpretation of or stance toward the vegetable world.) Turner, on the other hand, stresses that in botany Muir found a new kind of "work," far from the drudgery of farm and machine shop (and even Greek and Latin): "with botany the actual work of hunting, collecting, and analyzing plants was the same to him as play, releasing aesthetic impulses, inspiring imagination, revelation after revelation unfolding as in the opening of a flower's petals" (99). Elizabeth Keeney (chapter 6) discusses the change from interpreting botany as "work" to viewing it as "play"—both constituting differing interpretations of "self-improvement"—over the course of the nineteenth century.

15. Muir's intense botanical gaze contrasts sharply with Thoreau's desire to "let [his] senses wander": "I must walk more with free senses. . . . Be not preoccupied with looking. Go not to the object; let it come to you. When I have found myself looking down and confining my gaze to the flowers, I have thought it might be well to get into the habit of observing the clouds as a corrective, but no! that study would be just as bad. What I need is not to look at all, but a true sauntering of the eye" (quoted in O'Grady, 25). As we shall see, Muir would gaze at his surroundings in a disciplined, focused, non-Thoreauvian manner at least until his first winter in California, and in many ways for long after.

Moreover, Muir understood botany in specifically religious terms, as a literal religious practice. From the start, the discovery of botany gave him yet another approach to the "great book of Nature" as a source of religious insight. Interestingly, while the published *Story of My Boyhood and Youth* presents Griswold as suggesting to Muir the connection between botany and religion, in the original version of the autobiography it is Muir himself who supplies the religious interpretation, after Griswold has described botany in more neutral terms, as "simply a natural system" (see 46:11822). In any case, Muir would have soon encountered such an interpretation in his textbooks. The 1860 edition of Alphonso Wood's widely used *Class-Book of Botany* (some version of which Muir used consistently for years) begins with a discussion of the religious meanings of botany. Wood argues that the natural sciences in general train the human mind for "the recognition of Intelligence by intelligence," the discernment of the God-given design in nature, "making it all luminous with the Divine Presence" (10). In particular, the study of botany serves as "a source of the purest pleasure," and more importantly affords occasion for the discipline and enlightening of the human mind: "Entering life as a mere germ, the soul expands into intelligence and virtue through the teachings of surrounding objects and influences. In this good work the beauty, purity and wisdom displayed in the vegetable world bear a full share" (9). The teaching function of botany includes moral education as well as the specific tenets of Christianity: the individuality of plants and the seed's triumph over death "declare that nature sympathizes with humanity in the circumstances of the Fall, the Redemption, and the Life" (12). Wood concludes with a statement of the practical good of botany: "The ultimate aim of its researches is the development of the boundless resources of the vegetable kingdom for our sustenance and protection as well as education; for the healing of our diseases and the alleviation of our wants and woes. This branch of botanical science is called . . . APPLIED BOTANY" (14). Despite (or perhaps because of) his valuation of nature as expressive of God's design, Wood clearly interprets the natural world in terms of human use and benefit—much as had Muir's teenage hero Mungo Park. Thus, on a variety of levels, Wood's *Botany* provided Muir with a way to literally act out a religious relationship with the world, a structure of activity and of thought (embodied in an actual book) that guided his engagement with the "book of Nature."[16]

16. As Keeney notes (103), taxonomic botany's emphasis on empirical observation and classification fit well with much nineteenth-century Protestant philosophy of science, based as the latter was in Baconianism. As we have seen, the Baconian approach was especially influential among the Campbellites/Disciples, and so Muir would have been familiar with it (and attracted to it) both as a general mode of reasoning and as a method for natural theology. On the uses of botany in natural theology, see Keeney (chapter 7).

Although this religious dimension placed botany on a continuum with the other sciences, in professional and social terms it held a unique position at midcentury. At the beginning of the nineteenth century, according to Elizabeth Keeney, almost all botanizers were "amateur," in the sense of undertaking the activity from sheer love of the subject; in that context, local collectors made major contributions to the science even when their primary motivation was moral, cultural, and aesthetic "self-improvement." As the century progressed, however, there emerged a growing split between amateurs interested in botany as natural history and professionals seeking a more rigorous, laboratory-based botany stressing biology and physiology. As professionalization advanced, the local activity of the amateurs would eventually lose contact with and influence on the more scientific, institutionalized practitioners, and become more of a sheer pastime or hobby—"amateur" in the sense of nonprofessional and, by implication, nonrigorous. These changes would also affect the cultural meanings attached to amateur botany, including religious, educational, and gender dimensions.

In the Wisconsin of Muir's day, botany was perfectly poised between the amateur and the professional realms, allowing it to function on multiple levels in his intellectual, social, and cultural lives. In the 1861 *Catalogue* of the Wisconsin State University, botany was defined as the study of "The Plant being first considered as an individual in reference to the nature and processes of vegetable life; Second, its relation to other plants, or the Vegetable Kingdom; Third, its uses" (42); thus, the course supposedly included both biological and natural history approaches as well as a more practical component. As taught by Professor Carr, however, whose primary interests were in chemistry and agriculture (as suggested by his later book on agriculture and the Grange in California), the natural history component was probably deemphasized. By contrast, Muir's enthusiasm was for the taxonomic approach exemplified in Wood, and it is not even clear that he ever took Carr's course. Rather, his particular interests and passions led him out of the formal university setting and into a more informal—but still culturally shaped—social world of botany.

Although *Boyhood* continues the account of his discovery of botany by stating that Muir "wandered away" for solitary botanizing whenever he could, Griswold reports that Muir immediately proposed that the two students meet regularly to walk and to botanize. Both by necessity and by choice, the amateur botanizers of the nineteenth century participated in a wide-ranging network of companionship and support, and Muir stepped directly into the social and cultural patterns of this network. In doing so, he did not necessarily forsake all status as a "scientist"; indeed, one of the leading American botanists of the day, John Torrey, was himself an amateur whose high position depended on his placement in the network of amateurs, for whom he acted as a clearinghouse in the exchange of specimens and information. (At the other end of the clearinghouse stood Asa Gray of Harvard, who held a unique place as one of the very few professional botanists of the mid-nineteenth century.) Increase A. Lapham, a Milwaukee land speculator and developer, served as a major link between Torrey and Gray and the local amateurs in Wisconsin— including those around Madison (Keeney, 30–36). Although it would take Muir some time to become fully integrated into this network, the midcentury coexistence of amateur and professional botanical culture placed his first exposure to botany in a wider social and intellectual context.

As a first step in this process, Muir both drew upon and transformed his immediate familial and social relationships in constructing his personal "practice" of botany. In particular, the common view of botany as a particularly appropriate activity for children and for women fit in well with Muir's own past constructions of religion, home, and personal relationship.[17] Interestingly, his descriptions of his first attempts at botanizing—e.g., that he went on long expeditions every Saturday (46:11822)— seem to recapture some of the feelings of his early wanderings with (male) playmates and with his grandfather in the Scottish countryside; perhaps the activity itself evoked a more companionate, less rigid mode of relating to Griswold and other men than he had exhibited while lecturing the soldiers in the army camp. Moreover, Muir had long made important associations between women and plant life, from his aunt's "sacred" lilies in Dunbar to his long walks in Wisconsin fields with his sisters, the "God of Trees" poem to the Peltons, the images of the girls gathering flowers on campus, and the practice of exchanging bits of moss, wood, and so on with his sisters and with the Peltons. Thus, his own personal experiences and patterns of relationship were reflected in and amplified by the existing social configuration of botany.

On the symbolic level as well, the culture of amateur botany was intimately intertwined with women, children, and domestic life. One form that this connection took was the "culture of flowers" of nineteenth-century Europe and America. In poetry, art, and popular botanical manuals of the day, the sentimental "language of flowers" was defined in terms of its feminine character and its function of representing emotions and

17. See Keeney, chapters 4 and 5. Alphonso Wood himself was an instructor at a girls' school. In general, the categories of gender and age were intimately intertwined with those of religiousness, social and geographical location, and scientific validity, somewhat as follows: women/children/religion/home/amateurs vs. men/adults/secularity/institutions/professionals. At the same time, Vera Norwood (chapter 1) argues that women themselves helped create the gendered character of botany as a response to their exclusion both from the natural world and from the economic realm; thus, botany was an arena in which the ideology of domesticity could attempt to influence the public sphere.

relationships. As far as I can tell, however, Muir did not utilize this sentimental language of flowers; rather, he used the *scientific* language of flowers, i.e., botany, for many of the same ends—expressing emotion, cementing the bonds of human relationship, evoking religious values and aesthetic beauty, and establishing an affective relationship with flowers themselves. Thus, like his personal invention of Scotland, Muir's own culture of flowers was a unique and idiosyncratic process, rooted in the specifics of his individual experiences and development but dependent on the existence of the public culture as a context in which such a privately constructed system could have meaning and could work as a way to relate to others. Indeed, if Muir's general mode of relating to friends and family can be characterized as "Christian love," it may not be too much to say that the language and activity of botanizing would come to constitute his *practice* of Christian love—an active mode of physical, emotional, intellectual, spiritual, and (as we shall see in later chapters) erotic relationship with significant persons, with the natural world, and with the divine.[18]

By the end of his time at the university, for example, Muir's love of botany had subtly refashioned his relationship with his sister Sarah. Responding to his expressions of scientific enthusiasm and enjoyment, a letter of Sarah's from April 1863 described her own interest in the study of the beauties of the natural world, "whether the grand and sublime or the most simple and passing" (including "the tiniest flowers"), as a means of seeing the "skill" and "wisdom" of "that silent but mighty Power that makes everything spring to fresh life and vigor" (1:280). After revealing that she had cried over a photograph of himself that Muir had sent her, and promising one of herself in return, Sarah also explained that she was sending to John a specimen of an unknown vine she had found on a walk—for purposes of identification, not solely sentimental exchange. In June, Muir responded that he could not identify the plant without the flower, but that he intended to return to the Fountain Lake homestead to collect his own specimens for a herbarium. In this context, his description of a twenty-five-mile botanical walk carried some of the feelings of his earlier walks with Sarah. He obviously was pleased by his sister's interest: "You would like the study of botany. It is the most exciting thing in the

18. According to Jack Goody, "[F]lowers are . . . part of culture: firstly, because they have been brought under cultivation by mankind and, secondly, because they are used throughout social life, for decoration, for medicine, in cooking and for their scents, but above all in establishing, maintaining and even ending relationships, with the dead as with the living, with divinities as well as humans" (2). To Goody's analysis, I would add the cultural, emotional, and spiritual meanings of individuals' relationships with flowers in themselves; thus, for Muir, flowers and botany served as symbolic mediators for his relationships with the natural world as well as with humans and with the divine. Norwood (12–18) briefly describes the sentimental "language of flowers" in nineteenth-century America.

form of even amusement much more of study that I have ever known" (1:290). This exchange is particularly striking in light of the fact (noted above) that up to this point Muir had hardly mentioned his studies in his letters to his family; apparently botany resonated sufficiently with the patterns and interests of his relationship with Sarah that he chose to begin to blur the sharp dichotomy between his academic and his family lives. It is also perhaps important that Muir was at this time preparing to leave the university (and was aware of the potential disruptiveness of this change), and so may have felt especially deeply the need to tie together whatever parts of his life he could, in constructing a stronger pattern of self and world with which to confront the unknown future.

Further, despite his deeply felt allegiance to Scotland, the religious meanings and emotional associations of botany began to allow Muir to experience his local Wisconsin landscape in more intimate and positive ways. As one indicator of this change, note that Muir in the autumn of 1861 had walked the entire distance from the farm back to Madison but had then written a letter home with no mention of the landscape he saw along the way, focusing rather on his joy at seeing the buildings and people of the university (see 1:146); indeed, it is striking that none of the letters written before his discovery of botany contain any extended description of his natural surroundings at all! By 1863, however, as we have seen, his immersion in the sciences had provided a disciplined means of attending to the details of his immediate environment, with a different emotional and intellectual coloring than he had experienced on the farm, and his passion and enthusiasm for the land were leading him on strenuous botanical expeditions.

The character of this new engagement with his surroundings is suggested by an 1863 essay on the Wisconsin prairies, which (judging from its dramatic tone and rhetorical style) may have been written as a lecture or an article for a school publication. Probably drawing upon his own years of experience and observation as well as upon formal botany texts, Muir described the yearly cycle of life on the prairie, in particular the distinctive "oak openings" (natural meadows in the forest, dotted or surrounded with oaks). As his earliest preserved piece of nature writing, the essay shows that he was capable of turning his scientifically trained eye upon his immediate surroundings as well as upon distant Scotland; at a deeper level, it reveals a growing emotional attachment to those surroundings, expressed through the same romantic and religious imagery through which he also interpreted his childhood homeland.

In part, his valorization of the local environment was accomplished through romanticizing it, utilizing imagery such as that of medieval warfare.

An annual battle is fought by the trees and prairie for supremacy. The windy weatherbeaten oaks stand around cased in mail thick corky bark holding their strong angular knotty arms over the wished for territory & casting handfuls of acorns upon it every fall but in vain. Fire the Maker and Preserver of prairies befalls the invader[s] the saplings are cut off by the ground but they do not yield. The old oaks safe in their corky mail still shake acorns. (31:111)

At the same time, his disciplined, careful, structured engagement with the details of his present surroundings provided the basis for a more positive interpretation of them. For example, fire is here described as a creative force, the "Maker and Preserver of prairies"; his scientific understanding of fire's ecological function helped effect a profound transformation of his initial experiences of prairie bonfires on the frontier, which his father had used to suggest the terrors and pains of hell. In another passage, a melancholy description of the barren prairie in early winter sets the stage for an ecstatic, hopeful evocation of the return of life in spring, conveying the regenerative powers of nature through the religious image of resurrection. Interestingly, Muir had in an earlier letter to Mrs. Pelton presented the analogy the other way around, using the general image of leaves in spring as a metaphor for his religious faith in heaven (1:200–201); similarly, but in a somewhat darker context, he had elsewhere contrasted the appropriate, timely fall of leaves in autumn to the unnatural death of soldiers on the Southern battlefields, in emphasizing the injustice and horror of the un-Christian war (1:251). Here, however, seasonal change was itself the primary subject of Muir's description, and he used religious imagery as metaphor in emphasizing the power and goodness of his immediate natural surroundings.

Thus, the cultural, social, and intellectual meanings of botany—in the context of his emotional heritage and of his important interpersonal relationships—allowed Muir to take the first tentative steps toward a transformed relationship with his immediate natural environment. By the end of his university years, what sense he had come to possess of positive identification with the "New World"—which, for both geographical and cultural reasons, was for him "Wisconsin" more than "America"—did not come through enthusiasm for any public institutions or political ideals (which avenue, always distant to the young frontier farmer, was ultimately foreclosed by the war). Rather, his public, national identity remained Scottish, but he was able to develop a more private, local bond with the land itself, grounded in continued contact with, cultural and religious assimilation of, and psychological appropriation of his natural and social surroundings.

# Three

# *Where Many a Moss & Fern Find Home*

## Canada West, Indiana, and Wisconsin, 1863–1867

In June 1863, Muir completed his final term at the Wisconsin State University. On the one hand, his departure was not as entirely formless as he and most later interpreters have presented it. In the absence of formal graduation or a degree, the administration recognized his academic achievements by asking him to give a commencement lecture, on the properties of heat. For longer-term prospects, he had thoughts of studying medicine at the University of Michigan in the autumn, having consulted with Professors Carr and Butler and having obtained a letter of introduction from Chancellor Sterling (1:300). This plan of becoming a doctor, though tentative, was very real to Muir: his most important male role model at the time, Carr, had originally been a physician before becoming a professor; moreover, Muir probably saw medicine as a way to address Civil War suffering (Wilkins, 38). As we shall see, the possibility of a medical career would reemerge at various points in Muir's life; interestingly, his brother Dan eventually would become a doctor.

On the other hand, it is important to realize that Muir's time at the university had not essentially changed his position with respect to work and society from what it had been when he first left home. After the failure of his apprenticeship, academic study gave him a structure within which to grow personally and intellectually, but not socially or vocationally: since neither his class background nor his personal interests inclined him toward business or government and he was unwilling to commit to a professional career, his college work was essentially meaningless with respect to a more developed public identity. Given the social place of higher education at the time, this probably would have been true even had he obtained a formal degree. As before, his family held out no real future life path for him, and there is no mention of William Duncan or

114

any other neighbor giving further advice, direction, or encouragement. His continued disgust at the war and the very real possibility of his being drafted added to his sense of confusion and unease; in addition, Muir was complaining of sheer physical and emotional exhaustion from his strenuous academic work (see, e.g., 1:293, 296). On top of it all, Frances Pelton died in April, after a long illness that had followed upon the infant Fannie's death a year earlier. Although no letters record Muir's initial response to her death, his grief must have been deep.

As suggested in the previous chapter, it was not coincidental that at this time Muir finally began to write home about his newfound love of botany, as one attempt to consolidate a stable sense of self and to tie together his disparate worlds. In another, more definite act (which was to become paradigmatic for the rest of his life), Muir responded to this sense of confusion, uncertainty, and ill health by taking a long botanizing trip down the Wisconsin River, accompanied by two Madison companions. Arriving at Prairie du Chien for the first time since Frances' death, Muir visited her grave, taking away a tuft of grass as memento (1:308). Given his overlapping emotions toward the Pelton women, he probably transferred at least some of his various layers of affection, respect, and Christian love both for Mrs. Pelton and for Fannie to the one surviving female, Emily, adding to the strong bonds already apparent between the two. As Linnie Marsh Wolfe suggests (86–87), many of the circumstances pointed toward a marriage between John and Emily, for which this visit provided a clear opportunity. Although Muir chose not to initiate marriage (again suggesting that it was he, not she, who had the power to set the terms of their relationship), he was surely emotionally affected by the visit; his feelings became even more confused a few days later, when, attempting a second visit with Emily, he was unexplainably rebuffed by her uncle Mr. Pelton, suggesting some tensions surrounding Muir's relationship with the family (and with Emily in particular). According to Wolfe, this situation (and the loss of his two traveling companions) left Muir feeling "desperately alone and friendless." His original plan had been to continue up the Mississippi to Minnesota and thence to Lake Superior; after Prairie du Chien, however, finances, tiredness, the desertion of his companions, and Muir's emotional state led him to cut the trip short after "only" three weeks and four hundred miles.

Although we have no contemporary account of this first extended wilderness adventure, Muir wrote two letters the following winter that describe the trip. No less than the trip itself, these acts of writing out his experiences in letters to loved ones were the beginnings of a lifelong pattern. In the first letter, written in December to his brother Dan, he began by stating that he would describe the beauty and glory of nature; interestingly, however, the subsequent text contains very little actual description of what he saw on the trip. Rather, the narrative reads like a lighthearted, mock-epic adventure story, focusing on his and his companions' experiences of searching for lodging or campsites, incidents of hunger and of finding food, the drama and humor of their attempts at rafting the river, and so on, with only a little scientific description (and religious rhetoric) filling out the framework of the narrative.

Later that winter, responding to Emily's request for a detailed account of the trip, Muir interpreted his experiences more elaborately through traditional literary and religious forms. Beginning with his adventures at the Mississippi (i.e., after his visit to Emily in Prairie du Chien), his account takes the form of a series of letters to her, dated retroactively but certainly written long after the event, along with four long poems further describing various scenes or incidents. Much of his narrative echoes his letter to Dan, presenting Muir's growing self-image as a romantic male adventurer. At the same time, the letter reveals the continued importance of his usual pattern of associating botany and religion in his relationships with women: in writing to Emily, Muir paid somewhat more attention to specific landscapes and flowers than in his letter to Dan, and more clearly expressed his responses in terms of religious joy and piety. His continuing Christian interpretation of nature often sounds fairly conventional, as in the poem describing nature's recognition of the Sabbath, various references to Christ's presence in nature, and so on. In general, however, Muir in both letters focused more on a stylized adventure story than on any extensive description of his natural surroundings.

Despite the evident enjoyment and inspiration that he derived from the trip, Muir returned home for the summer to the same set of uncertainties that he had tried to escape. Changing his mind about his future plans for medical study, he was thinking now of staying in Madison and studying with a local doctor through the autumn, but still going on to Michigan later (see 1:296). Perhaps in part because of his lack both of external support and of inner direction, he did not follow through on any of these plans; instead, he stayed on the farm through the summer and autumn of 1863 and into the winter. To Dan, he stated his reasons for not going to Michigan as being the expense and the uncertainty of the draft, but this does not explain his failure to pursue a medical career in Madison. His initial break from home had not equipped him either psychologically or socially to move out of his old life grounded in family and farm; doing so would require a creative act of courage and vision that—once again—he would have to achieve essentially on his own.

On one point, at least, the situation had changed for the better: Muir was able to live with Sarah and David Galloway, and so was not in direct contact and conflict with his father. At the same time, he still searched out older male role models. In a letter to Ambrose Newton, Frances Pelton's father, Muir wrote of his felt need for the wisdom, experience, and continued friendship of "aged Christians" (1:336). A series of letters between Muir and Newton shows the former's continued reliance on Christian love for emotional sustenance, with a special tone of respect for and desire for guidance from the older man. The sense of melancholy and of "Christian resignation" in these letters, partly expressive of Muir's continued sadness over the death of Frances Pelton, also suggests his own feelings of being stuck, the dampening of joy and spontaneity arising from his inability to move on with his life. In this respect, then, although his relationship with Newton may have helped him to endure the disappointments of his present state, it did so only through the reestablishment of earlier emotional and spiritual patterns, not through helping him to a new orientation.

A more active response is revealed in the long December letter to Dan mentioned above, in which Muir himself vigorously took on the role of the "experienced Christian man" with respect to his younger brother. Significantly, their other brother, David, after his unsuccessful semester at the university, had gone into the haberdashery business in Portage and had married a childhood sweetheart; while David was thus moving away from John's interests and life path, Dan and John were moving together through their shared interests in medicine, inventing, and botany. When younger, John had been closest to David, but from now on it would be Dan with whom he would share his deeper thoughts and adventures. As had happened earlier with Sarah, separation allowed John to reformulate his relationships with his brothers in terms of his adult interests and concerns.

Interestingly, Dan had been able to move out of the family circle with somewhat more ease than had John, going to Canada to find work (and to escape the draft) sometime during the past year; thus, John may have felt both admiration and envy toward Dan, along with a need to reassert his own place within the family. In his December letter, following his descriptions of his mock-heroic adventures on the trip the previous summer, Muir abruptly broke off this narrative to shift into a "man-to-man" discussion of his and his brother's present situations and prospects. Noting David's recent marriage, Muir insisted that he and Dan must not marry for at least five or six years, to give sufficient time for study (and perhaps other experiences such as travel, adventure, and general youthful independence). Supporting Dan's decision to leave the country, John complained of the continued tensions between himself and their father and of the continued presence of the war: "War seems to spread everywhere. It seems difficult for a peaceable man to find a place to rest" (1:325). For his part, Muir stated that if not drafted, he would travel to Scotland in spring 1864, mentioning that he had been studying Scottish "history and manners" in preparation for the trip.[1] He encouraged Dan to come with him, and in any case he would stop in Canada to visit (and to obtain British currency) on the way. Muir concluded with a long section of fatherly and Christian advice to his younger brother, calling for Dan to strive to be useful, to serve both Christ and other people, and especially to discipline his mind through study. The ultimate goal of this life is "Christian benevolence": "To what end do we receive life and health from God if not to do good and to be good[?]" This Franklinesque emphasis on (almost obsession with) duty, perhaps an attempt to balance Muir's own feelings of aimlessness and stagnation, ends the letter: "May God always bless you and make you useful."

Reasserting the values and role of a paternal authority figure toward his younger brother, Muir strengthened his own sense of inner authority; further, this inner father merged with the more comradely, adventurous persona expressed in the first part of the letter to constitute a deepened male identity, still grounded in his own familial experiences but emerging as a somewhat more independent self than before. In striving to find a way out of his present stagnation, however, he could only imagine a return to a former life in Scotland. Given the deep power that his (reformulated) image of Scotland held for him, a return there would have been envisioned or undertaken not merely as an enjoyable visit but as a significant step in establishing his own self-chosen life direction; as I read the materials, he was (at least at times) planning to return to Scotland for good. In the face of the dissatisfactions and uncertainties of his present life in America—economic, social, cultural, and political, as well as deeply personal—such a plan offered a way to solve these problems by definitively reasserting (and, of course, further reshaping) his identity as a Scot.[2]

1. I should note that it is possible that this study of Scottish "history and manners" was what resulted in the notebooks on Scottish geography and history discussed in chapter 2. The microfilm editors have placed these notebooks in Muir's university years, but I can find no evidence supporting this dating; at the same time, although this remark in the letter to Dan is the only mention of such study I have found, it isn't enough to firmly place the notebooks at this period either. In fact, the precise date is not essential for my general purposes, because the long process of Muir's developing image of Scotland spanned all of these years; it seems clear that a wide range of past and present images and ideals shaped his decision to return there and the feelings and expectations with which he carried out that decision.

2. Most Muir scholars have downplayed the importance of Scotland as a factor in Muir's decision to go to Canada. According to Fox (42) and Turner (110–12), Muir was mainly fleeing the possibility of a draft, while Linnie Marsh Wolfe states that Muir wanted to "wander for a while in the Canadian wilderness" (90) in order to meditate and to reevaluate his life. Although all these interpreters do acknowledge the importance for Muir of his Scottish identity, they regard his statements about returning to Scotland as expressions of his uncertainty and indecision, not (as I am doing) as a means of forging a path out of that uncertainty and indecision.

Of course, an immigrant's return to the home country was not un-known—and indeed was much more common in nineteenth-century America than is usually thought. For a wide variety of reasons—having to do either with their own personal situations or with their experiences of American public realities—many immigrants failed, refused, or did not want to "make it" in the United States, and so turned back to Europe with new eyes and renewed longing. In Wilbur Shepperson's words, "For many, the very thought of home became a flight of the imagination rather than the recollection of a reality. . . . They felt an urgency to escape from the cataclysm of America" (26). Thus, Muir was by no means unique in choosing a return to Scotland—or at least a vision of such a return—as a way to respond to his own experience of "the cataclysm of America."[3]

At the same time, the vagueness with which Muir presented his plan suggests that he was still tentative and uncertain. There is no evidence that he was in contact with any supportive mentor figures (such as William Duncan or his Madison professors) during this period, nor is there any indication that he discussed his intentions with his family; his mention of the plan in the letter to Dan reads as if he were revealing a deeply private decision that he had not shared with anyone before. Because Dan had broken from home himself, Muir may have felt that his brother was the only person he could trust with the news, while he may have feared that it would have hurt or caused controversy among the family members closer to home. In any case, it seems clear that—for the first time in his life—Muir made this decision wholly on his own, without any particular person acting as role model, support, guide, or companion (except for some amount of inspiration coming from Dan himself). Rather, it was Scotland itself that provided the impetus, the goal, and the (imagined) companionship for this new turn of his life; and it was his strengthened sense of self that allowed and was expressed by this decision.

In this context, Muir's letter to Emily describing the previous summer's Wisconsin River trip—written as he was about to leave for Canada in February 1864—was shaped by the emotions of his present situation as

---

3. According to Shepperson, a wide range of factors motivated this reverse immigration: on the one hand, straightforward conditions such as climate, political disagreement, or the inability to find an economic place in America; on the other hand, a more vague (but no less deeply felt) dissatisfaction with the New World on cultural and emotional grounds, whether expressed in terms of coarseness, immorality, irreligion, excessive materialism or conformity, or a chaotic degree of individualism, diversity, and rootlessness. Some immigrants "easily mastered the details of American life but found it difficult to fill the emotional void which immigration had created" (27). Whatever the reason, an individual's inability or refusal to "become an American" often led to a sense of disenchantment with previous hopes for and idealizations of America, an increased loyalty to and love for the home country, and an active decision to return home.

well as by his memories of the past. As in his letter to Dan, Muir re-counted to Emily his (and his companions') attempt at a raft trip up the mouth of the Wisconsin, dramatizing their struggle and ultimate failure as they tried to row against the strong current of the river flowing into the Mississippi; expanding upon the incident, he also added as a postscript a long dramatic speech directed toward the raft itself, which they had de-cided to abandon by pushing it out into the Mississippi and letting it flow downstream. Bemoaning the noble craft's fate of being left to wander in the strong currents of the river, Muir perhaps expressed his own feelings of uncertainty and lack of direction that still underlay his decision to set out on his own. His language in addressing the Mississippi as "mother" (strikingly, one of the first times he used the familiar "nature as mother" imagery in his letters) may or may not signify a deep psychological depen-dence on and/or fear of the powerful presence to be found either at home or in nature; in any case, he clearly saw his own life as subject to the same sorts of controlling currents as the river. By contrast, in the poem "Noon Rest," a particular landscape reminds him strongly of the familiar grounds of the university; in other passages, the narrative repeatedly (and dramatically) describes the adventurers' quests for lodging and their suc-cess in finding it in the homes of friendly strangers.

Thus, Muir's account of the previous summer's adventure represents contrasting themes—aimlessness and direction, freedom and attachment, familiarity and strangeness, leaving home and finding home—that be-spoke his emotions upon leaving for Canada/Scotland. The conclusion of his letter to Emily expresses his ambiguous feelings even more poignantly: "I am to take the cars in about half an hour. I really do not know where I shall 'halt.' I feel like Milton's Adam and Eve—'The world was all before them where to choose their place of rest.' . . . I have already bidden all my friends goodbye. I feel lonely again. Goodbye Emily" (1:351). Much as had his letters to his sister Sarah at the end of his university years, Muir's writing to Emily as a trusted friend in Christian love allowed him both to express his inner troubles and to allay them through the evocation of a whole range of nurturing and supportive relationships, patterns, and images: familiar natural surroundings, male identity and privilege, female associations, botany, religion, and literary images, along with the felt sense of the presence of Emily herself as an Eve-like companion. Not sur-prisingly, this whole inner constellation with which he began his travels strongly shaped his experiences in the next period of his life, his two-year sojourn in Canada.

Although Muir left little evidence of his precise locations and actions during his first six months of wandering in Canada West (present-day Ontario), it is possible to reconstruct a general outline (see L. M. Wolfe,

91–94, or Turner, 113–17). He left his family's home in Portage on March 1, 1864. After crossing through upper Michigan and leaving the United States at Sault Ste. Marie, he wandered around Lakes Huron and Ontario for much of the spring and summer before meeting up with Dan near Niagara Falls in early September. After some camping and botanizing together, the two decided to spend the coming autumn and winter (at least) in Meaford, by Lake Huron, at a sawmill and factory where Dan had briefly worked before. They were welcomed there by the owners, a family of Scots Disciples. Dan would stay until late spring of the following year, at which time he would return to Michigan for more profitable employment; John would end up staying in Meaford until February 1866.

Muir's autobiographical reflections, in language clearly shaped by his later experiences and by an Emersonian philosophy of nature, stress the positive feelings of joy and freedom he felt during these first months in Canada, which constituted his first solitary immersion in nature: "I traveled free as a bird, independent alike of roads and people. I entered at once into harmonious relations with Nature. . . . I felt a plain, simple relationship to the Cosmos" (quoted in L. M. Wolfe, 91). As in the case of his childhood reminiscences, however, his actual experience was probably not so clear-cut. For one thing, he was not in fact as solitary as his later statements would imply (and as his later self-image and public persona would require). Although he had no constant companions, he stayed many (if not most) nights in people's homes, often fellow Scots immigrants to the New World frontier; he stayed all of June with the Campbells of Bradford, Ontario, and at one point he even met some folks from Dunbar. Additionally, he spent the last month or two with his brother. At the same time, of course, even if his solitude did not measure up to the mythic aloneness of the later Muir, he was still on his own to a far greater extent than ever before, and nothing in his life to this point had prepared him to handle such aloneness. We can only speculate as to the widely contrasting waves of freedom and melancholy, ecstasy and loneliness, that must have passed through him during these months.

The only concrete description we have about a specific incident from this trip, his famous discovery of *Calypso borealis* at the end of a long day wandering in a dark swamp, was not written until a few years after the experience itself. Because it uses language that he had probably learned in the interim, I will not discuss it in detail until reaching the time of composition. Still, we may here note the parallels between this incident and Mungo Park's experience when, lost, alone, and despairing after being robbed in a remote forest region of Africa, he came upon a small moss in flower. Attracted first by its "extraordinary beauty," Park found religious consolation in the scene: "Can that Being (thought I) who planted, watered, and brought to perfection, in this obscure part of the world, a thing which appears of so small importance, look with uncon-cern upon the situation and sufferings of creatures formed after his own image?—surely not!" (223). Given the depth of Muir's Scottish orienta-tion at the time, we can only presume that his admiration for, knowledge of, and identification with the Scots explorer both shaped and were fur-ther strengthened by his own experience with Calypso.

Upon arriving in Meaford (a small town on the Georgian Bay of Lake Huron), John and Dan immediately began working in the factory and living with the owners. In one of his first letters, Muir described his new "family" to his sister Mary. William Trout, "an unmarried boy of thirty summers," and Charles Jay, "a bird of twenty-five, who . . . is created like a blue-jay, with bristly hair and good-natured and vociferous as any parrot," were partners in the factory and "the rulers of the two scotch heather Muirs." Mary Trout was "perhaps more than thirty years, an un-married lady of a great many good qualities," while her sister Harriet was "a very happy and sportive fish who employs herself in giggling and mak-ing giggle for hours at a time, is about twenty years of age, 5-1/2 ft. long and will perhaps sometime join affinity to the Jay who whistles and coos and gesticulates so funnily to her" (1:359–60). The tone of this letter, partly intended as affectionate entertainment for his younger sister, ex-presses something of the atmosphere of the household itself: youthful, playful, intimate, free. At the same time, the group was intellectually in-teresting and challenging for Muir; although he kept up his habit of lec-turing his friends, he focused less on religious and more on scientific themes, which gave rise to "a good deal of spirited but congenial ex-change" (Turner, 117). In particular, Muir held forth on botany and as-tronomy, both in the informal setting of the home and in more formal lectures to Sunday school students and teachers.[4] Thus, according to a later (and admittedly idealized) comment by Hattie Trout, "Was there ever more freedom of speech, thought, and action felt on earth than in that 'hollow'[?] We were all equal, everyone did as he chose" (1:435). Living for the first time with neither parents nor parental figures watching over him, and with a range of vivacious young adults to stand in for his siblings and previous friends, Muir felt more free, energetic, and expres-sive than in any living situation since Scotland.

4. While at the university, Muir had occasionally taught at local schools in Wisconsin to supplement his income. Both the public schools and the Sunday school setting would have brought him into further contact with the religiously defined culture of botany as a means of moral education and natural theology, and (presumably) with representatives of the informal networks that made up the world of amateur botany.

At the same time, later letters make it clear that he utilized many of the tactics that had previously been successful in bringing forward the felt presence of his family: arranging moss and flowers inside his room, treasuring drawings and photographs of home, writing to ask for news from the family, and so on. This construction of his new home in terms of the old seems to have provoked some confusion and guilt with respect to his original family. In another letter to his sister Mary (1:365–66), Muir provided a fanciful model for the kind of letter that he wanted her to send him, one full of details and daily occurrences of the family's home life. The content of his "model" is suggestive: he describes how the farm animals have moved into the house, and the people are living in the barn! Everything is upside down, free-floating, changing; although again this was partly his mode of playfully relating to his younger sister, it also seems to signify his real confusion over what is "family," and some level of anxiety or guilt over the changes that he has wrought in his own family. In any case, his new "family" did not completely replace the old: in a late letter from Canada (December 24, 1865), written just after Daniel Muir had sold the farm and moved the family into a nearby town, John wrote to his sisters Mary and Annie that "I often think of you and wish with all my might that I could see you and chat with you. Were it not that I have no time to think, I would grow homesick and die in a day or two. My picture of home is in my room, and when I see it now I feel sorry at the thought of its being sold" (1:393).

Within the supportive and liberating context of his new living situation, Muir's most important relationship was probably that with William Trout. As the oldest male and the primary owner and director of the factory and sawmill, William possessed some amount of fatherlike authority in the group; in the long quotation above, Muir refers to the possibility of William's electing a "lady mistress of Trout's Hollow," implicitly casting him in the role of "master." At the same time, Trout genuinely liked and respected Muir for his mechanical abilities, intelligence, and character, and so the two seem to have related as equals and as friends. This is nowhere more evident than in their discussions of religion. As noted above, the Trouts were Scots and Disciples, and so shared much of the cultural and religious background of the Muirs. William seems to have been fairly conventional in his own religiousness, but he possessed two qualities that made him a good debating partner for Muir: a high degree of open-mindedness and a keen interest in science. Although no direct evidence of their discussions survives, an 1870 letter (from Muir in California to Trout in Canada) perhaps reflects the overall temper of their relationship. Responding to a previous letter in which Trout had raised the question of "the Darwinian theory of origin of species," Muir stressed his commitments both to science and to religion by describing Darwin as "a most profound and righteous philosopher, an earnest seeker after truth," "striving with honest scientific ardor to read the laws under which the Lord creates" the "vast ocean of organic forms": "If I had time I might set forth a great many facts in favor of Darwin's theory but a far greater number against it[;] as far however as our Christian religion is concerned I cannot see that it injures it in the least" (Muir to Trout, May 28, 1870; typescript of letter in the Holt-Atherton Department of Special Collections, University of the Pacific). Again, while this indicates Muir's particular opinions in 1870, it also suggests something of the character and tone of his intellectual and personal relationship with Trout during his sojourn in Canada in 1864–65. Such discussions with Trout gave Muir a chance to express, to work through, and—perhaps most important, and most in contrast with his relationship with his father—to feel heard and respected in his increasing religious liberalism.

Similarly, his activity as mechanic and inventor was fully supported and affirmed in the Trout factory. It is important to remember that at this point in his life, both in his own and in society's eyes, Muir was an inventor more than anything else. In a later reminiscence, university friend Harvey Reid states that when he thought of Muir after leaving Madison, he "expected to hear of him as a great inventor or mechanical expert" (Letter, 3), and this image of Muir was probably held by the rest of his friends, family, and supporters. In Canada, with William fulfilling some of the functions of "master," Muir's work proved a more successful "apprenticeship" than had his abortive attempt in Prairie du Chien. According to Linnie Marsh Wolfe (based on a later reminiscence by Trout himself), William "was a master mechanic and millwright with several patents to his credit. During the early months he had taught the younger man everything he knew, 'but I felt,' says he, 'that I could by no means take rank with him'" (96). The group's first major project was an expansion of the factory, with John, Dan, and the others working under the direction of William; by September 1865 Muir had reached a more independent and equal footing with his employer, having signed a contract to improve the machinery so as to reach a production goal of 30,000 broom handles and 12,000 rakes. Reflecting his status as a semipartner, he would receive half the profits from this venture.

Alongside his interest in and success at inventing, Muir's fascination with botany—and his association of it with significant women—grew during his Canadian years. Although he became close friends with the Trout sisters both on emotional and on intellectual levels, his most significant relationship continued to be that with Emily Pelton. He began a May 1865 letter to Emily somewhat formally: "I sincerely trust Emily that you are well and happy in the enjoyment of good friends and of those blessings so plentifully bestowed upon all those who love duty." Soon, however, Muir took on a more personal tone, wondering if Emily was lonely and expressing his own feelings in childlike language: "poor *me* is left in Canada, *farther* from home and *longer* from home than *me* ever was before. You will not wonder then to hear that I am at times touched with melancholy or loneliness" (1:368). In this context, and to a greater extent than in any previous letter, he described an ordinary natural scene in original language saturated with religious meaning and personal emotion.

> Our tall, tall forest trees are now all alive, and the mingled ocean of blossom and leaves, wave and curl, and rise in rounded swells farther and farther away, like the thick smoke from a factory chimney. Freshness and beauty are everywhere. Flowers are born every hour, living sunlight is poured over all and every thing and creature is glad. Our world is indeed a beautiful one, and I was just thinking on going to church last sabbath that I would hardly accept a free ticket to the moon or to Venus or any other world, for fear it might not be so good and so fraught with the glory of the Creator as our own. (1:369)

While phrases such as "every thing and creature is glad" and the reference to church and Sabbath echoed the conventional and pious writing of his long letter to Emily of a year earlier (describing the Wisconsin River trip), Muir's language and sensibility had grown more focused, intense, and individual. In large part, the goal of such language was to create an avenue for intimacy and emotion between himself and Emily, much as he might have done if they were together in person: "I wish Emily that you could be so near or I so near that we could take an occasional ramble together to botanize and to admire these glorious manifestations of creative skill. I hope we may at some time. I shall take great delight in showing you my specimens, I have some rare ones and I know that you would appreciate them" (1:369)

On important levels, Muir's loneliness and longing for Emily increasingly were powered and colored by the sexual energies of a young man, but again, it would be incorrect to interpret the erotic element in their relationship as primarily sexual in nature. That is, his biologically based urges and attractions were not associated with the appropriate range of images, behaviors, and relationships to constitute "sexuality," "sexual activity," or a particular "sexual orientation" in the modern sense. Rather, those energies—combined with other physical, psychological, aesthetic, and spiritual dimensions—were aligned with a unique set of behaviors, images, and relationships to constitute a nonsexual eros, in particular a reshaped form of Christian love. As in his university years but with a different texture, color, and visceral power, Muir's Christian love—as "practiced" through his botanical friendship with Emily—was a personally, socially, and culturally created pattern of erotic relationship with other persons, with the natural world, and with the divine. Thus, on the one hand, Emily continued to hold a special place in Muir's heart and to be an important part of his images of self and of world (particularly nature); on the other hand, her imagined presence augmented the camaraderie of the Trouts to allow Muir's life at Trout Hollow to be touched by the freedom and feeling of romance.[5]

Despite the intensity of emotion suggested here, there are indications during these years of a widening gap between Muir and Emily, probably caused not only by distance but also by his personal changes and needs. For one thing, his growing liberalism in religious matters probably moved beyond what Emily was prepared to understand or to support. Muir himself tried to assert otherwise: "Those miserable hymns such as these— 'This world is all a fleeting show / For man's delusion given'—do not at all correspond with my likings and I am sure they do not with yours" (1:369). However, Emily's own letters reveal her to be fairly conventional, and in future letters he seems to write more cautiously, as if not to offend her. He filled his next letter to her with botanical descriptions and discussion (indeed, this letter represents his most extensive and specific botanical writing to date), but his tone was less personal and less religiously expressive than before. At one point, however, his continued longing for her presence reappeared: "I would take pleasure in showing you my collection of ferns. The eyes are so few that appreciate such beauties" (1:390).

To further complicate their relationship, Muir almost surely again felt the need to draw back from the possibility of marriage with Emily. Many of his letters from this period make some (negative) reference to marriage, as in his admonitions to Dan not to marry until after taking time for study and travel, and similar advice to Mary (see 1:324, 366). In the letter to Emily, he grouped marriage with sickness, craziness, and anger as possible reasons why she had not written to him for a while. Not only social expectation but his own needs and desires continued to make marriage a

5. In a similar way, according to Frederick Kirchhoff, the young William Morris created his new home Red House as an expression of his own and his culture's youthful romantic visions: "Living at Red House, [Morris] almost realized the self-image he had conceptualized as a late adolescent—the ideal of a self sustained by a set of fraternal relationships and commitment to a life of sensuous, quasi-medieval beauty [and, though Kirchhoff does not stress it here, to the architectural and design work that engaged Morris and his friends], including the sensuous, quasi-medieval beauty of the woman he had married. Psychologically, Red House was an extension of Morris' body, an outward form approximating an inner notion of the self" (113).

major issue for him and gave an intensity and edge to his rejection of that possibility. Given the history and character of his relationship with Emily, and after as expressive of letters as the ones quoted above, Muir may have felt the need to either go forward to marriage or draw back from that level of emotional intensity. Faced with this dichotomy, he could only choose the latter. In any case, whether from one or all of a range of reasons—an increasing lack of understanding between the two, the difficult push and pull of the possibility of marriage, or the sheer effects of prolonged distance—his subsequent correspondence with Emily carried less emotional and intellectual weight than the intimate and expressive letter of May 1865.[6]

Of crucial importance for Muir, this shift away from Emily coincided with the emergence of a new letter relationship with Jeanne Carr, the young wife of his favorite professor at Madison, Ezra Carr. Interestingly, the two had met even before he had entered the university, because she had been a member of the committee that had given Muir an award for his inventions at the state fair, when he first left home. During his university years, Muir spent much time in the Carr household as student, as friend, and as companion to the Carrs' two young boys; thus, he certainly felt Jeanne as a maternal presence, evoking the treasured but painful presence/absence of his relationship with his own mother, with many of the same dynamics that had shaped his relationship with Frances Pelton. At the same time, Carr was only twelve years his senior, and so their relationship carried other layers as well: an element of sibling companionship, especially given their shared respect for and deference to her older husband; a sense of student collegiality, again given their relationship to the professor; and a strong current of sheer friendship. They seem not to have corresponded at all for his first few years away from the university, and they resumed contact only when Jeanne answered a letter that Muir had originally sent to Ezra (Fox, 45). Whatever the status of their previous contacts, their letters from late 1865 onward show that she brought to their relationship a keen scientific and literary interest, an immersion in transcendentalist thought, and a sense of supportive respect, admiration, and encouragement for the younger man—without raising the difficult

6. This by no means marked the end of their friendship, however. The long-term importance for Muir of their relationship is suggested by an 1872 letter to her in which he remembered "your kind words to me the first day I saw you. Kind words are likely to live in any human soul, but planted in the breast of a Scotchman they are absolutely immortal, and whatever Heaven may have in store for you in after years you have at least one friend while John Muir lives" (quoted in Stanley, 54). Moreover, the erotic element in their relationship would reemerge at various points over the years, especially during their 1874–75 reunion in California (O'Grady, 73–82).

emotional and practical issue of marriage. Thus, their correspondence picked up where his and Emily's was beginning to leave off, as an arena for the continued development of his patterns of relationship both with close female friends and with his natural surroundings.

That first letter from Jeanne Carr is now lost, but it must have touched a deep chord in Muir, for his response reveals that she had sunk deeply into his thoughts and imagination. Initially, the primary theme of their letters was not actual botanical description but the larger question of his future life and work. Despite his successes at the factory, by this time Muir had begun to feel some tensions and contradictions surrounding inventing. A letter to Emily from the autumn of 1865 reveals that she was encouraging him to think of himself as an inventor, but also expresses some resistance on his part: "You seem to think that nature has designed me for an inventor. . . . It seems as though I should be dragged into machinery whether I would or no" (1:389). By the time he wrote to his younger sisters in December, his frustrations with the demands of his work had grown (at moments at least) into the deepest sense of disorientation since he first left home for Madison: "I have been exceedingly busy. . . . My bed sets me on my feet at five, and I go to bed at eleven, and have to do at least two days' work every day, sometimes three. I sometimes almost forget where I am, what I am doing, or what my name is" (1:393). Significantly, his first letter to "Mrs. Carr," dated September 13, 1865, shows him grappling with questions of personal and public identity, of who he might become in the future, with a young man's sense of impatience and confusion.

> Since undertaking a month or two ago to invent new machinery for our mill, my mind seems to so bury itself in the work that I am fit for but little else. And then a lifetime is so little a time that we die ere we get ready to live. I would like to go to college, but then I have to say to myself, "You will die ere you can do anything else." I should like to invent useful machinery, but it comes, "You do not wish to spend your lifetime among machines, and you will die ere you can do anything else." I should like to study medicine that I might do my part in lessening human misery, but again it comes, "You will die ere you are ready or able to do so." How intensely I desire to be a Humboldt, but again the chilling answer is reiterated. And could we but live a *million* of years, then how delightful to spend in perfect contentment so many thousands in quiet study in college, so many amid the grateful din of machines, so many among human pain, so many thousands in the sweet study of Nature among the dingles and dells of Scotland, and all the other less important parts of our world. (1:376)

Even as he expressed his dilemmas, however, Muir was again able to use the imaginative space of a letter relationship to begin to create a clearer sense of his own self and future: "I was struck with your remarks about our real home as being a thing of stillness and peace. How little does the outer & noisy world in general know of that 'real home' & real inner life. Happy indeed they who have a friend to whom they can un-mask the workings of their real life, sure of sympathy & forbearance." (1:376). If in fact this letter to Carr was a "home" in which he could reveal his true self to a supportive listener, it soon becomes clear that his deepest intellectual and emotional leanings were toward not inventing but rather the study of the natural world. Directly quoting her own transcen-dentalist language from her previous letter, he spoke reverently of "'the pure and deep communion of the beautiful, all-loving Nature.'" By con-trast, his own language remained more traditionally Christian, as he wrote of "the glorious chart of God in Nature" (1:378); moreover, as with the Peltons and his own family, the language of Christian love and friendship helped support and contain a deep emotional bond between Muir and Carr. After extending thanks to Ezra Carr, "who first laid be-fore me the great book of Nature," Muir went on to express his own vision of nature study in an intimate image of Jeanne's own library/conservatory.

> O how frequently, Mrs. Carr, when lonely & wearied, have I wished that like some hungry worm I could creep into that delightful kernel of your house—your library, with its portraits of scientific men, and so bountiful a store of their sheaves amid the blossom and verdure of your little king-dom of plants, luxuriant & happy as though holding their leaves to the open sky of the most flower-loving zone in the world. (1:379)

Despite being indoors, the library seemed as expansive and life-giving as the "open sky"; imagining himself as a worm on one of the plants, Muir too shared in the life and delight of Carr's presence.

Carr quickly responded to Muir's interest, meeting him with equal inti-macy: "I wish you were here in the 'kernel' of the house. It looks very pleasant, especially with the wind howling without. I would give you your choice between talking and singing" (1:383). She went on to give further descriptions of her library and plants, noting especially her mosses, ferns, and lichens and mentioning an attempt to raise butterflies; she also imag-ined how Muir and she might arrange things for "rest" and "comfort," were he there. (Clearly, even at this early point their relationship—and their images of domesticity and of the natural world—involved both a maternal dynamic and a more equal, companionate, even erotic dimen-sion.) The opening of his next letter conveys some of the relief and joy that he felt in finding a kindred spirit: "Your last, written in the delicious quiet of a Sabbath in the country, has been rec'd and read a good many times." Reassured by her words, he expressed his increasingly liberal religious views more explicitly: "It may be a bad symptom but I will confess that I take more intense delight from reading the power & *goodness* of God from 'the things that are made' than from the bible. The two books however harmonize beautifully, and contain enough of divine truth for the study of all eternity. It is so much easier for us to employ our faculties upon these beautiful tangible forms than to exercise a simple humble living faith" (1:407–8). Again, he strongly associated the "beautiful tangible forms" of natural beings with Carr and her library: "I suppose that this evening finds you in your pleasant library amid books, & plants, & butterflies. Are you really successful in keeping happy sportive 'winged blossoms' in such weather as this?" (1:410). As he did also in a letter to Emily of the same period, Muir shared with Carr his own fascination with mosses and ferns.

Thus, in contrast to his visions of easy botanical rambles with Emily (and, earlier, his sister Sarah), in his letters to Carr Muir imagined a nature relationship located in a more secluded, contained, and explicitly domestic setting. At the same time, this setting was also infused with the intellectual intensity and power of the public (and male) world of official science. Carr's library was created by her and her husband out of her desire for an active intellectual life, within the bounds of the social and intellectual possibilities of nineteenth-century femininity; indeed, as with the Peltons, it was in part this desire to go beyond the limitations imposed upon her as a woman that fired her relationship with Muir as well. Similarly (but from the other direction), Carr's library symbolized for Muir a partial reconciliation between the predominantly male realm of formal science, represented by Ezra Carr, and the more informal religious and emotional meanings of botany that he had developed in the context of his relationships with women. Although he had seen models of "the intellectual life" in his professors at college, none of them touched him as deeply on an emotional level as did Jeanne Carr, and none of them were able to bring together his varied interests, motivations, and associations as strongly as did she. Having set for himself the question of his future life, Muir found the beginnings of an answer that would speak both to his social conditions and to his emotional state.

In this context, his invocation of Humboldt seems particularly significant and complex. It was probably not until his lessons from Madison had fully sunk in with the help of further independent study that Muir would have been equipped conceptually to understand Humboldt's ideas, but when he did he must have felt a deep sense of excitement and intellectual kinship. Laura Dassow Walls has summarized the core of Humboldt's philosophy as "the reciprocal interaction of all with all," and his field method as "explore, collect, measure, connect" (92, 98)—principles that clearly echoed Muir's scientific education and that would come increasingly to characterize his thought and activity. To be sure, Muir would never be as intellectually sophisticated as was Humboldt, and he would always be guided by moral insight and by personal experience more than by precise philosophical reflection; thus, it seems impossible (during this period, at least) to trace extensive influence of specific Humboldtian ideas on Muir's thought, as Walls does in the case of Thoreau.[7] More important than specific intellectual influences, however, was the figure of Humboldt the person.

In accord with much of nineteenth-century American and European culture, Muir regarded Humboldt as a sort of "representative man," the embodiment of a human life expressing itself fully in the disciplined yet passionate study of the natural world. As did the writings of Mungo Park, Humboldt's account of his explorations in the Amazon held powerful personal meanings for Muir, speaking to the latter's own experiences of travel and struggle far from home and native country. However, the German scientist was more emotionally inspired and aesthetically sensitive than was the British imperialist: "Amidst the overwhelming majesty of nature, and the stupendous objects she presents at every step, the traveller is little disposed to record in his journal matters which relate only to himself, and the ordinary details of life" (Humboldt, xix). Significantly, this model of the scientist as explorer extended the self-image as mock-heroic adventurer that Muir had tried on in his own writings about the Wisconsin River trip; going back further in his past, the young man's admiration for Humboldt also echoed his preadolescent emulation of Scottish heroes and adventurers: William Wallace, Robert the Bruce, the fabled North Sea sailors and pirates. For Muir as for most of us, the use of historical and cultural figures—encountered in the official culture of print and science as much as in the folk culture of story, song, and legend—as personal role models was important both in childhood and in adulthood.[8] Perhaps most important, Humboldt provided a role model of a mature and socially acceptable identity for an adult male, thus functioning for Muir in a way that the image of Carr's library—feminine, amateur, and domestic—could not. At the same time, as an imagined-yet-actual male persona, the image of Humboldt gave Muir an ideal figure without the

7. For a more complete discussion of Humboldt's philosophy, see Walls, 77–93; on his public figure and influence, 95–108.

8. Utilizing a concept from Bourdieu, Craig Calhoun comments: "The constant construction of identity that is the habitus is not entirely absorbed within the immediate situation. The habitus includes representations of historical memory" (63). The power of this process is captured in Bruce Springsteen's song "Backstreets": "Remember all the movies, Terry, we did see / Trying to learn how to walk like the heroes we thought we had to be."

pressures and associations of his own relationships with men, allowing him to fill that image with some of the emotional and personal tone that previously had characterized his activity of botany in relationships with women.

Thus, in differing ways, both Carr's library and the figure of Humboldt gave Muir deeply felt images of the scientific study of nature as a life pattern that would address his varied intellectual interests, emotional and religious sensibilities, and personal needs. These images not only gave him *something to do* that brought him into relationship with people and the world but also constituted *someone to be,* a distinctive identity that added another layer of depth, meaning, and strength to the activity and to the relationships. Together, Carr's library and Humboldt contributed crucially to the emergence of Muir's version of what Daniel Levinson has called "the Dream." For the young adult, the Dream is "a vague sense of self-in-adult-world. It has the quality of a vision, an imagined possibility that generates excitement and vitality" (91). Facilitating a sense of one's Dream are significant relationships with older adults, especially the "mentor" and the "special woman"—who for Muir at this time were combined in Jeanne Carr, with Humboldt functioning as a sort of imagined adjunct mentor. As Levinson stresses, however, the initial formulation of a Dream is only the first step; the task of actually establishing it as the guiding force in one's life is often a much longer and more tumultuous struggle, one which may very well end in failure or in the transformation of the initial Dream into a more adequate or practical form.[9] As we shall see, Muir was not in a position to fulfill his Dream of nature study for years, and in the end he modified it significantly in establishing an enduring public and personal identity. However, despite its provisional character, the importance of one's initial Dream as a guiding image can hardly be overestimated, and in fact Muir's vision of a life devoted to nature study would propel him forward through the most transformative years of his life.

Most immediately, this vision of a life devoted to the scientific study of nature was powerful enough to displace his previous guiding image of a return to Scotland. In concrete terms, his experiences with the Trouts and with other Scots immigrants in Canada probably fulfilled some of his longings for contact with his Scottish past, while at the same time providing a more satisfying and enjoyable life than he had previously found in

9. According to Levinson, "Though it has origins in childhood and adolescence, the Dream is a distinctively adult phenomenon: it takes shape in the Early Adult Transition and is gradually integrated within (or, in many cases is excluded from) an adult life structure over the course of early adulthood" (93).

the New World; in any case, his break from home and father, his experiences of travel, and his work as mechanic and inventor all helped him come to new levels of independence and of self-confidence. On intellectual and symbolic levels, Park gave way to Humboldt, and Muir's association of nature study with "the dingles and dells of Scotland" was in the process of being transmuted into a broader interest in the larger world, including America (North as well as South, his own Great Lakes region as well as Humboldt's Amazon). Thus, Humboldt's particular embodiment of "the science which is of no country" helped Muir move away from his image of Scotland and toward a deeper engagement with his present world, while at the same time keeping his distance (literally, symbolically, and emotionally) from the United States.

At the same time, it is important to remember that the ideals embodied in Carr's library and in the figure of Humboldt were in practical terms inaccessible for Muir. The role of naturalist was not regarded as a real "profession" at that place and time, especially for a person of his social standing. On the one hand, the wife of a university professor could undertake amateur botanizing within her own home and environs; on the other hand, the independently wealthy German baron could explore the world in search of scientific knowledge and philosophical wisdom. For a young farmer and mechanic such as Muir, however, botanizing in either form could afford no economic, social, or emotional security. Even if he was able to do it on a psychological level, it would have involved great risks and instability on a practical level.[10]

Thus, despite the emotional power of his vision of a life devoted to the study of nature, Muir's concrete public identity remained rooted in his activity and success as mechanic and inventor, with William Trout acting as mentor and model. Interestingly, an 1865 drawing of the Trout home suggests the split within Muir's consciousness (see figure 2): in the foreground are tree stumps, woodpiles, and other signs of industry, echoing his early drawings of Wisconsin homesteads and expressing his work and self-image as mechanic and inventor; in the background, however, the dense web of flowing branches and tree trunks provides a much more organic and welcoming setting for a home, an evocative image of a living and pulsing natural world that is reminiscent of his letters to Emily Pelton and to Jeanne Carr. Even in his letter relationships with Pelton and with Carr, however—which on one level served as creative spaces within which to work out a new vision of self-in-nature—the role of inventor continued to carry the most emotional, religious, and practical weight for his present

10. Again, see Norwood and Keeney for discussion of the cultural and social place of botany in the nineteenth century, stressing its feminine associations and amateur status.

Figure 2. The Trout home, Meaford, Ontario, 1865. (Courtesy John Muir Papers, Holt-Atherton Department of Special Collections, University of the Pacific Libraries. Copyright © 1984 Muir-Hanna Trust)

life in the world. In direct response to his outburst of uncertainty concerning his future, Carr's next letter (September 1865) proposed an alternative role model to that of Humboldt.

> I have thought much of you in reading lately of the life of Charles Goodyear, the "India rubber man," whose whole existence was a battle with adversity. He does not seem to have lived so near the heart of Nature, or found her balms for his wounded spirit, but he was haunted with inventions. They tortured him, sleeping or waking, until he worked them into visible forms. A great mechanical genius is a wonderful gift, something one should hold in trust for mankind, a kind of seal and private mark which God has placed upon souls especially his own. (1:382)

Despite the hints here of a division between the life of an inventor and that of a nature lover, we should keep in mind that for Muir the two were not clearly opposed. As in the case of botany, he had always interpreted inventing in religious and in ethical terms. As a teenager, he had tried to overcome his father's objections to Thomas Dick's *Christian Philosopher* on the basis of the useful contributions that science can make, basing his argument on the need for spectacles in order to read the Bible (*Boyhood*, 243). Numerous letters suggest the strong value he placed on duty and on Christian benevolence; for example, to his sister he wrote, "I trust

Mary that you are diligently employed in the acquisition of knowledge—prepare yourself for usefulness as a teacher and don't think of marrying for long years to come" (1:366). Similarly, he valued his own inventing and mechanical work in terms of its usefulness. According to a later reminiscence by Merrill Moores (whom Muir would meet after returning to the United States), Muir never applied for patents for any of his inventions, because "he thought that all improvements and inventions should be the property of the human race, and that no inventor had the right to profit by an invention for which he deserved no credit, as the idea really was inspired by the Almighty" (51:385). Thus, inventing and nature study in many ways occupied the *same* life realm: in their differing ways, both activities constituted compelling ways to engage (and to control) the natural world in the context of important personal relationships and symbolic meanings. Inventing, however, offered Muir a public and practical role that nature study (as yet) did not, and so he primarily used the former to express some of the deeper values that also grounded his vision of the latter.

At the end of February 1866, a fire unexpectedly destroyed the Trout factory and warehouse, including the 30,000 broom handles that Muir had manufactured in fulfillment of his contract. This abrupt turn of events opened up the possibility for him to change his life path, and his choices indicate much about his inner life at the time. His subsequent decision to leave Trout Hollow was in part motivated by a growing religious gap between himself and the Trouts (see, e.g., a letter to Dan [1:415]), as well as by the yearnings of a restless and ambitious young man to move beyond the isolation and familiarity of the hollow. On the one hand, he never reconsidered his earlier plan (and passion) of returning to Scotland, indicating again that his time in Canada had already served many of the emotional needs that had impelled that plan in the first place; on the other hand, despite the power of the image of Humboldt in his emotional life, Muir was in no position—either emotionally or practically—to emulate his hero by exploring the Amazon. Rather, with the Civil War over, his longings seem to have turned immediately back to the United States—not yet his fully chosen home, but deeply attractive to him for what it held of his past and what it might hold of his future. However, he clearly could not return to Wisconsin and his family, for his religious and personal development had carried him farther than ever from his father's unchanged worldview. Ultimately, although the factory fire might have given Muir an opportunity to give fuller expression to his Dream of nature study, he decided to return to the United States to pursue work as an inventor and mechanic, showing how deep a hold those roles maintained upon his sense of his possible futures.

After the fire, Muir's departure from Canada was little more directed or decisive than any of his earlier moves. He looked for work and botanized through New York, Ohio, Indiana, and Illinois before ending up in Indianapolis for what he thought would be a temporary stay (see his letter to Henry Butler [1:426]). Finding work with the manufacturing firm of Osgood, Smith, and Co., Muir tried to drown his doubts and dissatisfactions with machine work by throwing himself fully into his new job. In a letter to Dan, he declared: "I have about made up my mind that it is impossible for me to escape from mechanics. I begin to see and feel that I really have some talent for invention, and I just think that I will turn all my attention that way at once" (1:432). As in Canada, Muir quickly made a good impression upon his employers, progressing rapidly from mere sawyer to foreman and inventor. Along with constructing a new machine for automatic manufacture of wooden wheels, he conducted an innovative time-and-motion study to explore ways of increasing productivity in the shop; in Turner's words, "Muir had grasped the vision of the total factory as a machine in itself, where laborers, machines, and products were interchangeable, smoothly functioning parts," thus contributing to the further development of the "American System" of industrial production, in which "standardization and interchangeability were the revolutionizing concepts, and these had the tendency to rob workers of their humanity and the products of their individuality" (124). Here as during his years at the university, Muir's talents and personal temperament placed him in the forefront of an emerging culture of efficiency and control, in which human bodies were equated with machines and the natural world with raw material, both subservient to the demands of technology.

Alongside his success in a new work situation, Muir used familiar tactics for carving out a realm of personal and social life. After finding lodgings in the home of a good Scots family named Sutherland, he made the acquaintance of the prominent Merrill and Moores families (helped by an introductory letter from Professor Butler of Madison). These contacts provided Muir with another set of intelligent, remarkable women and adventurous young boys, all of whom would reflect and support his love of nature and the personal and religious emotions with which he associated the activity of botanizing. He became especially close to Catharine Merrill (who would become a professor of English literature at Butler University) and her nephew Merrill Moores (later a member of the U.S. Congress). As in the past, Muir spent his spare time botanizing and discussing religion and nature with women such as Catharine Merrill and Ellen Graydon and leading a group of Sunday school children into the fields and forests for botanical instruction, as well as undertaking more solitary rambles. At the same time, his correspondence with Dan centered as much on their shared interest in botany as on their respective factory work, maintaining a family (and male) presence in the circle of those with whom he was sharing his love of nature.

As in Canada, however, despite these successes Muir felt a nagging sense of dissatisfaction with his life and work, which emerged most explicitly as a growing conflict between being an inventor and being a naturalist, between living with machines and living with nature. The depth of these feelings is best expressed in a letter to his sister Sarah from May 1866. Encouraging Sarah and David Galloway to make a "fixed home" of the farm that they had recently bought, Muir stated that he "never before felt so utterly homeless as now."

> Much as I love the peace and quiet of retirement, I feel something within, some restless fires that urge me on in a way very different from my real wishes, and I suppose that I am doomed to live in some of these noisy commercial centres. Circumstances over which I have no control almost compel me to abandon the profession of my choice, and to take up the business of an inventor, and now that I am among machines I begin to feel that I have some talent that way, and so I almost think that unless things change soon I shall turn my whole mind into that channel. (1:443)

In part, this sense of being "doomed" to a life at odds with his own desires was grounded in the continued psychological legacy—and the immediate presence—of his father's religiously based worldview. In directing his son to follow only the will of God as revealed in the Scriptures, the elder Muir (as recently as a letter of February 1866) had imbued in him a deep mistrust of his own judgment: "When you know that man cannot will nor do, so as to please god, of himself, it is consequently best to do at all times according to god's judgements, & let him work in us to will & to do. . . . Everything that is opposed to his every word, is lies, whether it comes from the Devil, your own heart, or the world" (1:411–12). Although this imperative of religious obedience did not give Muir any helpful guidance—his father still asserted the sufficiency of "Christ and a good farm" (in a letter to Dan [1:403])—it did handicap his ability to believe in his own insights and to choose for himself.

Feeling himself trapped by machinery, Muir poignantly expressed his longing for escape in a letter to Butler's young son Henry: "I dreamed a few weeks ago that I was walking by a deep clear stream that flowed through a field of hay that was waving in the wind and changing in the light and ornamented with gorgeous flowers. Beautiful dream, was it not?" (1:426). After reading his words, Jeanne Carr responded by succinctly expressing his alternatives: "I like to think of you either in the good old mother's arms, or where men's work is the work of the ages"

(1:461). Using for the first time the imagery of the natural world as mother (and elsewhere in the letter referring to her favorite plants as "little children"), Carr was to some extent helping Muir to *create* a gender- and age-inflected dichotomy/conflict between work and nature, at the same time as she was trying to help him to some form of reconciliation. (Of course, this maternal and child imagery was in part based in the "language of flowers" and other domestic interpretations of botany, as filtered through Carr's own sensibility and philosophical orientation.) Despite her initial suggestion that "the good old mother's arms" and the arena of "men's work" could be equally attractive options, she implied a clear preference for the former: "I think you would love her ["Nature"] as well if she did not turn *mill wheels,* or grind any body's *grist*" (1:461). The power of these categories was increased by the deepening emotions of their personal relationship.

> I write you to ask you to come here this fall, . . . and make me, (us,) a good long visit, renew your old intimacies with children and books, and make new friendships with grown people and with the plants I have to show you. . . . You do not know how we hold you in our memories as one apart from all other students in your power of insight into Nature, and the simplicity of your love for her. . . . Besides, I like you for your individualized acceptance of religious truth, and feel a deep sympathy in it. (1:461–62)

Carr's wavering between "me" and "us," between the feelings of her individual relationship with the younger man and her status as a representative of her husband and marriage, suggests that her emotions toward Muir were testing the boundaries of their friendship in Christian love.

Muir responded with equal feeling: "I have not before sent these feelings and thoughts to anybody, but I know that I am speaking to one who by long & deep communion with Nature understands them, and can tell me what is true, or false and unworthy in my experiences. The ease with which you have read my mind from hints taken from letters to my child friends gives me confidence to write" (1:463). Referring back to Trout's Hollow, Muir described himself as "but an insect—an animalcula" in the midst of the grand natural setting. His descriptions show how both his literary skill and his sense of self were being shaped by the cultural references shared with Carr: "I have stood by a majestic pine witnessing its high branches waving 'in sign of worship,' or in converse with the spirit of the storms of Autumn, till I forgot my very existence, and thought myself unworthy to be made a leaf of such a tree" (1:463–64). The phrase "in sign of worship" was one of Muir's favorites from Milton (*Paradise Lost,* V:194), but he immediately offered a less traditional interpretation by suggesting that the pines are communing not with God but with "the spirit of the storms." In one of his first allusions to transcendentalism, the phrase "forgot my very existence" echoed Emerson's "transparent eyeball" passage at the beginning of "Nature," as Muir presented himself as engulfed in and overwhelmed by an impersonal Nature in a way not found in any writing up to this point; although he probably had not yet actually read Emerson himself, he would have associated such language with Carr and with his other Madison teachers. However, the references to feeling "unworthy" and "but an insect" betray an emotional experience grounded in the continued legacy of his father's Christian denigration of self—as well as in his own present sense of inner turmoil and exhaustion.

In an offhand remark, Carr had asked Muir whether he had ever encountered *Calypso borealis* while in Canada; by an unexpected route, his response to her would become his first published writing. A few months later, Carr would report that Professor Butler had stolen Muir's letter from her house and sent it to the *Boston Recorder* as an article, "The Calypso Borealis: Botanical Enthusiasm." The article appeared in December 1866 under Butler's name and referred to Muir only as "a young Wisconsin gatherer of simples . . . not a whit behind Thoreau as a scrutinizer and votary of nature." Butler's introduction frames the incident in heavily transcendentalist terms: "Who of us outsiders can fail to envy him [Muir] his esoteric raptures in his close communion with virgin nature? as well as to wish with all the heart that ours were such a vision and faculty divine, and that for us also culture or genius had added a precious seeing to the eye, transforming every weed to a flower, and transfiguring every flower with seven-fold beauty?"

The original context of the letter, however, was as an element of Muir's relationship with Jeanne Carr, and his description reveals how much he had been influenced by her imagery of plants as friends and as "little children"—but *not* by her (or Butler's) transcendentalist language. Remembering and reinterpreting an experience that was at that point two years past, Muir presented his meeting with Calypso in terms of a personal encounter between himself and an individual natural being.

> I never before saw a plant so full of life, so perfectly spiritual. . . . I felt as if I were in the presence of superior beings who loved me and beckoned me to come. I sat down beside them and wept for joy. Could angels in their better land show us a more beautiful plant? How good is our Heavenly Father in granting us such friends as are these plant-creatures, filling us wherever we go with pleasure so deep, so pure, so endless.

As shown in his early evangelical letter to Bradley Brown, Muir's understanding of religiousness had always centered on an experienced relationship with a divine Person; in this letter, Calypso had become that person, taking the place of Jesus in "the best place in the warmest end of [his] heart." Although strongly grounded in Christian language and patterns of thought, this shift involved a further rejection of traditional Christian views of the natural world: "I cannot understand the nature of the curse, 'Thorns and thistles shall it bring forth to thee.' Is our world indeed the worse for this 'thistly curse?' Are not all plants beautiful? or in some way useful? Would not the world suffer by the banishment of a single weed? The curse must be within ourselves." Strikingly, Muir still felt some need to valorize nature in terms of its usefulness within the divine order as well as its beauty, but even this served to place nature further within the same realm as the human and the religious, given his continued assertion of the fundamental spiritual and ethical importance of duty.

Thus, both Muir and Carr were striving to imagine and to experience nature in ways that would place it within the same realm of personal relationships as their human loved ones. Where before Muir could regard natural objects as "specimens" to be shared and analyzed, by this time his relationship with Carr had evoked a more intimate and personal sense of companionship in and with natural beings. On the one hand, this imagery allowed them to bring nature into each of their separate social and familial circles; on the other hand, it held a special meaning within the imaginative space of their own deepening relationship, opening up a shared emotional and physical realm in which their feelings for and images of each other could have freer play. The power and energy of this language were increased by their use of religious imagery, through which natural objects were brought into the sphere of their friendship in Christian love. Moreover, although on some levels the natural realm symbolized human and religious meanings and relationships, on other levels it was the natural objects and relationships that were themselves "primary," and we should understand the human and the religious as allowing or energizing a deepened relationship with the natural world—a relationship that was itself of fundamental importance both to Muir and to Carr.

At some point during the winter or early spring of 1867, this process was further shaped and extended by Muir's reading of Alphonse de Lamartine's *Stone-Mason of Saint Point* (1851). The long route by which he came to read it is indicative of the probable weight that the book carried both in his and in Carr's mind and heart. As far back as September 1865 (in his long Humboldt letter), Muir reported to Carr that upon her recommendation he had sent for the book, and in the meantime was reading a life of Lamartine's mother. The following autumn, in the letter inquiring about Calypso, Carr also asked Muir if he had found a copy of "my beautiful book" (1:461); in his reply, Muir claimed he had been looking for it "a good deal," but had not yet acquired it (1:464). In December, Carr finally sent him her personal copy, which Muir read at some point over the winter; by April 3 he told her that he had read it "with a great deal of pleasure" and promised to write his thoughts upon it later. No such letter survives to attest to the book's specific impact upon Muir, but the novel itself reveals much about the imaginative and emotional world that he and Carr shared.

Within a pious Christian framework, Lamartine's novel—largely a theological discussion between the humble peasant stonemason Claude and an educated, spiritually seeking narrator—echoed and extended many of Muir's and Carr's own explorations of "the sensation of the divinity in nature" (Lamartine, 99):

> I feel a foolish tenderness, but a tenderness that I can not conquer, for all
> the rest of creation, especially for those living creatures of another species,
> who live beside us on the earth, who see the same sun, who breathe the
> same air, who drink the same water, who are formed of the same flesh
> under other forms, and who appear truly less perfect members, less well-
> endowed by our common father, but still members of the great family of
> God. I mean these animals. . . . I feel [this tenderness] also for trees, flow-
> ers, and mosses, that do not move from their place, and do not appear
> to think, but live and die there round me on the earth, and especially for
> those that I have known, like the ferns and heaths on the edges of these
> rocks in this enclosure. (47, 49)

Claude's sensitivity to the spiritual dimension of the physical world leads to a correspondingly physical sense of ethical relationship with the world, including other humans, as he interprets the will of God as consisting in "loving all that he has made, sir, in order to love him himself in his works; and in serving all, in order to serve him himself in all the world. . . . It seems to me that I am one with all men, sir; that they are a part of my own flesh, and that I am part of theirs" (43, 47). Moving beyond sheer morality, Claude's sense of the spiritual in the physical suffuses his love for the beautiful Denise, herself "as wild and timid as the young roebucks and roe that are sporting beside our wild flowers in the morning"; as roebuck and roe, the two lovers "amused ourselves with trying who could run quickest down the slippery grass slopes of the mountain; who could leap best over the trenches that were made to water the meadows; who could first discover the brightest stone under the running water, the loveliest flower under the moss, the prettiest nest under the bushes. . . . It seemed the me that the whole world, heaven and earth, had entered into me with her" (61, 85–86, 89). Through such images, Lamartine's story helped both Muir and Carr to create new ways of imagining and sensing the presence of God in the world—and to invigorate and to channel the energies of their own feelings for each other. Impressed into his mind by Carr's enthusiasm as well as by his own long quest to obtain the book, many of the story's images and motifs would reappear in Muir's writing over the next few years.[11]

Thus, paradoxically, Muir's close contact with machines in Indianapolis forced his connections with natural objects to be mediated by memory, reflection, symbol, and human relationship in ways that both reinforced his previous patterns and made imaginative room for new experiences. On the one hand, he became more at ease with his work situation than most commentators have realized. His letters from the autumn and winter of 1866 indicate that he had begun working less, was taking more time for himself and for botanizing, and was in better health and spirits than he had been over the summer; by January 1867 he could write (to Dan), "I like my home here very much. . . . My health is better than it was in the summer and I take things a bit easier in the shop" (1:480). On the other hand, this emotional reconciliation with work helped prepare him for a future engagement with the natural world more intense and deep than what had gone before. Most concretely, he began to plan to live out his dream of being "a Humboldt," in the form of a long tour through the southern United States, South America, and Europe (see, e.g., 1:492). Significantly, the only way he could conceive of fully expressing his ideal of nature study was still through the culturally validated model of the adventurous male explorer, on a trip that would take him away from machines for an extended period but from which he would return to a life of continued inventing. However, a sense of paralysis and inability to act remained with him, and he found it impossible to do more than look at maps and imagine.

As with the fire in Trout's Hollow, Muir would be pushed into his next move not by his own decision but rather by an unexpected, destructive accident. In early March of 1867, while working late at the factory, he suffered a severe injury to his right eye, which lost much of the aqueous humor and became completely blind. Within hours, the left eye too had gone blind in sympathetic reaction, and his entire body slipped into a

---

11. The novel also echoes Muir's Disciples legacy, explicitly opposing "the word of God" to "the inventions of men" and asserting even the poor man's ability "to discover by his conscience where good is and where evil is" (Lamartine, 111). Further, Claude's rejection of the religious strife of his own country parallels Muir's revulsion against the churches' participation in the violence of the Civil War: "[A] religion which imprisons, burns and curses can not flow from a good source, or must have been very much changed on its way, and instead of giving men the water of heaven to drink, gives them the blood shed by executioners" (107). I am indebted to Bonnie Gisel for stressing the importance of Lamartine to Muir and to Carr.

state of shock that confined him to bed and made it impossible to eat or to drink for two or three days. A doctor pronounced his right eye gone, ordering him to stay in his darkened room for weeks in order to give his left eye a chance to heal. In a letter to Sarah and David Galloway a month later, Muir described his agony while lying in his room: "My days were terrible beyond what I can tell, and my nights were if possible more terrible. Frightful dreams exhausted and terrified me every night without exception" (1:528).

According to Linnie Marsh Wolfe, an eyewitness at the factory reported that Muir first responded to the accident by saying, "My right eye gone! Closed forever on all God's beauty!" (104). Most commentators have interpreted the accident as leading to a decisive resolution of the dilemmas with which he had been struggling, by turning him away from inventing and machines and toward a life of seeing "God's beauty" in the natural world.[12] However, the real process of change was more complex and more drawn out. On an experiential level, the accident—or, more precisely, his specific process of *recovery* from the accident—eventually would impel him to more intense patterns of engagement with his natural surroundings, but this response did not involve a clear image of a long-term "life in nature," as naturalist or as anything else. Indeed, for the first days after the accident he seems to have hung onto his self-image as inventor in order to protect himself from the pain of what had happened, writing to his mother that he "hope[d] to be at work again in a month or two" (1:492). After finding that he would in fact recover his sight in both eyes, Muir indicated in his next letter to his mother that he had accepted Osgood and Smith's proposal that he eventually take complete control of a new factory they were building (1:495). Although he may have been saying this partly to allay his mother's concerns about his future prospects, it seems probable that the continued assertion of his identity as an inventor helped him to maintain a sense of hope in the face of what had befallen him.

Although it did not immediately change his sense of public identity or

---

12. For example, John O'Grady claims: "Following the recovery of his eyesight, he decided to commit his life and love to the study of nature" (52). Turner, though more aware of Muir's uncertainty and indecisiveness regarding his future, still speaks of a "final escape" (126) from factories. In most accounts, the story goes straight from the accident to the Southern walk, without much consideration either of the period of his recovery during the spring or of the events of the following summer—the details of both of which I consider crucial in understanding Muir's development. Clearly, this sense of a sudden conversion to nature is shaped by the influence on Muir (and on his commentators) of the image of Paul's blindness and conversion on the road to Damascus, during which he (like Muir) lay in bed for three days without food or drink (Acts 9:9).

his career path, the experience of physical trauma led him into (and helped shape) a transformative emotional and spiritual trauma as well. Writing to Professor Butler at the end of April, Muir reported that in the first days after the accident he "was weak in mind as in body—all of my lessons of fortitude were forgotten—the comforts of religion did not come to me, because my mental powers were stricken down" (1:545). Perhaps most viscerally, the accident struck directly at his body, which he had always been able to control and through which he had succeeded at controlling his world, and which therefore was for him a major source of pride, identity, and sheer survival. Muir was baffled by and perhaps ashamed of his injury, as he wrote to his mother on March 9: "I am surprised that from apparently so small a shock my whole system should be so completely stunned" (1:493). Further, the accident brought him to a decidedly unmanly position, as he lay inactive in a darkened bedroom and was waited on and accompanied by women and children (especially the Merrills and Mooreses) for the long weeks of his convalescence. He expressed his feelings of a loss of adult masculinity to Jeanne Carr, writing that "my hard, toil-tempered muscles have disappeared, and I am feeble and tremulous as an ever-sick woman" (1:511) and that "the shock on my nervous system made me weak in mind as a child" (1:517).

In the face of this disorientation and suffering, Muir wrote to Butler, "all that my spiritual appetite craved was sympathy and of this your letter was full" (1:545). He longed above all for human support and presence, and he found it in the women and children who read and spoke to him in his bedroom, as well as in letters to and from his family and friends. In particular, his correspondence with Carr reveals some of the inner dynamics of his process of recovery—and the crucial role that she played in it. In his first letter to her after the accident, dated April 3, Muir bemoaned his fate: "The sunshine & the winds are working in all the gardens of God—but I—I am lost!" (1:511). The tone of the letter, for example his reference to "my immense blank days," suggests that it was not only the injury to the eye itself but also the extended immobility and confinement that were wearing on him and sapping him of hope and energy.

A few days later, Muir received his first letter from Carr (written on March 15, before she had heard from him). Taking a more overtly maternal role than in previous letters, she imagined him as an injured Civil War soldier, to whom she wished to

whisper some of those sweet promises which fasten the soul to the source of Light and Life . . . to speak the words of hope and faith and courage of which my heart is full. . . . [L]et us *believe* that nothing is without meaning and purpose which comes from the Father's hand. And let us try to emulate the courage & fortitude of those brave thousands, who have lately sacrificed so much of the beauty and joy of life, and yet go cheerfully on with what is left. . . . So my precious soldier boy, I put out my hands to ward off the consequences of the blow which struck you. (1:496–97)

The rest of the letter shows that she was concerned primarily with the implications of the accident for Muir's life path and future occupation. Strikingly, in this arena (as in others) she was undergoing her own process of change, in large part as a result of her experience of their relationship; although most commentators have portrayed her as a somewhat static teacher and guide for the younger man, it was precisely because she too was being transformed by their relationship that she could speak so deeply to and with Muir about his own condition and needs. In contrast to her past encouragement to continue to think of himself as an inventor, in this letter she imagined other possibilities for him: "Dear John, I have often in my heart wondered what God was training you for. He gave you the eye within the eye, to see in all natural objects the realized ideas of his mind. He gave you pure tastes, & the sturdy preference of whatsoever is most lovely and excellent. He has made you a more individualized existence than is common, and by your very nature, removed you from common temptations."

It is important to realize that the "eye within the eye" is not—in religious terms—very different from the "mechanical genius" that Carr had earlier lauded both in Charles Goodyear and in Muir himself: both concepts refer to the ability to see divine order, design, and value in the material world, whether one is doing so by the process of botanical observation or by mechanical creation. By this point, however, she no longer envisioned Muir as exercising this "gift" solely in the field of inventing. At the same time, the rest of the letter makes equally clear that she did not see him becoming a naturalist: "Perhaps [God] only wants you to love and to speak of Him. Perhaps He will not let you be a naturalist, but calls you by this suffering away from that pleasant path, to speak to other souls those messages of His your soul has heard" (1:496). In practical terms, she seems to have meant this as encouragement to become a minister or preacher—a role which, as we have seen before, Muir had declined in the form modeled by his father but which had remained as an option in his mind and in the minds of his Christian friends. Butler too hoped that Muir would respond to the accident by becoming more actively religious: "In all the blasting of your hope may you find Christ to be more precious than your right eye!" (1:501). Later, Carr wondered if the accident might return him to his previous plan of becoming a doctor (1:524), another occupation in which he could place both his personal experiences of suffering and his intellectual talents at the service of helping others.

Alongside her concern for his future life and occupation, Carr expressed her sympathy and concern—and evoked a sense of mutual physical presence—by writing of her and Muir's shared love of nature. In her first letter, she suggested that "Hepaticus and violets will tell you a good many things which I do not care to say at second hand, or through an interpreter" (1:497). (Muir had his letters read to him by friends, especially Catharine Merrill; we may detect a note of jealousy when Carr refers to her as "Miss (or Mrs.?) Merrill" [1:524].) Her next letter contained a long philosophical quotation from an unnamed "best beloved friend"—who was in fact the Reverend Walter Brooks, a popular Baptist minister.

> I had a fancy that there is a universe of spiritual bodies and forms of which the material plant and animal are the exact counterpart in the physical world—that there is a pre-existent spiritual body for every moss, lichen, & plant of every kind; growth is an actual "clothing upon" of themselves by these spiritual beings. They gather from nature its substances to make themselves a garment exactly fitting their persons. . . . So the poor things get a relation to us and our life which will make them nearer and dearer when they and we all are spiritual bodies again. (1:521–23)

Shifting to her personal experiences of such "relations" with natural beings, Carr continued in her own voice: "I feel myself shaken with a strange inexplicable emotion in hearing the notes of some solitary birds— as if they called me to the silences of unknown worlds. They are the only true lovers I have known (as the flowers are your beloveds) and we shall exchange the secrets of our existence soon. Have they grief and pain also, these sinless creatures? Do they rejoice to be gathered?" (1:523–24). Whatever she may have meant by saying that she and the birds "shall exchange the secrets of our existence soon," such writing served as a way for her to exchange her deep secrets and feelings with Muir.

A few weeks later, perhaps as a result of her own increasing sense of the role of nature in his life and in their relationship, Carr for the first time envisioned an actual career as naturalist as a possible future for Muir. "Who knows but we shall see South America yet?" she wondered. "You will gather seeds for us in South America, and we will have a Conservatory Fund and by and by we will appoint John Muir F.R.B.S. Bot Prof. and director . . . and he shall have a little study in the greenhouse. . . . All this if you don't make a minister" (1:536). As an aside, she mentioned another possible place he might go, not so much as a naturalist but as a fellow devotee of nature: "Get some good friend to read you a description of the Yo Semite Valley, and try to realize what God's landscape gardening is. Oh this house of our Father! I would like to know all its mansions—and after to meet and compare notes with you who love it with the same fervent love" (1:537).[13] In any setting—South America, a greenhouse, or California—contact with the natural world, as an implicit (maternal) companion to the divine Father and in the midst of his human companions, was what she prescribed for his condition: "The dear old mother will heal you fast when you get upon her lap once more" (1:536–37).

Muir himself does not seem to have absorbed fully Carr's loftier thoughts on career paths or on spiritual philosophy, for he responded in a more visceral way to the emotions of his relationships both to her and to his immediate natural surroundings. (Interestingly, a letter to Sarah indicates that he experienced a sharp recovery at about the time he received Carr's first letter: "I could scarce feel more completely a new man than had I risen from the grave but the cup is removed and I am alive" [1:528].) Referring to Carr's descriptions of some of her plants that had died of an unexpected frost, he revealed something of his own recent relationship to her: "How could they grow cold and colder and die without you knowing—they must have called you[.] Could any bedroom be so remote you could not hear[?]" (1:549). Her letter had made no mention of bedrooms, and in past letters their descriptions of her plants had centered around her library and conservatory; clearly, he was the one who, lying in his bedroom during his own weakness, felt truly heard and known by her. In contrast to her image of him as an explorer and scholar, he could envision himself only as a student at the feet of both of the Carrs: "I am sure that when in the Yo Semite Valley and following the Pacific Coast I would obtain a great deal of geology from Doctor Carr, and from yourself & friend I should win the secret of many a weed's plain heart" (1:550–51). Similarly, he confessed his inability to follow her friend's spiritual philosophy as quoted in her previous letter but responded to the more intimate, even erotic feelings underlying it. Perhaps taking his cue

13. Interestingly, in 1864 the landscape architect Frederick Law Olmsted had written a report for Congress as part of the process by which the valley was granted to California for the express purpose of preservation as a public park. Stating that "the union of the deepest sublimity with the deepest beauty . . . constitutes the Yo Semite the greatest glory of nature" (16), Olmsted stressed the aesthetic, spiritual, and health benefits of the Yosemite experience. The report was never published, however, and so could not have been the direct impetus for Carr's interpretation of Yosemite in terms of landscape gardening; at the same time, the very mention of Olmsted, already famous for Central Park, may have implicitly suggested such an interpretation to her.

from her own mention of mosses and lichens (which we have seen were long of special interest to them both), Muir noted that he read her letter "upon a moss-clad fallen tree" before giving his own careful observations on their lives and clothing: "The dear little conservative spring mosses have elevated their capsules in their smooth shining shafts, and stand side by side in full stature, & full fashion, every ornament & covering carefully numbered and painted & sculptured as were those of their Adams and Eves; every cowl properly plaited, . . . their fashions never changing because ever best" (1:549–50). The sexual imagery and emotional intensity of this language were probably indicative of his feelings both for Carr and for the mosses themselves, as he deepened his patterns of relationship both with human and with natural companions.

At the same time, Muir felt limitations in those relationships. In a letter to a new female botanical friend, Mrs. O. A. Flanner of Indianapolis, he described himself in more restrained terms: "Although a fervent lover of botany, I know very little about it—God's precious plants are dear indeed to me, but when I walk among them I feel that I am with strangers. I am not intimately acquainted with a single flower" (1:551). Later, discussing botany with Carr, he claimed that "I have no skill whatever in the matter" (1:572). Rather than taking such statements simply as indications of Muir's intellectual and personal humility, I read them as real expressions of his longing for a certain sort of emotional relationship with natural beings that he had not yet fully established. His letters to Carr were not sheer reports of experiences he was having in his regular life but (in part, at least) the occasions within which he was *creating* new ways of observing and of experiencing the natural world. It would only be later, when he got the chance to live out these new modes of relationship with nature, that they would come to feel fully real to him; for now, they existed not so much in his actual life as in the potential spaces between him and the mosses and flowers and between him and Carr—within which they still possessed enough reality to serve as powerful sources of motivation and of desire.[14]

By early summer, Muir's eye had healed well enough for him to botanize but not to go back to work in the factory, and this fact more than anything else kept him from following his often-repeated plan of resum-

14. For a more developed case of this process, see Christopher Benfey's study of Stephen Crane, which details the ways in which Crane's writing provided a pattern for action and identity that he only later embodied in his life. As do I, Benfey uses Winnicott's concept of transitional phenomena in describing this process. For another example of the use of object relations theory in a historical biography, see Frederick Kirchhoff's study of William Morris.

ing his life as inventor and mechanic. Rather, he decided to leave India-napolis and, accompanied by his young friend Merrill Moores, to travel and to botanize through Illinois and on to Wisconsin for an extended visit with family and friends. Although he wrote to Carr that he "hopes to go south towards the end of the summer" (1:561), he made no explicit mention of Humboldt or of a botanical career, and his future plans seem to have been much less certain than his immediate interests. Nevertheless, in the same letter, he was able for the first time to interpret the accident as a life-transforming event: "I am thankful that this affliction has driven me to the sweet fields rather than from them." Strikingly, his language of being "driven" echoes the sense of will-lessness that marked his previous inability to leave the family farm and, later, to stop inventing, though he was at least able to put his feelings and will more fully behind this fate than before.

It was during this ramble with Merrill that the ideas, feelings, and psy-chological dynamics surrounding Muir's accident and recovery came to transform his patterns of experiencing nature on an immediate, even bodily level. In understanding the process by which this took place, we must keep in mind the physical conditions both of Muir and of the trip itself. In contrast to the rigid, straining, controlling bodily experience of factory work and to the sense of weakness and loss of an adult male body during his convalescence, his letters describing the summer in Illinois and Wisconsin are filled with the freedom and sensuousness of a restored or reborn body. In particular, Muir took great delight in the actual feelings of climbing, touching, and walking, as well as in the play and presence of light; indeed, his descriptions of nature are both more tactile and more visual than ever before. At the same time, as Turner (128–29) notes, the recovery of his eyesight was still tenuous and mysterious, and the cloud that continued to haze the vision in his left eye was a constant reminder of the fragility of his body and of the uncertainty of his present strength and joy. He was not "reborn" into the same body as before, but one more delicate and precious, and this sense of newness within himself may have opened him up to a deeper experience with the natural bodies he encountered.[15]

15. In a draft essay that he wrote for the Merrills at the end of the summer, Muir was drawn to describe a sort of rebirth in nature—the emergence of the flower *Anemone nuttal-liana* from the late winter cold. As the first flower to bloom in early spring, Anemone rises up out of "the cold and the drear marks of winter," in order to do its "work of beauty & love" (34:1963). His special interest in this flower, as evidenced by his choice to try to write an essay about it even though "I never sat down to describe a flower before" (1:579), may have arisen because it served to reflect his own bodily and emotional "rebirth." The essay

Further, he was quite drawn to his young companion Merrill, whom he had promised Catharine Merrill and the boy's mother, Julia Moores, he would watch over and whose actions and attitudes seem to have evoked in Muir some of the feelings and associations of his own childhood. A six-page letter to Merrill's family reveals the intense interest that Muir took in the boy, and some of the effects of this relationship: "Yesterday forenoon I helped him to dam the meadow brook and to make a waterwheel for it. My own days of juvenile millwrighting came back with very full recollection" (1:565). Merrill was eleven at the time, the same age at which Muir had first come to Wisconsin from Scotland; beneath his conscious recollections, Muir may have felt the resurgence of some of his own responses to the landscape of that earlier time. In any case, his recent experience of being "reborn" made him particularly sensitive to the emotions and psychological patterns that he observed in the young boy.

After spending time in Illinois with Merrill's relatives, the pair went up to the Muir home in Portage and then to Sarah and David Galloway's new farm at nearby Mound Hill. John and Merrill soon made their way back to the Muir family's original homestead at Fountain Lake (also called Muir's Lake). A drawing probably executed around this time (but touched up at a later point for publication in *Boyhood*) suggests that Muir's attention was drawn almost wholly to the natural aspects of the place, especially the "garden meadow"; in sharp contrast to his earlier drawings, all signs of habitation (fences and a single stump) are confined to a small corner of the drawing (see figure 3). Writing to Carr, Muir described his homecoming in a letter characterized by pastoral idealization and bliss undercut—but also allowed—by an awareness of continued separation.

> The dear flowers of Wisconsin are incomparably more numerous than those of Ca[nada] or Indiana. With what fervid unspeakable joy did I welcome those flowers that I have loved so long—hundreds grow in the full light of our openings that I had not seen since leaving home. In company with my little friend I visited Muir's lake. We approached it by a ravine in the principal hills that belong to it, we emerged from the low leafy oaks and it came into full view all unchanged, sparkling & clear with its edging of rushes and lilies, and there too was the meadow with its brook, &

---

also gives a more welcoming view of nature than that of his late-university-era paper on the Wisconsin oak openings, in the detail of the annual fires that keep the openings clear of most vegetation. In the earlier piece, Muir used military imagery to describe the "battle" between the fire and the oaks themselves; here, he incorporates the imagery of landscape gardening (first suggested by Jeanne Carr in reference to Yosemite) as he describes how the fires "dress and keep" the openings, making them into the new immigrant's first "orchards" and "gardens" (34:1961).

Figure 3. Fountain Lake (Muir's Lake) and the "garden meadow," Wisconsin; originally drawn ca. 1867 and later finished for publication. (Reprinted from *The Story of My Boyhood and Youth*, plate facing p. 62)

willows, and all the well known nooks of its winding border, where many a moss & fern find home. I held these poor eyes to the dear dear scene and it washed me once more in its fullest glory. (1:572)

Despite his earlier declaration to Mrs. Pelton that "*Scotland* alone will ever be Scotland to me," after years of separation and longing it was Wisconsin that carried the weight of nostalgia and the emotions of his return home. Moreover, in contrast to his earlier letters to family that had expressed his increased love and longing for them, in writing to Carr he downplayed the emotions of his human relationships in favor of his feelings for the landscape itself. This deflection of emotion from the familial to the natural environment allowed him to hide the factors that had kept him away from home for so long—his relationship with his father, his disgust at American society, and his own choice and ambition—and thus released him from some of the more problematic psychological claims that that place might make upon him. Indeed, his ability to control the terms of his relationships with home and with family was grounded in the privilege granted him as a male in nineteenth-century American society, a privilege that he was using for his own emotional and imaginative purposes—including the creation of a somewhat alternative male identity. In fact, his chosen stance set up an impassable barrier between himself and that particular familial and natural "home"—and it was precisely this emotional barrier that, by defusing the difficulties of his actual home, allowed him to carry forward some of his very real feelings toward place and people by constructing a more idealized, literary image of home.[16]

Although Muir presented this home as primordial and unchanging, and his feelings toward it as a direct legacy of his childhood, it is clear that the ways that he perceived the natural environment were shaped by his recent experiences and ways of thinking. Despite the passivity implied by the statement that the "dear dear scene" "washed" him, he entered into the environment with the active skills of observation and classification that constituted his practice of botany—which was itself saturated with the emotions of his relationship with Carr: "I wish you could see the ferns . . ." (1:572). Most significantly, Muir brought forth into his homecoming some of the erotic power and aesthetic insight that had characterized his recent letters to her, as in his description of an underground stream.

> The opening of this dark way is extremely beautiful. I wish you could see it, it is hung with a slender meadow sedge whose flowing tapered leaves have just sufficient stiffness to make them arch with inimitable beauty as they reach down to welcome the water to the light. This I think is one of Nature's finest pieces most delicately finished & composed of just this quiet flowing water, green sedge & summer light. (1:572)

Further, the tone of longing that infuses the letter arises not only from his past separation from the place but also from his present separation from

16. Garber (in "Pastoral Spaces") identifies the central meaning of pastoral as the enactment of a desire for a return home—the most significant instance of a more general return to origins, to the "used-to-be" and the "place of absolute beginning." However, this act of return, arising from and expressed in nostalgia (the pain that arises from a deep longing for home), is impossible, "an uncompleteable act"; this impossibility is itself enacted as a tension between a surface text of presence, fulfillment, and bliss and a subtext of absence, loss, and melancholy. Garber assumes that the desire for return is unfulfillable because it is blocked by historical conditions, such as the familiar pastoral themes of urbanization and the expansion of technology (themes clearly relevant to Muir as he returned from Indianapolis and the factory accident). However, it is crucial to view Muir's own choices and goals as part of the "historical conditions" that shaped his experience; from that perspective, it was in part his own values, emotions, and ambitions that made a return to that home an impossibility. Interestingly, Garber himself suggests this perspective in his later study of Thoreau, when he writes of the latter's inability to fulfill his "central obsession": "to find a way of being everything that he wanted to be and *also* find a way of being at home in the world" (*Thoreau's Fable,* 5). The implication is that the two goals may be in conflict, as they certainly were for Muir with respect to his familial home.

Carr herself: the erotic tension in his description of the sedge is deepened by the melancholic wish that they could see it together. As with an actual return home, however, such a union was both for social and for personal reasons an impossibility; rather, it was through partial gestures such as a temporary visit or an impassioned letter that Muir found a safe space for the imaginative creation and expression of such intense and powerful emotions and images.

Thus, within his idealized, pastoral description moved opposing currents of union and separation, passivity and self-assertion. In trying to resolve (or at least to contain) these tensions, Muir was led by scientific observation and religious imagery to a deepened experience of the immediate, loving presence of God in the natural world.

> Can it be that a single flower or weed, or grass, in all these prairies occupies a chance position, can it be that the folding or curvature of a single leaf is wrong or undetermined in these gardens that God is keeping[?] The most microscopic portion of plants are beautiful in themselves, and these are beautiful combined into individuals & undoubtedly are all woven with equal care into one harmonious beautiful whole. . . . To me all plants are more precious than before. (1:573)

In somewhat less erotically charged language, but more strongly restating Carr's own earlier imagery of God as landscape gardener, Muir described for Catharine Merrill the view of prairie and woodland from a nearby hilltop.

> Ah! these are the gardens for me. There is landscape gardening—while we were there, clouds of every texture & size were held above its flowers & moved about as needed, now increasing, now diminishing, lighter & deeper shadow, & full sunshine in small and greater pieces side by side as each portion of the great garden required. A shower too was guided over some miles that required watering. The streams, & the lakes, & dens, & rains, & clouds in the hands of God weighed and measured. Myriads of plants daily coming to life, every leaf receiving its daily bread—the infinite work done in calm effortless omnipotence. (1:581)

As another aspect of his return home, this perception of God as landscape gardener was infused with domestic feelings and associations, just as the mosses and ferns were fed and cared for in their homes by Fountain Lake.[17]

17. As suggested by Carr's earlier conjunction of landscape gardening and "this house of our Father" (Yosemite), her and Muir's shared imagery drew on the domestic meanings of gardens. Norwood (chapter 4) discusses the relationships between women, domesticity, and the activity and values of landscape gardening. Even when undertaken by men—preeminently Olmsted and Downing—landscape gardening had a strong domestic dimension, and

In the context of his recent experiences—the weakness of his own body, the disruption of his work plans and of his masculine identity, the care and attention of female friends and children, the evocation of his own childhood emotions, and the joy yet impossibility of his return home—this religious language expressed Muir's deeply felt sense of reassurance in and dependence on the physical/natural world. This was his version of his father's imperative to trust wholly in the will of God; although he was no less passive than before, he had found an object of trust more attractive than his father's God, in the divinely established order of the natural world. Interestingly, Muir does not use Carr's language of "Father" and "Mother" in describing God and the natural world; however, the tactile, detailed, evocative descriptions and the tone of dependence suggest that Muir was experiencing his natural surroundings as a child would a loving, protective parent in a welcoming domestic setting. In particular, Muir's God is in part both a reflection of and an implicit critique of Daniel Muir, as a farmer/gardener and as a father caring for his own children. On a deeper level, Muir's deep sense of confidence and trust both in God and in the natural world recaptures some of the feelings that must have characterized his earliest childhood relationship with his mother, Ann, the felt loss of which had been a powerful source of motivation, hope, and energy throughout his life. Saturated with these and other images and emotions, the familiar Wisconsin prairies had become an immense, harmonious whole in which not only the flowers and weeds but Muir himself was strongly yet gently held and cared for, even in the face of his accident, his uncertain future, and the tensions and contradictions of his own desires and choices regarding home and family.[18]

---

indeed it may have been one way for men to express their own domestic longings and values. For example, A. D. Gridley asserted that moral values and emotional associations should be paramount principles of landscape gardening: "May we not so plan and plant our grounds, as both to awaken and to express some of the loftiest sentiments of the soul? . . . The Creator, it is believed, has given to each vegetable structure and form its own expression, and these, variously combined, may be used to typify some of the noblest ideals and purest emotions" (159–60). Paralleling the "language of flowers," Gridley discerns various levels of meaning and association for trees and shrubs: historical, mythological, emotional, religious, and—finally and most importantly—domestic. Thus, through proper landscape gardening, "[w]e find a new charm added to domestic life, which grows stronger with every passing year, and makes home the full realization of its sacred name" (166). These religious, emotional, and domestic dimensions would have resonated powerfully in the context of Muir's particular symbolic world and his relationships with his parents, Carr, the Merrills, and others.

18. To continue my Thoreauvian comparisons: Lebeaux argues that Thoreau's childhood experience with his mother left him with a sense of basic *mis*trust, and so as an adult he "sought in nature the security that his mother did not offer him in those early years. Returning to nature was like returning to the mother's breast" (48). Lebeaux goes on to

In short, as a gift from the world and as a creative act of his own doing, Muir was able to *love* this Wisconsin landscape with his whole being and to *feel loved by it* in return, to plunge into the flowing meadows and flowered prairies with his senses wide open, to feel the welcoming landscape kiss his open senses as warmly and intimately as a dive into Fountain Lake, to feel meadow and lake and sky and all that they contained embrace and hold his entire body and mind and heart until he became whole once more.

By the end of the summer of 1867, Muir was able to use this felt sense of protecting care to experience his surroundings in a way that brought together into creative tension many of the facets and dimensions with which he had been struggling all along. A glimpse of this process can be seen in a letter to the Merrills describing his trip in mid-August to the Wisconsin Dells. Jeanne Carr had requested that Muir visit the Dells in order to look for a certain type of fern that the premier botanist of Wisconsin, Increase I. Lapham, had told her could be found there (1:582); thus, Muir would have carried her presence within him as he visited the spot, accompanied also by his trusty friend Merrill. The expedition illustrates well the cultural pattern of men and boys collecting botanical specimens for women and girls, emphasizing that the proper place for a female botanist was not in the field but in the home (see Keeney, 75–76). Thus, the relationship between Muir and Carr was defined in part by their gender-based positions in the network of amateur botany; on this trip to the Dells, they were themselves flanked by the older authority Lapham and the young novice Merrill.[19]

---

interpret much of Thoreau's adult relationship with the natural world in terms of a preferred alternative to undependable, impure, or stifling human relationships. However, Lebeaux does not explain *how* Thoreau was able to find such security in nature; if indeed his experience of his mother's breast was undependable, then turning to the natural world as a regressive return to the breast might only be more so. (This is not to imply that a person could not, even with an uncertain maternal experience, attain a unique relationship with nature that *does* contain a sense of basic trust, only to suggest that such an achievement would call for more explanation than Lebeaux gives.) Indeed, as Garber has argued, Thoreau's adult relationship with the natural world was much more complex and ambiguous than Lebeaux realizes; this complexity and ambiguity may have been the real legacy of Thoreau's childhood experience of basic mistrust. By contrast, as I have argued, Muir's initial experience was one of basic trust, which would inform his adult relationships both with other women and with the natural world. At the same time, I have stressed that his experiences and images of nature were shaped not *solely* by the legacy of his early mother relationship, but also by the powerful influences of later experiences and dynamics, including his changing relationships with and inner representations of self, father, siblings, friends, the divine, and particular places and natural beings.

19. Unfortunately, the letter describing this trip is undated, which has caused much confusion. Turner (108) presumes that the letter refers to Muir's 1863 trip down the Wis-

The Wisconsin Dells are a series of narrow, rocky chasms and gorges through which the Wisconsin River winds and surges powerfully, creating one of the more singular landscapes in the state, and Muir's letter (see 1:306–7) is correspondingly ecstatic: "The thousandth part of what we enjoyed was pleasure beyond telling." His description of the river itself is marked by the romantic and medievalizing imagery characteristic of his youth but not evident since the university-era essay on Wisconsin prairies: "The invincible Wis[consin] has been fighting for ages for a free passage to the Mississippi & only this crooked & narrow slit has been granted or gained." Flowing past "black yawning fissures & beetling threatening rock brows," the river itself takes the military form of "fierce legions" of waves at war with the banks: "they rush to battle clad in foam—rise high upon their ever-resisting enemy & with constant victory year by year gain themselves a wider and straighter way." Significantly, Muir opened his description by mentioning that he and Merrill floated down the river "on a raft of our own construction," and as the passage proceeds his own perspective subtly merges with that of the river itself. In particular, the river perhaps evoked or expressed something of Muir's sense of masculinity: the warrior imagery reflects his childhood games and ideals of manhood; his perceptions of the rocks and banks brought to the fore his geological understanding, which was closely associated with his male mentor Professor Carr; the pounding, exuberant river probably paralleled some of the youthful emotional and erotic energies that were surging within him. Especially after the loss of adult masculinity that he associated with the accident and with his long bedridden convalescence, such an affirmation of his own masculine body probably felt powerfully exhilarating. Given his long and continued sense of will-lessness and weakness, it was this identification with the river—not his own will—that allowed him to emerge as an energetic presence in the landscape.

   The second half of this letter, an impassioned description of the flowers and ferns found in the rocky gorges that flow into the main river, contrasts

---

consin and to the Mississippi, while Stanley (110–11) takes it as describing a different trip immediately after that one; the editors of the microfilm collection have catalogued it as written to Sarah and David Galloway in July 1863 (see 1:306). However, these attributions cannot be correct, for a number of reasons. For one thing, the Dells are upstream from Madison, and so a trip there could not have been part of the trip down the Wisconsin. The "Mrs. Davis" referred to in the last lines of the letter was a friend of Catharine Merrill (see 1:610), and thus Muir could not have known her until 1866. Finally, Merrill Moores, in his later reminiscence of Muir (reel 51), describes an August 1867 trip to the Dells in ways that correlate with the circumstantial evidence concerning this trip (e.g., Muir's goal of finding a certain plant for Carr). Interestingly, there is a typescript of this same letter located at frame 570 and identified as sent to the Merrills in August 1867, which attribution I believe to be correct.

to (or, better, complements) the first half in a number of interesting ways. The object of Muir's attention has shifted from the powerful, elemental river and rocks to the more delicate and organic plant life, and his modes of perception and of feeling have shifted as well. Instead of military metaphor, Muir utilized religious and domestic imagery, infused with an affectionate, childlike tone: "Those ravines are the most perfect, the most heavenly plant conservatories I ever saw. Thousands of happy flowers are there but ferns & mosses are the favored ones. No human language will ever describe them. We travelled two miles in eight hours & such scenery such sweating scrambling climbing & happy hunting & happy finding of dear plant beings we never before enjoyed" (1:307). Muir's implied perspective is no longer one of identification with the landscape (as with the river) but rather one of loving relationship to it, with individual objects personified in a more gentle and accessible way (as "dear plant beings"). Although he is still an energetic presence in the landscape, the character of that energy has changed: instead of the aggressive feel evoked in the river scene, these descriptions convey a more controlled but no less intense passion, appropriate to the contained space of the ravines and to the delicacy, softness, and beauty of the ferns and mosses. Significantly, his scientific frame of reference has shifted from geology, with its more "male" and "objective" orientation, to the female-associated language and practice of botany, opening up a more emotional and relational set of images and patterns of response.

Accordingly, his descriptions become more evocative, even erotic:

> The last ravine we encountered was the most beautiful & deepest & longest & narrowest. The rocks overhang & bear a perfect selection of trees which hold themselves towards one another from side to side with inimitable grace forming a flowering veil of undescribable beauty. The light is measured & mellowed. For every flower springs too & pools are in their places to moisten them. The walls are fringed & painted most divinely with the bright green polypodium and asplenium & allisum & mosses & liverworts & gray lichens & here & there a clump of flowers and little bushes. (1:306–7)

Along with their aesthetic sensuousness and botanical specificity, these descriptions embody metaphors of the female body: the womblike ravine; the image of the banks "bearing" the childlike plants; the protecting or seductive veil; the moist, nurturing presence. A further image combines both feminine and masculine physical imagery: "Over all & above all & in all the glorious ferns tall perfect godlike, here & there amid their fronds a long cylindrical spike of the grand fringed purple orchis." Whether or not it was associated specifically with Carr, such imagery suggests an erotic dimension to Muir's patterns of relating to the natural world itself. However, as in the case of his relationship with Emily Pelton, we should not understand Muir's attraction to and experience of this natural setting as—or, only as—"sexual" in the modern sense, as an expression of sublimated sexual desire for actual women such as Jeanne Carr or Catharine Merrill. Rather, this experience was a unique and (primarily) nonsexual construction of the erotic in the context of a whole range of images, emotions, and energies—drawn from relationships with women, men, and natural beings themselves, and involving intellectual, religious, psychological, and domestic dimensions—that came together in his consciousness at a particular place and time with respect to a particular natural setting. Whatever its precise character, this erotic dimension was further held and intensified by the nurturing and protective presence of the maternal landscape of the riverbanks.[20]

Finally, Muir's conclusion once again brings religious and domestic dimensions to the fore: "But who can describe a greenhouse planned & made & planted & tended by the Great Creator himself. Mrs. Davis wished a fernery—tell her I wish she could see this one & this rock work. We cannot remove such places to our homes but they cut themselves keenly into our memories & remain pictured in us forever" (1:306). This larger awareness of a protective, caring God, whose hand is seen (and literally and concretely *felt*) in the order of nature, supported Muir in the integration—or, at least, coexistence—of diverse sides of his personality and experience: nostalgia and ambition, ecstasy and dependence, masculinity and female associations, assertiveness and receptivity, childhood and adulthood. At the same time, this sense of the presence of God was itself an integration of a whole range of relationships, associations, emotions, and images from his past and present lives—including his immediate experience of the Wisconsin prairies, lakes, and rivers.

Significantly, this simultaneously pastoral and religious ideal of the Wisconsin landscape was grounded in, but moved beyond, the visions of nature study that he associated with Jeanne Carr and with Humboldt. In

---

20. Terry Tempest Williams and others have used the term "erotics of place" to describe this sort of multilayered relationship with the natural world; in Williams' words, "We call out—and the land calls back. It is our interaction with the ecosystem; the Echo System. We understand it intellectually. We respond to it emotionally—joyously" (82). As my exploration of Muir's childhood suggests, however, we must understand an erotics of place as (at least potentially) incorporating emotional responses other than sheer joy, including more "negative" elements such as a quest for control and an aggressive sexuality—considered as techniques for the creation and maintainance of the patterns of relationship and of selfhood that express the core of eros. For further discussion of Muir in terms of an erotics of place (taking an example from a later stage of his life), see Holmes.

contrast to the former's enclosed library of books and specimens, the prairies and lakes constituted an entire concrete landscape, whole and alive, that could not be "remove[d] . . . to our homes"; unlike the latter's Amazon, this was a landscape close at hand, with which he had strong personal connections of memory and relationship. Thus, Muir's scientific knowledge and activity were essential in bringing him into disciplined contact with his natural environment, but by this point his goal was a deeper engagement with that environment than mere "study," an engagement that drew upon a wider range of personal emotions and concrete life experiences than ever before.

Finally, we can surmise that this process of integration was not the result of any single, direct experience of the natural world but arose through a repeated dialectic of engaging his surroundings and then writing about it to his friends. He clearly had some powerful experience at the Dells, but also had a powerful experience when he sat down to write, re-creating the experience in his mind through a form, language, and meaning that were not "there" a few days earlier. Thus, writing constituted a continuing inner act of emotional evocation and association, as Muir utilized his whole experience of the Dells as a way to bring about closer and more revealing relationships with the Merrills and with Jeanne Carr—which relationships in turn further shaped the character and meaning of his experience of that particular natural place. As at many other points in Muir's life, the process paralleled Wordsworth's juxtaposition of nature and sister in "Tintern Abbey":

> . . . these steep woods and lofty cliffs,
> And this green pastoral landscape, were to me
> More dear, both for themselves and for thy sake!
>
> (ll. 157–59)

Perhaps most important, this inner constellation of language, insights, relationships, and imagery allowed Muir to maintain a positive, emotion-laden relationship with a natural environment that held a strong place in his memory and affection, without the necessity of relating it to his actual home, either past or future. With such a place "cut keenly into his memory," he could carry it within himself as he stepped forward into an ambitious and uncertain future.

In the midst of these deeply powerful personal developments, a little incident with more public import should not be overlooked. In an 1895 address to the Sierra Club, Muir discerned the roots of his environmental activism in his early experiences in nature: "The preservation of specimen sections of natural flora—bits of pure wildness—was a fond, favorite notion of mine long before I heard of national parks." In particular, Muir recalled, at the end of the summer of 1867 he tried to buy a plot by the Fountain Lake homestead in order to fence it off and protect the flowers and grasses from farm animals, telling his brother-in-law: "I want to keep it untrampled for the sake of its ferns and flowers; and even if I never see it again the beauty of its lilies and orchids are so pressed in my mind that I shall always look back to them in imagination, across seas and continents, and perhaps even when I am dead" (Address, 276–77). Unfortunately, David Galloway refused to go along with such an impractical scheme, and so the land was not preserved; when Muir returned to the area years later, the garden meadow was trampled into mud.[21] The desire to preserve such places, however, was planted deep in Muir's heart. Thus, alongside its personal importance, Muir's emotional homecoming to the farmstead and lake gave rise to his original attempt at land preservation, the seed from which his commitment to the idea of the national parks would spring—with long-term implications for the history of environmentalism in America and in the world.

21. Stanley (116) places this initial attempt at preservation in 1864, just before Muir left for Canada. However, in the Sierra Club address Muir states that he did not return to Fountain Lake for eighteen years after the incident; this return in fact took place in 1885, at the time of his father's death, and so Muir must have been referring to his 1867 visit to (and departure from) Fountain Lake. In 1871 Muir again tried to purchase some Fountain Lake land in order to preserve it, but again failed; in the 1980s, a portion of the land was made the John Muir Memorial County Park.

# Four

# Strange Plants of a Strange Kingdom
## The South, 1867–1868

At some point during the summer of 1867, Muir finally made the decision to "be a Humboldt" by undertaking his long-planned journey to the Amazon. He had saved enough money from his years of work to be able to take an extended break from factories and inventing, and he needed such a break for his physical and emotional health; when he returned, he thought, he would again settle down to a career among machines. For now, though, setting out from Indianapolis, he would botanize his way through the South before finding passage by sail to South America. As it turned out, he would only get as far as Florida and Cuba before turning back to other regions of the United States; as with his time in Canada, however, the original destination that provided the fundamental motivation and self-concept for the journey must be kept in mind.

Despite his obvious emulation of his hero Humboldt, Muir described his resolution to go south as not so much a conscious decision as something that happened to him, a result of elemental forces that emerged from within him or that took hold of him from without—much as he had earlier felt himself dragged against his will toward machinery and inventing. Having returned to Indianapolis with Merrill, Muir wrote to Carr on August 30: "I wish I knew where I was going—doomed to be 'carried by the spirit into the wilderness,' I suppose. I wish I could be more moderate in my desires but I cannot, and so there is no rest" (1:587). In one of the first entries in the journal that he began keeping at the start of the trip, he stated that his only plan was to go "anywhere along lines of any direction wheresoever the Spirit attracts which evidently is southward" (23:22).[1] Still uncertain about his future, with noth-

1. As explained in appendix B, the very beginning of the journal is taken up with an introductory passage that seems to have been written at some time *after* the walk was completed; thus, I begin my consideration of the journal not with that introduction but with the first actual daily entry. Much later in his life, Muir would revise the journal in prepara-

ing to replace inventing for a career, and burdened by familial roles and responsibilities, Muir may have been using his recurrent sense of will-lessness for a positive purpose: to break through, or more precisely to avoid, some of the real obstacles standing in the way of his pursuing his Dream. After all of his time spent gazing at maps of the American South and South America over the previous year, he *should* have known where he was going, and surely on some level did; but he could not admit it to himself, or take full responsibility for the choices he was making. Thus, it was much easier—perhaps even necessary—to submerge all sense of self-will and of future goals and to externalize his motivations as some-thing beyond his control or understanding.[2]

In particular, he may have felt a special need to submerge his emotional attachments to loved ones in order to marshal the strength to leave them, and something of this sort is suggested in his letter to Carr after returning from Wisconsin to Indianapolis. The tone of the letter is somewhat aloof and formal, especially in contrast to the intensity of his recent letters to her. Even more striking is his reported avoidance of a proper leave-taking on his departure from Madison: "I feel myself deeply indebted to you all for your great & varied kindness not any the less if from stupidity and sleepiness I forgot on leaving to express it" (1:588). Most likely, it was not stupidity or sleepiness but an inability to face up to the emotional implications of his departure that led him to avoid the situation. At the same time, having reached such a deep level of intimacy in their botanical letters, Muir may have felt awkward and uncertain at actually being to-gether in the flesh with Carr; their relationship, somehow more than Christian friendship, could not be contained in any of the available pat-terns of interacting in person. It may have felt easier and safer for him to keep the emotions, ideas, and visions of their relationship within the bounds of botanical correspondence, exchanging continued emotional in-tensity and creative freedom for the realities of loneliness and isolation that separation would involve.

Thus, he set out on his walk to the South on September 1, 1867, with a certain necessary level of unconsciousness. This somewhat passive stance

---

tion for publication, but he died before the project was completed. William Frederick Badè further edited and expanded the work into the form published in 1916 as *A Thousand-Mile Walk to the Gulf*. Of course, I base my discussion primarily on the original journal, with reference to the microfilm.

2. Muir's situation had parallels with that of Thoreau: "Thoreau often seemed to surren-der to passivity, yet characteristically, he could usually experiment with passivity only by yielding himself to nature or the cosmos. At this point in his life, he could not surrender his will to other people precisely because he had already surrendered so much; he was threat-ened by the depth of his passivity, especially with relation to his mother" (Lebeaux, 100).

may have allowed him to take in his immediate surroundings with a heightened openness; at the same time, we can see that he was clearly shaping his experiences and perceptions of nature in very definite—and characteristic—ways. The journal reveals that he was most attracted to and fascinated by those particular natural beings that he had especially loved in Wisconsin: oaks, ferns, and flowers, especially when found in conjunction with a rocky setting and/or a body of water. He felt the oaks as a reassuring, even maternal presence, writing of "the bowers & caves of their ample branches" (23:22). In a passage written a few days later he named Kentucky as "the Eden, the paradise of oaks," speculating that here was the true and primal home from which the Wisconsin oaks had sprung, thereby implicitly reproducing his present surroundings as his own true home as well (23:28). Similarly, he was especially excited to find his beloved Wisconsin ferns living in the special microclimates around the mouths of the famous Kentucky caves: "[S]hrubs and bushes leaned eloquently over [his first cave] with shading leaves, & the very loveliest ferns and mosses were in rows & sheets up on its slopes & shelves. Lingered here a long happy while, pressing specimens & printing this beauty into my mind" (23:25). Later journal entries record his attraction to the "fern-clad lips" of Horse Cave (23:26), as well as meetings with his favorite ferns, Osmunda, and with other familiar sedges and mosses (see, e.g., 23:30, 33). His first letter to Carr reveals his interpretation of his environment as a welcoming, nurturing female presence, with a special place for her.

> These lofty curving ranks of bob[b]ing swelling hills—these concealed valleys of fathomless verdure & these lordly trees with the nursing sunlight glancing in their leaves upon the outlines of the magnificent masses of shade embosomed among their wide branches. . . . I often thought as I went along how dear Mrs. Carr would appreciate all this. . . . I have seen many caves. . . . I found two new ferns at the last. (1:591–92)

A few weeks later, in Tennessee, his encounter with his first mountain stream echoed his experience at the Wisconsin Dells: "Its banks are most luxuriantly peopled with rare & lovely flowers, & tall arching shadowy trees, making one of nature's most sacred places. Discovered two ferns. . . . Near this stream spent some joyous time in a grand rock dwelling full of mosses, birds, and flowers. Most heavenly place I ever entered" (23:34).

Appropriately, in this initial stage of the walk, one of his most common ways of relating himself to his natural surroundings was by describing them as his "bedroom." In the morning after his first night sleeping out of doors, "The sun was gilding the hilltop & bestowing a rich measure of mellow gold upon the flowers & hazels of my bed. . . . This was beyond comparison the most delightful sleeping apartment I ever occupied and I lingered about it a long time enjoying its shades & soft lights & music & sweet flowers" (23:23–24). Perhaps the privacy and individuality of the act of journal writing helped give rise to this private imagery of a bedroom. Similarly, he described himself to Carr in language that echoed his previous letters to her, but went the additional step of placing him—and even both of them—in a bedroom: "I am in the woods on a hilltop with my back against a mossclad log. I wish you could see my last evenings bedroom" (1:591).

Serving as more than a symbol of individuality or of male-female relationship, this imagery reemerged in his explicit contrast between these favored outdoor bedrooms and the indoor ones where he in fact usually spent his nights. Despite our usual image of him as the archetypal mountain man, it is important to realize that at this point Muir as a rule did not sleep outside but preferred to board at taverns, hotels, or accommodating farmhouses, for reasons of practicality and comfort but also emotional stability. A comment later in the journal reveals that he had promised his mother that he would not sleep outside unless no lodgings could be found (presumably for health reasons), a promise he seems to have tried quite consistently to keep (see 23:61). However, he often complained of his lodgings as "garrets" from which he was glad to "escape" each morning; in a characteristic entry, he "[e]scaped from the dust and dimness of my garret bedroom to the glorious lights and shadow of a Kentucky forest" (23:30). As the emphasis on darkness and light suggests, this daily escape reenacted his "rebirth" and emergence from his long confinement after the Indianapolis accident, and thus served as a continually present symbol of the underlying motives for and meanings of the entire walk.

At the same time, this contrast between natural and human-made bedrooms was linked to a more general escape or alienation from his immediate social environment. Paralleling his dislike of his lodgings, he soon came to feel "repelled" by the houses and towns he encountered in the South (23:25), a response that only intensified as his journey progressed: "Passed the rickety filthy thricedead village of Jamestown, no clump of huts in the darkest wild could be so repulsive" (23:31). Perhaps most deeply, he felt keenly the absence of the particular homes and rooms he had left behind in the North, and was delighted when he came upon a place that reminded him of his familiar domestic arrangements. He was overjoyed when (in Murphy, North Carolina) he "found a house decked with flowers and vines, clean within and without, and stamped with the comforts of culture and refinement in all its arrangements. Striking contrast to the uncouth transitionist establishments from the wigwams of savages to the clumsy but clean log castle of the thrifty pioneer" (23:38). In addition, he was increasingly repelled by signs of the destruction caused by the recent war, evident both in village and in countryside, and his re-awakened feelings of revulsion and condemnation of the war probably became associated with the landscape through which he was passing.

Contact with individual persons proved no more attractive or satis-fying. His first meetings with African Americans evoked some level of discomfort if not outright racism, as he described a little boy as "a queer specimen, puffy and jet as an Indian rubber doll and his hair was matted in sections like the wool of a merino sheep" (23:23). In time, he came to have a certain level of respect for blacks ("many of these Kentucky ne-groes are shrewd and intelligent, and when warmed upon a subject that interests them, are eloquent in no mean degree" [23:26]), but in general his language remained stereotypic: "[O]ne energetic white working with a will would easily pick as much cotton as half a dozen sambos and sallies" (23:43). Interestingly, most of the explicit statements against slavery found in the published version of the journal are later additions, written in a substantially different hand; during his time in the South, at least, he remained as racist as most of the rest of white America. Indeed, it may be more true to say that he *became* racist—or, became *white*—as a necessary tactic or stance on the Southern walk, as he encountered more black per-sons than ever before and had to forge new ways of understanding them and, more importantly in this context, of understanding himself. In doing so, of course, he availed himself of images and stereotypes that were long familiar to him but which took on new meaning and importance as they became directly relevant to his experience on the walk.[3]

His most significant and unsettling interpersonal contacts, however, came with the adult white males he encountered: the dangerous robbers that roamed the countryside, the practical and often civic-minded men that he met in the towns, and the "primitive" farmers and mountaineers of the Appalachian hollows. Muir seems to have experienced all these men as threats, the first category in a very physical way, the latter two

3. Noel Ignatiev and others have explored the ways in which "whiteness" is not a fixed, natural category but must be created and transformed in the face of particular social, eco-nomic, and cultural circumstances. Discussing another group of Celtic immigrants in nineteenth-century America, Ignatiev states: "To the extent color consciousness existed among newly arrived immigrants from Ireland, it was one among several ways they had of identifying themselves. To become white they had to learn to subordinate county, religious, or national animosities, not to mention any natural sympathies they may have had with their fellow creatures, to a new solidarity based on color" (96). As with his invention of ethnicity, however, Muir's invention of whiteness occurred on a strikingly individual level, in ways that participated in but also diverged from the larger social processes.

on more psychological levels. With respect to the "useful, practical" men of the towns, the journal conveys Muir's perception that behind their "kindness" and offers of assistance or work opportunities lay a narrow-mindedness, conformity, and sense of paternal authority that constantly challenged his intellectual desires, his hard-won independence from his own father, and his sense of masculine identity. Thus, his repeated "escapes" from these men amounted to a continual rejection of potential father figures or male role models.

Significantly, Muir seems to have understood and justified his rejection of the role models offered by Southern males in terms both of religious values and of sectional identity, as he came to assert and to find a sort of emotional refuge in his previously ambiguous identity as a (white) Northerner. In response to a blacksmith who questioned the validity of a strong, healthy man wasting time botanizing when there was so much hard and productive work to be done, Muir defended himself by pointing to the example and injunction of Solomon, who "was silly enough with all his wisdom to write upon weeds & blossoms. I warrant you he had many a long ramble in the mountains of Judea & had he been a Yankee he would likely have visited every weed in the land" (23:31–32). Feeling himself a "Yankee" (perhaps for one of the first times in his life), he could assert a superior sense of strength and wisdom over his Southern hosts. This is conveyed more strongly in the case of the "wild, unshorn, uncombed men" of the rural areas (itself "the most primitive country I have seen"), whom Muir described as narrow-minded, backward looking, and savage (23:36, 37). Belittling their gristmills as "boyish looking," he went on to implicitly equate manhood, technology, and sectional identity: "The machines of Ky and Ten are very far behind the age. There is not the faintest signs of that restless spirit of speculation & invention so conspicuous in the north" (23:36).[4]

However, at the same time as he was coming to feel and to hold his white and Northern identities more deeply than ever, Muir was not stand-offish or judgmental in his personal interactions with Southerners of ei-

---

4. Thus, for Muir both industry and botany were able to serve as the "equivalent of war" for which his contemporary William James was searching. According to Fredrickson (156–61), James felt guilt and a loss of masculine (and class) identity because he did not participate in the Civil War (as did his brothers and many friends and respected older men); interestingly, in 1866 James went on an expedition to the Amazon with Louis Agassiz, though his participation was cut short by smallpox and by some sort of emotional break-down after only a few days in Brazil. Though Muir seems never to have idealized the Northern soldiers or their cause as did James, and probably did not feel guilt for his avoidance of what he saw as Godless, sinful carnage, he probably felt some call to "prove" himself through industry and botany (as valorized in religious and masculine terms), especially as he encountered the places and people of the war face-to-face.

ther race. He was lonely, wanted company, and loved talking, and he had a tactful way of making himself a pleasant conversation partner with whomever he met. Because of his Scottish accent and obvious poverty, he would have been regarded with somewhat less suspicion than the usual carpetbagging Yankee, and he seems not to have pressed any positions that would have antagonized his hosts; indeed, his sense of white Northern identity, forged for purely personal purposes, did not include any strong political views on slavery, war, or reconstruction. Instead, he usually listened patiently to whatever his companion wanted to talk about, until he could turn the talk to a subject of mutual interest such as local botany or industry; in these areas, his skill and knowledge provided the basis for a certain camaraderie, establishing a masculine relationship that was important to him. Thus, his social experience in the South was divided, encompassing both a public, interpersonal aspect of friendly companionship with both blacks and whites and more private feelings of opposition and assertion of his own superior white and Northern identity.

In the context of these ambivalent experiences of men, Muir once again invoked the presence of his heavenly Father in response to a new natural environment—the mountains. (Remember that, for the pre-Sierra Muir, the Cumberland Mountains were by far the highest and most rugged he had ever encountered.) On first ascending the mountains, after having "escaped from a heap of uncordial kindness to the generous bosom of the woods," Muir was struck by "the most sublime and comprehensive picture that ever passed my eyes" as he looked back at the Kentucky forests, "adjusted to every slope & curve by the hands of God" (23:28–29). As he progressed further into Tennessee, the sense of the presence of the hand of God became stronger, expressed in masculine language but carrying a feminine aspect through the imagery of landscape gardening.

> The scenery is immeasurable grander than any I ever before beheld. Such an ocean of wooded waving swelling mountain loveliness is not to be described. Countless forest clad hills side by side in rows & clumps seemed to enjoy the rich sunshine and to remain motionless only because they were so eagerly drinking the light. All were united by curves & slopes of inimitable softness & beauty. Oh these forest-gardens of our Father[.] What perfection, what divinity in their architecture, what simplicity, what mysterious complexity. Who shall read the teachings of these sylvan sheets, of these flowers & all the glad brotherhood of rills that sing in these valleys & all the happy creatures that have homes here & the tender keeping of a Father's care[?] (23:37)

Clearly, we cannot at this point characterize Muir's relationship with his environment through a sharp separation between "nature" on the one hand and "society" or "civilization" on the other, as many commentators stressing Muir's ecocentrism (Oelschlaeger, Cohen, etc.) have done. Rather, we must envision a more complex configuration in which a range of familiar natural, social, and religious relationships and associations (involving women, motherhood, light, bedrooms, divine fatherhood and care, ferns, oaks, intellectual life, domestic arrangements, Northern identity, and so on) were aligned in opposition to another set of unfamiliar or antagonistic realities (threatening men, darkness, garrets, primitive living conditions, misguided paternal or civic authority, reminders of the war, narrow-mindedness, Southernness, etc.). To be sure, in some instances Muir was beginning to create out of these elements a dichotomy between "nature" and "man," as in his description of the hotel and grounds at Mammoth Cave in Kentucky: "I never before saw the grandeur of nature in so abrupt contact with the uneasy paltry gardens of man. The fashionable hotel gardens are in exact parlor taste. Many a beautiful flower cultivated to deformity blooms in gross abundance in mixed geometrical beds, the whole *pretty* affair a laborious failure side by side with the divine beauty, simplicity & universal perfection" (23:27). More precisely, however, this passage continues a debate that Muir had been carrying on both with Jeanne Carr and with Catharine Merrill about the relative merits of "Nature" and "Art" (see, e.g., 1:473, 574, and 579). It also reinforces the image of the Kentucky landscape as Eden, with its

> Flow'rs worthy of Paradise which not nice Art
> In Beds and curious Knots, but Nature boon
> Pour'd forth profuse on Hill and Dale and Plain.
> (*Paradise Lost*, VI:241–43)

Given the broad range of religious, human, and personal associations involved, it is impossible to interpret this attitude in terms of a present-day ecocentric viewpoint. In particular, it seems clear that what Muir was fundamentally reacting against was not "society" or "civilization" in the abstract, but the concrete and specific Southern social and physical environment with which he was in immediate contact.

Moreover, as the walk progressed, many of the distinctively Southern elements of the *natural* environment joined the configuration of the unfamiliar and the threatening. At the beginning Muir had almost ignored the new aspects of the Southern landscape, his few comments in the journal being confined to salty rivers and dense vines. While in Kentucky he saw cotton for the first time, describing it as "a coarse, rough, straggling, unhappy looking plant, not half as good-looking as a field of Irish potatoes" (23:28). Later, in the "primitive" country of Tennessee, he described being lost among the "terrible southern brambles" that scratched and clawed him like wild cats: "The south has a plant flycatcher, it also has a plant mancatcher" (23:33). However, as he was aware, his journey south-ward had not yet brought him to an essentially different climatic region, "the decrease in latitude being balanced by the increase in altitude" in the mountains (23:40). On the southern slopes of the mountains, by con-trast, he noticed the intermingling of the "plant-nations of north and south," prompting him to describe the area as "the Lord's artificial gar-dens"—language that echoed his negative reaction to the gardens around Mammoth Cave.

Upon arriving in the river country of Georgia, he could no longer so easily ignore the newness of his surroundings, and a deeper division emerged between those elements that he could assimilate into his familiar images and understandings and those that he could not. A hidden, shaded spring paralleled the one near Muir's Lake that he had described in a letter to Carr the previous summer, down to the ferns and grasses overhanging the water: "It is not often that the joys of cool water, cool shade, and rare plants are so delightfully combined" (23:44–47). In the same passage, his statement that he "must have been directed here by Providence" echoes the end of *Paradise Lost* (XII:647), and in fact his memories of Wisconsin were joined by his reading of Milton in guiding Muir toward certain natu-ral beings and settings. His description of the Chattahoochee River, with its "impenetrable wreathings & tasselings of the splendid Muscadine grape, whose ornate foliage so exactly adapted for bank embroidery was lighted with the glossy leafing of intertwining vines & the resplendent colors of countless flowers" (23:40), parallels the Garden of Eden in *Para-dise Lost,* with its "fringed Banks" and its

> . . . umbrageous Grots and Caves
> Of cool recess, o'er which the mantling Vine
> Lays forth her purple Grape, and gently creeps
> Luxuriant. . . .
> (IV:257–60)

Again, it was those natural beings that resonated with personal memory or with cultural heritage to which he responded most favorably.

However, as the contrast between Milton's thornless roses and the "plant mancatcher" makes clear, Muir was leaving a familiar Eden and entering a strange land: "Grasses becoming more tall and wandy, do not cover the ground with their leaves as at the north. Strange plants crowding about me now, scarce a familiar face among all the flowers of a days walk-ing" (23:47). As the landscape became dominated by the "dense impene-trable cypress swamps" (23:49), he often found it difficult to move or to find his way, and seems to have felt further frustrated and confined by the lack of the expansive vistas of the mountains, or even the familiar horizons and lines of sight of the oak openings of Wisconsin.[5] His feelings of strangeness and alienation grew more intense.

> Am in a strange land. I know hardly any of the flowers, & I cannot see any place for the solemn dark mysterious forest, I do not know any of the birds, & the winds are full of strange sounds—feel far from the people & plants & lighted fields of home. Night is coming on & I am beset with indescribable loneliness. Felt feverish, bathed in a black silent stream, nervously watchful for aligators [*sic*]. (23:50–51)[6]

While part of his emotional unsettledness surely sprang from the sheer length of time (now a full month) away from family and friends, this loneliness was strongly associated with—and deepened by—the foreignness of his surroundings, the lack of the "plant people" and "acquaintances" that carried the reassurance of familiar relationships with both natural and human beings.

At the same time, it is important to keep in mind that even in the face of his unsettled emotions, Muir kept up the activity that justified the whole trip—collecting botanical specimens—and that this was a way to respond to and to control both those emotions and the very "otherness" of the environment. The practice of gathering and pressing specimens served as a way for him to familiarize himself with his surroundings both intellectually and emotionally, as his characteristic language of "pressing specimens & printing this beauty into my mind" (23:25) suggests. Further, pressing specimens was a way to literally domesticate his immediate environment, by physically preparing it for future inclusion in his own collection back home—or perhaps in Carr's beloved library. Finally, bot-

5. Besides his personal history, other psychological factors were probably acting here as well. Kaplan and Kaplan propose that the common preference for areas characterized by "openness" and "spatial definition" depends on an automatic cognitive evaluation of the "presumed possibilities for action, as well as potential limitations" in a particular setting; that is, "what it is possible to do in the setting," especially whether it is possible to gain information through sight and to find one's way (32–37). This preference may constitute an evolutionary inheritance on the part of those peoples who evolved in a woodland or savannah setting, in which open lines of sight and a quick grasp of the possibilities for action and danger are essential to survival; rainforest peoples, by contrast, have a wholly different set of environmental preferences.

6. As Wilkins notes (53), despite his numerous expressions of fear concerning alligators, Muir would only see one of them throughout his Southern journey. His consciousness of them may have reflected his reading of popular accounts of Southern travellers that often took encounters with alligators as a dramatic high point of the adventure; however, Muir did not read the best known of these, William Bartram's *Travels through North and South Carolina* (1791), until a much later 1897 trip through the South (Wilkins, 203).

anizing gave him a physical activity, something to *do,* that engaged his bodily energies and brought him into controlled contact with a new world. If the usual emotional and symbolic meanings of his natural environment were disrupted, he could at least bring small bits of that environment into an intellectual pattern, with hope of future clarity and familiarity; if his own sense of bodily control and ease of physical movement were constrained by swamps and brambles, he could at least feel some sense of mastery of body and world through the activity of pressing plants.

It is in the context of this growing estrangement from his natural and social surroundings that we must understand Muir's experiences in Bonaventure Cemetery, outside Savannah. The journal account of his five-day stay at Bonaventure, waiting for a package of money to arrive from home, includes impassioned descriptions of the natural beauty of the place as well as long philosophical reflections on the meaning of death and the relationship of humanity to the rest of the natural world. Cohen and other commentators take these reflections as an indication that the experience left Muir "radically transformed" (18) and that it involved a major intellectual advance in his progress away from traditional Christianity and toward an ecocentric viewpoint. However, I find strong reasons to question both the chronology and the exact meaning of Muir's insights.

Upon close scrutiny, the language and the appearance of the journal entries reveal that, after a few descriptive pages that seem to have been written at the time, Muir temporarily stopped keeping his journal for the rest of the Bonaventure stay. Thus, the bulk of the account—including the philosophical reflections—was in fact written at least a few weeks (and probably longer) *after* the experience itself. This suggests that these insights were not the result of this experience alone but rather the cumulative fruit of the entire walk; I will therefore delay a more detailed discussion of these intellectual insights until later, when we can view them in the context of his development over this whole period. (For a full discussion of the writing of these passages see appendix B.) Rather than signaling a sharp transformation, Muir's encounter with Bonaventure Cemetery once again seems grounded in an essentially *conservative* psychological stance, an attempt (on some levels a choice) to hold onto the patterns of meaningfulness and familiarity that he had forged in his past life and world.

Considering only the initial journal entries, Muir was attracted to and touched by the Bonaventure graveyard not as part of a radical break with his past but, in some large part, because it once again evoked feelings and associations of that past. His approach to the place presented him only with a typically unfavorable Southern landscape: "The fields on both sides of the road are in wreck with the most cruel kind of southern cultivation. Scarce a memory of past beauty is left them—disordered half-confused weeds look woefully from the broken fences, & the sickly crops seem to feel that they are growing for lazy negroes only" (23:54). Entering the graveyard felt like entering a different world.

> You come to clumps of purple liatris & to living trees. . . . You hear the song of birds—cross a small stream & you are with nature in the grand old forest graveyard. The most open glory of Bonaventure is its noble family of live oaks, but there are thousands of smaller trees & clustered bushes as happy as they, covered almost from sight in the glorious brightness of their own light.

Despite Muir's later claim that all signs of human intervention had been obliterated by nature, certain features would still have set the cemetery apart from the surrounding landscape. The setting had previously been a country estate, cleared, cultivated, and planted with an avenue of live oaks; its use as a cemetery seems to have been limited, with only a few broken-down tombstones and monuments remaining. Thus, the place would still have had an open, parklike feel, with longer lines of sight and a freedom of movement that put it in contrast to the constricting forest and swampland through which he had been traveling. In addition, the graves and vines would have given it a somewhat Gothic air, adding a sense of beauty and drama that could not have been lost on one so steeped in Scott and Burns. Within this setting, the particular elements to which he responded—the moss-covered oaks and the stream, the nearby river with its "delightful fringe" of reeds and sedges, "the sweet songs of countless warblers hidden deep in their dwellings of leaf and flower," "myriads of the most gorgeous butterflies," even the "happy insects . . . in a perfect fever of joy & sportive gladness" (23:54–55)—all seem to echo the favored places of his past, perhaps especially his remarkable experiences during his Wisconsin homecoming the previous summer.

Additionally, the journal passage echoes *The Stone-Mason of Saint Point,* when Lamartine's narrator unexpectedly enters a remote mountain cemetery: "You breathed spring there. A cloud of insects floated and sported in the rays, which they made, so to speak, palpable. You felt that other guests beside man had discovered this asylum. Plants also multiplied at the foot of the rocks. Red pinks took root there, and waved over the mosses on the wall, like cherries half opened by the beaks of the birds. . . . The grass, though wild, seemed to have been cleaned with a rake" (29). Besides the general similarities, the curious switch to the second person and specific details such as the "sporting" insects make it likely that Lamartine's text shaped Muir's experience of Bonaventure, thus tying it even more closely to his past patterns of feeling and of meaning— including the felt presence of Jeanne Carr.

This is not to say that Muir projected an idealized or expected landscape onto his actual surroundings, or that his perceptions of his natural environment—in Bonaventure or throughout the walk—were wholly determined by his past experiences and associations. Rather, he came into unique and spontaneous relationships with the natural beings he encountered *in part* by placing them into the context of a familiar pattern of imagery and feeling—a pattern that he was in fact constantly creating and re-creating through these very acts of repeated response to the world. Indeed, this initial encounter with the place primarily operated on an emotional rather than an intellectual level, as his concluding remarks sound less like definite insights and more like tentative questions, only the beginnings of an attempt to understand an unexpected yet powerful experience: "The whole place seems a center of life. The dead do not 'reign there alone'" (23:55).

Muir camped at Bonaventure for five or six days, feeling that he would be more safe from dangerous strangers there than anywhere else. On the one hand, it served him as the most hospitable outdoor bedroom he had found since Kentucky, as he again slept with flowers and birds (as well as with a tombstone for his pillow). On the other hand, the worry, hunger, and fatigue he experienced while waiting for the money from home must have made it a difficult and trying time. The lack of food seems to have affected the workings of his perception, not necessarily resulting in a "mystical perspective" as Cohen (18) claims but probably allowing the experience to sink into his memory with an increased clarity and depth. Again, he seems not to have written in his journal for at least a few weeks, but events in the near future would move him to write of Bonaventure in greater detail—and to expand upon whatever intellectual insights he had made during the actual stay. Thus, although the later reflections that Muir retroactively associated with his Bonaventure experience may still constitute an important turning point in his thought, they must be understood as springing from a fundamentally different psychological dynamic than a straightforward "break" from religious tradition, human relationship, or "civilization in general." Indeed, as we shall see, in the face of an unfamiliar and threatening environment, those philosophical insights constituted yet another tactic to justify, and to carve out a space for, his love of the familiar places of home.

After Savannah, Muir took a steamship down the coast to Florida— the "land of flowers" where, he thought, he would finally meet "the

Lord's tropic gardens" for which he had been longing. However, his initial encounter did not meet his expectations, as he again experienced a sense of alienation, if anything with more intensity than in Georgia: "Everything in earth and sky had an impression of strangeness, not a mark of friendly recognition, not a breath, not a spirit whisper of sympathy came from anything about me, and I was lonely. I lay on my elbow eating my bread, gazing, & listening to the profound strangeness" (23:71). Plunging inland, he found he could not navigate or even penetrate the tangled swamps and forests, and so followed the railroad right-of-way as he resumed his activity of collecting specimens. He was simultaneously fascinated and intimidated by the newness of the "plant grandeur so unfathomable": "Sometimes tangled up in a labyrinth of armed vines like a fly in a spiders web. Now climbing a tree for specimens of fruit, etc., overwhelmed by the vastness & unapproachableness of the great guarded ocean of tropic plants" (23:72).

As in Georgia, he was relieved whenever he came to open grassy areas or to the "pine barrens," "as bounteously lighted as the 'openings' of Wis[consin]" (23:80). It was in such a spot that he encountered his first palmetto. Despite its bizarre appearance, he seems to have been attracted to it—and in some ways to have identified with it—because of its independence and solitude, in contrast to the clinging, impenetrable masses of the swamps.

> I beheld this first palmetto in a grassy place almost alone. Some magnolias were near it & some cypresses but it was not shaded by them, or made captive by vines. They tell us that plants are not like man immortal but are perishable—soulless—I think that this is something that we know exactly nothing about. However, this Palm was indescribably impressive & preached far grander things than was ever uttered by human priest. (23:73)

As the most "other" of the new natural beings with which he was able to create a positive and religiously inflected relationship, the palmetto opened a way for Muir to feel somewhat more at ease with the continued overriding strangeness of the place. (It may not be insignificant that Milton named palms as characteristic trees of Eden, along with cedar, fir, and pine.) Muir's drawing of the palmetto (see figure 4) includes a childlike representation of himself, arms stretched upward towards the towering plant. Suggestively, the next passage contains a stronger sense of the presence of a protecting divinity.

> Well I am now in the hot gardens of the sun where grows the palm, longed & prayed for & often visited in dreams, & though lonely tonight in this multitude of strange plants of a strange kingdom—strange winds

Figure 4. Muir and cabbage palmetto, "my first specimen near Fernandina," Florida, 1867. (Courtesy John Muir Papers, Holt-Atherton Department of Special Collections, University of the Pacific Libraries. Copyright © 1984 Muir-Hanna Trust)

too with a language I never learned, & strange birds, all things solid or
spiritual are full of influences that I never felt before—But I thank the
Lord my Maker with all my heart for his goodness in granting me admit-
tance to this magnificent realm of flowery plant people. (23:75)

With the palmetto as guide or role model, Muir could maintain his sense
of independence and purpose as he searched out the openings in a
murky land.

Thus, as he journeyed through Florida, Muir strained to take in everything that was new, but he was most consistently attracted to well-lighted,
open settings with grasses, ferns, flowers, and palms—all of which he
often implicitly or explicitly compared to their Northern counterparts. At
the same time, the character of these familiar associations was being
shaped by certain perceptual patterns that were unique to his experience
in the South, especially regarding sound and light.

Throughout the walk, his sensitivity to sounds had been growing.
While in the mountains, he had repeatedly characterized the streams he
encountered as "eloquent"; in one entry he analyzed the particular arrangement of rocks, banks, and falls that gave rise to "an immense multitude of sounds," and in a later passage commented that the sounds thus
produced evoked "multitudes of thoughts and feelings that we did not
know ourselves possessed of" (23:38). By the time of his arrival in Florida, however, what he was hearing in the landscape was not eloquence
but "profound strangeness," or in the words of a later letter "a burden of
sounds that no Northman can read" (1:607). In a later addition to the
published version of the journal, Muir recalled that—because of the influence on climate of elevation—the landscapes and sounds of Kentucky
and Tennessee were not substantially new, but his sense of strangeness
increased through Georgia and into Florida: "These palms and these
winds severed the last strands of the cord that united me with home. Now
I was a stranger, indeed. I was delighted, astonished, confounded, and
gazed in wonderment blank and overwhelming as if I had fallen upon
another star . . . [in particular, the sounds created by the wind] at the
coming-on of night had overwhelming power to present the distance from
friends and home, and the completeness of my isolation from all things
familiar" (*Walk*, 176–77).

Occasionally, the sounds of the new land were more welcoming, as
when he came upon "a most magnificent assemblage of tall grasses, their
splendid panicles waving grandly in the warm wind and making tuneful
changes" (23:81). More characteristically, in an encounter with a colony
of palms, it was apparently the stillness and calmness of the scene, the
profound silence, that made a deep impression on Muir, in part because
it reminded him of "the farthest woods of the pine" (23:91). However,

this effect was easily destroyed by the undignified rustling produced by a passing breeze, with an immediate emotional reaction on Muir's part: "In rank they are to me far below the oak & the pine. . . . They rustle & rock in the evening winds. I have seen grasses wave with far more dignity, & our northern pines spiring to the clouds speaking & bowing with the storm winds of winter, where is the prince of palms that could ask the allegiance of such a being[?]" (23:91). Muir later edited the passage to include a favorite quotation from Milton, referring to "our northern pines . . . waving 'in sign of worship'"; he had previously quoted the phrase in a letter to Carr from Canada, and the verses from *Paradise Lost* were probably close to his consciousness during the Southern walk:

> His praise ye Winds, that from four Quarters blow,
> Breathe soft or loud; and wave your tops, ye Pines,
> With every Plant, in sign of Worship wave.
> Fountains and yee, that warble, as ye flow,
> Melodious murmurs, warbling tune his praise.
>
> (V:192–96)

By the time he got to Florida, however, he listened in vain for such sounds of praise, finding instead only "profound strangeness."

Although Muir's sensitivity to sound usually carried messages of strangeness and of distance, he seems to have been able to overcome that strangeness in part through a different mode of sensation: a changed way of perceiving sunlight. Besides his obvious preference for open, lighted settings, there are indications that he was increasingly perceiving light as a presence in itself, an entity distinct from the objects it illumined. In Bonaventure, he had commented that many of the plants were "covered almost from sight in the glorious brightness of their own light," and this perception of the light as a sort of shield or covering became more common in Florida. In describing his first palmetto, he paid particular attention to its "most noble crown" of leaves, "over which tropic light is poured, & is reflected from its slanting mirrors in sparks & splinters & longrayed stars" (23:75); when he encountered the tall grasses, he was most attracted to "the glistening light that is flashed from their bent columns" (23:81); and even as he disparaged the sounds made by the colony of palms, he was "enchanted" by their "glorious crowns," each tree "capped with a sphere of leaves bright as a star" (23:91).

A number of factors may have gone into this pattern of perception. On a sheerly physical level, it was probably an effect of the changed intensity and angle of light in the southern latitudes (especially in contrast to the weak light of the northern autumn), along with the distinctive reflective surfaces of many Southern plants; in a letter to the Merrills written the following winter, Muir observed that "the sunbeams so glance & blaze upon the glossy thick evergreen leaves of the trees which are so abundant that the whole green of the landscape is mixed and whitened. I have repeatedly gone up to examine a bush that seemed to be white with flowers but which had only bright leaves" (1:607). At the same time, his perception of light may also have been related to the continued oversensitivity of his injured eye or to increased fatigue or hunger. Whatever its physical or physiological origins, this new way of perceiving light was important in serving a complex psychological role: it provided a way for him to overcome his sense of alienation from the Southern surroundings without necessarily assimilating them into his images and patterns from the North—but also without necessarily encountering them on their own terms. In dissociating light from the natural objects themselves and treating it as a semi-independent being, he was as much distancing himself from his immediate environment as he was coming into closer contact with it.

Moreover, as these passages suggest, light was also taking on a religious dimension as itself the carrier of divine meaning and beauty, through increasing association with the terms "glory" or "glorious." It is impossible to overestimate the importance of the notion of glory in Muir's published writings, where no other single image carries more emotional or religious weight; later, Muir himself would wryly admit his habitual overuse of—one might say obsession with—the term, describing his own process of editing as "slaughtering gloriouses." It is therefore striking to note that he used the term relatively rarely before the Southern walk. In an 1865 letter to Emily Pelton, he had associated "the glory of the Creator" with the "living sunlight . . . poured over all"; after his nostalgic return to the sparkling waters and dancing flowers of Fountain Lake the previous summer, he had written to Carr that he "held these poor eyes to the dear dear scene and it washed me once more in its fullest glory." (In addition, he had used the adjective "glorious" in a few other letters of summer 1867, as when he referred to the "glorious ferns" at the Wisconsin Dells.) Only while on his walk through the South, however, did "glory" become Muir's characteristic term for describing natural beauty and religious value, usually if not always in conjunction with the distinctive pattern of perceiving light that he had developed on the walk. At one point, suddenly aware that the Southern forest itself was much more dark and closed than its Northern counterpart, he exclaimed that "all the flowers—all the verdure was at the top, all the glory was up in the light" (23:80).

For one as steeped in the Bible as Muir, his decision to use the term would not have been random, and in fact his usage of "glory" exactly parallels its Hebraic origins. The biblical writings often indicate the presence of the divine in the world through a certain sort of self-existing light (burning bush, pillar of fire) and term this light "the glory of God."[7] The image is also found in Milton:

> Eternal King: thee Author of all being,
> Fountain of light, thyself invisible
> Amidst the glorious brightness where thou sitt'st
> Thron'd inaccessible.
>
> (III:374–77)

My point is not only that Muir's use of the term was shaped by biblical influences but also that he began to use such language precisely at the point when his actual mode of perceiving light began to approximate the experience suggested in the Bible. Muir used the term not as a general expression of religious valuation but as a way to describe the specific perceptual experience he was having, as a result of a whole constellation of emotional, physiological, and intellectual circumstances. Perhaps most important, it allowed him to give a religious and emotional meaning to his "strange" Southern environment—even when the particular individual objects themselves remained "strange."

Thus, the newness of the natural environment of the deep South both energized and alienated Muir. On some levels, he interpreted it in terms of his familiar Northern images; on other levels, he forged new modes of religiously and emotionally charged relationship with it, whether in terms of Milton, sound, or "glorious" light; on yet other levels, he felt unsettled and repelled. This ambiguity and complexity are nowhere more evident than in his description of coming upon the home of a black family deep in the woods, an encounter that constituted a sort of inverse Eden (see 23:82–83). Overhung by protecting grasses, flowers, and trees, encircled in a "globe of light" cast by a "glorious" fire, the black family was "primitive" in an ambiguous sense, connoting both original innocence and "unsurpassable simplicity" *and* a less than human degradation. The adults themselves emit both a "radiant presence" and a "frightful" stare, are simultaneously "twin devils" and loving parents; a "black lump of something lying in the sand" turns out to be the couple's child, who "[h]ad he emerged from black muck of a marsh as he did from this sand we might have believed that the Lord had manufactured him direct from the earth

---

7. According to the editors of the *New Oxford Annotated Bible*, "In the priestly view, *the glory of the Lord* was an envelope of light (associated with the pillar of cloud and fire . . .) which veiled his being. Though men could not see God they could behold the glory which signified his presence" (87–88).

Figure 5. "Come sonny, eat you hominy": Muir and a black family in the woods, Florida, 1867. (Courtesy John Muir Papers, Holt-Atherton Department of Special Collections, University of the Pacific Libraries. Copyright © 1984 Muir-Hanna Trust)

as he did Adam." In his drawing (figure 5), Muir stands on the margins of the scene, in an odd gesture of reverence toward and distance from the grotesque figures at the center. The home is both a primal Eden and "not in harmony with Nature"—not so much because of the Adamic child's being naked as his being "in the dirt" and "nestless." This home is not a home.

Thus, again, we find that Muir's experiences and responses were leading him not to a straightforward value dichotomy between wilderness and civilization but rather to a complex array of emotionally charged associations and images, with natural and human elements in complex juxtaposition, held together by a personal psychological logic. At the center of this logic lay a desire for and image of a religiously and emotionally satisfying home, these desires and images grounded in his past but open to dynamic transformation in the present. Ultimately, however, he was unable to relate to his Southern surroundings as home. Despite certain religious and emotional connections, he could not in Florida find a bedroom, a providential "place of rest."

> Slept in the "barrens" at the side of some logs. Suffered from cold & was drenched in dew. What a comfort a companion would be in the dark loneliness of such nights, when a fire cannot be indulged from the danger of

discovery by robber negroes who would not hesitate to kill a man for five dollars—Had long walk after dark vainly hoping for the shelter of a roof—thirsty & often drank eagerly from slimy standing pools groped for in the grass hurriedly for fear of alligators. (23:89)

Muir's response to the South thus parallels what Aldous Huxley imagines Wordsworth might have experienced had the poet traveled to the tropics:

> Wandering in the hothouse darkness of the jungle, he would not have felt so serenely certain of those "Presences of Nature," those "Souls of Lonely Places," which he was in the habit of worshipping on the shores of Windermere and Rydal. The sparse inhabitants of the equatorial forest are all believers in devils. . . . The jungle is marvellous, fantastic, beautiful; but it is also terrifying, and it is also profoundly sinister. . . . [I]t is not loneliness that oppresses the equatorial traveller; it is too much company; it is the uneasy feeling that he is an alien in the midst of an innumerable throng of hostile beings. (114–15)

As we shall see, however, Muir's response was not—at least, not at this point in his life—the "falsification of immediate experience" that Huxley sees in the later Wordsworth's choice "to pump the dangerous Unknown out of Nature and refill the empty forms of hills and woods, flowers and waters, with something more reassuringly familiar—with humanity, with Anglicanism" (117).

Upon arriving at Cedar Keys on the Gulf of Mexico in mid-October, Muir fell prey to malaria and was laid up in bed for a month—a macabrely appropriate capstone to what was supposed to be a trimphant scientific march to South America. As with the accident the previous spring in Indianapolis, the feelings of bodily weakness and helplessness left him baffled and frustrated, "for I never was sick before." In addition to this sense of weakness and bodily "failure," he may have felt a specifically childlike sense of helplessness. Upon first smelling the sea, he had experienced a "restoration" of his childhood memories of Scotland (see 23:97); perhaps influenced by this visceral wash of memory, his account of his convalescence at Cedar Keys begins with him lying on the beach gazing at birds—natural beings in which he had not shown much interest so far on the walk, but which we saw in chapter 1 *were* an important aspect of his childhood experiences of nature, especially at the time he immigrated from Scotland to America. Through February 1868, while spending a month in the harbor at Havana, "the childishness of sickness as well as its weakness prevented me from spending a single night from the vessel" (23:120). On the one hand, these child associations may have helped open him up further to new ideas and ways of perceiving, and to a new level of accepting the natural environment on its own terms; for example, in one of the passages of the Bonaventure account that I am regarding as having been written after the illness, he describes himself as "one new born new arrived from another world" (23:57). On the other hand, the sickness and the childishness must have joined with all of the other strange and unsettling elements of his Southern experience to constitute a huge challenge to his sense of adult identity and to his understanding of the world and of his place in it.

It is in this context of emotional homelessness and bodily weakness that we must understand the series of intellectual insights that Cohen and others have seen as crucial elements in the development of Muir's later ecocentric perspective. These insights involve the equal status of humans and all other natural beings as regards "rights" or moral standing (found especially in his comments on alligators and bears); the harmonious interpenetration of life and death in nature, and in particular the acceptance of human death (associated with the Bonaventure experience); and the assertion that the world was not made primarily for human use, but for the worth and happiness of each individual being (in a discussion introduced by his observations on destructive forces such as malaria).[8] In each case, Muir not only was continuing the ethical and theological reflection that he had undertaken for years (both grounded in and in tension with his religious heritage) but also was attempting to respond to the psychological ambiguity and emotional unsettledness of his experience of his immediate natural and social surroundings. This is not to say that these intellectual insights were "determined" by his psychological state; on the contrary, they were creative attempts to understand and to address the complexities of the concrete situation in which he found himself.

Muir's account of the Southern walk (as compared to his later writings) is remarkable in the extent to which his elevation of nature to equal status with humans is couched in a somewhat misanthropic tone that ends up *devaluing* humans to the level of the rest of nature. In my view, this was

---

8. Indeed, it is these insights that have led many scholars to read *A Thousand-Mile Walk to the Gulf* as the most important prelude to Muir's Yosemite experiences. For example, Turner describes Muir's departure as "the beginning of one man's singular rediscovery of America" (131), thus placing this event at the very center of his biography (entitled *Rediscovering America*). Similarly, Oelschlaeger claims that "Muir's idea of wilderness perhaps pivots on his one-thousand-mile journey to the Gulf of Mexico" (180), while Cohen, O'Grady, and others begin their substantive analyses with the walk, after a perfunctory page or two of biography. By contrast, on my reading what is most important about these insights (and the walk as a whole) is the way in which they show how deeply Muir was embedded in previously developed patterns of imaging and approaching nature; indeed, these patterns provide the basis for the philosophical depth and power of his insights at the end of the Southern walk. Moreover, it was these earlier patterns that would most decisively shape his experiences in Yosemite and after.

a logical conclusion to his experiences in the South: having regarded his recent human contacts as "primitive" and "barbarian," narrow-minded and spiritually dead, he expressed his feelings in an attack on their worldview and self-image. Conversely, those humans with whom he was in closest emotional contact (Carr, the Merrills, etc.) were not physically present—except when he was able to feel their presence in certain natural beings and settings. Thus, "pure nature" (associated with his Northern friends) comes to be elevated above "humanity" (in the form of the Southerners with whom he was in immediate contact); in part, then, what is often thought of as his ecocentrism actually reflected an alignment with one group of humans over against another, on personal, regional, gender, and class levels. At the same time, his insights express his emotional orientations toward different natural environments as well, all of this as interpreted through his developing scientific and religious thought. Ultimately, it is most correct to say that Muir was neither ecocentric nor anthropocentric but *religiocentric,* placing the divine—whether found in a deity or in the natural world—at the center of value and power.

Underlying Muir's insights was a perspective that saw human and nonhuman beings as part of the same natural world, as existing together and subject to the same dynamics and laws. This perspective is suggested by passages in which he used religiously inflected scientific language—in particular, the terms and concepts of chemistry that he had learned at the university—to talk about both human and other beings, and to begin to describe the relationships between them. Previously, he had related the human and the nonhuman mainly through a pattern of humanizing nature, as when he and Carr would refer to their favorite plants as "children" or when he compared the "sensitivity to feeling" of various vines along the roadside in Tennessee (23:30). As both humans and nature became more strange to him, however, he viewed both through the more "objective" eyes of science, which at the same time was the perspective of God, in whose sight "we are all only microscopic animalculae" (23:81; recall his university scientific notebooks, 31:65). This swing from enthusiastic personification of the natural to equally enthusiastic naturalization of the human is not as drastic as may seem at first sight, for both are ways of expressing the relationship between the creation and the Creator. At the same time, his experiences of the Southern environment forced him to view this relationship from a somewhat different perspective than before; as we shall see, this new perspective did not wholly displace his previous imagery, but it did expand and transform it into a more encompassing view. Either as children or as microscopic animalculae, both human and natural beings stand beneath the Father, God—with the emotional power of this imagery grounded both in the legacy of his familial and other relationships and in his varying experiences of actual environments.[9]

Perhaps significantly, an addition to the journal records a long discussion with a Mr. Cameron in Georgia, whose interest in "e-lec-tricity" seems to have made an impression on Muir and perhaps reawakened his own interest in and understandings of electricity and chemistry. By the time he was in Florida he conceived of the human "antipathy" toward alligators as a parallel to the forces of electricity: "Repulsion & attraction are wisely balanced in the creatures of the mineral kingdom, & why are we so slow to recognize the same divine wisdom in the corresponding repulsions & attractions of the animal kingdom[?]" Asserting that "an inherent principle of our being repels crocodiles, snakes, etc.," he goes on to say that humans in their self-centeredness ignore the "*rights* of all the rest of creation," and elevate this natural antipathy into a moral law, when they call such beings "evil" or "diabolical." From the divine perspective, however, "Those creatures dwelling happily in these flowery wilds are part of God's own family, pure in their lives, unfallen, undepraved, & cared for with the same species of tenderness & love, as is bestowed upon angels in heaven or saints on earth." It is important to realize that this positive religious valuation of alligators does not eliminate, but rather reinforces, the existence of real antagonisms or oppositions within nature, and between humans and nature: "[W]e observe a few healthy natural [antipathies] among animals & doubtless some of ours are such" (23:78). Such patterns of attraction and repulsion are part of the divinely ordained system—or family—to which both humans and other beings belong. Thus, Muir learned at least part of the lesson that Huxley would have had the tropics teach Wordsworth, that "the diversity and utter strangeness of Nature are at least as real and significant as its intellectually discovered unity" (128).

By contrast, Muir's discussion of death in relation to Bonaventure Cemetery ends with the assertion that all things are related in "friendly union." Writing at least a few weeks after his actual experience in the graveyard (and very likely after he had arrived at Cedar Keys), Muir mingled his initial favorable perceptions of the place with further reflection and experience to produce new insights:

---

9. Lawrence Buell, in discussing the personification of nature, argues that "the rise of formal science did not so much discredit the notion of 'an occult relation between man and the vegetable,' in Emerson's quaint phrase, as translate it. Indeed, the evolutionary hypothesis intensified the claim of kinship by blurring the boundary between *Homo sapiens* and other species" (188). Muir's form of this "translation" was "to imagine God as having created the universe as a vast interwoven fraternity of absolutely equal members" (193).

Bonaventure is called a graveyard—a town of the dead, but the few accidents of graves are powerless in such a depth of life. A few scattered leaves do not mar the freshness & the strong life of a summer forest. The rippling of living waters, the song of birds, the cordial rejoicing of insects, the joyous confidence of flowers, the calm undisturbable grandeur of the oaks, mark this Bonaventure of mortals' darksome loathsome graves as one of the Lord's most elect & favored fields of clearest life and light.

Our ideas of things are governed by our experiences & teachings & upon no subject are they more warped and pitiable than upon the subject of *death*. We are taught that the thing called death is an Evemade accident, a deplorable punishment for the oldest sin, the enemy—the "Archenemy" of life. But let a child walk with nature, let him behold the beautiful blendings & communions of death & life, their joyous inseparable unity as taught in woods & meadows, & plains & mountains, & streams & seas of our lovely star, and he will learn that death is stingless indeed, & beautiful as fragrant life, & that the grave has no victory for it never fights. All is in harmony divine. (23:57–59)[10]

Again viewing humans as part of the natural system, this time informed by his awareness of the chemical processes of decomposition and new growth, Muir ends up laying most emphasis upon the harmonies that exist in that system rather than (as in the meditations upon alligators) upon the antipathies. One reason for this apparently contradictory interpretation may have been the emotional associations of the specific natural environments involved: as we have seen, the dark and dense swamps and forests within which the alligators (and blacks and "barbarians") lived were settings toward which Muir himself clearly felt antipathy and repulsion, while Bonaventure was aligned with the feelings, human relationships, and images he brought from the North and the past. Thus, we can see that his emotional/symbolic responses cut across his scientific and ethical interpretations of the "one continuous system of nature": while a strong emotional alignment *with* one environment (and the humans he associated with it) led him to see human-nonhuman interactions as harmonious, an equally strong reaction *against* a different environment (and its associated humans) was also understood in the context of human-nonhuman interaction, but in a more competitive or antagonistic manner.

By the end of his journey through Florida, and especially after his near-

---

10. Again, Muir's conclusions parallel—and extend—those of Lamartine, whose narrator describes the mountain cemetery as "a kind of funereal garden, where life disputed the soil with death"; later, Claude relates his own experiences of lying in the sun on the grass of the graveyard, "with the murmuring of these thousands of insects in my ears," when "I feel shudderings of life and death over my whole body, as if God had really touched me with the end of one of his sun's rays; as if my father, mother, sisters, all those I loved, came to life again . . . and drew me toward them" (50).

fatal bout with malaria at Cedar Keys, Muir had begun to think and to feel that he simply did not belong in the unfamiliar and threatening environment of the South. It was this realization that underlay the last of his long philosophical ruminations on the relationship between humans and nature: "The world we are told was made for man. A presumption that is totally unsupported by facts" (23:110). Again, the discussion may have been occasioned specifically by his reaction to Milton's Eden, where God "fram'd / All things to man's delightful use" (IV:691–92), as well as by his continuing devaluation and mockery of the specimens of humanity (and especially men) with whom he had recently been in contact.[11] On a more visceral level, however, the depth and power of his intellectual insight were grounded in Muir's own experience of a part of the world that was obviously not made for *him*. Beginning with an inventory of the dangers, diseases, and man-eating animals that threaten human life, Muir noted that humans are no more immune to danger and misfortune than any other being. Indeed, despite the orthodox exaltation of humanity, "the lord of creation" is "subjected to the same laws of life as his subjects" (23:112). He rejected the view that explains the paradox as the effect of the Fall and of the influence of Satan, and instead asserted that the explanation is in the very nature of divine creation: humans are not the pinnacle of creation, and the rest of the world was not made solely for human benefit and use. Rather, "The Lord's primary object in constructing all of his creatures was . . . the happiness first of all of each one, not the mere provident creation of all for the happiness of one. . . . The universe would be incomplete without Lord Man, but it would also be incomplete without the smallest transmicroscopic creature that dwells beyond our conceitful eyes" (23:112). As we have seen, such valuation of nature on its own terms was not new: a year earlier, in his letter to Carr

11. This discussion also includes another wonderfully biting critique of conventional religiosity. Writing of the views of the majority of respectable men, Muir says that it "is not more possible to be guilty of irreverence in speaking of *their* God than the idol institutions of the Hindoos. He is a civilized & law-abiding gentleman, in favor of a Republican form of government of a limited monarchy, believes in the literature & language of England & is a warm supporter of the English constitution & of all well-gotten-up sabbath schools and missionary societies, & in all respects is as purely a manufactured article as any puppet of a half penny theatre" (23:111). Although this passage is probably indicative of his changing attitudes toward Milton's God, it would be a mistake to take it as expressing a sharp break by Muir away from his own religious background. Indeed, this is another standard Disciples critique of the "human inventions" with which most denominations have obscured and made an "idol" of God; in particular, the specifically English focus may have echoed a Scots view of the Anglicans, Methodists, etc. It is in applying such a perspective to the human place in nature that Muir did go beyond the traditional theology to which he would have been exposed by his father or anyone else.

describing his encounter with *Calypso borealis*, he had rhetorically asked, "Would not the world suffer by the banishment of a single weed?" Then, he had argued against the notion of a "thistly curse" by asserting, "Are not all plants beautiful? or in some way useful?"; now, he could dispense altogether with human judgments of use or beauty, seeing each natural being as possessed of its own worth in the eyes of God.[12]

As in his discussion of alligators, it is crucial to realize that even when he placed human and nonhuman beings on the same cosmic, scientific, and moral plane, Muir strongly asserted their differences and even oppositions. He was arguing both that the entire world was not "made for man" and that humans were not "made for" every environment. This was the lesson he drew from his recent illness: "When man is taken to humid portions of the tropics & perishes amid deadly malarias, he cannot see that he was 'never intended' for such climates. No, he will rather accuse his first mother of the difficulty" (23:114). In asserting that humans were "never intended" for certain environments, Muir may have been drawing on the latest scientific understandings (with which he, as a onetime medical student, would probably have been familiar), according to which diseases inhabit their own proper regions: "[M]any diseases have geographical limits as definite and oftentimes as difficult to account for as the boundaries of the various Floras and Faunas of the world" (Woodward, 29).[13] Such a view was grounded in an interpretation of some diseases as

12. Keeney (121–22) notes a parallel decline in the importance placed on the usefulness of plants by the botanical culture in the late nineteenth century. For much of the century, the "utility" of botany—both for practical and for moral improvement—was promoted as an incentive to its study. By the end of the century, however, amateurs were more concerned with pleasure and recreation, while professionals viewed a proper "science" as its own justification. In his own idiosyncratic way, with characteristically religious concerns, Muir at this point was participating in this general shift.

13. In particular, he was probably familiar with the phenomenon of "typho-malarial fever," which had emerged as a "new" disease during the Civil War and which Joseph Woodward had classified as "the characteristic camp fever of the army at the present time" (74). The category of typho-malarial fever, understood as a distinct disease resulting from the combination of the causes of typhoid and malaria, was associated with the Southern latitude and climate, and was seen as particularly harmful to Northern soldiers who came from a different environment (something of a precursor to the more modern scientific idea of acquired immunity). While gaining scientific credence from the generally accepted view of the geographical and climatic distribution of disease, this creation of a new class of diseases was also the product of social and cultural factors: as a uniquely Southern disease, typho-malarial fever served as a correlate to the growing sense of Southern sectional identity as put forth (with different moral inflections) both by the North and by the South (see D. C. Smith). Although Muir does not seem to have understood his own illness as typho-malarial fever, he clearly saw it as arising from swamps and bad air, and in general from the distinctive—and unhealthy—natural environment of the South.

caused by "miasma," a technical term referring to the atmospheric "influences" arising from the decomposition of vegetable or human matter. Not an independently existing disease-causing agent (i.e., a germ), miasma was the hypothesized mechanism through which a particular environment itself gave rise to a disease; the particular character of this "influence"—gas, spores, electrical charges, etc.—was controversial (15, 30). In affected regions, exposure to night air was a key "cause" of disease, especially around marshes and swamps. Thus, the "black muck of a marsh" that Muir imagined as having given rise to the Adamic black child was also understood as the source of his own life-threatening disease. While some "influences" within nature could restore to him his childhood memories, as did the smell of the sea, other "influences" might kill him—especially distinctively Southern ones.

Thus, for Muir the South was a primal, powerful environment, experienced with great intensity and somehow Edenic—but its ultimate character was profoundly ambivalent and disturbing. Having begun the walk with a somewhat passive sense of being "carried by the spirit into the wilderness," Muir found in the South equally mysterious currents and elemental forces that pushed him *away* from that particular wilderness. Struggling to understand and to address his emotional alienation from his natural surroundings, Muir both solidified his connections with the beloved landscapes of the North and created new techniques for coming to terms with a strange environment, including philosophical insights that—however much they would prove useful in his later thinking—were at bottom a codification and defense of his feelings of alienation. Rejecting any view that places the responsibility for human suffering and limitation on the immoral, Satanic influences of either mother earth or mother Eve, Muir was drawn to the conclusion that there are parts of the world for which humans were "never intended"—and that, for him at least, the deep South was one of them. While it might be a happy home for alligators and "primitive" humans, it was not a home for him.

# Five

# These Pure Mansions of Crystal Foam
# & Purple Granite
## California, 1868–1872

By mid-January 1868, Muir had recovered enough to think about resuming his journey. Despite his loneliness and weakness, he still intended to push on toward South America, writing to his brother Dan that "I wish you were with me, I am sometimes lonely but I dispel my sore thoughts with the hope of seeing the snow-capped Andes and the flowers of the Equator" (1:611; see also 603). He left Florida on a vessel bound for Cuba, where he stayed for a month in an unsuccessful attempt to continue his voyage southward. As he admits in the published version of the journal, his inability to find passage to South America was fortunate, since in his still-weakened state the Amazon might well have killed him. He decided instead to sail to California (by way of New York) as a place for further recovery and botanical exploration. While waiting in the harbor at New York, he felt lonely and confused, writing to his brother David that "the labor of living among strangers is hard to bear . . . I wish that my travel work was done" (1:617). To the Merrills he wrote, "I often feel the absence of the plants I am acquainted with" (1:620), and he probably felt deeply the absence of his human acquaintances as well. As he sailed toward the Isthmus of Panama, he was still struggling to understand his ambivalent experiences in the South; even as he asserted that what humans see as "dismal swamps" are lighted by the presence of God, he again admitted his sense of alienation: "The deep mysterious gardens of the hot south seem to be made and kept in beauty for other eyes than those of man—he is fenced out by wild beasts & pestilence & countless gatherings of armed plants" (23:147).

Interestingly, the major explanation that he gave for choosing California was a medical one: the cold, clean air of the North and of the mountains would strengthen him and accelerate his convalescence. Again, this

189

understanding was probably informed by his scientific background, since authorities such as Woodward recommended dry, bright, airy, cool places—the exact opposite of the dark, hot swamps that cause disease—as most conducive to recovery.[1] In his continuing visions of South America, it was now the flowers of the Andes rather than the Amazonian jungles and rivers that attracted his interest, and he may have initially imagined California as a substitute for those appealing southern mountains. In any case, for a long time he continued to write of California as merely a stopping point before his eventual continuation on to South America. One wonders if he felt compelled to follow his Dream of "be-[ing] a Humboldt" in part because he could not yet imagine any other identity or life to return to or to create; in the end, he would transform that life model significantly, but throughout this whole period it remained essential in giving him a literal sense of direction and a context for his actions and self-understandings.

Muir arrived in San Francisco at the end of March 1868, and with a companion (an Englishman he had met on the trip) immediately set off for the interior. In a letter to the Merrills of July 19, Muir summarized much of what he had seen and felt during his first days in California. Although he described the Santa Clara Valley as "Eden from end to end," and the pass through the Diablos (of the Coast Range) as a "mountain home," he wrote most enthusiastically about the broad, level Central Valley,

> the floweriest piece of world I ever walked—one vast level flower-bed—a sheet of flowers—a smooth sea ruffled a little in the middle by the tree fringing of the river, and here and there of smaller cross streams from the mountains. Florida is indeed a "land of flowers," but for every flower creature that dwells in its most delightsome places more than a hundred are living here. Here, here is Florida. (1:635)

Along with the superlatives and imagery, Muir brought his customary scientific attentiveness to bear on the landscape, including a tally of the

---

1. In an 1869 series of articles in the *Atlantic Monthly,* Henry Bowditch discussed tuberculosis in just these terms. Bowditch argued that it was the location of a house or village, especially with respect to the moisture in the soil, that determined the prevalence of tuberculosis in a specific area. (Interestingly, he referred to the Andes in particular as one of those places whose location and climate gave "blessed immunity" from the disease.) Stressing sunlight, cool and fresh air, dryness, and other environmental conditions as conducive to health in general (and to the eradication of tuberculosis in particular), Bowditch interwove these with observations on Christian virtue, divine providence, and so on, in a way continuous with the cultural presumptions and imagery from which Muir was drawing. Much later, one of Muir's own favorite ways of describing the benefits of the wilderness experience would be in terms of its effects on health.

various orders and species represented, with a precise total of open flowers (165,912—a number clearly arrived at through calculation rather than by actual counting) and a more general estimate of the flowers in bud ("say 100,000"). He took special note of the different layers of vegetative matter, happy to find a world of mosses in flower underneath the taller stems. As always with Muir, such precise observation led him back to beauty and the self-sufficient order of nature, and to the sense of the presence of a protecting deity that had marked his letters to the Merrills the previous summer in Wisconsin:

> The color-beauty of these mosses, at least in the mass, was not made for human eyes, nor for the wild horses that inhabit these plains, nor the antelopes, but perhaps the little creatures enjoy their own beauty, and perhaps the insects that dwell in these forests and climb their shining columns enjoy it. But we know that however faint, and however shaded, no part of it is lost, for all color is received into the eyes of God. (1:636)

The letter ends with his desire to share these scenes with the Merrill women, as he repeatedly asks them to join him in "these oceans and gulphs and bays of plant loveliness"—"Can you not come[?]"

Muir must have remembered his earlier discussions with Carr concerning Yosemite, for that valley seems to have been his goal from the start (although there is no evidence of further correspondence on the subject in contemporaneous letters or journals). Muir and his companion followed the Merced River up to Yosemite, where they camped and explored the valley for a few weeks; they then went back down the river to the Central Valley, arriving in Hopeton sometime in June (at which point his companion left). It is important to keep in mind that initially Muir was much more attracted to the flowers of the Central Valley than to the grandeur of the Sierra. In describing his journey through the Diablos he had referred to the "poor human insect invader" overcome by the "terrible grandeur of these mountain powers" (1:635), and the Sierra and Yosemite would have been much more terrible and overwhelming than the comparatively gentle Coast Range.[2] He was clearly impressed by the Sierra, declaring to the Merrills that "Yo-Semite alone is worth the expense and danger of any journey in the world" (1:636), but also felt unsettled by and unworthy of them. Thus, he chose to stay away from the high mountains for the rest of his first year in California, thus remaining in an environment that was more psychologically (as well as physically) accessible.

---

2. Paralleling Muir's sense of awe before God and nature, Lamartine writes of "the poor insect called man who hollows the rock, probes the earth, and studies the sky, there to seek him who calls him without ceasing . . . his God!" (100).

After spending some months doing odd jobs at ranches and farms around Hopeton, in the late autumn Muir began what would be a five-month stint herding sheep for "an illustrious Irishman named Smoky Jack." Alone in his little shepherd's hut in gentle, expansive Twenty Hill Hollow, from the beginning he felt the entire landscape as his home. On January 13, 1869, he wrote to his sister Margaret and brother-in-law John Reid:

> The Merced [River] . . . passes me at speaking distance on the south. Smooth domey flowing hills with the tree-fringe of the Tuolumne, bound me on the north. The lordly mountain wall of the Sierra meets the sky and plain on the east, and the far blue mountains of the Coast on the west. And now, this, *this,* is my home. This mean twisted cabin is but a kennel where I sleep. The bright green fields are my home. Think of a glowing arch of sky resting on such a rim. Is it not a palace indeed? (2:692)

Within this welcoming setting, which he would come to compare to "un-cursed Eden" (23:180), he settled into a rhythm of life that was more stable and leisurely than he had experienced since Canada—or probably even since childhood. He had time to explore one place and to familiarize himself with new beings from a variety of encounters and perspectives. He lay on the ground looking for germinating seeds, and took the time to count 550 mosses on one-quarter of a square inch of rock. Equally impor-tant, he was able to relax more than on his previous travels, and to open himself up to experiencing nature through his body in a receptive rather than an aggressive, controlling way. One early entry in his journal for the period (for January 7) emphasizes his emotional response as he opened himself to the landscape: "The clear sunsets of these plains are all most exquisitely most intensely beautiful, & when one in full repose opens himself to their influence he will find pulsings & gushings in depths he hardly knew himself possessed of" (23:169).[3] Another entry, from Janu-ary 16, conveys a more purely physical experience: "The ordinary tranquil purple of evening and morning divinely laid on. A bright balmy genial day. Read in my shirt-sleeves, or lay with closed eyes, when my sheep also became meditative, & soaked & steeped in the sunbeams & they reached to the joints & marrow" (23:172).

Significantly, he had mentioned in his letter to the Merrills that he had lost his botanical books, and he remained bookless throughout the fol-lowing winter and spring (see also 2:713). We can thus give a fairly pre-cise—but partial—answer to Cohen's rhetorical question "John, when

---

3. An edited version of this Twenty Hill Hollow journal is available in *John of the Moun-tains,* chapter 1. I have used the original version throughout, with references to the microfilm.

did you stop carrying that plant press, and why?" (30). Although Muir in fact continued to take specimens for the rest of his life, it was during these first months in California that the activity of botanizing began to be less important to him. As Cohen notes, collecting and classifying plant specimens is a profoundly anthropocentric activity, and one that gives a false notion of plants by tearing them out of their natural context, their network of living relationships. Further, as I have stressed all along, the activity of botany gave Muir a way to control and to "domesticate" his environment (and his own body) both intellectually and physically, as a practice that carried with it a whole range of emotional and symbolic meanings. Thus, the inability to do botany—not chosen because of a changed way of thinking, as Cohen suggests, but resulting from the accident of a lost book—along with his increased settledness and leisure and the physical recovery and strengthening of his body, put him once again into a position in which he could (and perhaps was impelled to) reconstruct his ways of relating to and experiencing his natural surroundings.[4]

Appropriately, some of Muir's earliest journal entries while in Twenty Hill Hollow convey these feelings of flexibility and openness to new ways of understanding and even of perceiving nature. On January 4, after a winter rain flooded the nearby creek and left a fresh unmarked sheet of sand and mud on its banks, he precisely observed the profusion of animal markings that soon covered the area, and then compared the process to the human mind: "In like manner every human heart is written upon so soon as created & in all lives there are periods of change when by various floods their pages are smoothed like these sand sheets preparing the whole page for a series of new impressions, & many an agent is at once set in motion to print & to picture it" (23:167). Although the passage uses the imagery of "impressions" and "printing" familiar from the

4. Kaplan and Kaplan (chapter 6) propose that natural settings can act as "restorative environments," relieving the mental fatigue that results from the constant level of focused, concentrated attention demanded by the patterns of modern life. (Interestingly, Muir himself used such language in his later writings, as part of his own understanding of the healthy effects of wilderness.) In particular, in order to act as restorative, an environment must offer certain types of experience: escape, the sense of an interrelated whole (perhaps larger than what one immediately perceives), fascination, and a compatibility between the environment's possibilities for action and the individual's desires. For Muir, the Central Valley afforded just these aspects of experience—in sharp contrast to the environment of the South, where the dense undergrowth, short lines of sight, and animal and human dangers frustrated his desires for holistic perception and for active engagement. Moreover, his inability to do botany led him to direct his attention in less focused, more free-floating and playful ways. Thus, the Kaplans' assertion that a generalized "wilderness environment" can afford restorative experience must be qualified by a consideration of the particular characteristics of the environments, activities, and persons involved.

Southern walk and earlier, it also suggests that no single impression is final, definite, or comprehensive. The next day, he was impressed by the effects on perception of peculiar atmospheric conditions in which "all magnitudes [were] greatly exaggerated."

> Sheep at a short distance looked like oxen, & hills at a mile's distance appeared to be at least ten miles away. These conditions are oftentimes reversed. . . . Variations, mirages, etc. of all kinds are common upon these plains, but I seldom have seen any landscape so wonderfully disturbed as this one. If the Creator were to bestow a new set of senses upon us, or slightly remodel the present ones, leaving all the rest of nature unchanged, we would never doubt that we were in another world, & so in strict reality we would [be,] just as if all the world besides our senses were changed. (23:168–69)

In such a "wonderfully disturbed" landscape, and feeling as if he possessed a "new set of senses," Muir felt his own mind and heart flooded, smoothed over, and prepared for a new series of impressions.

In particular, his journals and letters of the time reveal three intertwined themes: the admission that much of the pattern and order in nature are beyond human understanding; a more imaginative and playful way of perceiving the relationships between natural beings; and a more purely sensuous and elemental experience of his natural environment in terms of texture, shape, color, sound, and light. All of these themes would be characteristic of his later thought and writings, and so it is striking to pinpoint their emergence in the perceptual patterns and language of the isolated shepherd in Twenty Hill Hollow.

With respect to the first of these, we have seen that one of the legacies both of his scientific education and of the recent Southern walk was the intellectual apprehension of the myriad relationships and interconnections within and between natural beings and elements. In California, he continued to delight in discovering pattern and relationship in nature, as when he made precise observations of cyclical patterns in the development of flowers (23:164; see also 187). In a common move, he immediately related this to the grander system of nature: "Like comets in the far points of their orbits, plants & animals seem to be moving out of all specific limits, but, by paths & motions calculable or otherwise they return to whence they set out" (23:166). At the same time, as the phrase "calculable or otherwise" suggests, he was becoming more impressed by the mystery and incomprehensibility of these interconnections and patterns, their independence from human thought or order: "I used to imagine that . . . there was a more or less clearly defined correspondence in the laws of Nature with our own, but here out from the tyranny of Man in the free unplanted fields there is no visible instance, no sound of a single rule humanly defined No rectilineal sectioning of times & seasons. All things *flow* here in indivisible measureless currents" (23:162). Still asserting his faith in the existence of pattern within nature, Muir—perhaps in part because of his present inability to impose order on nature through botany—had to admit that such patterns could not be fully seen or understood. In describing the markings of the flooded banks of the creek, he commented: "[H]ow soon will writing above writing in countless characters be laid upon this beautiful sheet making it yet more beautiful but also carrying it far beyond the best analysis of our limited mind. There are no unwritten pages in nature—everywhere there is line upon line" (23:167).[5] Given his lifelong faith in the "book of Nature," this inability to read it must have had a double-sided effect on him, evoking a greater sense of wonder and awe but also firing his desire for closer scientific study. Muir was not one to accept any limitations easily, be they physical or intellectual.

In the absence of the structured understanding afforded by scientific categories, Muir gave an imaginative and even playful aspect to his perception of natural relationships through a distinctive type of metaphor in which he describes one type of natural being in terms of—or *as*—one that according to normal perception would be its opposite. Again, we can find this pattern of imaginative inversion at the end of the journal of his Southern walk, particularly in his descriptions of the sea: "If we inhabited the bottom of the sea—ocean atmosphere—foam of wavetops would be clouds & their shadows would be finned birds" (23:147).[6] On a few occasions he had described the ocean as plains (when calm) or hills (when stormy), and in the Twenty Hill Hollow journal he reversed the imagery: "[C]loud shadows drifted gradually about the brown plains like islands

5. This is the first dateable reference to his image of the natural world as a palimpsest, so crucial to his later approach to nature. The published version of the journal of the Southern walk contains a statement of the idea, but this is clearly a later addition—perhaps from the Twenty Hill Hollow period, though again it is impossible to say. Patricia Roberts gives a good account of the way Muir developed this idea into a philosophy of "reading" the "book of Nature," especially with respect to the glacial origins of Yosemite; further, this concept of reading has clear parallels to Alexander Campbell and the Disciples' tradition of reading the written Scriptures (though Muir does not seem to have directly borrowed language or imagery from Campbell or anyone else). However, note that in this present germ state Muir used the imagery to stress the *indecipherability* of nature, the *inability* of humans to read it.

6. As noted in chapter 4, his encounter with the sea at the end of the Southern walk had brought back memories from his childhood and thus may have given him a sense of fluidity and an openness to playing with the things of the world, or at least with his perceptions and descriptions of them.

of solid darkness in a sea of light" (23:161). Other examples abound: clouds are "sky mountains" or "grand islands & rocks of the finest textured cirrus," rain is "cloud waterfall," while in another scene "flower suns are rising in every quarter of the valley sky & mingle their gold with the silvery gleaming crystal stars of quartz so abundant here" (23:176, 186, 182). As these examples suggest, he was delighted to find a way to compare airy beings such as clouds with fixed, rooted mountains, or to cast the ground as the sky and vice versa, or to dissolve the barriers between misty cloud and solid rock, inverting the perspectives through which we usually view and categorize the world.

In further describing all he was seeing and hearing through that first California winter and spring, Muir used an increasingly sensuous tone, constructing natural scenes in terms of elemental qualities—texture, shape, and color. During the winter, he was fascinated by the different qualities and connections of mist, cloud, and earth: "Great, warm soothing mist sheets are upon the mountains this morning, bathing the tree buds & myriads of quickening seeds with a gentleness of gesture & touch that has no word symbol on earth. How indescribable in texture, how exquisitely do they conform to the sloping & waving of the hill bands" (23:164). As the season progressed, he often referred to groups of flowers as blankets or sheets covering the ground in layers: "The glorious sheet-gold soon to cover all these hills & hollows & rocky banks like a sea" (23:177). He constantly painted earth and sky, sunset and flowers, in "Nature's three great colors" (23:181), yellow, purple, and green: near the end of January, he described the progression of a week as it "developed from day to day like a flower in atmospheres of purple and gold—by far the sweetest brightest balmiest cluster of radiate January days" (23:175). (He later edited the technical botanical term "radiate" to "radiant.")

As these last examples suggest, Muir was especially drawn to sunlight as the source of color, warmth, and life itself, and the journal records his increasing joy with the clear spring days: "Sun-gold to sun-gold with not a cloud to separate" (23:187). In contrast to the somewhat hard, harsh, "glancing" light of the Southern walk, this California sunlight was more fluid and supple, "gushing" with "warm balmy life" that it poured forth into both birds and flowers: "Sunshine gushed through jagged openings [of clouds] which turned in the breasts of the blessed larks to the sweetest song" (23:162). Indeed, the sunlight saturated the entire landscape: "The fields are lovely. The warm rains of the past week have doubled the depth of plant life & opened whole lakes & seas of color. . . . The wavy hills are mantled in the most abundant, most divine of all gushing, living plant gold. The most glowing landscape the eye of man can ever behold" (23:186, 187). At times, as when he was "steeping & soaking" in the sunlight, he felt it flowing into him as well, as suggested by a wonderfully ambiguous passage: "Four cloudless April days filled in every pore & chink with unsoftened undiluted sunshine" (23:188). *Whose* pores and chinks—those of the landscape or of the days, or Muir's own?[7]

In the midst of all this life and beauty, he could only wonder at what might exist beyond the reach of his limited human senses and understanding.

> Lark song . . . is about the only bird song of these plains that has been made with reference to our ears. . . . Wind also gurgles & vibrates about the angles & hollows of every surface grain of sand—each sand grain making a perfect song, but not for us. How spiritual must be the tunes that are born in the groves of these golden daisies. How the wind will pulse among the curves & points of these lovely corollas & among the pistils & the stamens with their sculptured pollen, but not one note is for mortals. But thank God for this arrangement of the wind beneath the feathers of a lark & for every wind vibration that our ears can read. (23:173–74)

As the last sentence suggests, Muir still felt the presence of God in nature: "Parents sometimes lecture children for snipping paper into fanciful shapes. How busily the Creator is at work today upon ornamental fl[owe]r tissue!" (23:180). In other passages, he invoked a parental, nurturing divine presence both in female and in male forms: "Almost every bundle of plant life has been unrolled & Mother Earth is brooding her beautiful children with loving appreciation of their coming glory" (23:174); "Only the fingers of God are sufficiently gentle & tender for the folding & unfolding of petalled bundles of flowers. Gorgeous sunset sky" (23:183). (He had conspicuously *not* used "earth as mother" imagery in Florida.) The "fingers of God" are sunbeams, and (as on the Southern walk) Muir closely associated light with religious meaning, as in the entry for March 6: "Fields are in full gush & blaze of glory" (23:185). In

7. At such times, Muir's experience may have echoed that of Lamartine's stonemason: "I lie down in summer, in the middle of the day, in the grass or the sand, on my back, with my eyes half closed and turned toward the rays which fall from the sky on my face; in this manner there rains into my eyes and into my soul a dazzling flood of rays as rosy as the flowers of the eglantine. This flows, illumines, warms me to the depth of my heart, as if one were plunged into a lake of light, which entered into one's limbs and veins, and even into one's spirit. Then, sir, I figure to myself that these rays, this dazzling light, this warmth, is the ocean of God in which I swim, and that I am carried deliciously across space, light and transparent as the air, to I know not where—it is a grief to me when I open my eyes and see only the sun. I thought that it was He, and I am ready to weep at having lost the feeling of his presence" (42). By this point, however, opening up his eyes would not have seemed so jarring to Muir as it was for Claude, for Muir's divinity had suffused into the entire landscape as well as the sunlight; thus, it is most correct to say that Claude's ways of sensing the presence of God taught Muir new ways of relating to the natural world.

some moments, he interpreted the entire sun-drenched landscape as the glory of God:

> Perhaps I do not understand the request of Moses, "Show me thy glory," but if he were here I would like to take him to one of the observatories of Twenty Hill Hollow, & after allowing him time to drink the glories of flower, mtn, & sky I would ask him how they compared with those of the Valley of the Nile and of Mt Pisgah, & then I would inquire how he had the conscience to ask for more glory when such oceans & atmospheres were about him. King David was a better observer, "The whole earth is full of thy glory." (23:182)

However, it is significant that Muir here did *not* use the image of God as landscape gardener, so important to him a year ago in Wisconsin. In general (though with some exceptions), Muir at this time was not so much concerned with God as an external force shaping the landscape as with the landscape itself as an active force, imbued with a divine light and life energy and flowing according to laws hidden from humans but ultimately beneficial to all beings.

Also significant were those times when Muir himself appeared as an active force in the landscape: "I welcomed [a new sheet of flowers] to the world—congratulated them upon the goodness of their home & blessed them for their beauty, leaving them a happy flock in keeping of the Great Shepherd, while I turned to the misshapen half-manufactured creatures of mine" (23:182). Along with lying on the ground and gazing at sunsets, Muir spent a fair portion of that winter and autumn running after a flock of sheep; more passive and receptive than before with respect to the natural world, he was still active and assertive in his human duties. If the absence of a botany book encouraged him to look at flowers in a less controlling manner, he still had to exert control over "this mongrel, manufactured, misarranged mass of mutton & wool called a sheep band," living in "wretchedness & unmitigated degradation" (23:179). Viewing the sheep as "manufactured," Muir responded with the same sense of order and efficiency he had used as an inventor: "I studied the disposition of the brutes, and found that their greatest fault was a tendency towards total disintegration. . . . [After working with them for a while,] the whole fifteen hundred became a unit in all things & as manageable as a trained dog" (23:178). It was with respect to the sheep that Muir further developed the negative associations of the term "civilization."

> After an experience of a hundred days, I cannot find the poetry of a shepherd's life. If ancient shepherds were so intelligent & lute-voiced, why are modern ones in the Lord's grandest gardens so muddy & degraded? Shepherds become sheepish. . . . The whole business, with all of its tendencies,

exerts a positively degrading influence. Milton in all his darkness bewailed the absence of "flocks & herds," but I am sure that if all the flocks & herds, together with all the other mongrel victims of civilization, were hidden from me, I should rejoice beyond the possibility of any note of wail. (23:185–86)

Similarly, when he found a pair of little pigs dead in the field after an unexpected February snowfall, Muir laid the blame on civilization: "Man has injured every animal he has touched" (23:181). His evident sense of pity for the pigs may have been colored by some of his childhood memories: *The Story of My Boyhood and Youth* contains a number of stories of animal deaths, including a pig shot by an Indian (88–89) and a squirrel frozen in a tree (135–36). Strikingly, Muir wrote to his little nephew George (Sarah and David Galloway's son) about all the lambs that died in the storm; in an earlier letter to Merrill Moores, he had also written about dead sheep. On some level, then, he associated dead animals with boyhood, and such feelings may have mingled with memories of his own boyhood on the farm to add to his negative valuation of the sheep and of the shepherd's life—and of "civilization" in general.

On April 17, 1869, four days before his thirty-first birthday, he summed up his present life in a letter to Dan. He still felt deeply the question of occupation, congratulating his brother on the latter's decision to become a doctor and wondering if he should have followed that route. Although most commentators have taken his statement that "I think I might preach Nature like an apostle" as presaging his future career as nature writer and activist, he had no conception of such a future at the time; indeed, the context makes it clear that he meant this in reference to his previous thoughts about becoming a minister, but he was sure that no congregation would want him for long.[8] He did not even know where he would be living in a year: he still had tentative thoughts of going to South

---

8. Although he would eventually turn primarily towards scientific and literary pursuits, the continued importance of religious work as a possible career for Muir places him squarely in a pattern that Robert Crunden has discerned in the lives of many of those who (like Muir) became part of the Progressive movement. According to Crunden, the typical Progressive came from an overtly religious family and seriously considered a ministerial or other religious career before his or her college experience opened up other ways of expressing deep social commitments and personal values. Under the guidance of a mentor, he or she then worked through a prolonged period of travel and experimentation before finding—often, creating—a profession that would fulfill his or her ideals, usually in social work, academics, journalism, or politics; whatever the field, the Progressive's life and work retained an aura of religious mission and commitment. Interestingly, Muir came from a somewhat different class background from that of many of his fellow Progressives, suggesting that this pattern of a personal life trajectory was at least as important as class issues in defining and fueling the Progressive character and movement.

America the following November, and then on to Europe (probably including Scotland) before going back home to Wisconsin. (He repeated and expanded upon these future possibilities in a letter to his sister Mary [2:726].) However, the sense of happiness and acceptance that he had found in his shepherd's hut in the Central Valley left him able to hold some of these uncertainties and worries at bay, and to put the rest of his life "on hold," at least for now.

> As for myself I am lost—absorbed—captivated with the divine & infathomable loveliness & grandeur of Nature. Somehow I feel separated from the mass of mankind, & I do not know whether I can return to the ordinary modes of feeling & thinking or not. I work hard for the means of traveling, & find myself able to make what is called a fortune in a great variety of ways, but bread & sunshine, birds & flowers & open sky are enough for the comfort of my existence. (2:720)

Having completed his time shepherding Smoky Jack's sheep and with his heart set on a return to Yosemite, Muir signed on to work for another local rancher, Pat Delaney, as the latter moved his flocks up into the mountains for the summer for better pasture than the sun-scorched valley would afford. It was the journal of this trip that, revised and published in 1911 as *My First Summer in the Sierra*, would present a particular version of his entry into Yosemite both as the key to his personal biography and as a normative pattern of wilderness experience open to all. As argued in appendix A, however, the earliest surviving account of this period—found in three notebooks from 1887—is most probably already heavily revised, and so cannot be taken as a straightforward description of Muir's inner experiences at the time. In particular, we must bracket many of the most powerful and influential (even archetypal) images and themes that we usually associate with Muir's entry into Yosemite: his intuitive apprehension of the glacial origins of the valley; detailed ecological insight into the interconnections between natural beings; an immediate, "mystical" bond with Yosemite as his "real home"; his language and experience of an ecstatic "blending with the landscape"; a dramatic "conversion" and total reorientation of his life. Although he clearly did come to these insights and images by 1887, we cannot use the existing notebooks as evidence that he held them in 1869; rather, we must understand them in the light of his experiences and trajectory over the whole period *between* 1869 and 1887. Accordingly, we must search other sources to grasp the specific importance of the summer of 1869 in this development. In fact, on my reading, this whole process was much more extended and gradual, much less an instantaneous "conversion" or "mystical bond," than the traditional myths suggest. To put it briefly, my sense is that Muir did not suddenly *find* a new home in Yosemite, but rather *made* one there over the course of years.

Thus, in exploring the categories, images, and associations that guided and gave meaning to Muir's initial experiences in the mountains, we must begin not with the published *First Summer* or with the 1887 notebooks but with his letters of the period—particularly those to Jeanne Carr. During the Southern walk, Muir's correspondence with her had suffered from the uncertainty of his location, but the intensity of their feelings for each other—and their association of each other with nature—had if anything increased. In the spring of 1868, soon after Muir had arrived in California, one of Carr's letters finally reached him: "I feel your presence and sympathy in all the gladness of the opening season, but I also feel very keenly the loss of you in my life" (1:626). (Her sense of loss again accentuates the fact that it was Muir whose gender position gave him most power to stop and to restart their relationship on his own terms, through his own decisions of travel and work, revealing a basic inequality at the core of what was on other levels a mutually supportive relationship; indeed, it was his unequal freedom and privilege that were part of what made Carr value their relationship so deeply and miss it so keenly.) In his response, dated July 26, 1868 (after his brief stay in the Sierra early that summer), he referred to their discussion of Yosemite in their Indianapolis letters: "I thought of you, Mrs. Carr, when I was in glorious Yo Semite, and of the prophecy of 'The Priest' that you would see it and worship there in company with your Doctor, priest and I. It is by far the grandest of all the splendid temples of Nature I was ever permitted to enter. It must be the sanctum sanctorum of the Sierra, and I trust that you will all be led to it" (1:640). In November he again referred to the possibility of their meeting in Yosemite, writing that "I know too the abode of many a precious mountain fern. I gathered plenty for you but you must see them at home" (1:660). Thus, from the beginning he interpreted Yosemite through familiar categories—the love of ferns he shared with Carr, and the contrasting joys of gathering specimens for her library and of meeting plants in their own homes.

As it happened, Professor Carr had resigned his post at the Wisconsin State University that summer, and he and Jeanne were considering where they should go next. She spent part of the summer in her native Vermont; sometime the following fall or winter they decided on California, eventually settling on the San Francisco area, with hopes of the Doctor's obtaining a position at the University of California. It is unclear whether Mrs. Carr had a say in the decision, and if so whether her relationship with Muir was a factor. In any case, he responded to news of her unexpected closeness with excitement: "I have thought of you hundreds of times in my seasons of deepest joy, amid the flower purple & gold of the plains, the fern fields in gorge & canon—the sacred waters, tree columns & eternal unnameable sublimities of the mountains. Of all my friends you are the only one that understands my motives and enjoyments" (2:694). Referring to their past connection through friendship and ferns, he immediately began to plan a future meeting with her in Yosemite: "I thought when in the Yosemite valley last spring that the Lord had written things there that you would be allowed to read sometime. . . . You must prepare for your Yo Semite baptism in June" (2:694–95). Her response, written on Easter Day, similarly merges past and future images and emotions: "I am 'drunk' with [flowers'] gorgeous colors and rich profusion. . . . My thoughts are unto you-ward, dear Shepherd, and there is no other soul with whom I would prefer to keep this spotless day sacred to the holiest memories and hopes" (2:711–12).

By May 16, he was writing detailed directions and instructions for her voyage to Yosemite, displaying his excitement and concern in extended speculation as to the possible routes she could take, what scenery she might enjoy best, warnings to bring enough blankets, and so on.[9] His overt feelings about their meeting had increased even further: "Dear friend, the thoughts of again meeting with you & with the mountains make me scarce able to hold my pen. . . . My soul is athirst for mountain things. . . . I intended to enjoy another baptism in the sanctuaries of Yo Semite whether with companions of 'like passions' or alone, surely then my cup will be full when blessed with such company" (2:727). Clearly, his excitement and anticipation were directed not only toward Carr but also toward Yosemite itself; on some levels, he had already merged the two into an emotional unit. Thus, his feelings toward Yosemite, in particular the psychological and religious meanings it would carry for him, were already being shaped by the emotional presence of Carr, while his relationship with her was itself being transformed by their sharing an imagined experience of Yosemite. Just a few days later, he again wrote her with plans and suggestions, urging her to travel to Yosemite via the Mariposa grove of sequoias, which he termed the "Mountain kings":

9. Here, as in most of his letters, he included a sentence or two expressing his hope that Professor Carr could come as well. Although Muir probably still regarded the Doctor as an important mentor, the feelings of that relationship were muted by the power of his feelings toward Jeanne. At the same time, it seems likely that one of the things that united Muir and Mrs. Carr was their shared admiration for her husband, as an epitome of the role of scientist to which both of them were attracted but from which they still felt excluded. (Both of them consistently refer to him as "the Doctor" or "the Professor.") On this level, the implicit presence of Professor Carr allowed Muir and Jeanne Carr to relate as equals—siblings and/or fellow students—in a way that directed attention away from themselves and toward scientific study and (through science) the natural world itself.

"I hope you may be able to spend a good long time in worship amid the glorious columns of this mountain temple. I fancy they are aware of your coming & are waiting. . . . I am in a perfect tingle with the memories of a year ago, & with anticipation glowing bright with all that I love" (2:731). Waiting and tingling both for Carr and for the mountains, Muir expressed his anticipation and longing in more bodily terms than ever before.

Thus, as he journeyed toward Yosemite in early June with sheep and fellow workers, Muir brought with him all of the patterns of perceiving his environment that he had developed over the previous winter and spring—openness to mystery, imaginative inversion and playfulness, and sensuousness—along with heightened levels of excitement and of desire. In exploring his responses to his new mountain surroundings, the 1887 notebooks do contain one type of information that seems reliable: the basic structure of what he did and saw, the sheer record of *what* he was looking at, rather than how he was seeing it. Expressing the standard interpretation, Stephen Fox states that for Muir, the mountains "seemed eerily familiar—like returning to a home he had never known, or recognizing a friend he had never met" (8). However, the specific patterns of perception revealed by the sequence of the notebook entries suggest that in the mountains he found—or, better, created—connections with particular homes and friends he *had* known in the past.

During the first part of his ascent into the mountains, when he stayed for about a month with his sheep and fellow herders in a camp in the foothills by the Merced River, Muir's attention usually was directed not toward the occasional grand panorama but toward the humbler, more enclosed natural beings he saw close at hand—the familiar ferns, trees, and flowers to which he had been attracted in the Midwest and the South. Again, as on the Southern walk, this is not to say that Muir's perception was wholly and forever determined by the past, but rather to suggest that he used familiar patterns as a means of coming to an emotionally satisfying and sustainable relationship with an unfamiliar environment—which relationship he could then develop further in new ways, in creative response to the new elements of that environment. In particular, his entries (and drawings, some of which seem to be originals cut out and pasted into the notebook; see, e.g., figure 6) suggest his fascination with the ferns, mosses, sedges, and oaks of the riverbanks, along with the lilies (recall his aunt's "sacred" lilies in their backyard garden in Dunbar, which Muir himself later associated with these California lilies [*Boyhood*, 12]). In this welcoming, familiar but new landscape, Muir found another "bedroom": a large, flat-topped, moss-covered rock resting in a wide pool in the river, surrounded by lilies and the leaves of carex and alders leaning over the water, where he spent at least one memorable night.

Figure 6. Cascade and pool on North Fork Merced River, California, ca. 1869. (Courtesy John Muir Papers, Holt-Atherton Department of Special Collections, University of the Pacific Libraries. Copyright © 1984 Muir-Hanna Trust)

After a few weeks, however, he began to shift his focus from these enclosed spaces to the sky overhead. It is important to keep in mind that this first camp by the Merced River was down in a valley that afforded few expansive views of the mountains themselves; the notebook entries at this point refer to the sky much more often than to the mountains. As during the previous winter and spring in Twenty Hill Hollow, he was quite attentive to and drawn to the sunlight, and kept up his practice of noting wind and cloud cover daily.

Although specific incidents must remain forever hidden behind the revisions of the 1887 notebooks, there must have been some particular events and environments that made deep and powerful impressions upon Muir, or he would not have chosen to revise the original journal in the ways that he did. For example, consider the ecstatic "conversion" passage in the notebook entry for June 6, which (in the published *First Summer* form) I have already quoted in the introduction. On that day, Muir crossed from the hot, lowland Upper Sonoran life zone to the more forested and alpine Transition zone; live oak are replaced by black oak, sabine pine (which Muir himself compared to the palm family) by sugar and ponderosa pines, and the general richness of vegetation increases dramatically. (For a detailed description of Muir's route, see Fiske.) This sharp change, which on one level he may have perceived as going from a Florida-like environment to one more closely approximating Wisconsin, was probably so physically striking and emotionally evocative as to have brought about a sudden rush of feeling. In any case, it seems quite likely that he had a powerful experience of *some* sort at this point, perhaps on a milder scale than the present language suggests but nevertheless of importance in the development of his perceptions of and feelings toward the mountain environment.

Given the lack of letters from this initial stage of the journey, the emotional presence of Jeanne Carr becomes evident only in her absence, when she and Muir failed to make their long-awaited rendezvous in Yosemite. After leaving the Merced camp on July 8—somewhat later than he had originally planned—Muir and the sheep moved up toward Yosemite, arriving at a temporary camp on the north side of the valley itself by July 13. (Interestingly, the notebooks convey Muir's continued preference for fern-fringed meadows and stream-watered flower gardens over the rougher, rockier areas of the higher elevations they were entering.) However, Carr, after having arrived in Yosemite a few weeks earlier, unexpectedly had to leave sooner than she and Muir had hoped (in order to talk over with Ezra his imminent appointment to a post at the University of California); thus, with Muir's late arrival, they did not meet at all. Her letter informing him of this situation reached him by July 11, and his immediate written response revealed the depth of his feelings.

> I need not try to tell you how sorely I am pained by this bitter disappointment. . . . Thus far all of my deepest purest enjoyments have been taken in solitude, & the fate seems hard that has hindered me from sharing Yo Semite with you. . . . The sun has set & these glorious shafts of the spruce & pine shoot higher and higher as the darkness comes on. I must say good night, while bands of Nature's sweetest influences are about me in these sacred mountain halls & I know that every chord of your being has throbbed & tingled with the same mysterious powers when you were here. Farewell. I am glad to know that you have been allowed to bathe your existence in God's glorious Sierra Nevadas & sorry that I could not meet you. (2:734–35)

In a postscript dated July 17, he bombarded her with questions concerning her exact whereabouts while in Yosemite. The intensity of his questioning suggests both that he continued thinking of her after their non-meeting and that his association of her with Yosemite—and thus his incorporation of that environment into their shared construction of an emotional and erotic relationship with nature—continued to deepen even in her absence.

Perhaps significantly, the moment at which Muir's emotional focus on a meeting with Carr dissolved coincided with his arrival at his long-sought destination, the rugged, dramatic mountains and valleys of Yosemite and the High Sierra. In sheer perceptual terms, this involved an important shift of perspective: instead of focusing on familiar things within an enclosed space or gazing upward at the sky, his attention and energy were drawn outward, across and into a complex and expansive landscape filled with mystery and with the possibility of exploration and contact. According to the 1887 notebooks, his first view of Yosemite Valley came in a dramatic and hair-raising adventure on an extremely narrow ledge beside Yosemite Falls, looking out from within the falls as it plunged three thousand feet straight down;[10] in our only contemporaneous evidence concerning this incident, however, Muir merely wrote to Carr that he had "had a most heavenly piece of life among the domes & falls & rocks of the North side & upper end of the valley" (21:735). A number of other references to domes suggest that he found them to be the most interesting new geographical feature.

As both the 1887 notebooks and his contemporaneous letters indicate, Muir responded to this new landscape by energetically exploring it, climbing around many of the peaks and valleys north of Yosemite itself. In addition, sketching became one of his major activities and even preoccupations, as a way to begin to grasp and to take in the new landscape (in the continued absence of his botany books and plant press); he wrote to Mrs. Butler in August that he was "sketching and absorbing from the inexhaustible treasures of glory that are gathered here" (2:745). Significantly, however, the notebook entries continue to describe sky, clouds, and storms more often than mountains or rocks. In fact, he seems to have learned how to look at mountains by first looking at clouds, whose grandeur and sheer magnitude would still have been much more familiar and accessible to him.[11] The numerous comparisons and interminglings of cloud and mountain in the 1887 notebooks may well reflect his original responses, especially given that he had already developed just such a perceptual technique of imaginative inversion over the previous winter and spring. In a letter to Carr in October, Muir copied out a journal entry from September 2 that pictures clouds as "anchored in dense massive mountain forms" and describes mountains mainly in terms of their

10. Interestingly, a number of later entries mention his subsequent resolution to stay away from such dangerous situations and his feelings of giddiness as he looked out over similar precipices, suggesting that he was not as intuitively comfortable in the mountains as we usually assume.

11. In the Twenty Hill Hollow journal, he had often compared California clouds and storms to those of Wisconsin, with the latter often coming out ahead: "This is like a Wisconsin summer sunset only the clouds are upon a smaller scale" (23:169).

"cloud caps," concluding that he had "[n]ever before beheld such divine mingling of cloud and mountain" (2:756).

Strikingly, however, this copied journal entry—the only surviving entry from the original journal—ends not with mountains, sky, or waterfalls but with ferns, flowers, and domestic imagery. Walking through a narrow cleft in the granite on the north wall of the valley, he found that its borders were "splendidly decorated with ferns and blooming shrubs, the most delicate of plantlets in the gush and ardor of full bloom." Noting that such places are usually thought of as "desolate and gloomy," beset by snow, storms, and rocks, he marveled at how the protective hand of God allows "these sweet and tender children of the plants" to "live in safety and innocence." In particular, he was overjoyed to find cassiope, "the long-looked for mountain child," in its "dwelling place." (He had earlier written to Sarah that "I am with Nature in the grandest and most divine of all her earthly dwelling places" [2:742].) Muir's encounter with cassiope strongly echoes both his discovery of *Calypso borealis* in the woods of Canada and his joyous experience at the Wisconsin Dells with young Merrill Moores, as well as the "gush and ardor" he had felt in the landscape more recently (as expressed in the previous spring's journal and letters to Carr). Poignantly, Muir concluded the letter by sympathizing with what he imagined were the emotions raised by the Carrs' recent move to California: "I hope that you will all be very happy in your new home, and not feel too sorely the separation from your loved places and people of Wis[consin]" (2:756–57). If his comment indicates his own emotions upon arriving in California, such feelings may have been part of what led him to re-create in Yosemite the world of associations and images from his own "loved places and people" of his past.

Thus, even at the end of his first extended immersion in Yosemite, Muir's emotional and imaginative responses to the place were strongly continuous with his previous patterns of experiencing his natural surroundings, from childhood through his recent winter and spring in the Central Valley. He came to his eventual relationship with Yosemite not through a sudden, dramatic "conversion" but rather through a gradual process that would develop only over years of living in that place and that was grounded in specific patterns and images that were deeply rooted in the experiences and relationships of his entire life.

In August 1869, Muir wrote to Sarah from Yosemite: "I am captive, I am bound—love of pure unblemished nature seems to overmaster and blur out of sight all other objects and considerations" (2:742). His words echoed almost exactly his letter to Dan the previous spring (2:720), suggesting that even after his summer in the Sierra it was "nature" in general, not Yosemite in particular, that was the object of his love. In fact, back down in the foothills in September, he was still unsure as to what he should do next; writing to Mrs. Butler, he stated that "I will likely leave Cala some time in December or Jan' for some other of our Father's gardens" (2:745). Letters to Dan and to David reveal that he was still thinking of South America as his next destination, suggesting also the continued importance of the role model of an international explorer and botanist à la Humboldt; thus, his love of "nature" might still have carried him away from Yosemite.

Moreover, he was lonely, and he missed his family and friends back in the Midwest even more than before: "Though my lot in these years is to wander in foreign lands my heart is at home. I still feel you all [his family] as the chief wealth of my inmost soul and the most necessary element of my life. . . . I have but gone out a little distance to look at the Lord's gardens" (2:795–96). Again, his description of his present situation as his "lot" obscures the very real goals, desires, and privileges that allowed him to choose a life of freedom and wandering; at the same time, his struggle with loneliness was equally real, and the continuing presence of family and friends in his emotional life would last throughout his time in Yosemite. Stanley (chapter 9) cites numerous letters from Muir's early Yosemite years that illustrate his continued interest in and concern for the details of his parents' and siblings' lives, and the readiness with which he sent them advice and financial assistance as well as botanical specimens.

By mid-November, however, he had decided to return to Yosemite for the time being, to see the winter weather and to botanize: "I am bewitched—enchanted & tomorrow I must start for the great temple to listen to the winter songs and sermons preached & sung only there" (2:767). He had not seen snow and ice since leaving the Midwest two years earlier, and his letters make clear that memories of the familiar Wisconsin winters were part of what moved him toward the mountains. Echoing Carr's language from her very first mention of Yosemite over two years before (see 1:537), he described Yosemite in domestic terms, as "the grandest earthly *mansion* that the Lord has in all the open world" (2:776) and as "the Lord's mountain house" (2:778). Accordingly, he immediately found a human family and friends with whom to share it.

Finding work at James Hutchings' hotel (one of two in the valley at the time), Muir quickly became close to the women and children of the Hutchings family; their friendship was based largely in their shared love of nature and of botanizing, infused with all of the familiar emotional and religious associations that he had developed earlier with his own family and with the Peltons, the Trouts, and the Merrills. In addition to doing odd jobs around the house and hotel, Muir built and operated a sawmill with another young man, Harry Randall, and the two lived together in a shack close to the hotel. The steady stream of tourists through the valley, many of whom Muir despised, nevertheless brought him various other like-minded, nature-loving companions, such as the British countess and writer Thérèse Yelverton (who would base her novel *Zanita* directly on the Hutchingses and Muir). Whether or not Muir was romantically involved with either Elvira Hutchings or Thérèse Yelverton—a subject of much debate—they clearly were a part of his erotic relationship with nature in at least some of the ways that had characterized his previous relationships with women; similarly, whether or not Muir and James Hutchings were rivals for Elvira, they certainly held rival ways of relating to Yosemite—Muir's way religious, scientific, and aesthetic, Hutchings' primarily economic and political. Thus, for Muir, Yosemite was not only a natural environment but a social one, with both aspects approachable through familiar patterns from his past life (while at the same time open to creative transformation in the present). Although he had initially planned to leave that spring, by February 15, 1870, he was telling Dan that he would stay at the sawmill all summer (2:789).

The first December storm fulfilled his hopes for winter beauty: "I rode to the very end of the valley, gazing from side to side, thrilled almost to pain with the glorious feast of snowy diamond loveliness" (23:202).[12] Interestingly, the phrase "gazing from side to side" echoes his descriptions of his first botanical expeditions (see 1:323), and indeed he called snow-flakes "the floral stars of the fields above" (23:203). His attention was focused mainly on the valley floor and on the snow itself, with a reverent if somewhat distanced stance toward the mountains: "Tissiack [i.e., Half Dome] stood like a god, a real living creature of power & glory, awful, incomprehensible" (23:202).[13] For the rest of the winter, sky and storms were his major interests, as a May letter to Professor Butler suggests: "The power & the beauty & the wondrous *works* of the sky which the Lord laid over this mountain gulph are far beyond description. A great many

12. Happily, Muir's original journal from his first winter, spring, and summer in Yosemite has survived. An edited version is available in *John of the Mountains,* chapter 2; my references are to the original on microfilm.

13. Interestingly, despite his reverence for and love of Half Dome, Muir felt overwhelmed by and distanced from it for a long time. In late 1871, describing two smaller domes by which he camped one night, he would write: "They are not vast and over-spiritual like Yosemite Tissiack, but comprehensible and companionable and capable of human affinities" (2:973). Thus, if my focus on home is a parallel to Robert Orsi's use of the term "domus"—the unity of family and house—as the center of the moral and symbolic world of Italian Harlem, perhaps at this point Tissiack was only a half-domus for Muir.

of our winter days were full of the most tangible wide open of natural phenomena which were intensely interesting" (2:815).

With spring, however, his attention turned back to the ground and its emerging plant life, to "the Lord's gardens" and his old favorites: the deep green of the grasses, the sedges and ferns, the breckans and "forests of fronds," and the flowers "like yellow stars on a green sky" (23:221). On April 21—his birthday—he reflected in his journal upon the new intensity with which he was experiencing his surroundings.

> Part of all these beautiful days remains with me enriching my life. These atoms-sheets-oceans of beauty divine do not exist as mere pictures—maps hung upon the walls of memory to brighten at times when touched by the will or by the force of association & sink again like a landscape in the dark but they saturate themselves into every part of the body & live always. (23:219)

As we have seen, from the Wisconsin Dells through the Southern walk, the imagery of "pictures cut into memory" had long been his favorite way of conceiving the process of memory. At times, however, he had modified this informal psychological understanding in a somewhat more organic way, as when (on the Southern walk) the smell of the sea brought back memories of Scotland with unexpected power: "How imperishable are all the impressions that ever vibrate upon our life. We cannot forget anything. Memories may escape the action of will—they may die a kind of sleep, but when the right influence does but touch them lightly as a shadow they flash into full stature & life with all parts in place" (23:97). This sense of a bodily locus of memory, and by implication a more bodily interconnection between himself and his natural surroundings, was extended in the April 21 journal entry into the imagery of natural scenes "saturat[ing] themselves into every part of the body." Muir developed this language further in a letter to Carr the following summer.

> [July 29, 1870.] I have spent every Sabbath for the last two months in the spirit world, screaming among the peaks & outside meadows like a negro Methodist in revival time, & every intervening clump of week-days in trying to fix down & assimilate my shapeless harvests of revealed glory into the spirit & into the common earth of my existence, & I am rich, rich beyond measure, not in rectangular blocks of sifted knowledge or in thin sheets of beauty hung picture-like about the "walls of memory"—but in unselected atmospheres of terrestrial glory diffused evenly throughout my whole substance. (2:858–59)

Where for the teenage Muir it was the memory of the heart that had decisively shaped his experience of religiousness (as in the evangelical letter to Bradley Brown), by this point it was the memory *in the body* that carried the weight and meaning of many of his closest relationships—religious, interpersonal, and natural.[14]

In the years that followed, Muir drew upon a whole range of resources and tactics—intellectual, symbolic, emotional, behavioral, imaginative, relational—in a conscious and creative attempt to "assimilate" his natural surroundings into the deepest dimensions of his being, "into the spirit & into the common earth of [his] existence." In exploring the dynamics of this process, we can begin by looking at the ways in which Jeanne Carr's emotional presence allowed Muir to come into deeper relationship with specific places and phenomena in Yosemite. Interestingly, in the autumn of 1869 the Carrs had offered to let Muir stay with them rather than return to Yosemite. His refusal to do so—perhaps motivated by the awkwardness that he would surely have felt at living in a normal, socially constrained manner with a person with whom he had shared such intense words and feelings—clearly did not signify any lessening of his desire for her companionship; rather, he imaginatively brought her up to Yosemite with him. In particular, where he had earlier felt her presence in the placid streams and springs of Wisconsin and of the South, during his early Yosemite years he most often associated her with waterfalls.

In the summer of 1869, after they had failed to meet in Yosemite, Muir's letters to Carr questioned her closely about the waterfalls that she had visited while there, and it seems likely that he had already begun to associate her with those waterfalls. For her part, in a letter from June 30, Carr looked forward to when "in God's own time and way we are once more permitted to enjoy face to face communion," giving a specific location for such a meeting: "I have trodden these paths in your footsteps. We will talk of it all ere long. Oh the divine blessed harmonies I have *heard*, even more than I have seen in these days. . . . I have left only one word for you on the bridge between the Vernal & Nevada fall, 'The Lord bless thee & keep thee,' and this I wish always" (2:739–40). In December, Muir responded: "I read your word of pencil upon the bridge below the Ne-

---

14. The parallel images and phrases in these three passages illustrate the way in which Muir carried forward and refined ideas from journal entries into letters—and eventually into his published works. The April 21 passage would reappear in the concluding sentences of one of his first published articles, the 1872 "Yosemite Valley in Flood": "Visions like these do not remain with us as mere maps and pictures—flat shadows cast upon our minds, to brighten, at times, when touched by association or will, and fade again from our view, like landscapes in the gloaming. They saturate every fibre of our body and soul, dwelling in us and with us, like holy spirits, through all of our after-deaths and after-lives" (350). As we shall see in a number of instances below, such a process of self-borrowing and revision would characterize most of Muir's published writings. For a detailed analysis of one case—emphasizing also Muir's habit of borrowing insights and phrases from other people's writings—see Ronald H. Limbaugh's study of the writing of Muir's story "Stickeen."

vada & I thank you for it most devoutly. No one nor all of the Lord's blessings can enable me to exist without friends & I know that you are a friend indeed" (2:778). Feeling her presence as friend and as religious protector set in motion a chain of emotional associations: the brown and yellow oak and maple leaves that littered the valley floor evoked memories of Madison, and the adiantum ferns in a nearby cave reminded him of dulse on the seacoast of Scotland.[15] He then adapted a sentence from a previous letter of hers: "You speak of dying and going to woods I am dead & gone to heaven" (2:779)—thus setting up a complex emotional equation of Yosemite (as "the Lord's mountain house") with Madison, Scotland, heaven, and the presence of Carr. Within this general context, her own references to "divine harmonies" guided his specific perceptions of the falls: "I have been wandering about among the falls & rapids studying the grand instruments of shapes and curves & echoing caves upon which those divine harmonies are played" (2:778–79). Her response to this letter (in January) further intensified her association with the place: "John Muir, I wish I *could* tell you how full of God his Universe seemed when I stood on that little bridge by the Nevada fall. I never was *interfused* with the interior life of things as that day" (2:783).[16]

Over this same period, Muir's growing fascination with Yosemite's waterfalls is recorded in his journal as well, but without explicit reference to Carr. At one of the falls in mid-January, he "gazed upon the mighty torrent of snowy cometized water whether in or out of the body I cannot tell such overwhelming displays of power & exquisitely beautiful grandeur almost wrings the life out of our feeble tabernacle" (23:209). In the remarkable passage that follows, Muir placed flowers and waterfalls together at the center of his scientific attention and emotional desire. Expressing his longing for passionate contact with nature, he imagined himself as possessing the freedom to "study Nature's laws in all their crossings & unions," following magnetic streams and the rays of the aurora to "the very center of our globe." "But," he concluded, "my first journeys would be into the inner substance of flowers & among the folds & mazes of Yosemite's falls. How grand to move about in the very

15. There may have been other, more subtle ways in which the Yosemite landscape reminded him of Scotland—the lush but sparse and low vegetation, the rockiness, the semi-tundra-like feel. Of course, such associations would not have been totally consistent with the Wisconsin image/construction that I have been stressing; such internal dynamics often aren't logically consistent, but include a wide range of elements held together by their own emotional logic.

16. Interestingly, it was at another bridge by a ravine that Lamartine's lovers, Claude and Denise, first revealed their love for each other; their idyllic love—and eventual tragic separation—may have further intensified both the power and the ambiguity of the relationship between Muir and Carr.

tissue of the falling columns & in the very birthplace of their heavenly harmonies looking outward as from windows of evervarying transparency & staining. Alas how little of the world is subject to human senses!" (23:210–11). (His perception of falling water in terms of "tissue" echoes his imagery of God's "ornamental fl[owe]r tissue" of the first spring in Twenty Hill Hollow, suggesting a transfer of some of the emotional meanings of flowers to falls.) Despite his final qualification, in the spring he began to get his wish: "[April 10] Spring genial gushing balmy in all the sky & in every sound & song. Falls in glory that excelleth. Caverns & arched openings in the falling columns. Saw & heard things of unwritable grandeur at the base of upper Falls. Plant life rapidly maturing" (23:215).

On May 17, 1870, Muir wrote to Carr not of waterfalls but of the melting snow and flooding rivers of springtime: "Our valley is just gushing, throbbing full of open, absorbable beauty, & I feel that I must tell you about it. I am lonely among my enjoyments; the valley is full of visitors, but I have no-one to talk to" (2:823). By July 29 (in a letter already partly quoted above), his ability to feel her presence in and through ferns, flowers, and waterfalls had set the stage for the imaginative realization of their long-hoped-for meeting in Yosemite.

> In all my wanderings through nature's beauty, whether it be among the ferns at my cabin door or in the high meadows and peaks or amid the spray and music of waterfalls, you are the first to meet me and I often speak to you as verily present in the flesh. Last Sabbath I was baptized in the irised foam of the Vernal & in the divine snow of Nevada, and you were there also & stood in real presence by the sheet of joyous rapids beneath the bridge. (2:859)

Through an intimate history of hope and action, Muir was finally able to meet Carr in the flesh in Yosemite—rather, in the flesh and blood of Yosemite rocks and water, a setting safe and strong enough to hold and even to magnify the erotic currents flowing between the two friends in Christian love.[17]

To be sure, Muir did not associate waterfalls with Carr alone. In the

---

17. John O'Grady, stressing Muir's "passion and aesthetic response to cascades, torrents, floods, and flows of any sort," writes that in experiences such as these, "Muir was wildly and innocently making love with the world" and that "we should not restrict our interpretation to the merely sexual" (61, 58, 63). However, a detailed exploration of the complex construction of the nonsexual eros that was shared by Muir and Carr affords us a deeper model of what such lovemaking with the world is (or can be) than does O'Grady's somewhat blanket use of the terms "desire" and "the wild." O'Grady is correct in noting the ways that this pattern of experience was heightened by relationships with various women (including Emily Pelton), not only Carr; I focus on the latter relationship not to argue for its exclusive importance but as one way to pinpoint the specific processes by which such patterns of experience came into being.

same letter, he referred to a night spent at upper Yosemite Falls with two male friends, and yet another more recently: "I passed, no I *lived* another night there two weeks ago—entering as far within the veil amid equal glory, together with Mr. Frank Sharpleigh of Boston." (These seem to have been his first instances of "entering into," or behind, the falls.) It was with Carr, however, that he incorporated such experiences into the most extensive and powerful set of images, associations, and meanings.

As always, their shared emotional world included a strong religious dimension; in particular, this passion for waterfalls fit well with the imagery of baptism, which by this time Muir was using to express his most profound experiences of his natural surroundings. (Given his Disciples background, baptism would have carried much more theological weight and personal resonance than conversion, at this time of his life; see chapter 2, esp. note 1.) Interestingly, Muir's use of the term as a metaphor for an intense experience of nature had begun just the previous year, when in the spring of 1869 he wrote of a "cloud waterfall" (thunderstorm) giving a "flower baptism" (23:186). Later that spring, he had written to Carr about her hoped-for "Yo Semite baptism"; in a half-mocking, half-serious letter to David of April 1870 (2:806), he denounced conservative religionists (such as their father) by describing his own three recent baptisms in Yosemite, first in sunshine (which he compared to immersion), next in the beauty of flowers (pouring), finally in the spray of Yosemite Falls (sprinkling). Muir's most intense and memorable baptisms, however, such as the one reported in the July 29 letter, were in waterfalls and in the presence of Carr. Moreover, alongside of and expanding the theological meanings of baptism was the actual physical experience of Muir's encounters with Yosemite rivers and lakes, as the clear and rushing waters caressed and pounded his whole body with an invigorating embrace; especially given the dirt and sweat of his work and the continued lack of human touch, Muir's immersions must have helped him to feel his body anew, to live in his body a new way, perhaps to rise from the waters a new man. Thus, these waterfall baptisms replaced botanizing as the central activity and image that constituted his religious practice—his practice of Christian love as a nonsexual construction of eros—by evoking, solidifying, and valorizing the emotional bonds that united him with Carr, with the divine, with his own body, and with particular places in Yosemite.

Despite the sense of repetition and even ritualization surrounding his waterfall experiences, Muir's first two years in Yosemite saw no lessening of the intensity with which he felt them. Indeed, this repetition added to the richness of the experience by providing deeper layers of associations and of interpretive and emotional frameworks (which is just the goal of ritualization at its best). Thus, the next spring, on April 3, 1871, he wrote an even more evocative waterfall letter to Carr (see 2:906–10).

O Mrs. Carr that you could be here to mingle in this nightnoon glory. I
am in the Upper YoSem falls & can hardly calm to write but from my first
baptism hours ago you have been so present that I must try to fix you a
written thought. In the afternoon I came up the mountain here with a
blanket & a piece of bread to spend the night in prayer among the spirits
of this fall. But now what can [I] say more than wish again that you might
expose your soul to the rays of this heaven.

As he went on to describe the music of the falls and to comment on the
"magnificent double prismatic bow" standing bridgelike at its base, Muir
implicitly reconstructed this scene in terms of his and Carr's shared Nevada bridge experience. Further, he crawled out into the falls along a narrow seam in a way that replicated his Yosemite Falls adventures of past
years; this time, however, he was almost washed off the ledge when a shift
in the winds brought the full force of the plunging water down upon him.
On the one hand, the sheer physicality of his predicament made him more
aware of his own body than before: "I suppose I was in a trance but I can
positively say I was in the body for it is sorely battered & wetted." On the
other hand, despite—or perhaps because of—the danger, his attention
and emotions were primarily turned toward the falls and the scene itself:
"And every atom of the magnificent being from the thin silvery crest that
does not dim the stars to the inner arrowy hardened shafts that strike
onward like thunderbolts in sound & energy, all is life & spirit, every
bolt & spray feels the hand of God. O the music that is blessing me
now[!]" [18]

The heightened—even ecstatic—emotional and physical feelings of the
experience moved Muir to develop further his 1870 language of natural
scenes "saturat[ing] themselves into every part of the body," as he created
a new language—at once scientific, religious, and emotional—for describing his intimate connections with the natural world.

How little do we know of ourselves[,] of our profoundest attractions & repulsions[,] of our spiritual affinities[.] How interesting does man become
considered in his relations to the spirit of this rock & water[.] How significant does every atom of our world become amid the influence of those
beings unseen, spiritual, angelic mountaineers that so throng these pure
mansions of crystal foam & purple granite. (2:909–10)

Beneath and within his serious yet playful sensitivity to light, color, texture, and unseen energies lay a creative vision of the deepest workings of

18. Muir would rework this part of the letter repeatedly in succeeding years, and a
number of versions can be found throughout his journals and notebooks. It would appear
in various places in his published writings, including one of his first overtly political essays,
"The Treasures of the Yosemite," written in 1890 as part of the campaign to make Yosemite
into a national park.

nature. As we have seen, since the Southern walk Muir had used chemical and electrical concepts such as attraction, repulsion, affinities, and magnetic currents to describe human relationships with the natural world (often, in the South, as a way to emphasize his own *separation from* living beings such as alligators). In this letter to Carr, Muir's language in effect constituted his own environmental psychology based in chemical language and concepts, which he used to stress his sense of physical, emotional, and spiritual *connection with* natural beings; thus, for Muir, chemistry provided a metaphorical rather than a scientific basis for the development of ecological and relational modes of thought. Interestingly, some of his later Yosemite journals would be kept on the back pages of his old university notebooks on "physics and natural philosophy," suggesting that he carried the intellectual legacy of his study of chemistry with him into the mountains in a physical as well as in a symbolic manner.

Moreover, the term "affinity" had taken on a technical meaning in the popular religious discourse of the day, mainly in association with spiritualism. Muir was clearly aware of and intrigued by spiritualism and other currents of thought, from his references to spirit rapping and phrenology in *The Story of My Boyhood and Youth* to his skepticism at a spiritualist seance in San Francisco in 1873 (see L. M. Wolfe, 172–73).[19] Despite his rationalistic rejection of spiritualist thought as such, the metaphor of "spiritual affinities" gave him a new way to understand his relationships to all of the "unseen beings"—from *Calypso borealis* to cassiope to "the spirit of this rock and water"—that he encountered in nature, thus bringing the natural world into a language that was usually reserved for discussion of human (or human-divine) relationships.

Finally, given Carr's strong imagined presence in the scene, the passage implicitly expresses the emotions of Muir's relationship with her as well as those of his relationship with the waterfall itself. Interestingly, Muir's description again may have been shaped by his and Carr's shared reading of *The Stone-Mason of Saint Point*. Muir: "I cannot refrain from speaking to this little bush at my side & to the spray drops that come to my paper & to the individual sands of the slopelet I am sitting upon" (2:909); Lamartine: "Is there not between her [the earth] and us a true relationship

19. To be sure, there is only one concrete reference to spiritualism or related popular religious thought during these early years in Yosemite (see 2:881, quoted below, where he writes of "souls . . . allowed to go rapping & visiting where they please"); the revised journal of the "first summer" contains a reference to "the new fangled doctrine of the elective affinity of souls" (31:486), but there is of course no telling when between 1869 and 1887 this passage was written. Given his lifelong interest in such issues, however, he surely associated the term with these religious meanings as well as with scientific ones, especially in the context of passages such as this.

of body, so that when we take up a handful of sand, or a clod of earth from the hillocks which have borne our weight, we can say to this grain of sand, 'Thou art my brother;' and to that clod of earth, 'Thou art my mother or my sister'?" (49). Moreover, Lamartine himself applied the language of attraction and repulsion to human relationships: "Some [persons] attract us like the magnet, others repel us like the serpent, without our knowing why. But nature, she knows it; we ought to listen to these repulsions and attractions, as sensations and warnings of the instincts of the soul" (52). If, in listening to the divine music of the waterfall, Muir heard more clearly the natural instincts of his soul, he may have felt his attraction to Carr more powerfully than ever before. (In a letter of October of the next year, Muir would more clearly—though also more ambiguously—use chemical language to express his feelings toward Carr: "my attractions & repulsions are badly balanced tonight & I will not try to say any more" [2:1191].)[20]

In such metaphors, Muir's experience of human relationship was at points indistinguishable from that of relationship with nature. Indeed, chemical language and imagery tied together all of his modes of understanding the world—geological, botanical, religious, medical, psycholog-

20. Of course, the use of metaphors from the physical sciences to express the workings of psychological phenomena was (and is) a common occurrence; perhaps most famous is Freud's understanding of psychic drive-energy according to an electrochemical neurophysiological model. Thus, Muir's language constitutes an informal or vernacular version of the same sort of thing that was going on at more formal scientific levels. Indeed, Muir and Lamartine were by no means alone in the specific metaphors that they chose; as a random example, the Unitarian minister Newton M. Mann published in 1867 a pair of articles— "Attraction" and "Repulsion"—that discerned parallels to these and other physical forces acting in the human world: "There is a wonderful likeness between the law which, representing the divine Activity, brought together at first diffuse, chaotic atoms, and formed the vast globes, and now maintains their accustomed motions, and the law of life which draws mankind into families, communities, and states, and preserves the orderly courses by which they acquire growth and power." After discussing cohesion and affinity as social energies, Mann considers magnetism: "That power which holds two magnets together, fast as though they were one, acts again with surprising similitude in the lover's clasp, and is observable always in some degree in the influence of personal presence, in the fascination of pleasant converse, in the force of impassioned eloquence" (469). Like Muir, Mann's vernacular psychology used chemical metaphor to express both patterns of observed human action and religious/ moral values and ideals.

Interestingly, Muir's metaphors turn out to have been more subtle than Freud's, or at least more open to creative revision: one of the mid-twentieth-century founders of the object relations approach, W. R. D. Fairbairn, would replace the Freudian idea of "energy" with that of "fields of force which could merge or repel each other according to their compatability" (J. D. Sutherland, 109)—imagery strikingly close to that of Muir. Moreover, Muir also presages my own expansion of object relations thought to include relationships with natural and with supernatural as well as with human beings.

ical, social—into a unified realm of body, energy, and relationship. Thus, in this passage, scientific, religious, and literary language combined to image his connection to a specific place in the presence of Jeanne Carr *and* to evoke his connection with her through his experience of that place.

At the same time, the intensity and intimacy of this ritualized relationship—with the waterfall and with Carr—were motivated in part by Muir's desire to overcome some very real distances and differences that had arisen between him and Carr over the preceding two years. That is, the feelings and visions expressed in his letters may have been created in an attempt to fill up some painful gaps that were appearing in his own inner experience of their relationship. The most obvious such gap was their continued failure to actually meet, in the Sierra or anywhere else; a summer 1870 trip by Carr to Yosemite was again unexpectedly cut off by business back home, and Muir refused to "come down" from the mountains any farther than the foothills in the autumn and winter seasons. Given that they had not been together in person since the summer of 1867, it surely required more and more emotional and imaginative energy for Muir to feel her presence in particular instances (and to create such instances in letters). Moreover, there is much evidence that, in important ways, Muir was beginning to move away from the scientific and emotional world that he had long shared with Carr.

In October 1870, she excitedly wrote to him to suggest that he join a colonizing expedition to the Amazon. Initially, he seems to have taken the proposal quite seriously, saying that "[i]t must be that I am going soon for you have shown me the way. . . . You are a prophet in the concern of my little outside life, & pray what says the Spirit about my final escape from Yosemite[?]" (2:879). In December, however, after first claiming that it was only practical matters that delayed his immediate departure for South America, he displayed a deeper emotional reluctance: "Why do you wish to cut me from California & graft me among the groves of the Purus[?] . . . This Pacific sunshine is hard to leave. If souls are allowed to go rapping & visiting where they please I think that unembodied I will be found wallowing in California light" (2:881). By the spring of 1871, refusing either to leave for the Amazon or to visit Carr in Oakland, Muir more strongly resisted her will for his life—and even deposed her from her long-standing role as his "prophet": "'The Spirit' has again led me into the wilderness, in opposition to all counter attractions and I am once more in the glory of YoSemite. . . . I am very happy here and cannot break for the Andes just yet" (2:898–900). After such a forceful stance in "opposition" to her "counter attractions," a few weeks later Muir attempted in the moonlight waterfall letter to Carr to reestablish the emotional relationship with her that was being threatened by his own actions—with the effect of adding to the intimacy and intensity of the more immediate relationship that remained available to him, that with the waterfall itself. Moreover, the tension and ambiguity that were emerging between them both shaped and was shaped by a strengthening of Muir's relationships with men. Strikingly, many of his new companions were introduced to him by Carr herself, and in fact his male relationships—and his own changing male identity—were often grounded in the same patterns of imagery and emotion that he had long shared with her. One of the first of these friendships was with J. B. McChesney, superintendent of the Oakland public schools, who during his visit in 1870 was a favorite companion of Muir's on trips to Yosemite Falls. Muir's later letters to McChesney sometimes sounded like those to Carr: "You belong to all of my moonlight wanderings at the upper falls. I have been there many times by night and day since seeing you, and you always are present as one who is susceptible of the spiritual influences that so gloriously abound there" (2:935). Other important male friends would include another educator, John Swett, and the artist William Keith.[21]

Perhaps the best expression of Muir's own newly strengthened male identity comes in one of his most remarkable letters ever, written in sequoia sap to Jeanne Carr in the autumn of 1870 and headed "Squirrelville, Sequoia Co., Nut time." Describing sequoias as "columns of sunshine, tangible, accessible, terrestrialized," Muir imaged them as earthly incarnations of the heavenly Father, and extended the Christian symbolism by naming them "the King in his glory." Thus, he established a personal relationship with sequoias as overtly male divinities, placing them in the role of Jesus from his evangelical letter to Bradley Brown—a role that also had been occupied, in a more feminine form, by *Calypso borealis* and other flowers. In writing of sequoia, his language was more en-

21. Despite the presence of a shared erotic aspect in Muir's and his male companions' experiences of the natural world, I find no evidence for a "homosexual" dimension of his relationships with men. At the same time, it may be unnecessary or inappropriate to define the erotic aspects in his relationships with women as constituting a clear "heterosexual" identity, either. In general, the question of Muir's sexual orientation—as formulated in such a way as to be applicable in the nineteenth century—would require a more detailed analysis than I can give here, incorporating evidence from his later life (especially his marriage and male friendships). Such a project, although potentially important, would not disrupt the general outline of my analysis of the erotic dimensions of his relationships with the natural world.

I also can find no evidence for autoerotic experiences such as those described by Whitman: "You sea! . . . / We must have a turn together . . . / Dash me with amorous wet, I can repay you" ("Song of Myself," section 22). The "Lord Sequoia" letter, discussed next, seems the most likely candidate, but is hardly conclusive. In general, Muir's erotic life was not often expressed through explicitly sexual desires or activity.

thusiastic and energetic than ever: "I'm in the woods woods woods, &
they are in *me-ee-ee*. The King tree & me have sworn eternal love—sworn
it without swearing & I've taken the sacrament with Douglass Squirrel
drank Sequoia wine, Sequoia blood, & with its rosy purple drops I am
writing this woody gospel letter" (2:883–84). This language of being "in"
the woods, and feeling the woods "in" him, foreshadows the passage in
*My First Summer in the Sierra* in which he asserts his "conversion experience": "We are now in the mountains and they are in us" (20; the full
passage is quoted in the introduction, above). Strikingly, however, it is
with respect to the sequoia, *not* to the mountains, that Muir first uses this
language, indicating again that the process by which he came to such an
(imagined) relationship with the mountains was more complex and gradual than has usually been thought. At this point in his life, the sequoia
were the largest beings with whom he had established so personal and
personalized a relationship; significantly, this new relationship was one
that allowed a new self to emerge, as the towering woody columns drew
something out of Muir that mosses and flowers had not.

Saying that he has "left all for Sequoia," Muir termed this a "manly
treely sacrifice" before placing himself in his own New Testament role: "I
wish I was so drunk & Sequoical that I could preach the green brown
woods to all the juiceless world, descending from this divine wilderness
like a John Baptist eating Douglass Squirrels & wild honey or wild anything, crying, Repent for the Kingdom of Sequoia is at hand." This biblical "wilderness" represents one of his first extended usages of the term,
so important in his later writings and self-image; strikingly, in none of his
passionate letters to Carr does he refer to waterfalls (or to himself) as
"wild." Rather, wildness seems here to emerge in symbolic relationship
with a male being: "I wish I were wilder & so bless Sequoia I will be"
(2:884). Similarly, instead of his usual flowery companions, Muir was
most delighted with "Squirrel Douglass, the master spirit of the tree
tops," who is "charged with magnetism" and whom Muir imagines himself eating "for the lightening he holds."[22] Indeed, the letter closes with
Muir and squirrel in a most intimate relationship: "The sun is set & the
star candles are being lighted to show me & Douglass Squirrel to bed

22. The passage parallels that in *Walden* where Thoreau, seeing a woodchuck at night,
"felt a strange thrill of savage delight, and was strongly tempted to seize and devour him
. . . for that wildness which he represented" (140). (It is uncertain whether Muir had read
*Walden* by this point.) A century after Muir, Edward Abbey (at the beginning of his *Desert
Solitaire*) actually kills a rabbit—without eating it—as an "experiment" (37). Such images
and actions seem to serve—for men, at least—as a means of creating a new, "wilder" persona in relationship with the natural environment, or a new interpretation of that environment as "wilderness."

therefore my Carr good night" (2:885). Strikingly, Muir does not invite Carr into this bedroom, but leaves her "a thousand fathoms deep in dark political quagg" (a reference to the circumstances that caused her to cancel a planned trip to Yosemite the summer before). Nowhere in the letter does he repeat his usual refrain of asking her to come for a visit. Rather, he seems quite happy without her, and with his new companions: "You say, When are you coming *down*? Ask the Lord—Lord Sequoia."[23]

The next spring, after Muir had again refused to "come down" at Carr's request, another of her acquaintances came up to Yosemite— Ralph Waldo Emerson. According to his own later reminiscence, during the visit Muir told Emerson, "You are yourself a Sequoia. Stop and get acquainted with your big brethren" (*Our National Parks,* 135), and Muir would elsewhere describe Emerson as "the most serene, majestic, sequoia-like soul I ever met" (*John of the Mountains,* 436). The parallel between Emerson and "Lord Sequoia" suggests the reverence—and also the energetic intimacy—that marked his encounter with the older man. Interestingly, however, I have found no evidence that Muir had read any of Emerson's writings before Carr sent him a copy of "The Song of Nature" while he was in Twenty Hill Hollow in 1869; his response to that poem was approving but fairly subdued. Of course, he knew of Emerson as a cultural figure and a hero to many, including the Carrs, James Butler, and others; thus, his initial orientation toward Emerson was not as a thinker but as a role model and inspiration.

Their meeting in May 1871 is usually discussed in terms of their contrasting life trajectories—Emerson at the end of his creative life, Muir at the beginning; the older man protected by his entourage from the cold night air, the younger man warmed by energy and enthusiasm. However, from the perspective of Muir's psychological development what is most striking is the way in which he strove to *identify with* Emerson, denying— or even reversing—their obvious differences. After overcoming his shyness enough to give the celebrity a letter asking for an interview, Muir acted in a possessive, almost controlling manner, aggressively telling the Sage of Concord how he should best experience Yosemite. Although Muir surely looked up to Emerson as a father figure, that very relationship seems to have brought out Muir's own fatherlike persona. At the same

23. The reference to "political quagg" and his vehement refusal to "come down" mark another step in his construction of a negative image of "civilization"—particularly in the context of his developing concern for "wilderness" as its opposite. More commonly in these early Yosemite journals and letters, the worst aspects of civilization are represented by his opinions of tourists. Indeed, he often refers to tourists in much the same way that he described the sheep he herded during his first winter in the Central Valley, which (as we have seen) he condemned as exhibiting the "degrading influence" of civilization.

time, he tried to forge (one might say force) a sense of identity through the opposite approach: as John McAleer notes, Muir "seemed to think he could invest Emerson with his own boyishness" (602), and in later letters he would try to "infus[e] Emerson with his own zest and strength" (606).

Despite Muir's insistence and cajoling, he and Emerson did not camp out together under the sequoia. What they *did* do together in Yosemite, however, was not without its own powerful and complex set of meanings. For most of the final two days of his visit, Emerson climbed up into Muir's little shack by the waterfall, where the two of them pored over his collection of botanical specimens, rock samples, and drawings while they talked of nature, religion, and Yosemite. In his own domestic space, Muir's ambitions and desires for emotional contact, for male relationship, and for a model for public identity were brought inside the familiar patterns of action and meaning that had once made him long so deeply to be with Carr in her botanical conservatory. In fact, Muir tried to give his best specimens to Emerson, striving to make human contact with him in the deepest way he knew.[24] At the same time, Muir's energy and enthusiasm could not be wholly contained within such patterns, and in fact it was he who did most of the talking, expounding his knowledge of the natural world with the great man almost literally at his feet. When Emerson was about to leave the valley, Muir's desire for companionship expanded to include all of Yosemite: "And now once more in the name of Mts. Dana & Gibb, of the grand glacial hieroglyphics of Tuolumne Meadow & Bloody Cañon . . . In the name of a hundred cascades that barbarous visitors never see . . . & in the name of all the spirit creatures of these rocks & of this whole spiritual atmosphere Do not leave us now" (2:925). Later, Muir went alone to camp out by the fire on ferns and sequoia branches. Thus, as in the case of the moonlight waterfall letter to Carr, Muir's powerful but ambivalent encounter with Emerson was ultimately deflected into a deeper sense of relationship with the natural world.

At the same time as he was striving for richer interactions with men, Muir also was becoming increasingly interested in a more male-associated branch of science, geology—which again had implications both for his

---

24. After Emerson had returned to Massachusetts, Muir would send him numerous specimens, some of which found their way to the eminent Harvard botanist Asa Gray. Muir would come to establish his own botanical relationship with Gray, and indeed Gray—along with America's other premier botanist, John Torrey—would come to Yosemite for a week-long botanical expedition in 1872. Muir must have been impressed by the warm friendship between the older men, as he later recalled sitting around the campfire with them: "They told the stories of their lives, Torrey fondly telling all about Gray, Gray about Torrey" (Wilkins, 87).

relationship with Carr and for his patterns of engaging the natural world. Indeed, although he probably had a whole range of reasons for not wanting to follow her suggestion of a botanizing expedition to South America (possibly including his memories of illness and isolation in Florida), a significant aspect of his decision was his desire to continue his investigations of Yosemite glaciers. Muir's first reference to glaciers was in the July 29, 1870 letter to Carr: "I have been tracing glaciers in all the principal cañons towards the summit" (2:858). (Although there obviously must have been some extended process of observation and meditation leading up to his interest, I have found no indication of it either in his correspondence or in his original journals.) Interestingly, this first reference to glaciers was pointedly directed not toward Jeanne but towards "the Doctor"—unlike flowers and birds, rocks and glaciers were phenomena most naturally appearing in relationships between men, and in particular (for Muir) with representatives of the official scientific community.

Soon, however, it was not to Ezra Carr that Muir turned for a geological companion, but to Joseph LeConte. LeConte, a professor at the University of California and a friend of the Carrs, journeyed to Yosemite in the summer of 1870 with a team of students to study glaciers, but his expansive intellectual and spiritual vision encompassed much else as well; upon first seeing Vernal Fall, for example, he wrote in his journal:

> Oh, the glory of the view!—the emerald green and snowy white of the falling water; the dizzying leap into the yawning chasm; the roar and foam and spray of the deadly struggle with rocks below; the deep green of the somber pines, and the exquisitely fresh and lively green of grass, ferns, and moss, wet with eternal spray; the perpendicular rocky walls, rising far above us toward the blue arching sky. As I stood there, gazing down into the dark and roaring chasm, and up into the clear sky, my heart swelled with gratitude to the Great author of all beauty and grandeur. (52–53)

With such an aesthetic and religious sensibility, it is not surprising that when LeConte met Muir during the course of the expedition (again at the instigation of Jeanne Carr), the two struck up a close friendship. According to LeConte's journal (67–68), by August 7 the two had discussed Yosemite geology and glaciation extensively, again indicating the speed with which Muir had mastered the details of his new passion.

Of course, this shared scientific interest swam in an ocean of other personal associations and cultural references that united the two men. For example, in an August 20, 1870 letter to Jeanne Carr, Muir described one experience with his new acquaintance: "After moonrise LeConte & I walked to the lakeshore & climbed upon a big sofa-shaped rock that stood islet-like a little way out in the shallow water & here we found another beauteous throne of earthly grace & I doubt if John of Patmos saw grander visions than we & you were remembered there & we cordially wished you with us" (2:863–64). Instead of his usual "bedrooms" with Carr, Muir preferred to construct a "living room" with LeConte. A string of detailed geological letters between the two suggest the importance to Muir's intellectual development of his first real scientific mentor in years, as well as the personal respect and admiration he felt toward the older man: "I remember the week passed in your company with a great deal of solid earnest pleasure & will be exceedingly happy to accompany you again in rambles to any portion of our glorious star" (2:873). Interestingly, however, when Muir discovered his own living glacier in July 1871, he first wrote of it not to Ezra Carr or LeConte but to Emerson, using language that he had learned from Jeanne Carr: "The dear Mother has told me one magnificent truth since you were here" (2:942).

By the autumn of 1871, Muir was totally committed to and engaged by his glacial work: "The grandeur of these forces & their glorious results overpower me and inhabit my whole being, waking or sleeping I have no rest. In dreams I read blurred sheets of glacial writing or follow lines of cleavage or struggle with the difficulties of some extraordinary rock form" (2:958). Strikingly, Muir's language strongly echoes Carr's earlier comments on Charles Goodyear, who "was haunted with inventions" that "tortured him, sleeping or waking, until he worked them into visible forms" (1:384), by which she tried to persuade Muir to further develop his inventing skill during his years in Canada (see chapter 3). According to Linnie Marsh Wolfe (96), Muir somewhere described his own work in the Trout Hollow factory in exactly these words; whether he did so in a contemporaneous account or a later autobiographical reflection, this shows how deeply Carr's words had sunk into his consciousness. The re-emergence of this language with respect to his geological work suggests that he had finally found a mode of activity that could engage his mental, physical, and creative faculties—and his newly strengthened male identity—as fully as had inventing.[25]

Thus, in his defiance of Carr's wishes, it was no longer inventing that Muir had to reject but botanical exploration conceived along lines that both of them had long idealized. In a fascinating exchange of letters during the winter of 1871–72, Muir and Carr consciously admitted and tried

25. For fuller accounts of the character, development, and results of Muir's glacial studies, see Turner (193–201) and Cohen (chapters 2 ["The Glacial Eye"] and 4 ["The Way of Geology"]). Cohen's descriptions of Muir's rather unscientific "method," including its imaginative and bodily aspects, are especially good. Additionally, see Cohen (104–11) and Roberts on Muir's metaphor of "glacial manuscript" as his method of "reading the Book of Nature."

to come to terms with their growing differences. Responding on January 8 to some negative comments of hers on glaciers, Muir's mocking and cajoling tone overlay a real sense of hurt and confusion.

> I am astonished to hear you speak so unbelievingly of God's glorious crys-
> tal glaciers. "They are only pests," & you think them wrong in tempera-
> ture, & they lived in "horrible times" & you don't care to hear about
> them "only that they made instruments of Yosemite music." You speak
> heresy for once, & deserve a dip in Methodist Tophet, or Vesuvius at
> least. . . . I have just been sending ice to LeConte, & snow to McChes-
> ney, & I have nothing left but hailstones for you. . . . You confuse me.
> You have taught me here & encouraged me to read the mountains. Now
> you will not listen. Next summer you will be converted—*you will be iced.*
> (2:1008)

Interestingly, this passage contains one of Muir's first uses of conversion language—used to express his intense desire for a change in *someone else's* orientation toward nature, not his own. Feeling deeply the gap that had emerged between him and Carr because of his changing environmental preferences, he wanted the gap closed through a sudden transformation—on *her* part.

Accordingly, in the astonishing passage that follows, Muir attempted to restore the emotions and associations of their relationship by describing glaciers in terms of their familiar shared patterns of imaging the natural world. As we have seen, he had long referred to snowflakes as flowers; more recently, he had extended the equation with the image of glaciers as born of numberless compacted snowflakes. Further, in following the ancient flow of glaciers over rock he had found it useful to envision them as waterfalls and rivers. Developing these notions dramatically, he gave Carr an imaginative interpretation of glaciers that incorporated much of the emotional, domestic, and religious imagery that had shaped and energized their previous shared experience of flowers, fields, woods, and waterfalls.

> You like the music instruments that glaciers made, but no songs were so
> grand as those of the glaciers themselves, no falls so lofty as those wh[ich]
> poured from brows, & chasmed mountains of pure dark ice. Glaciers
> *made* the mountains & ground corn for all the flowers, & the forests of
> silver fir, made smooth paths for human feet until the sacred Sierra have
> become the most approachable of mountains. Glaciers came down from
> heaven, & they are angels with folded wings, white wings of snowy
> bloom. . . . The busy snowflakes saw all the coming flowers, & the grand
> predestined forests. They said, "We will crack this rock for Cassiope
> where she may sway her tiny urns. Here we'll smooth a plat for green
> mosses, & round a bank for bryanthus bells.["] Thus labored the willing

flake souls linked in close congregations of ice, breaking rock food for the pines, as a bird crumbles bread for her young. & when food was gathered for the forests & all their elected life, when every rock form was finished, every monument raised, the willing messengers unwearied unwasted heard God's ["]Well done["] from heaven calling them back to their homes in the sky. (2:1009–10)[26]

Like *Calypso borealis* earlier, snowflakes and glaciers here are personified as divine messengers; moreover, in their actions of feeding and arranging plants they have taken over the roles of "mother nature" and of the divine landscape gardener, creating domesticated space and peopling it with other natural beings as well as with humans.

In her response, dated February 4, Carr began by describing the early spring beauty of ferns, flowers, mosses, and trees, and then acknowledged her differences with Muir in a tone both of resignation and of regret.

> I am so possessed at times with the memory of [the plants'] life. . . . If you had written me your glory, glacial letter then, dear John, I couldn't have answered it—no more can I in this intermediate state, but I should have liked to feel your footstep! It is beautiful, though, that we can understand each other—while in such singular apartness, you dwelling in the house of forces, becoming *elemental* yourself through sympathy, and I living only among such forms of these as are charged with personality. . . . My spirit was converted by your lovely sermon, but my flesh isn't, and when your track is from lands of snow to lands of sun, only then shall I be able to follow you. (2:1040)

Her measured response set the tone for much of their subsequent relationship. Disappointed though Muir perhaps was at not "converting" Carr, her philosophic but firm acceptance of their differences had the effect of freeing him to pursue more fully his own interests without having to make a final choice between glaciers and her. At the same time, the division of their loves had a huge impact on the emotional character of their relationship, and henceforth much of the erotic, throbbing energy of their previous letters would fade. (To be sure, there are some significant exceptions to this, such as the 1873 letter published as "A Geologist's Winter Walk," which O'Grady characterizes as the "most fluid" of all of Muir's "parables of desire" [67].) However, this lessening of eros did not imply a lessening of the importance of their friendship, but rather its transformation: Carr would remain an important mentor and friend, and in particu-

---

26. This letter would provide the basis for a passage from Muir's first published book, *The Mountains of California* (1894); see 16–18. In a move characteristic of his later writing, however, all reference to God would be deleted, the snowflakes being referred to instead as "Nature's agents."

lar her encouragement and advice would be crucial in convincing Muir to publish his glacial theories and thus to step upon the public stage as scientist and writer. Indeed, in July 1872 he would write to her, "I need a talk with you more than ever before" (2:1133)—not to share the secrets of nature but to discuss his writing. In August, he expressed their continuing, if muted, emotional bond: "I am learning to live close to the lives of my friends without seeing them. No miles of any measurement can separate your soul from mine" (2:1143).

Moreover, these letters reveal that Muir's movement away from botany and Carr and toward glaciers and male associations did not mean that he had rejected the emotions and imagery of his important shared experiences of nature with women and children. Rather, his domestic interpretation of glaciers was the beginning of an attempt to integrate many of these familiar themes into his new environment and activities—and thus to express the meaning and power of his new experiences in terms of the imaginative world that was still closest to his heart. Increasingly, this integration was centered not in an imagined relationship with another person—his water-filled romance with Carr was the greatest of those—but rather in a complex and highly charged image of the natural world as home.

After the dramatic—even traumatic—experiences of Muir's childhood and teenage years, the intermingling of nature and home had been a central imaginative and psychological dynamic in his life, coming into fullest flower with his 1867 homecoming to Fountain Lake—which, as we have seen, was saturated by the emotions of his relationship with Carr as well as with a whole range of other meanings and associations. Although his continued quest for a home in nature was frustrated during the Southern walk, the image reappeared—transformed—during his months herding sheep in the Central Valley and on up into the Sierra. Almost from the beginning, he referred to Yosemite as a house or mansion, and he carried this language forward into his glacial investigations, as suggested by a sentence interspersed among the drawings and precise measurements of an 1872 geological notebook: "That these domes were united by removed rocks is as palpable a truth as that the ruins of a house walls were not made as ruins" (23:263). As he became more familiar with the particular environment of Yosemite—and as he developed deeper and more intense emotional bonds with it, in part through the imagined presence of Carr—the metaphor of home took on much more emotional and religious weight, as an encapsulation of the whole range of his images of and relationships with the natural world. Even in the most remote and desolate places, Muir searched out—or, as in the glacial letter to Carr, imagined—flower friends such as cassiope living in domestic harmony, cared for and nurtured by the divine forces of nature; and Muir felt such places and forces as caring for and nurturing him as well. If the angelic glacier snow-flakes had returned to their homes in the sky, Muir found his own home in the Yosemite landscape that they had created on earth.[27]

In accord with the gradual, overlapping development that I have discerned throughout his life, Muir did not come to this sense of home through any single experience or event but rather as the culmination of a lifetime of relationships, gifts, cultural resources, social structures, and personal creativity. As only one of many possible incidents that illustrate where this process took him, consider a letter from September 19, 1871, to Clinton Merriam, director of the Smithsonian Institution.[28] After having been "stunned and dazed" by yet another of Carr's failures to come to Yosemite, Muir set out at the end of the summer on his longest excursion yet, to work on his glacial theories with an eye toward writing an article or book. One of a series of letters to Merriam opens with the following passage.

> Last evening I camped in a glacier meadow at the head of the Cascades' Eastmost tributary. The meadow was velvet with grass and compassed with a wall of Williamson spruce. I made a great fire and the daisies of the green sod rayed as if conscious of a sun. As I lay on my back in the silence, feeling the presence of the trees gleaming bright against the outer dark, all gushing with life and circling closer and closer about me, and saw the small round sky coming down with its stars and doming the 'lumined trees, I said, Never was mountain mansion more beautiful, more spiritual. Never was mortal wanderer more blessedly homed. The sun rose and my forest walls were removed—the charmed trees returned to the common fund of the woods, and my sky flake fused back into the fathomless blue, and I was left upon common ground to pursue my daily glacial labor. (2:968)

27. Muir's application of domestic imagery to remote areas reversed Ruskin's emphasis on terror and awe as the "sublime" response to wilderness; as Michael Smith states, "Muir . . . played the trickster with Ruskin's categories by extending the feminine qualities of the meadows and groves to the highest, most rugged Sierra summits" (96). Cronon has proposed the term "domesticated sublime" (75) for Muir's ecstatic yet gentle response.

28. Interestingly, in his first letter to Merriam (2:955) Muir had offered to work for the Smithsonian not as a geologist but as a botanical specimen gatherer, in California or wherever he would be useful—including South America. Thus, even at a point when his overriding interest in geology and glaciology had been expressed in letters to friends such as LeConte and Carr, in seeking to establish a formal scientific position he fell back to his earlier identity as botanist and potential Humboldt. Moreover, even a position such as this probably would not have constituted an actual "career" as botanist: as Keeney notes, the Smithsonian regularly used amateurs as specimen gatherers, supporting them with equipment and some funding but often not according them real professional status. As it turned out, Muir would be engaged in glacial work for only a few years before undertaking one of the projects mentioned to Merriam, a study of Sierra forests.

Clearly, this passage is a more polished narrative than most of the writing we have yet considered; thus, it reflects a point at which the self-conscious creation of a literary style was becoming more important to Muir.[29] At the same time, the passage provides a window onto the ways in which he constructed his lived experience of the natural world, out of elements of style and intellect as well as more personal wells of feeling, image, and association.

The passage begins and ends with glaciers, both as the power that created the meadow and as the object and purpose of Muir's presence in it. Fittingly, the description initially suggests a remote and potentially barren location, at the very head of the easternmost (and therefore the highest) tributary, as far from "civilization" as one can get. The scene itself, however, is happily composed of Muir's old favorites—"velvet" grass, a stream leading to a cascade, daisies brought to life by a metaphorical sun—as well as trees "gushing" with their own life, reminiscent of his more recent waterfall and sequoia letters. Muir is in familiar, even familial company here. (A drawing from around this time, although probably representing a different location—and clearly touched up for later publication—suggests Muir's habitual attraction to walled, watered, and welcoming meadows such as this one; see figure 7.) The glacier meadow with its "circling" trees is mirrored by the "small round sky"; thus imaged, earth and sky carry strong mythic overtones, as the firmaments above and below. Within this configuration, Muir himself is initially active in building the fire, but soon comes to occupy a passive position, lying on his back; the movement of the narrative comes from the natural beings themselves, as the daisies "ray," the trees gush and encircle him, and the sky approaches and "domes" the "walls" of the trees. Indeed, the erotic flow within the scene is not so much a straight line between Muir and any particular natural being as a circular current encompassing them all, not so much a waterfall as a whirlpool in which Muir and companions luxuriate; both his passive, receptive position and this circular energy suggest an erotic stance that is less aggressive and stereotypically male than ever before—without being any less throbbing, liquid, or "gushing" than (for example) his moonlight waterfall letter to Carr.

The passage places this passionate companionship with daisies, trees, and meadow at the heart of the process of homemaking with the natural world. Significantly, despite the fact that the meadow is literally Muir's

29. Indeed, the passage is included (with little revision) in his first published article, "Yosemite Glaciers" (December 1871); the entire article is based largely on these letters to Merriam. Curiously, it is there presented as a journal entry, and it may well have been one before going into the letter, since Muir was obviously summarizing much material from his notebooks and journals in describing his glacier work to the Smithsonian. For a detailed literary analysis of this passage as it appeared in the published form, see Holmes.

Figure 7. Glacier meadow, on the headwaters of the Tuolumne, California; originally drawn ca. 1869 or early 1870s and later finished for publication. (Reprinted from *My First Summer in the Sierra*, p. 274)

sleeping quarters for the night, the "walls" of spruce, the "great fire," and the sheer abundance of natural beings suggest not so much a private intimacy as a communal one; the setting is not so much a bedroom as a large hall or a house. At the narrative center of the passage, then, Muir's own act of speaking interprets the natural elements as a "mansion." The lines of activity intersect curiously here: He *says* that it is the place itself that has homed *him*, but in terms of the narrative it is Muir who speaks this house into existence. That is, despite his usage of the odd verb "homed" to imply the active power of the environment itself, the structure of the passage (perhaps against Muir's own conscious intent) suggests that it was both the environment *and Muir's interpretation of it* that "homed" him—gave him a home, and allowed him to feel at home in it.[30]

The next day, in the presence of the actual sun, this personal sense of home is not dissipated but rather is expanded to include the whole world, as "my" walls, trees, and sky/dome recede into the "common fund" of the forest and the "fathomless blue." On one level, Muir himself is the

30. Muir's instinctive use of the image of home to express—and, at the same time, to create—a sense of intimate relation with and security in the natural world accords with Bachelard's observation that "all really inhabited space bears the essense of the notion of home. . . . [T]he imagination functions in this direction whenever the human being has found the slightest shelter: . . . the imagination builds 'walls' of impalpable shadows" (5).

remaining offspring of the evening; "left upon common ground," he has been born (or reborn) of the mythic union of earth and sky. Moreover, the odd term "sky flake" suggests that the sky that had come down to him in the dark was but another form of the creative power that, as snow-flakes and then as glaciers, had created the entire landscape. In this con-nection, the phrase "glacial labor" carries with it connotations from other passages of Muir's writings in which glaciers are described as creating and nurturing the mountains themselves; later in this same letter, he describes the hollow space between two domes as "the womb of the glacier." Thus, Muir is a child of the glacier itself as well as of earth and sky.[31]

At the same time, "my daily glacial labor" refers to his own present scientific activity, the intellectual, physical, and imaginative efforts that bring him to and through the landscape; Muir himself thus embodies the creative and procreative forces of the universe, and his work stands as a fit companion to that of the glaciers themselves. It is only in relation to this "blessed home" and to the other beings that constitute and inhabit it, and with the promise of their return with the cycles of the day and night, that Muir's individual daily activity is given structure, life, and meaning. In turn, it is Muir's energized and reshaped patterns of work, selfhood, and eros that allow him to imaginatively build such a home in the high Sierra.

Moreover, a home must be constructed upon a many-layered founda-tion of personal memory and meaning—not only visual images, "mere pictures hung upon the walls of memory," but living experiences made present and whole through one's body, heart, and sense. As an initial layer, this Sierra scene answered Muir's frustrated quest for a welcoming "place of rest" during his Southern walk, as his mountain meadow consti-tuted a striking—almost eerie—inversion of the anti-Edenic home of the black family that Muir had found in Florida. There, at the center of an-other fire-lighted globe of grasses, flowers, and trees, making a "glorious," "primitive," and "radiant" scene, had lived "twin devils" and a "black lump of something" that had turned out to be a young boy lying in the

31. The "Yosemite Glaciers" article also contains a somewhat muted version of the imaginative interpretation of glaciers from the letter to Carr; in this version, glaciers are described in subtly maternal imagery as giving birth to the landscape of Yosemite. See Co-hen (55–61) for a related discussion of more explicit womb imagery in Muir—and Muir in imagined wombs. Discussing Muir's description of an 1872 journey into a glacial crevasse, Cohen writes: "Indeed Muir was reborn as a son of Mother Nature when he returned from the glacial womb. He had acquired a deeper appreciation of his own relationship to the wilderness by living with the agents which shaped it and are still shaping it. He learned to see not as a man but as a glacier might" (61). A similar process applies to his experience this night in the glacial meadow.

fire, "nestless." In the environment of Yosemite, however, Muir himself could lie by the fire and be homed, arising the next morning a newborn man.

Deeper: The dancing flowers, overhanging trees, living walls, and elegant, graceful simplicity recall both his ecstatic homecoming to the glorious banks of Fountain Lake and his later encounter with the Wisconsin Dells, "a greenhouse planned & made & planted & tended by the Great Creator himself," both scenes which had "cut themselves keenly into our memories" as he undertook his youthful botanical labors. Muir's implicit and actual companions from that 1867 trip—his own family, Jeanne Carr, the young Merrill Moores, the shining lake and pulsing river, and the "dear plant beings" of his midwestern homes—may have had their long shadows cast by his bonfire onto this night scene in the Sierra.

Deeper: The contours of this mountain meadow may have been further shaped by the loved places and images he had shared—in imagination and in reality—with Jeanne Carr, from Yosemite waterfalls to Carr's library/conservatory, the "delightful kernel" of her home in Madison, "with its portraits of scientific men" from Humboldt to, perhaps, the same Clinton Merriam to whom Muir was now writing. Places of comfort and challenge, rest and activity, conservatory and meadow each constituted a "little kingdom" where both the plants and Muir himself were "luxuriant and happy" under "the open sky of the most flower-loving zone in the world."

Deeper: This "mountain mansion" rebuilds the bright "princely mansion," "the home of our Saviour and Father," of the early evangelical letter to Bradley Brown, within which the weary traveler—here, the "mortal wanderer"—receives refreshment, love, and hope from a "lord" who "watches over you . . . as tenderly as the fond mother over her sick child" before "send[ing] you on your way with a glad heart." There, however, the bright heavenly mansion was a refuge from the forbidding storms and dangerous powers of both the natural and the human worlds during Muir's teenage years; here, the mansion is literally created, constituted, and made sacred by the powers of the mountains, earth, and sky. Thus, at the highest point in the Sierra, "above the region of storms," the meadow becomes "that bright mansion of the blessed"—a "blessed home"—where Muir meets again his "gay warm company," "to part again no more forever."

Yet deeper: This walled-in bit of welcoming and pulsing nature must owe something to the loved and intimate places of Muir's childhood in Scotland, perhaps most profoundly the backyard garden of the family's home, warmed and brightened by both Ann and Daniel Muir as they created a place of beauty to lovingly share with their daughters and sons.

Indeed, in a later description of a mountain meadow Muir makes this connection explicit: "And notwithstanding the scene is so impressively spiritual, and you seem dissolved in it, yet everything about you is beating with warm, terrestrial, human love and life delightfully substantial and familiar. The resiny pines are types of health and steadfastness; the robins feeding on the sod belong to the same species you have known since childhood; and surely these daisies, larkspurs, and goldenrods are the very friend-flowers of the old home garden" (*Mountains of California*, 128). But this Sierra meadow may have evoked a wider range of childhood experiences as well: the round ruins of Dunbar Castle, site of adventure and safety both, where a young heart and body could test its strengths in companionship with imagined heroes and real playmates; the rocky cliffs of the coast, wettened and enlivened by the surging and embracing sea; the sunny walls of Lord Lauderdale's gardens, where with his grandfather the little boy ate apples and figs; even the snug bedroom that Muir shared with his brother, in which they explored the known world and relived the vast sweep of history only to fall asleep in strange positions under their blankets—and to find themselves lovingly rearranged by their mother in the morning.

Perhaps deeper: The earliest bliss and fluid brightness of family, a newborn body held warmly by parents and siblings, felt need and answering care, a mother's breast, even her womb. Lying in the wet roundness, perhaps some depth of Muir reentered what Bachelard describes as the original home, a well of being, "a sort of earthly paradise of matter, dissolved in the comforts of an adequate matter. It is as though in this material paradise, the human being were bathed in nourishment . . . gratified with all the essential benefits" (6). Nestled in the familiar grass and flowers, the adult Muir was able to let the energies and feelings, hopes and needs of his earliest being well up inside him, safely held by the circling trees.

Thus, this Sierra home was touched and blessed by a whole range of the beloved persons and beings—human, natural, and divine—with and within whom Muir had lived the most memorable and powerful days of his past life. At the same time, it did not merely replicate the past. Rather, through his glacial labor Muir was able to create a path out of that meadow that was not an escape or a leaving behind but rather a cyclical adventure and welcoming return, allowing the power and spark of childhood and youth to saturate his adult life and work. Despite his strong love of the people and places he had known, he held them loosely enough— or, they held him loosely enough—that he could leave them safely in the background as he looked forward, opening himself up to something new, using the power and insight and resources that they had given him to *create* something new.

In doing so, he did not leave his past loves *behind,* but in the background; the foreground was this simple Sierra meadow. In its specificity and detail—*that* evening, *this* meadow, *these* Williamson spruce, *those* daisies—the scene stood before Muir as a unique and present reality, to be encountered and met with all the spontaneity and grace of which he was capable. As only the latest in a long and gradual series of such encounters, this meadow was enveloped in a wide and deep blanket of associations and meanings; as a single present reality—just as were all the previous encounters, in their own time—this meadow grasped and held Muir in its immediacy and power. There and then, within the potential space and time of that Sierra evening, Muir—or, rather, Muir and the meadow together—created a new experience and a new reality; held by each new experience in turn, Muir over time was able to enter a blessed home, and to live a new life within it.

# Conclusion

# The Bonds That Open Our Hearts
# to the World

If someone were to fall into intimate slumber, and slept
deeply with Things—: how easily he would come
to a different day, out of the mutual depth.

Or perhaps he would stay there; and they would blossom and praise
their newest convert, who now is like one of them,
all those silent companions in the wind of the meadows.
—Rainer Maria Rilke, *Sonnets to Orpheus*

A friend tells me that Rilke's term for "companions" (*Geschwistern*) could as well be translated "brothers and sisters," or even "playmates." If so, perhaps the term captures something of what his mountain meadow— or, more generally, the natural world—was for Muir, or what he made of the "things" of that world. At the same time, part of my argument is that Muir did not come to such multilayered, intimate companionship with the natural world so easily, through any process so gentle and unconscious as a fall into deep slumber. Rather, on Muir's part, it took work; it took thought; it took luck; it took guts; it took creativity; perhaps most of all, it took time, endurance, and memory. On the part of those around him, those silent and talkative companions in his world, it took effort and care as well: the love of family and friends; the ambiguous support and demand of social structures and cultural institutions; the unseen but strongly felt (and feared) power of the divine; the bright, rough, engaging, welcoming presence of the particular meadows, lakes, rivers, and forests he encountered, from Scotland through Wisconsin and the Midwest to California. As one slice of this creative work, of course, on some levels the process *was* as unconscious as sleep, perhaps a form of sleepwalking, imbued with the ease, uncertainty, and power of a dream; and Muir's life was surely shaped by his own dreams, asleep and waking, as well as by what Thomas Berry has called "the dream of the earth," that "mutual depth"—or potential space—between and within humans and the natural world.

As it turned out, of course, Muir did not "stay there" with the silent companions of his Yosemite meadow, but came to a "different day" in a larger world. Over the next few years, he would expand his felt experience of a "blessed home" to include all of Yosemite, and would give more explicit philosophical formulation to this experience; under the pressure and possibility of cultural, historical, and personal forces, these images and ideas would undergo further transformation after he left Yosemite and returned to "civilization." A brief consideration of these further developments will set the stage for some concluding reflections on the weight and meaning of Muir's imaginative achievement of a home in the wilderness.

As an important element of what he chose to *do* in his new home—his continuing intellectual, emotional, and spiritual labor—over his next few years in Yosemite Muir would come to break down even further the traditional philosophical distinctions between human, natural, and divine beings. Of course, such a task was not completely new: scientifically, he had seen humans as part of "the great system of nature" at least since his university days; ethically, the Southern walk had led him to view humans and the rest of nature as possessing equal moral status and rights in the eyes of God; emotionally and sensuously, his first years in California and in Yosemite had opened him to a greater sense of concrete connection with his surroundings than ever before. At the end of the letter to Merriam, Muir again used the notion of "spiritual affinities" to evoke the connections between the human, spiritual, and natural worlds: "Why is night so intensely impressive[?] Is it because of an indefinite bodyless something nothing that we call wildness, weirdness, etc., or is it because of the activity of our own spiritual affinities concentered by the darkness, and made to act with more force upon the spiritual beings about us, and made more susceptible of their influences[?]" (2:974). Grounded in his emotional experience of being homed in Yosemite, however, Muir was able to develop an even more complete imaginative and intellectual integration of the human, the natural, and the divine; a few passages from his letters and journals of 1872 and 1873 suggest where he takes these ideas, or where they take him.

Going beyond the metaphor of "affinities," Muir increasingly understood humans as literally composed of the same stuff as the natural world: "Man is so related to all of Nature that he is builded of small worlds. . . . Squeeze all the universe into the size & shape of a perfect human soul & that is a whole man" (23:433). Accordingly, the human emotional response to natural beauty is itself an elemental process. In discussing Ruskin, Muir speculated that "[p]erhaps we owe 'the pleasurable emotions wh[ich] fine landscape makes in us' to a cause as radical as that wh[ich] makes a magnet pulse to the two poles. I think that one of the *properties* of that compound wh[ich] we call man is that when exposed to the rays of mountain beauty it glows with *joy*" (2:1191). Conversely—and in direct contrast to Ruskin's denigration of the "pathetic fallacy"—the natural world possesses the same properties as do humans.

Gravitation universal
So also music
" " life
" " love
properties of *Matter* (23:337)[1]

Such assertions do not constitute "anthropomorphism" or "personification" because of Muir's profound religiocentrism. As at the end of the Southern walk, his humanization of the natural and his naturalization of the human were but two sides of a single impulse: the assertion of a world infused with divinity. He ultimately valorized music, life, and love in religious terms—as properties of the divine, or as evidence that "Matter" was itself divine. Where earlier he had imaged God as a landscape gardener whose power and love consists in protecting and caring for the things of the world, after his immersion in Yosemite Muir understood divine presence as existing in and through the world itself: "The warm blood of God through all the geologic days of volcanic fire & through all the glacial winters great & small flows through these mountain granites, flows through these frozen streams, flows through trees living or fallen, flows through death itself" (23:483). Similarly, where he had once perceived the beauty of natural objects as the "glory" of God, i.e., as an expression of a Divinity that is still separate and hidden, he came to write of such natural beauty and objects as literally filled with God.

1. This journal entry may have been inspired in part by Muir's reading of *Observations on the Growth of the Mind* by Sampson Reed, a Swedenborgian. Emerson had sent the book to him, and in late 1872 Muir wrote Carr that "[i]t is full of fountain truth" (2:1192). Discussing gravitation as a "uniform" and "all-pervading" principle, Reed asks, "[W]hat all-pervading power is there by which gravitation is itself produced, unless it be the power of God?" (31). A little later, he describes music as "that harmony which pervades . . . all orders of creation; the music of the harp of universal nature, . . . the voice of God" (57). Although the book exalts the spiritual above the material to a degree that soon would be unacceptable to Muir, he may have learned from its descriptions of the parallels and interpenetrations between the two realms. Limbaugh (53–54) briefly discusses the long-term influence of Swedenborgianism on Muir's thought and writing, especially with respect to Muir's story "Stickeen."

Trees in camp bright & grasses & weeds impressive beyond thought. So palpably Godful in form & in wind motion, wind is the breath—the blood of God. The pines spiring around me higher higher to the starflowered sky are plainly full of God. God in them, they in God. & these brown weeds & grasses, that we say are dying in autumn frosts are in a gushing glowing current of life, they too are Godful and immortal. Oh the infinite abundance & universality of Beauty. Beauty is God—what shall we say of God that we may not say of Beauty. (23:361)

As the final component, Muir imaged the human and the divine worlds as interpenetrable, writing that "there are no stiff frigid strong partition walls betwixt us & the spiritual worlds—between us & heaven there are blendings immeasurable & untraceable as the edges of melting clouds" (23:302). Earlier (e.g., in the moonlight waterfall letter to Carr) he had spoken of our contact with the spiritual realm in terms of "angelic" beings, but he now could refer directly to God; in telling Carr of his plans for a long mountain excursion in the late summer of 1872, he exclaimed: "I will fuse in spirit skies. I will touch naked God" (2:1148). Most striking, instead of his long-standing construction of God in terms of a divine Person with whom one might have an individual relationship, Muir now wrote of the love of God—or, the Love that is God—as overflowing the boundaries of any one person or relationship and running though the whole world, natural and human together. To Catharine Merrill's statement that good men are "nearer to the heart of God than are woods and fields, rocks and waters," he responded:

Such distinctions and measurements seem strange to me. Rocks and waters, etc. are words of God and so are men. We all flow from one fountain Soul. All are expressions of one Love. God does not appear, and flow out, only from narrow chinks and round bored wells here and there in favored races and places, but He flows in grand undivided currents, shoreless and boundless over creeds and forms and all kinds of civilizations and people and beasts, saturating all and fountainizing all. (2:1123)

As the tone of the letter makes clear, Muir was aware of how far he had come from the religiousness of his previous life; the reference to "round bored wells" may have arisen from his memory of the well that he as a teenager had been forced to dig (through solid rock) as a result of his father's narrow, harsh ethic. More recently, the passage also echoes Muir's letter to Catharine after his 1867 homecoming to Fountain Lake; there, however, God's presence was envisaged as a landscape gardener giving measured portions of life-giving water and sunlight to the Wisconsin prairies, whereas here God's love flows more wildly and unbounded through land and humans alike.

Significantly, this letter to Catharine also contains some of the first clear evidences of the specific intellectual and literary influence of Emerson. After their meeting in Yosemite, Muir and Emerson had begun an occasional correspondence that would last until the latter's death. The Concord sage repeatedly called for Muir to go east to start a formal scientific and literary career among the best minds of the day; Muir refused, instead sending botanical specimens and other Yosemite tokens to Emerson. For his part, Emerson sent a two-volume copy of his own essays. Thus, in a book received from the author's own hand, Muir finally read the famous passage at the beginning of "Nature": "Standing on the bare ground,—my head bathed by the blithe air, and uplifted into infinite space,—all mean egotism vanishes. I become a transparent eye-ball; I am nothing; I see all; the currents of Universal Being circulate through me; I am part or particle of God" (Emerson, 10). In writing to Catharine, Muir advised her to "bathe in [the sea] . . . and allow the pure and generous currents of universal uncolleged beauty to blow about your bones" (2: 1123). Similarly, one of Muir's early published works, "Twenty Hill Hollow" (also from 1872), interestingly modified Emerson's words: "Presently you lose consciousness of your own separate existence; you blend with the landscape, and become part and particle of Nature" (86). The transparency of these adaptations—virtual quotations—suggests a young man in the process of searching for an acceptable literary voice by trying on the style of a revered cultural figure; it was perhaps the style itself, more than any specific philosophical content, that was most useful to Muir at this point in his attempt to reimagine his possible place in the world, both in cosmic terms and as a budding writer.

Eventually, as his later writings show, Muir came to be more successful in creating his own voice, a fusion of Emersonian images, scientific insight, and Muir's own religious faith and fervor. For example, by 1873 Muir could write in his journal:

> Now all of these varied forms high & low are simply portions of God radiated from Him as a sun, & made terrestrial by the clothes that they wear, & by the modifications of a corresponding kind in the first God essence itself. The more specially terrestrial a being becomes the higher it ranks among its fellows, & the most terrestrial being is the one that contains all the others, who has indeed flowed through all of the others & borne away parts of them, building them into itself. Such a being is man, who has flowed down through other forms of being & absorbed & assimilated portions of them into himself thus becoming a microcosm most richly Divine because most richly terrestrial. (23:594–95)

Whatever meaning he may have intended in scientific terms, the language of this passage echoes the long quotation from Carr's friend Walter Brooks ("the Priest") that she had sent Muir during his convalescence after the 1867 factory accident in Indianapolis (quoted above, chapter 3): "[T]here is a pre-existent spiritual body for every moss, lichen, & plant of every kind; growth is an actual 'clothing upon' of themselves by these spiritual beings. They gather from nature its substances to make themselves a garment exactly fitting their persons" (1:521–23). However, where that quotation had ended with human and natural beings shedding their material bodies and uniting in the spiritual realm, Muir's reformulation united the human and the divine in the "terrestrial."[2]

Moreover, we can again discern powerful traces of the writings of Emerson. Muir's passage both incorporates and responds to an Emersonian view of nature: "The world proceeds from the same spirit as the body of man. It is a remoter and inferior incarnation of God" (Emerson, 42). More concretely, Emerson had sent a handwritten copy of "The Song of Nature" to Muir in 1872 (see 2:1044–45), the same poem that Carr had sent to Muir in 1869, when he had newly arrived in California. The central conceit of the poem clearly parallels the main theme of Muir's "terrestrial divinity" passage, describing the numberless achievements and creations of Nature and the processes by which "out of spent and aged things / I formed the world anew" in elemental and living forms. However, one final creation has not yet appeared: "And still the man child is not born / The summit of the whole." Thus, the formation of a divinely human being from the inner processes and materials of the natural world, and as the "summit" of that world, may have guided Muir's philosophical assertion that humans are "most richly Divine because most richly terrestrial." In fact, the passage is quite unlike Muir (but very like Emerson) in exalting humanity as the crown of creation, and that particular aspect is seldom if ever expressed again in his writings. Thus, Emerson's writings— not only as philosophical doctrine but also as story and imagery—by degrees gave Muir yet another way to envision the merging and interrelationship of the human, the natural, and the divine, and thus to sound

2. Passages from Brooks's published writings are similarly suggestive of Muir's insights: "The earth around us, in its variety of creature and life, is not merely a varied form of matter; it has a meaning; it is a revelation; the character of God is spread over it, and the thoughts of God are revealed in it. . . . So in the world there is a living God, a divine and moral meaning; and if we see not this we do not see the world" (20). However, it is unclear how much actual contact Muir had with Brooks's writings or sermons, outside of Carr's mediating letters. Again, Muir also may have been influenced by the Swedenborgian Reed: "As we behold the external face of the world, our souls will hold communion with its spirit; and we shall seem to extend our consciousness beyond the narrow limits of our own bodies, to the living objects that surround us. The mind will enter into nature by the secret path of him who forms her; and can no longer be ignorant of her laws, when it is a witness of her creation" (90).

the deepest meanings of his continuing explorations of Yosemite—and of himself.

For all the long intellectual and geographical distances he had come, however, Muir was still tied by indissoluble bonds to the people and places of his past. From an 1873 journal: "To ask me whether I could endure to live without friends is absurd. It is easy enough to live out of material sight of friends, but to live without human love is impossible. Quench love & what is left of a man's life—the folding of a few jointed bones & squares of flesh? Who would call that life[?]" (23:594). Indeed, it was these very bonds of love—at times constraining, at times painful— that energized and empowered him as he moved forward into his future. Thus, we cannot read any of Muir's insights during this period as abstract philosophical assertions; rather, they are always tied to his own experiences of particular persons, places, and natural beings. His intellectual discoveries, literary images, and mystical insights constituted not so much a general worldview as a situational psychological tactic, an intellectual, imaginative, and emotional orientation that made sense in Yosemite but would not have made sense in San Francisco, or—most likely—in the swamps of the South or the jungles of the Amazon. For Muir, the confidence and security implicit in his integration of the human, the natural, and the divine arose from and were continually supported by a particular, contingent experience: the multilayered and deeply felt sense of being "homed," grounded in prolonged, intimate, and creative contact with the particular natural and domestic places of his past and of his present.

Despite the depth and power with which he felt homed in his Yosemite mountains and meadows, Muir also felt continuing challenges and goals, gaps and desires that drew him away from that place and forward into a new future. On the one hand, the question of work was still unanswered; he needed to find or to create a career that would provide a socially recognized adult male identity, solve the practical issue of money, serve as an arena for intellectual engagement and for religious/literary expression, *and* allow him to relate to the natural world in the way he knew best, as an amateur—that is, as a lover. On the other hand, more personal challenges remained as well: How would he live with other people? How would he live with his own body? Would he ever be comfortable enough with both body and relationship to help create a family of his own? Muir felt all of these questions deeply, and the fact that they were not solved easily by his imaginative construction of a home in nature does not reveal the inadequacy of the latter but the human complexity of the questions themselves—and Muir's commitment and courage in facing them.

In fact, Muir's decision to leave Yosemite to engage such issues did not shatter his relationship with that place, but rather creatively transformed it yet again. Indeed, in many ways it strengthened it. By the end of 1871, Muir had come to feel "homed" by specific natural environments that he encountered within Yosemite. However, he never in those years made any special claim for the Yosemite region itself as the only or even the best place where he could be homed; his letters to LeConte, Merriam, and others make it clear that he would be happy to travel to anywhere he could be in intimate and engaged contact with natural surroundings. It was only after repeated experiences of leaving and then returning to Yosemite throughout the 1870s that he came to commonly refer to that specific place as his "true mountain home"; this process was especially powerful after he had begun to make a literary career on the basis of his descriptions of Yosemite and had begun to be strongly associated with that place in the public mind. Just as his most powerful symbolic reconstruction of the family homestead at Fountain Lake as an ideal and emotionally charged environment emerged only in the process of returning to it for a brief visit after a long absence, so too Yosemite took on the force of a symbolic center only after he had left and then returned to it—with no plans of actually staying there to live. Thus, Yosemite gained meaning precisely through marked *contrast* with his actual homes of the period; freed of many of the requirements for a literal home, Yosemite could serve as a locus of religious and symbolic meanings in the context of a developing literary career and personal identity.

Muir's achievement of "at-homeness" in Yosemite again invites comparison with the case of Thoreau. In *Walden,* according to Marilyn Chandler, "[u]ltimately the cabin, having served its purpose, falls away. . . . It is not the cabin but the kind of life engendered in such a dwelling that matters. Once achieved and fully embraced, that way of life can sustain itself in other places, having become internalized. . . . The house is a prop, an aid, in a spiritual journey whose end is to rise above dependency on setting and circumstance" (27). Similarly, Muir's "mountain mansion"— not an actual cabin but a deeply felt experience of a concrete place, based in part upon previous actual homes but more in an imaginative reinterpretation of his natural surroundings—could engender a new way of life, and experience and life could both be internalized and carried forward into the larger world. To be sure, Frederick Garber argues that Thoreau eventually found that he could not always "rise above dependency upon setting and circumstance"; in his later writings, especially *The Maine Woods* and *Cape Cod,* he struggled to bring his internalized sense of at-homeness in Walden to those more harsh and inhospitable environments, ultimately failing in the attempt. In the far more harsh environment of the Sierra—and eventually those of Alaska, the desert, and elsewhere—

Muir seems to have done a better job of rising above circumstance than did Thoreau. Muir's admission into his domed mountain mansion answers Thoreau's admission of failure: "We look up to the gilded battlements of the eternal city, and are contented to be suburban dwellers outside the walls" (quoted in Garber, *Thoreau's Fable,* 3). To make such a claim, however, one would have to compare in more detail their experiences of home: the place of home in their lives, their respective standards for at-homeness, the character and meanings of their constructions of home. Thoreau, the Concord homebody, was probably more sensitive to the vagaries of actually dwelling in one place, and open to the real differences and difficulties that would confront one in trying to make an actual home in a new place. By contrast, as we have seen, Muir throughout his life approached new environments through a more fixed lens, with a much more strongly developed imaginative and emotional constellation, drawing especially upon religious faith and the felt presence of family and friends. Thus, his experiences in Yosemite provided the basis for a powerful image of home that would shape and guide him as he moved forward into the new places and challenges of his future.

To fully detail this process—to say nothing of the twists and turns over the remaining forty years of Muir's life—would take as much time and effort as understanding his development up to 1871. For the rest of his life, a complex (and changing) construction of particular natural environments as emotional and religious homes would give Muir a context within which to continue his long-term process of "assimilating" those environments into himself. Despite his own attempts to portray them as static, Muir's relationships to the natural world were (and continued to be) as complex and changing as his relationships with family, friends, human society, and his own self-image—all of which were themselves intimately interrelated with each other, in dynamic and unexpected ways, over the course of his entire life. Having come to at least a provisional resolution of a certain trajectory, however, we may stop and reflect: What have we learned from Muir, or from my modes of exploring Muir's life? I hope that each reader will come away with his or her own set of conclusions, growing from his or her own set of questions, concerns, and passions; thus, what follows is only one possible "conclusion" to this book, or rather some brief hints of one possible way of continuing this discussion into the future.

In constructing a framework for environmental, religious, and psychosocial biography, I have taken an object relations perspective on a transactional person-culture-environment whole, viewing relationship and change as inherent to an individual's being and meaning. Such a framework helps us to see that the development of Muir's relationship with his natural surroundings was not characterized by a sudden, individual, timeless, ecstatic conversion from civilization to wilderness, nor was it a monochromatic growth in inherited wildness or in nurturing domestic bliss. Rather, it involved a series of gradual, relational, creative, and bodily grounded transformations of his visions of and emotions toward various emotionally and symbolically charged environments. In this process of repeated self-transformation, Muir was by no means solitary and independent but rather was crucially supported by a wide range of cultural and social patterns of nineteenth-century America, including family and friends, Christian imagery and Christian love, sexual patterns and erotic possibilities, male identity and privilege, social structures such as apprenticeship and higher education, scientific institutions such as the network of amateur botany, and much more. At the same time, Muir creatively appropriated all of this social and cultural support and did something *new* with it, imaginatively and courageously creating new patterns of relationship with persons and places and new images of nature as home. As an aspect of the wider growth of his person, these creative transformations were both patterned and spontaneous; they were both expressions of something within him and reactions to external forces; they were shaped and motivated by—and creative resolutions of—complex, interconnected layers of need and desire for selfhood, for human relationship, for the power of spiritual experience and religious symbol, and for contact with natural objects in themselves.

In particular, I have emphasized Muir's creation of enduring erotic relationships with certain natural beings and phenomena—relationships that drew upon the energies and images of his relationships with important women but that were ultimately nonsexual in character (at least given our usual genitally focused understandings of male sexuality). As a deep layer of his personal development, this erotic dimension incorporated cultural images and social patterns as well as emotional and physical needs and desires, unifying his mind, heart, and body in a unique dance of passionate and joyous connection with the world. Indeed, Muir's later creative life—his nature writing, environmental activism, and agricultural work—can perhaps be understood as the procreative or generative activity that arises from erotic experience of nature, just as his family life was the generative expression of his later sexual activity. More immediately, his life suggests that an erotic relationship with nature may be an aspect of *everyone's* life, a powerful but as yet ignored dimension of human psychological and spiritual growth.

Moreover, out of the complex array of forces and freedoms that was Muir's life, at each point in his journey he created an image (and a reality) of a favored or idealized environment that was contrasted to a negative or rejected one—both of which were simultaneously human, natural, and religious. That is, his positive image of "nature" never encompassed the whole of the natural world, but always forced some natural objects and places into a negative, feared, or devalued category; and this was not a temporary oversight or inadequacy, but rather an essential characteristic of the images one constructs to understand and to negotiate one's natural surroundings. Such a pattern is common in other realms of human life: for example, in Melanie Klein's notion of the infant's experience of a "good mother" and a "bad mother," or in the near-universal coexistence of God and the Devil (or their correlates). Moreover, both Muir's "good nature" and his "bad nature" never wholly excluded the human and religious realms; indeed, it was in the rich and complex context of intermingled natural, human, and religious objects and relationships that particular beings and places came to be experienced as "good" or "bad," or even defined as "natural" at all.

Paradoxically, it was only with such an array of images of nature—loved *and* feared, attractive *and* repulsive—that Muir could feel "held" by his specific natural surroundings. For an overarching image of "Nature" (like "God") to be psychologically and spiritually supportive and powerful, it must help a person to maintain his or her sense of connection with those loved beings—human, natural, or divine—that are the sources of vitality and aliveness, at the same time as it allows (and even encourages) experimentation, individuality, and the capacity to move forward into new relationships and situations. Correlatively, in those cases where a particular natural being is of such a quality as to allow or evoke a new primary relationship, that being and relationship must be clearly demarcated—even grasped and held—as special and precious, distinct from others that may be more threatening, painful, or ambivalent. Indeed, I take it as one of the discoveries of this study that for Muir, despite his later rhetoric, *not* every natural object could act in his psychic economy in a positive manner, either as a transitional or as a primary phenomenon. Thus, Muir negotiated these varied natural realities in part through the construction of appropriately distinct representations of them, just as distinct images are required in the human (and indeed the religious) realm, in order to feel held by and to hold onto the specific beings that were the sources and expressions of his growing passion and selfhood.

Perhaps most simply, Muir's changing orientations toward nature were part of his lifelong quest to love himself, other people, and the world more fully, deeply, and richly. At the heart and the end of this quest, we find a homecoming—or, rather, a series of homecomings, each of which also constitutes a homemaking, the act of making a place a home. Again, of course, Muir is by no means unique in this, only human; as Robert Orsi has observed, "When poor men and women are asked to tell the story of their lives, if they have been fortunate enough to have built a house, they make the event of this building the centerpiece of their autobiographies" (*Madonna*, 64). In fact, what makes Muir distinctive is not the centrality of homemaking but the equally recurrent motif of home leaving; for Muir, a home—whether human or natural—is a place of rest and restoration only as part of a recurring cycle of exodus and return. Each dynamic process required the other, and it was only through the balance of both that Muir was able to express his longing and his love.

The point is crucial, and so I must stress here that I am *not* talking about a balance between wilderness and civilization. That dichotomy is one that Muir did not construct until later in his life, and in fact he never did really *live* it, structure his life around it; leaving all his human contacts for "pure nature," for good, was never a real possibility for him. Instead, his emotional bonds to home cut across "wilderness" and "civilization," or rather the natural, human, and divine realms, resulting in complex and shifting configurations of the desired and the defiled. Thus, Muir's life has something to teach us in response to what we can now see as the inadequacy of his own mature thought: any equation of "nature" with "wilderness" is as dangerous emotionally and spiritually as it is environmentally, for it consigns most of the natural beings we encounter—trees encased in concrete, in culture, or in imagination—to the devalued and forgotten realm outside of the equation. Rather, we need language and myths that describe and evoke the natural worlds in which humans actually live, the *world* as a whole, with all its interconnections and intricacies of the natural, the human, and whatever others there be.

Similarly, in his call for "rethinking the human place in nature," William Cronon argues that the traditional dichotomy between nature (as "wilderness") and humanity (as "civilization") must be overcome, in order to "discov[er] what an ethical, sustainable, *honorable* human place in nature would look like." Rather than being idealized as an escape from responsibility and work, the natural world must be revisioned as a—perhaps *the*—"place we actually live," i.e., as continuous with human civilization and culture in all its forms: "[W]e need to discover a common middle ground in which all of these things, from the city to the wilderness, can somehow be encompassed in the word 'home.'"[3] Cronon con-

3. Interestingly, Cronon's repeated use of the verb "discover" reveals some lingering essentialism; I would suggest that we need to *create* this middle ground, as a new historical-natural reality in our own time (though perhaps with historical-natural antecedents or parallels).

cludes: "If wildness can stop being (just) out there and start being (also) in here, if it can start being as humane as it is natural, then perhaps we can get on with the unending task of struggling to live rightly in the world—not just in the garden, not just in the wilderness, but in the home that encompasses them both" (81, 87, 89, 90). Just as our traditional images of Muir have contributed greatly to the wilderness/civilization dichotomy that Cronon is eager to overcome, a new perspective on Muir can contribute to more adequate understandings of actual human lives-in-nature.

The equation of nature with wilderness is difficult for late-twentieth-century Americans to shrug off, however—especially when it is infused with other layers of meaning regarding gender and domesticity. For example, even when calling for an increased sensitivity to the problems and possibilities for contact with the natural world on the part of adolescent girls, Stephen Trimble writes: "They may develop rich relationships with the land, *but* these most often come from a relatively restricted circle around home, and social experiences within that circle: gathering plants with a group of women, tending a garden with other women" (Nabhan and Trimble, 72; italics mine). What is the force of this "but," which everyone understands and accepts? It reveals that the presumptions behind the discussion are that "wild," "distant" nature, separate from home and encountered in solitude, is still considered the "real" experience of nature, while a natural world experienced in domestic or interpersonal settings is somehow less valid or valued. Even for such a "wild child"—and a "wild man"—as John Muir, however, the core of his experience of his natural surroundings was always much closer to the patterns of the adolescent girls that Trimble describes than to any programmatic vision of solitary, distant wilderness. Clearly, girls and women *should* possess other possibilities and cultural patterns than those they have traditionally had/made/been given; but the power and meaning of those traditional patterns must not be overlooked, and indeed they should probably be acknowledged as in fact the dominant—and healthy—patterns through which most people have always found and created meaningful relationships with their world, men and boys included.

To be sure, Muir may not be the best person to exemplify all of these "new" (actually quite old) perspectives and concerns; he may even come in for critique on the basis of some of them, especially as he came to promote (and to stake his self- and public image on) the "solitary wilderness experience" model. At the same time, I do not want to throw out that model, either; it too is deep and powerful, and still has a lot to teach us about the natural world, about religious power, about the sources and limits of interpersonal relationship, about ourselves. What I find most fascinating about the young Muir is the way that his life encompassed both models (and more), the complex intensity with which he felt human connection *and* solitude, familiarity *and* adventure, domesticity *and* wildness. That said, I will not claim for him some sort of superhuman status as ungendered or as androgyne; rather, his breadth and complexity came from the specific conditions of his life, his particular human relationships, cultural images, religious and natural influences, biographical circumstances, and creative choices. It is not as a straightforward model of any clear or definite form of relationship with nature, but as a felt companion in the murky and uncertain process of forging our own lives and relationships, that Muir has most to offer as a mythic figure today.

From this perspective, Muir emerges as a figure not to follow but to walk beside, to converse with and to learn from—just as Muir would sit with the plants he encountered, to hear what they had to tell about their life and ways. In doing so, one realizes: You don't have to be a John Muir to love and care for and dream of and draw strength from the natural world. Muir himself wasn't even a John Muir, for most of his life. You— I—don't need wilderness, solitude, adventure, etc., though that can often help. Rather, you and I can claim and celebrate our circles of human and natural friends and loved ones, and can expand those circles. We can risk inviting the world into our homes, and can risk rebuilding our homes as part of the larger world. And—not least of all—we can risk leaving our homes, venturing out into the unheld and unholding free spaces of the world, in pursuit of whatever re-creations and revelations of self, of other, of passion, and of truth we may find there. Whether at home or away, we can cultivate our capacities for intimate, mutual companionship with all of the beings that inhabit our worlds. To adapt the words of the Quaker George Fox: May we walk cheerfully over the world, answering that of God in everyone—and every*thing*.

At the same time, we can—indeed, we must—acknowledge the pain, the fear, the unknown, the uncaring, the dying, sometimes the sheer evil that exists within ourselves and in our world. For all our striving toward love and passionate companionship, those beings and forces that work against brightness and life are equally real, and our visions and understandings must include a place for them as well. To deny them is folly; to try to eliminate them is probably futile. Rather, we must invite them in, too, and learn to live with them, have a talk with them, sit together in silence by the hearth. It is in such sitting with the real threats to relationship and selfhood that our capacities both to love and to be alone will perhaps be most fully tested and proved; if they endure—and they may not, for again the threats are real—the spark from this love and this aloneness may in its turn kindle a new fire, to cast our surviving worlds in a new and different light.

For Muir as a young man, living in Yosemite was ecstatic—because he was living with beauty, with the divine, with his longtime companions and family, with truth, with the fundamental powers of his world, with himself. The challenge of the new Muir myth may be: How can we live in beauty, justice, and love? How can we shape our lives—our work, our social relations and political values, our communities, our life paths and prospects, the ways we touch and are touched by other persons, by the natural world, and by the divine—how can we shape our whole lives toward beauty, justice, and love?

*Appendices*
*Works Cited*
*Source Acknowledgments*
*Index*

# Appendix A

# The Journal of the "First Summer"

*My First Summer in the Sierra* is one of John Muir's best known and most influential books; generations of readers have taken it as an authentic account of a dramatic, transformative immersion in Yosemite in the summer of 1869 and as the center of his biography. What is less well known, among popular readers at least, is that the published *First Summer* is based not upon an original journal but upon three handwritten notebooks that date from 1887; whatever journal he actually kept during the summer of 1869 is now lost. Oddly enough, this fact has occasioned very little critical scholarly discussion of an obvious and very important issue: Can we take these 1887 notebooks as a faithful transcription of Muir's original journal? Do the notebooks constitute a reliable record of his experiences during the summer of 1869, or do they represent a revised—or even completely rewritten—story of that summer? If so, is it possible to guess as to the extent of the revisions?

To be sure, given the popularity of the story, a few scholars have discussed the autobiographical reliability of the published version. Michael P. Cohen and John Tallmadge both stress the revised character of *First Summer*, treating it as a literary creation that expresses Muir's later ideas, language, and imagery. Given their focus on Muir's "mature beliefs," however, neither of them pursues the implications of his analysis of *First Summer* for our understanding of the 1887 notebooks themselves, or of Muir's original encounter with Yosemite; and in fact, both of them essentially follow the traditional model in interpreting the biographical importance of the summer of 1869 as an element of a dramatic transformation, a "conversion" (albeit a two-year one, beginning with the Southern walk) for Tallmadge and a Buddhist/Taoist "awakening" for Cohen. Unfortunately, other scholars have been much less critical even with respect to *First Summer:* writing at the same time as Cohen, Frederick Turner regards the published book as a "faithful depiction" of Muir's experiences (377); similarly, the two most recent biographies, those of Thurman Wilkins and Millie Stanley, along with numerous more specialized studies (e.g., those of O'Grady and Fleck), take *First Summer* as an accurate account of Muir's initial experiences in the mountains.

That *First Summer* cannot be used as a guide to Muir's initial experiences in Yosemite should be apparent. But the questions remain: Can the 1887 notebooks? Why should we believe that those notebooks represent an accurate copy of Muir's original journals? If not, how should we regard them? I have approached these questions in the light of three considerations: (1) the internal organization, style, and inconsistencies of the account given in the 1887 notebooks; (2) the relationship between this account and the two original journals for the periods *surrounding* the summer of 1869; and (3) a comparison of another 1887 notebook account of a completely different journey with the account found in an original journal. As a result of these considerations, I conclude that the account of Muir's "first summer" that is found in the 1887 notebooks can probably be trusted only in a very limited way: the sheer record of the places and objects that Muir encountered in his travels is in large part reliable, but much of the narrative structure and interpretive language of the 1887 notebooks is the product of an extensive process of revision that was undertaken at some as-yet-unknown time(s) between 1869 and 1887.

1. Like the published *First Summer,* the 1887 notebooks constitute an engaging and evocative story of one individual's powerful relationship with the natural world. However, a close reading—especially in the light of other materials from the period—reveals a number of oddities and inconsistencies that should call into question the authenticity of this account on sheerly textual grounds. (Indeed, most of my argument here applies to the published version as well as to the notebooks; keep in mind, though, that my focus here is on determining the status of the latter.) The initial entries in the first of the 1887 notebooks are long summary descriptions of Muir's fellow sheepherders, mundane aspects of camp life, David Brown the bear hunter, and so on, many of them even longer than in *First Summer;* given the amount of work that Muir was doing, one might ask how (or why) he could have found the time for all this writing. Moreover, keep in mind that there are very few surviving letters from this period. Even on the Southern walk, his journaling was paralleled by continued letter writing to friends and family, even in the face of the difficulties and uncertainties of his journey; thus, if he had time for writing as he journeyed up to Yosemite, we might have expected he would spend at least some of it in writing to friends—but he did not. Moreover, many of these initial passages in the notebooks are written in the distant past tense: "Here for the first time since leaving the plains we found green untrodden pasturage . . . & Mr. Delaney determined to seek a first perma-

nent camp next day" (34:144); the long description of shepherd Billy is another good example of a clearly distant past tense. In later entries, Muir's descriptions of the landscape contain much natural history that he probably would not have known yet; he often gives botanical names for plants, but (as discussed in chapter 5 above) he still did not have any botany texts at this point. Detailed sections of pure natural history writing are often set off with section headings ("Libocedrus," "Bower Cave," etc.)—an unlikely structure for a personal journal.

A number of particular incidents are especially confusing. For example, Muir's initial mention of glaciation (in the entry for July 11; see 31:312–13) seems to be quite out of place: the passage starts abruptly, presenting his glacial theory full blown, with no preceding entries showing any process of intellectual development or observation of glacial action at all. Perhaps most strikingly—and obvious only in the light of my detailed study of his previous months in California—he has up to this point expressed no interest in questions of the origins of the landscape, or any indication that he was ever thinking about it. Additionally, these entries again seem based on much more extensive knowledge of the landscape than he could have had at this early stage, as in his detailed descriptions of ouzels at Yosemite Falls and of Yosemite Creek basin. One begins to wonder whether these entries reflect later additions of ideas and observations that Muir had made over the succeeding years and that were then written back into the 1887 account of the summer of 1869.

Another odd passage gives the same impression. The entry for July 7 gives a summary reflection on his experiences in the first Merced camp: "Its features are fairly grown into me as part of my body, not pictures on memories' walls hanging against a surface or even painted or burned into it, but living love pervading filling mind & body alike." However, this statement is immediately followed by a number of scenes that *are* referred to as "pictures" (see 31:194ff.). Well, John—are these scenes "pictures" or aren't they? The mystery perhaps becomes more clear when we read Muir's letter to Carr from July 29, 1870 (discussed in more detail in chapter 5 above), where he writes: "I am rich, rich beyond measure, not in rectangular blocks of sifted knowledge or in thin sheets of beauty hung picture-like about the 'walls of memory'—but in unselected atmospheres of terrestrial glory diffused evenly throughout my whole substance." Given his common habit of selecting and refining passages from journals and letters as elements of his published writings, we might suspect that the phrase "not merely as memory pictures" was one that Muir mined out of this letter and then inserted into his 1887 account of the "first summer"—without, however, adjusting the surrounding passages that record his original reactions (in terms of "pictures"). (In the published version, by contrast, the whole passage is made consistent by the deletion of any reference to such scenes as pictures.)

Happily, another perplexity can be resolved much more definitively. In the notebook entry for September 2, Muir suddenly comments at length—in the past tense—that he had been looking for the flower cassiope the whole summer, but had not yet found it; one is struck both by the backward-looking tone and by the intensity of his sudden interest in something he supposedly hasn't seen. A subsequent entry reports that he finally did find cassiope on September 7. However, we happen to have an outside source that throws light on the matter: In a letter to Carr from October 1869, Muir writes out what he says is a journal entry for September 2, which claims that he in fact did find cassiope on that day and which uses language and imagery found in both of the entries in the 1887 notebook. If the letter contains the original journal entry (or, at least, a not too extensively revised version of it), the 1887 notebook seems to reflect a later decision to separate that one incident into two, probably for increased dramatic effect. Significantly, this quoted entry in the letter to Carr is much shorter than, and contains none of the philosophical reflections of, the revised version in the 1887 notebook; this pattern accords well with my discoveries below.

2. At this point, then, internal evidence suggests that the 1887 notebooks are not a straightforward copy but rather a revision of the original journal. A similar conclusion follows from looking at the structure and content of the 1887 notebooks in the context of the journals for the periods before and after the summer of 1869, both of which journals are original. In fact, the "Twenty Hill Hollow" journal of January–May 1869 (23:152–96) and the "Yosemite Yearbook" of November 1869–August 1870 (23:197–236) are strikingly similar to each other in structure. (Edited versions of these journals are available in *John of the Mountains*, chapters 1 and 2.) After long introductory sections that recount how Muir got to his present position and note his living situation, both journals primarily contain brief descriptive entries, usually introduced with observation of wind and cloud cover (many days having nothing more than this). These brief entries are occasionally punctuated by longer narratives about particularly noteworthy events like storms or adventures, or passages of philosophical or religious reflection on particular experiences. By contrast, the 1887 notebooks have much longer entries, with a much more complete and developed narrative structure. (The differences are particularly striking when we remember that he was working harder and traveling more during that summer, and so would not have had as much free time for writing as during the previous spring and following winter;

how then did the summer entries come to be so much more detailed and extensive?) Additionally, as is discussed more fully in chapter 5 above, certain key themes of the traditional account of Muir's "first summer"— glaciation, "conversion," a feeling of "immortality," and so on, all of which are found in the 1887 notebooks as much as in the published *First Summer*—are simply not present in the journals or letters of the periods that precede and follow. Other themes, such as an experience of "melting into the landscape" described in language of "pores," "pulsings," etc., are found in both of these original journals at equal levels of usage and intensity—far below that of the 1887 notebooks—suggesting that he in fact did *not* undergo a marked transformation during the summer between Twenty Hill Hollow and the first Yosemite winter. Thus, these original journals exhibit a high degree of continuity in style and content over this whole period, but the 1887 notebooks contain much seemingly anachronistic structure, language, knowledge, and modes of experience.

3. Fortunately, other materials allow us more detailed insight into what Muir probably did when he sat down to write the 1887 notebooks. In fact, there is a whole series of 1887 notebooks that contain accounts of various of Muir's travels and studies during the early 1870s; these notebooks are similar in form, handwriting, and presentation to the 1887 "first summer" notebooks, suggesting that all were the product of the same bout of literary work in 1887. However, for some of these 1887 notebooks, unlike the "first summer" notebooks, the corresponding original journals still survive. We can therefore gain a glimpse into the patterns that guided Muir's process of revision and rewriting by looking at a test case: two accounts of an early spring 1873 trip to Yosemite Falls— the first from the original journal (still in existence), the second from the corresponding 1887 notebook. (In the microfilm, the sections I am considering are found at 23:558–67 [original] and 31:689–700 [1887 notebook].) Keep in mind that my concern here is not primarily with the specific content of these two accounts, but with what the comparison between the original 1873 journal and the 1887 notebook can tell us about Muir's process of revision—and thus about the probable reliability of the 1887 account of the "first summer."

In the case of this 1873 trip to Yosemite Falls, both the original journal and the 1887 notebook include the same basic sequence of places and objects that Muir encountered on the trip, along with some specific details: sunrise in the valley on the first day; observations on vegetation and birds; signs of a recent snow avalanche; a drink in a cascade; the huge ice cone in front of the falls; a pine log he saw washed over the falls; and so on. At one point in the 1887 notebook, an observation on the timing of the sunrise is moved ahead of a few other entries as found in the original, but there are few other transpositions such as this. Many of the original drawings are carefully redrawn in the notebook.

However, this 1887 notebook is about twice as long as the original 1873 journal, the additions coming in a number of ways. Some passages in the notebook have no parallel in the original, and were clearly added to help a future reader by setting the stage, clarifying the narrative structure, or adding necessary information and interesting ideas. The first three pages of the 1887 notebook, for example, are wholly new additions, comprising introductory descriptions of the valley and establishing the account as a narrative ("Today I having no winter cabin rolled some bread & tea in a pair of blankets" [31:689]). Other notebook passages expand upon the brief, fragmentary entries of the original, adding both grammatical correctness and descriptive power; for example, "Huge mass of Yo Pt stood over me like spirit" (from the original, 23:567) becomes in the notebook "The huge mass of Yosemite Point, the lofty brow to the east of the fall, was impressively brought forward into the moonlight & seemed to be immediately over me towering with gestures so lifelike it seemed like some spirit of the mountains" (31:700). Perhaps most important for my purposes, the 1887 notebook contains much religious and literary language that is not found in the 1873 original. To the original journal's description of pines drenched by the spray of the falls, the notebook adds that the pines were "bowing devoutly their acknowledgements of the marvelous blessing" (31:696); instead of merely stating (as in the original) that the stars are scattered "orderly," the notebook says that they "are scattered through the heavens in glorious harmony, all in joyful subordination to the law of love" (31:696); in a second-person description of standing close to the falls, the notebook stresses "the sights & sounds & tremendous energy of the crowd of waters preventing all knowledge of yourself" (31:699); in describing the mist rising from the falls, the notebook adds to the original journal the statement that "the beaten rainbow dust makes all divine adding glorious beauty & peace to glorious power" (31:700). This is not to say that the original journal contains no interpretive or religious language; interestingly, an interpretation based in more traditional Christian themes, "Yosemite fall is a bible it contains Christ's Sermon on the Mt" (23:561), is not found in the 1887 notebook at all. On the whole, however, far more of such language was added to the account when it was written into the notebook than was taken out of it in the course of this revision process.

If these are the patterns that guided Muir's preparation of the 1887 account of this particular (1873) trip, we may be justified in thinking that the same process applied to the 1887 notebook account of the summer of 1869, thus confirming and extending my arguments in (1) and (2) above. Thus, a critical evaluation of the 1887 notebooks suggests that they are not a straightforward copy of the original journal, but are already substantially revised with an eye toward publication. Accordingly, we cannot take the account found in these notebooks as reliable evidence of what Muir experienced—what he thought, felt, imagined, hoped, dreamed, or feared—in Yosemite during the summer of 1869. However, if my analysis of the general patterns of his 1887 process of revision is correct, we *can* take these 1887 notebooks as a fairly reliable guide to the sheer facts of the places and natural objects that Muir encountered that summer.

In retrospect, the style and character of the published *First Summer* should have given rise to questions such as these long ago, but the power of the Muir myth has been too strong. In large part because of his own success in the creation of a public image, as well as the ways that subsequent writers, scholars, and environmentalists have used and reinforced that image, the thought of a John Muir without a "first summer"— i.e., an ecstatic conversion upon entering Yosemite—has been almost inconceivable.

Although my conclusion actually fits in with my general approach better than does the standard interpretation of the "first summer," I was in no way looking for it, and never even considered the possibility until all of the documentary evidence was staring me full in the face. A fuller exploration of the process of revision would give us a fascinating window upon Muir's development and thought between the years 1869 and 1887; indeed, the imaginative *creation* of "Muir's first summer" could be seen as one of his major projects during that period. I will not undertake such a study here, however; the question that this discovery poses for me has to do with understanding his experiences during the summer of 1869 itself.

# Appendix B

# The Journal of the Southern Walk

The first step in using the journal of the Southern walk is to acknowledge the obvious and heavy editing and additions that Muir made at a much later date, when he was intending to publish it. As much as possible, I have been careful to use only the descriptions and language of the original text, which is usually clearly distinguishable from the modified words or added or rearranged passages. These acts of rewriting and editing are fascinating processes in themselves, and would have been important aspects of Muir's inner life at the time they occurred; however, in discussing his experiences and interpretations at the time of the walk itself I confine myself to considering the original passages.

Furthermore, Michael P. Cohen (4) has raised the possibility that the entire existing journal is not the original one, but rather a copy made later, perhaps in Yosemite or even after. Cohen notes that a few anomalies in the journal require explanation: the introductory passage, whose language suggests it was most probably inserted at some later date; the fact that some of the drawings were cut out of an original position and pasted into their present locations. (Another seeming anomaly—the existence of a number of places where the narrative is written continually in a distant past tense—Cohen takes as a sign of Muir's hyper-forward-looking consciousness during the walk.) Although all of these issues are clearly important, and to my knowledge no one besides Cohen has given them the consideration they deserve, I believe that they can be explained in other ways than by supposing that the journal was copied.

First, it is clear that many if not all of the pasted-in drawings were originally part of the present journal, filling up the gap between pages 64 and 71; the stubs of the cut-out pages are clearly visible, and on many of the sheets containing drawings one can find an appropriate page number (often on the reverse side from the drawing itself). Many of the drawings are still in their original locations, written directly on the page; one can note that Muir often made his drawings on a completely separate sheet from the ones he used for writing, especially so through the first half of the journal. This allows us to explain the first anomaly, the anachronistic introduction, by supposing that he left the first page and a half blank after drawing on the verso side of the first sheet, and added the introduction later, as part of a subsequent process of revision (I have no better guess than Cohen as to when). Finally, the long passages written in the past tense can be understood by assuming that at some points Muir went many days without writing in the journal, intentionally leaving room to fill in later on, and that he eventually did go back and complete the journal at later times during the trip, possibly even after he had made it to California. Thus, I believe that Cohen was partly right, in that certain significant segments of the journal were written at some time after the events actually occurred; the journal as a whole, however, seems to be original.

In particular, a number of issues have led me to conclude that much of Muir's account of his experiences in Bonaventure was written somewhat after the fact. The beginning of the account appears to have been written down at the time of the events. After the first few pages, however, the handwriting, margins, and verb tenses change abruptly when we come to the following sentence: "It was in October that I first beheld Bonaventure, the most impressive assemblage of animal and plant creatures I ever met" (23:55). Both this new handwriting and the sudden dramatic and self-conscious use of a distant past tense continue for many pages, including a passage where he says that the money for which he was waiting "did not arrive till the following week" (23:60). In addition, it seems highly unlikely that his descriptions of some details—such as his weakness from hunger and its effects on perception—were written as he was experiencing them; thus, it seems likely that Muir only began writing this whole section sometime after the entire experience was complete. This sense of a recollected or reconstructed narrative continues through his account of the steamship trip from Savannah to Fernandina, Florida, including some meandering comments on Georgia people and places that look as if they may have been inserted to fill up extra space. My hypothesis, then, is that Muir stopped writing in the journal after the first few pages of the description of Bonaventure and did not begin again until he was well into Florida, at which point he left open a number of pages so that he could then go back and fill them in at some future time. In fact, a whole section of drawings originally filled pages numbered 64–71 in the journal, and he may well have executed these drawings before going back to complete the written account. Although the written comments on pages 71–73 seem contemporaneous, the narrative then goes back into past tense until around page 87 (though I can't make a very definite judgment as to when he began writing again).

Perhaps a more important—and certainly more difficult—question is, When *were* these recollected or reconstructed passages written? Without making a definite claim, my hunch is that it was not until after he was struck down with malaria at Cedar Keys (on the Gulf coast of Florida) that he went back to fill in the uncompleted parts. For one thing, he claims on page 56 of the journal that fear of malaria was one of the things that led him to camp out in Bonaventure; curiously, none of the contemporaneous entries either before or after this time betray any such fear. Coming back to the journal after an actual bout with the illness, however, may have led him to project that awareness back into his past motives. Further, his month-long convalescence at Cedar Keys was the only time he would have had for such extended meditation and writing as went into these passages; in particular, after his illness—much more severe than his hunger at Bonaventure—he would have had good reason to think about death. Strikingly, Muir gives almost no hint of his thoughts or feelings in his accounts of his illness and convalescence; perhaps he felt the need to distance himself from the experience by projecting those inner responses back into more philosophical, less personally focused reflections upon his recent past. Thus, the Bonaventure incident proved useful as an occasion for working through and expressing some thoughts about death that were more immediately related to Muir's later experiences in Florida than to the Bonaventure experience itself.

# Appendix C

# Theoretical Frameworks
# for Environmental Biography
## Toward an Object Relations Approach

Since mid-century, a small but growing group of scholars and thinkers in a wide variety of fields have explored the inner dimensions of human interactions with the physical environment, both built and natural. Most of this work, however, has all but ignored the *emotional meanings* and the *developmental dynamics* of relationship with the environment in the lives of *individual persons*—issues crucial in understanding and writing an individual's environmental biography. Noting this problem in her 1995 *House as a Mirror of Self*, Clare Cooper Marcus begins by echoing the pioneering proposals of Bachelard and Searles (mentioned in my introduction): "At the base of this study is a very simple yet frequently overlooked premise: As we change and grow throughout our lives, our psychological development is punctuated not only by meaningful emotional relationships with people, but also by close affective ties with a number of significant physical environments, beginning in childhood." Such a perspective, however, is still a minority view, even in those fields where it is most relevant: "Psychologists whose domain is the study of emotional development view the physical environment as a relatively unimportant backdrop to the human dramas of life. Those who *are* interested in people-environment relations—geographers, anthropologists, architects, and the newly emerging field of environmental psychology—have for the most part ignored issues dealing with emotional attachment" (4).

A glance at a few representative works bears out Marcus' critique. One of the classics of humanistic geography, Yi-fu Tuan's *Topophilia,* takes as its title a term of Bachelard's, which Tuan redefines as "the affective bond between people and place or setting." The real concern of the book, however, is not emotional bonds at all, but rather "[p]erception, attitude, value, and world view" (1)—issues of cognition, image, and action rather than of emotion and meaning. Moreover, Tuan usually discusses larger groups—whole societies or cultures—rather than the lives of particular individuals. Similarly, the field of environmental psychology—rooted strongly in behavioral and cognitive approaches—analyzes environmental experience in terms of perception, classification, and preference, in order to address such issues as cognitive maps and route finding, territoriality, and stress. Traditionally concerned with the built environment (including home settings), environmental psychology has in recent years taken more of an interest in nature; in one recent summary of this literature, the psychologically important roles of the natural environment are characterized as "(1) nature restores; (2) nature facilitates competence building; (3) nature carries symbols that affirm culture or the self; and (4) nature offers, if nothing more, a shift in the stimulus field—inherently pleasing to an organism fueled by a need to investigate" (Knopf, 786). Clearly, while it affords interesting and valuable insights, such analysis runs the risk of becoming overly reductionist and atomistic—and in any case offers few opening for an appreciation of the emotional meanings and dynamics of an individual's environmental experience.[1]

As a third example—with a more specific focus on the natural environment—consider the proposals for an "ecopsychology" that have emerged from outside of academic psychology, in part as the therapeutic community's response to the environmental crisis. In the most prominent example, at the core of Theodore Roszak's ecopsychology is the concept of a preexisting, transpersonal "ecological unconscious" connecting humans with the natural and spiritual worlds; this ecological unconscious is variously identified with the id, with the "living record of cosmic evolution" and the "newborn's enchanted sense of the world" (320), and with the sheer materiality of the earth itself. Ultimately, however, Roszak's assertion of humans' deep connection to the planet serves more as an environmental ethic or worldview than as a basis for an analytic psychology; despite its imaginative and moral power, I find such an approach unsatisfactory as an aid in my more descriptive work of analyzing those specific connections that are operative in (and in fact created by) concrete lives in particular historical and natural contexts.[2]

1. For a general introduction to environmental psychology, see Stokols and Altman; for a sustained focus on the natural environment, see Kaplan and Kaplan.
2. J. P. Reser, in an extended discussion and sympathetic critique of ecopsychology, identifies the essential lessons of environmental psychology for ecopsychology as the insights that "connecting with the planet must . . . take place at a local level, and that attachment, meaning and identity . . . are related to behaviour in complex ways which are not necessarily elucidated by psychoanalytic or Jungian exegesis. The impact of the ecological crisis and

Interestingly, Roszak directs us to a passage from Freud that hints at a more concrete approach to the development of an individual's emotional relationship with the physical environment. At the beginning of *Civiliza-tion and Its Discontents*, Freud discusses the "oceanic feeling" that char-acterizes the experience of religion or of love, the "feeling of an indissol-uble bond, of being one with the external world as a whole." Freud suggests that this feeling must have come about through a discernable "process of development," and looks in particular at the infant's first ex-periences with the mother:

> An infant at the breast does not as yet distinguish his ego from the exter-nal world as the source of the sensations flowing in upon him. He gradu-ally learns to do so, in response to various promptings. . . . One comes to learn a procedure by which, through suitable muscular action, one can dif-ferentiate between what is internal—what belongs to the ego—and what is external—what emanates from the outer world. . . . In this way, then, the ego detaches itself from the external world. Or, to put it more cor-rectly, originally the ego includes everything, later it separates off an ex-ternal world from itself. Our present ego-feeling is, therefore, only a shrunken residue of a much more inclusive—indeed, an all-embracing—feeling which corresponded to a more intimate bond between the ego and the world about it. (12–15)

The "oceanic feeling," then, is the occasional resurfacing of this primal feeling in adult life. But does the legacy of this primal bond surface only occasionally? Might it not rather be active in a wide variety of everyday situations, providing an emotional substrate for our later interactions with the world? Moreover, does the sense of "an intimate bond" with the physical world necessarily cease after earliest infancy? Might similarly powerful bonds—different in meaning, color, and character, to be sure—emerge in the context of the person's development at later stages of life? How might such bonds emerge in relationship with all the different mean-ings of "environment"—the social and interpersonal environment, the built environment, the symbolic environment, the natural world? Might such a perspective provide the groundwork for what I see as the goals of environmental biography—to describe the interior meanings and dynam-

---

motivational imperatives may need to be *experienced* at a local level and must *register* on one's cognitive, emotional, and personal map of the world" (249–50). At the same time, Reser concludes by stressing the moral, social, and political message of ecopsychology: "If environmental psychologists do not consider and address the spectrum of issues raised by ecopsychologists, . . . seriously and urgently, they will have truly lost their way as well as their credibility" (252).

ics of an individual's environmental development in all their richness and meaning, and to relate environmental experience to the full range of human emotional and imaginative life, to interpersonal relationships, and to cultural and historical context?

Happily, it is precisely these dimensions of Freudian thought that are addressed by one recent development within psychoanalytic theory, namely, the object relations approach. Indeed, I believe that an object relations perspective offers a more comprehensive conceptual framework that can encompass the concerns and contributions of humanistic geography, environmental psychology, and developmental psychology at the same time as it opens outward into the arenas of culture, social relations, and historical context that are so essential in understanding and describing the concrete realities of an individual life. However, object relations theory must be significantly expanded and transformed in order to make it into a useful tool for environmental biography.

Instead of the traditional Freudian focus on drives, object relations theorists take relationship as the fundamental given of human existence, and the longing for relationship as an irreducible human reality. That is, for the child and the adult alike, "behavior and experiences of human beings are not derived from a set of directionless tensions seeking release, nor constructed out of a thirst for various bodily pleasures which become secondarily altered and transformed into socially acceptable and desirable behaviors. . . . [Rather,] human experience and behavior derive fundamentally from the search for and the maintenance of contact with others" (Greenberg and Mitchell, 156). Moreover, not just anyone or anything can adequately serve as the "object" of a particular person's longing; rather, each person (at each point in his or her life) has a definite array of other persons who serve as "primary objects," relationship with whom is crucially important for the sustenance, stability, and aliveness of that person's emotional life.[3] Indeed, echoing the passages from Freud quoted above, D. W. Winnicott has famously stated that "'there is no such thing as a baby'—meaning that if you set out to describe a baby, you will find you are describing a *baby and someone*. A baby cannot exist alone, but is essentially part of a relationship" (quoted in Hughes, 133). It is the relationship between baby and mother—or, more generally, any primary

3. It should be stressed that the term "object," as used here, is not meant to "objectify" the other person, in the usual sense; rather, the term is used to indicate the direction of the subject's longings and capacities for relationship. Of course, depending on the particular character of the subject's longings and capacities (and on the object's capacities for resistance), he or she *may* objectify the other person; but the relationship may also be a more warm, interactive, mutually humanizing one.

caregiver—that defines the fundamental reality of the situation, for baby and mother alike (though in powerfully different ways).

In particular, the healthy development of the infant depends on the experience of being "held," which for Winnicott begins with "the physical holding in the intra-uterine life, and gradually widens in scope to mean the whole of the adaptive care of the infant, including handling" (*Home*, 27). This holding has important psychological as well as physical implications, for the infant "begins life in a state of 'unintegration,' with scattered and diffuse bits and pieces of experience. The infant's organization of his own experience is preceded by and draws upon the mother's organized perceptions of him. The mother provides a 'holding environment' within which the infant is contained and experienced" (Greenberg and Mitchell, 191). Thus, the infant's relationship with the original primary object—the mother—allows the infant to become real to him or herself: "In an environment that holds the baby well enough, the baby is able to make *personal development according to the inherited tendencies*. The result is a continuity of existence that becomes a sense of existing, a sense of self, and eventually results in autonomy" (Winnicott, *Home*, 28).

A crucial dimension of this process of individuation involves the development of inner images or representations of the objects of the external world; indeed, it is in part through the creation of such images that an awareness of inner and outer, of the subjective and the objective realms, first emerges. From repeated encounters with the important primary object(s) of the holding environment, a person constructs "object representations" that embody and allow the person's subjective experience of those objects, shaped by want, need, expectation, and imagination as well as memory in all its forms (tactile, somatic, visual, cognitive, emotional, etc.). It is through these object representations that much of the character, texture, and meaning of relationships with actual people ("object relations") are mediated, and indeed one might say that full psychological relationship is possible only through (or in the presence of) inner representations. Moreover, it is in the midst of these relationships and representations that the self is formed, called forth by the presence of others at the same time as possessing the power to shape them. Thus, in the words of Diane Jonte-Pace, "according to object relations theory, the person is not constituted by the isolated interactions of impersonal instinctual energies, but by the interplay of human persons, both as those relationships actually occur in the world and as they are internalized" (312).[4]

---

4. On object relations theory and its historical development, see also works by D. W. Winnicott, W. R. D. Fairbairn, Harry Guntrip, John D. Sutherland, Judith M. Hughes, and Greenberg and Mitchell, among many others.

The object relations and representations most prominently involve family members or caregivers as the fundamentally important primary objects. However, in Winnicott's view, certain human or nonhuman beings can come to be infused with the emotions and meaning drawn from relationship with primary objects. Such an object (for example, a teddy bear or blanket, or more precisely the infant's internal representation of them) can then function as a bridge from a state of dependence on or union with the primary object (most often, initially at least, the mother) to a more autonomous sense of selfhood, without threatening the loss of the essential vitality and emotions grounded in the original relationship— and in fact providing a way to bring that emotional power into the autonomous subject's new psychological world. Paradoxically, the meaning and power of these "transitional objects" are clearly not inherent characteristics of the object in itself, yet are nevertheless experienced by the subject as coming from outside his or her realm of control; therefore, Winnicott refers to the "intermediate area of experience" or "potential space" between the infant and the mother, an in-between realm that is not wholly self or not-self but is saturated by the longings, energies, patterns, and powers of the self-in-relationship. Within this potential space, an everyday object is re-created as significant and powerful, and thus able to serve as a transitional object, a means of extending the subject's sense of self and meaningful world into new and larger arenas of action and relationship. Indeed, although object relations theory has traditionally interpreted the child's use of a transitional object as a (so to speak) defensive maneuver in negotiating the loss of maternal presence, it may be equally understood as a creative technique for gaining psychological control of an otherwise strange and even chaotic external world, and for injecting familiar and powerful emotions and meanings into that world. That is, in understanding the function of transitional phenomena, we may shift our emphasis from the infant's concern with maintaining connection with the primary caregiver to his or her needs and desires for establishing new relationships with the larger world. In any case, the relative importance of each goal depends in large part upon the particular experiences and capacities of each child/person, including the quality and character of his or her earlier human and nonhuman relationships.

Winnicott further defines potential space as "what happens between two people when there is trust and reliability" (quoted in Milner, "D. W. Winnicott," 39), again suggesting that a certain quality of relationship between infant and mother—or, more broadly, between a person and a primary object—is required in order for the creative growth and expansion that are achieved through use of a related transitional object. This idea is related to the traditional psychoanalytic notion of transference, so it comes as no surprise that Winnicott goes on to suggest that not only teddy bears and blankets but people as well can function as transitional phenomena. Long after the toys and blankets are cast away, the energies and images of the child's world are carried forward into the adult's relationships with and memories of particular persons, further sustaining and elaborating the sense of selfhood and aliveness rooted in primal experience.

Moreover, if everyday nonhuman objects can carry some of the psychological weight of relationships with loved ones, this process would apply most strongly to those things with which we have the most intimate and long-term interactions, namely, the objects, spaces, and places of home. Toys, clothing, buildings, the arrangement or color scheme of a room, stray memorabilia and hand-me-downs, a favorite garden or feared corner of the basement—all possess deep emotional associations with the people in whose company one lives (or lived) with those things. At the same time, some slices of meaning and feeling arise not from association with another person but in the context of relationship with the domestic objects themselves—though inanimate, such beings may possess a certain psychological life of their own, thus standing as "primary" objects in their own right.[5] Whether considered as primary objects or as transitional phenomena, the material objects that constitute a home are best understood—psychologically speaking, at least—not as a set of discrete things but as a web of relationships, continuous with the webs of human relationship that constitute family, friends, and society; in addition, just as with human "objects," our internal representations of the objects of home can be psychologically powerful as well, up to and including an overarching image of "home" that incorporates cultural values and images as well as personal memory and experience. Thus, the language of home may carry with it a whole range of meanings, emotions, and relationships, encompassing both human and nonhuman objects—making the image of home a particularly useful tool or tactic in the continuing process of coming into familiar and energized relationship with larger and larger segments of the outer world. That is, home may be important not only as

5. As Samuel Abrams and Peter B. Neubauer note, psychoanalysis has traditionally interpreted a powerful orientation toward a nonhuman object as pathological, branding such an object a "fetish"; Winnicott's idea of everyday objects as transitional phenomena places such an orientation on a more healthy psychological footing. Abrams and Neubauer find variations between children in the tendency to turn toward an animate or an inanimate object as a preferred transitional phenomenon; indeed, such variations in "human orientedness" versus "thing orientedness" may be inherent or congenital. In addition, we might expect similar variations in children's tendencies to relate to nonhuman things as primary objects.

"where we start from" (in Winnicott's phrase) but also as where we are going—and even as the vehicle that allows us to move along with (relative) comfort and a sense of direction.

Indeed, according to Winnicott, primary relationships and transitional phenomena are the basis of the meaningfulness of all symbolic objects, whether in domestic, artistic, or cultural life. Initially, symbolic creativity occurs when a person uses elements of primary experience to create wholly new inner representations—of a soon-to-be-born baby brother, for example, or of the mysterious resident of the house three doors down, or of the monster beneath the bed; in a similar (and equally if not more common) way, external symbols are received and interpreted, made meaningful, through associations with inner meanings, feelings, and representations drawn from previous experience—or themselves created on the spot, through the power of imagination. In the absence of external correlates, these private or public symbolic representations can themselves serve as objects of relationship in their own right, actors in a psychological drama that takes place on a stage somewhere between inner and outer—but is no less real for that. In this way, cultural symbols, images, and actions in a wide range of spheres—religion, literature, art, everyday life, social relations, economic activity, and ethnic, national, or racial identity—come to carry weight and depth in our psychic lives. Even abstract ideas derive some portion of their full meaning—denotative as well as connotative—from their spidery connections with powerful persons, places, and things.

The implications of the idea of the transitional object for understanding symbolic and cultural life have been explored in most detail by a number of contemporary psychologists of religion, who have reinterpreted God as a personalized representational object, constructed out of images, memories, ideas, and dynamics first encountered in relationship with primary objects. In particular, God is a representational object that can function as a transitional phenomenon, helping the child (and later, the adult) to negotiate the difficulties and opportunities of both relationship and selfhood. According to John McDargh, "The child encounters the raw material for the object representation of God in the same place and in the same way as the material for super-heroes, and devils, monsters, and imaginary companions. The child brings to all these the same vital agenda, the problem of becoming a self which means the problem of negotiating the terrors and traumas of achieving a sense of self that is both separate and securely related" (123). Unlike the teddy bear or the imaginary companion, however, the object representation that is God has an unusual tenacity and endurance in the psychic economy of the individual, and remains real and available for creative use long after other such objects have faded (whether or not the person actually "believes in" God). This endurance is perhaps explained by the particular power and depth of the relationships and experiences that give rise to and shape the original God representation, or by the presence of an entire cultural and social system—organized religion—designed precisely to keep that representation alive; depending on one's theological orientation, of course, one might also propose that the God representation is ultimately supported by—and finds its deepest reality and power in—the experience of encounter with an actual divine being or realm. That is, as we explore the uses and dynamics of religious belief and experience as transitional phenomena, we should also keep open the possibility of understanding them in terms of primary relationship with the divine as well.[6]

Despite their rejection of certain Freudian emphases, many contemporary object relations psychologists of religion find inspiration in the work of Freud, as when Ana-Maria Rizzuto quotes a passage from *Leonardo da Vinci and a Memory of His Childhood:*

> Psychoanalysis has made us familiar with the intimate connexion between the father-complex and belief in God; it has shown us that a personal God is, psychologically, none other than an exalted father. . . . Thus we recognize that the roots of the need for religion are in the parental complex; the almighty and just God, and kindly Nature, appear to us as grand sublimations of father and mother, or rather as revivals and restorations of the young child's ideas of them. (Rizzuto, 15)

Although Rizzuto follows this quotation with the important object relations insight that early relationships other than that with the father need to be considered in understanding religious belief, we can also take Freud's words in another direction—as the germ of a new approach to the exploration of the psychogenesis of our relationships with and representations of the natural world. As object relations theory has been expanded to include everyday domestic objects and religious phenomena, it can be used to understand the meanings and dynamics of human relationships with the natural world. Such work can be undertaken at every level of experience, from the most specific to the most general. For example, again utilizing Winnicott, some clinical psychologists have considered the psychological and developmental meanings of pets and other animals as transitional phenomena (see, e.g., Volkan and Kavanaugh). More broadly, just as religious experience involves a much more complex and ambivalent set of relations and symbols than "the almighty and just God,"

6. In addition to Jonte-Pace and McDargh, religious psychologists incorporating an object relations approach include Ana-Maria Rizzuto, W. W. Meissner, Naomi Goldenberg, and James Jones.

Freud's "kindly Nature" is surely too narrow an image for the full range of meanings, feelings, and concrete experiences that characterize our interactions with our natural surroundings; in particular, the implication that the image of nature is grounded primarily in the early experience of the mother must come in for some hard examination. Opening up a whole array of concrete and theoretical issues such as these, an object relations perspective can help us to explore how the full range of natural realities—specific animals, plants, landscapes, lived environments, and other natural phenomena up to and including "Nature" itself, as an encompassing symbol or generalized reality—may serve as primary objects and as transitional phenomena in an individual's life.[7]

At this point, we might summarize by asking the simple question: What do we mean by "environment"? In traditional object relations (and, more generally, psychoanalytic) thought, the relevant environment is restricted to the interpersonal and the social, to those other human bodies and persons with whom the individual lives and grows. To this, traditional environmental psychology would add the built environment, and in newer versions (joined by ecopsychology) the natural world as well. Without denying the very real psychological, ecological, and moral differences between them, we might want to unite the built and the natural in the category of the physical—though given the importance of those differences, we might *not*, and in any case the exact relationship between the natural and the built (and even what we mean by those terms) is a subject of much debate. In any case, the realities and powers influencing our lives may extend further than the natural/physical world, and so we must include the possibility of the supernatural and the religious as well; we may conceive of all of these as constituting a continuum, various aspects of a more fundamental category of the "nonhuman" or the "other-than-human." From the psychological perspective, however, even the distinction between the human and the other-than-human environments can be broken down in fundamental ways, as both realms can be seen as subject to some of the same dynamics and patterns when considered as elements of individual development and meaning-making. In addition to the interrelations between other persons, the external physical world, and the religious realm, the individual's body is at some times an integral part of the "self," at other times more of an "environment"; the same can even be said of deeper psychological phenomena and structures. Thus, alongside Winnicott's assertion that there is never a baby, only a baby-and-mother,

7. Roszak (291–95), Barrows, and others have raised the possibility of an object relations approach to environmental psychology—without, however, following up this suggestion in detail.

we might say that there is never a person, only a person-in-the-world—more precisely, a person-in-a-*particular*-world, a body and mind and heart surrounded by and in relationship with a specific set of natural and built objects and scenes as well as persons, cultural symbols, and religious forces and realities.

In answer to our "simple question," then, we find that there may be no such thing as a mere "environment" at all. This conclusion parallels the holistic approach called for by some recent environmental psychologists; for example, Irwin Altman and others have proposed a transactional perspective, in which

> the unit of psychological analysis is holistic entities such as events involving persons, psychological processes, and environments. The transactional whole is not composed of separate elements but is a *confluence* of inseparable factors that depend on one another for their very definition and meaning. Furthermore, transactional approaches focus on the *changing* relationships among aspects of the whole, both as a tool for understanding a phenomenon and because temporal processes are an integral feature of the person-environment whole. (Altman and Rogoff, 24)

To be sure, the transactional approach at present stands more as an ideal than as a definite methodological framework within environmental psychology (Altman, 278); for purposes of environmental biography, it must be further refined. As two steps in this direction, I would first stress again that "environment" must be understood in the broadest possible sense, as encompassing all of the physical realities that surround and shape us throughout our lives: the bodies of other humans, and in different ways our own bodies as well; the everyday objects with which we live, usually centered on the home; all levels of natural phenomena and built artifacts, in all their confusing intertwinings; perhaps even the supernatural realm, if and when it touches us through our heart or senses with the immediacy and power of a physical object. Second, we must acknowledge the presence and importance of something *between* a person and his or her environment, something akin to what Winnicott calls potential space, a realm of imagination, interpretation, and meaning that exists in (and transforms) person and environment simultaneously. In a sense, to assert the existence of such a realm is just to try to pinpoint what welds a person and an environment into a whole, what makes a person-environment *whole,* by allowing (or even constituting) the transactional relationships of mutual definition and meaning. On an individual level, we might term this realm "the symbolic," perhaps incorporating any or all of the various meanings that previous theorists have attached to that term; on a social and historical level, we might prefer to call it "culture," as I (perhaps mainly for purposes of convenience) will do in what follows. Thus, adopting a transactional perspective and adapting particular insights from environmental psychology and other fields as needed, I employ an expanded object relations approach in exploring the dynamics of person-culture-environment wholes.

Implicit in my discussion so far is a developmental dimension, an awareness that the symbols and structures of relationship between self and world are not static but rather constantly in motion: the simultaneously personal and social world of individual meaning goes through different phases in a life, with the particular character of each phase building upon the particular configuration of the last. According to Rizzuto (179), after its origins in the object relations and representations of infancy and earliest youth, "[t]he psychic process of creating and finding God—this personalized representational transitional object—never ceases in the course of human life. It is a developmental process that covers the entire life cycle from birth to death. . . . The process of reelaborating the God representation also follows the dynamic laws of psychic defense, adaptation, and synthesis, as well as the need for meaningful relations with oneself, others, and the world at large"—including one's domestic and natural environments. Moreover, I would suggest that an individual's images of "home" and of "nature" itself, along with particular relationships with specific home-places and natural beings, undergo similar processes of reelaboration over the cycles and circumstances of a life.

In exploring this developmental aspect of environmental experience, I have found certain insights from the developmental traditions of Piaget and Erikson to be useful in an object relations framework. Jean Piaget's early studies of the intellectual growth of children led to the formulation of the idea of distinct stages of logical systems, each system constituting an equilibrium between the child's developing inner capacities and his or her experience of physical body and world; Robert Kegan has stressed the centrality of interpersonal relationship and affective life in Piaget's view (as well as the flexibility of each individual's progression through the "stages"). Similarly, Erik Erikson's influential notion of personal identity as involving dual aspects, "inner" and "outer"—both "a subjective sense of an invigorating sameness and continuity" and "a unity of personal and cultural identity rooted in an ancient people's fate" (19, 20)—accords well with Winnicott's emphasis on the paradoxically intersubjective character of the potential space wherein both individuality and culture are born. However, the usual Eriksonian (and Piagetian) formulations of development and identity in terms of distinct "stages" are less satisfying, especially to the extent that such stages are tied to a rigid age-based progression. Thus, I have come to interpret identity in more transactional terms, looking not for a single, permanent "achievement" of personal identity (as did Erikson) but rather exploring the ways in which a range of private and public forces—internal and external relationships, images, meanings, and narratives—are constantly in interaction, co-creating each other in every new situation. Despite this fluidity and inherent change, the successive moments of an individual's life are fundamentally connected— physically, symbolically, developmentally—in ways that constitute or allow a sense of enduring selfhood and biographical unity as a locus of meaning, direction, and choice (not to mention sanity). Thus, the language of identity will be a useful way to refer to a person's changing experience of a cumulative integration of selfhood over the life course, including the relationships between such experience and the other more traditionally developmental dynamics of psychological and physiological growth.[8]

Later psychologists of religion such as James Fowler and Sharon Parks have expanded the developmental perspective to include the phenomenon of religious belief and/or experience; that is, a person's mode of being religious goes through certain cumulative stages as the individual matures. Moreover, a developmental perspective can be similarly expanded to include relationships with the natural and built environments as well. In exploring the dynamics of these processes with respect to nature, a number of theorists have focused on a Muir-like connection between childhood and wildness. In the psychoanalytic tradition, Edith Cobb proposes that the Freudian "latency period" is a time when inner energies are not really latent at all but rather quite actively expressed in an arena other than family or sexuality, namely, in the task of exploring the natural world; Rachel Sebba outlines some of the particular aspects or qualities of the natural environment that allow it to hold such deep attraction and meaning for the child. However, an adequate developmental approach must interpret relationship with the natural environment not solely in terms of internally driven stages but also with reference to a whole range of conditioning forces such as sexuality, cognition, belief systems (including religion), gender roles, and so on—and must also locate the experi-

8. Interestingly, the transactional emphasis on change as an inherent aspect of "the person-environment whole" leaves open the possibility that the "directions of change [are] emergent and not preestablished," and so "the goal of transactional approaches is to understand the pattern and flow of particular events, by means of existing and emergent principles" (Altman and Rogoff, 13, 27). This perspective accords well with my insistence on the uniqueness of each life as a product (in part) of individual creativity and of the specificity of historical circumstance, thus requiring a primarily descriptive approach rather than one based in predetermined analytic or explanatory categories.

ence of nature within the patterns and dynamics of one's experience of the total environment, broadly conceived.

Moreover, childhood environmental experience is not as unfailingly positive as these (and many other) theorists imply. Concluding their discussion of the development of "place identity" in childhood, the environmental psychologists Harold M. Proshansky and Abbe K. Fabian state: "The cognitions that form the basis of place identity include affective responses to settings that range from attachment to aversion. Consequently, self-identity is informed by cognitions of the physical world that are not only self-enhancing and supporting but also threatening and potentially damaging as well" (36). Of course, in addition to shaping one's sense of self, negative environmental experiences can lead to fear or devaluation of the natural world in general. This broad and inclusive perspective seems more adequate than the narrower focus on purely positive attachment that characterizes most discussions of childhood experience of nature (as well as Tuan's "topophilia" and related notions in humanistic geography).[9] Most especially, I would want to look critically at any romantic idealization of childhood (such as that of Cobb) that sees it as a time of "direct," "unmediated," "pure," or otherwise privileged relationship with the natural world. As I argue in Muir's case, childhood experience of nature—like childhood itself—must be understood in the context of the entire range of human projects, conflicts, imaginings, and desires.

On one level, adapting insights from Winnicott, Cobb, Piaget, and others, we may view the individual's relationship with his or her environment as aspects of a common human structuring, a back-and-forth developmental pattern of orientation to "the other" and "the world," human and nonhuman alike. After the infant's focus on (even identification with) the mother, the toddler moves outward to discover the spaces and things of a simultaneously human, natural, and supernatural world; after the intense familial and sexual developments of the oedipal phase, the latency child is once again free to explore a larger world; after the adolescent focus on peer group identity, the young adult must create new sorts of relationship with an even larger world, and most crucially forge an individual life path in it. The process does not stop there, however, but continues in the form of the more or less dramatic shifts in focus on and concern for self, other, and world that recur throughout adult life. In adulthood, these shifts seem less tied to specific stages of physical, neurological, and psycholog-

---

9. To be sure, Tuan himself tried to rectify the limitations of *Topophilia* by writing *Landscapes of Fear;* it is the former work, however, which is considered a classic in the field and has exerted most influence in other fields, reflecting our culture's preference for positive views of natural experience in adulthood as well as in childhood.

ical development, more diffusely affected by personal experience and choice and by cultural influence and historical circumstance.

Indeed, it is important to remember that even in earliest childhood, each developmental moment is overlaid by a whole range of historical and cultural images, patternings, opportunities, and powers, as well as by a different range of individual textures, wants, barriers, and choices; as stressed in the introduction, my approach assumes both a radical historical embeddedness and an equally radical individual power of unique and spontaneous imagination, choice, and action. Thus, at each step the individual's capacities for creativity and for courage are both constrained and called forth, are given or denied shape, strength, and substance, by the whole historical world within which we live and move and have our being.

Alongside this historically conditioned developmental trajectory, however, we must overlay a more uniquely biographical one, the particular succession of environments that each individual encounters in his or her own life. At the same time as the cumulative emergence of psychological capacities, needs, and desires is busy shaping the individual's changing relationship with his or her surroundings, the surroundings themselves are changing as well, to greater or lesser degrees. Moreover, these biographical-environmental changes have an emotional power and psychological dynamic of their own; like developmental stages, each environment of our lives *actively shapes* the psychological, emotional, and imaginative meanings of the next. Joachim Wohlwill and Imre Kohn offer the following as a postulate of environmental psychology: "The individual evaluates an environment on a given dimension in terms of a frame of reference established through prior experience in previous environments" (Wapner et al., 30). To be sure, in seeming contrast, William H. Ittelson, Karen A. Franck, and Timothy J. O'Hanlon stress the creative dimension: "Environmental experience is the continuing product of an active endeavor by the individual to create for himself a situation within which he can optimally function and achieve his own particular pattern of satisfaction" (Wapner et al., 206). Both dimensions—the backward-looking and the forward-looking—must be considered in understanding a particular encounter with a new place. Moreover, the two positions may not really be in opposition: the use of familiar patterns to make meaning out of a strange new experience is on many levels a creative act. Less technically, David Lowenthal's comments on the shaping of landscape perception by the historical past apply as well to the personal past: "We need the past . . . to cope with present landscapes. We selectively perceive what we are accustomed to seeing; features and patterns in the landscape make sense to us because we share a history with them. . . . Without the past as tangible or remembered evidence we could not function" (5–6). (Such dynamics are intensified in the confrontation with drastically new environments, as in the case of immigrants and migrants such as Muir.)

Again, far from being merely an arena for the expression of intrapsychic or interpersonal developments, the physical environment is an active participant in the development of a person-culture-environment whole; even at its deepest levels, an individual's inner trajectory of environmental development depends on the specific environments in which (or *with* which) that individual comes into being. Considered as person-culture-environment wholes, Muir-in-frontier-Wisconsin-in-1856 is a different reality from Muir-in-Yosemite-in-1869, with the process of evolution between the two shaped *in part* by Muir's developing environmental attitudes and orientations—themselves shaped by the personal trajectories of his psychological and physical capacities, webs of images and relationships, and enduring sense of selfhood—but *also* by the concrete differences in the specific environments through which Muir moved and by the particular influences that those environments had on Muir's inner life.[10]

As a central developmental dynamic of each person's environmental biography—and as discussed with respect to Muir in the conclusion—the confluence of developmental and biographical trajectories calls forth (or, requires the creation of) a succession of paired sets of representations of the environment, one of each set being "positive" and the other "negative." Thus, at each point in life, a person has images of "good"—or attractive, beautiful, loved—natural places and beings that oppose images of "bad" ones; both of these categories intersect with more general images of "good" and "bad" built and domestic environments, leading to larger constructs of "good Nature" and "bad Nature," "good places" and "bad places," and even "heaven" and "hell." Each individual has an array of paradises shaped by cultural influences as well as by personal needs and experiences; these paradises—religious, environmental, and so-

10. In conversation, John Elder has suggested that I am taking a bioregional approach to biography, taking my subject's natural region as more than a mere setting but rather as a real actor in his life, with a shape, character, and influence distinctive to that region. From that perspective, the leading question of a life story would be: How has this person come to *inhabit* his or her particular bioregion, his or her particular place on earth? In studying Muir (and in reflecting on my own life), I have found that an equally important set of questions is: How does one move from one region to another, how is one able to abstract patterns of experience from one place and adapt them to (or perhaps impose them on) a different place, how is one able to stay open to a new place? As we shall see, Muir's particular trajectory of development led him through a succession of bioregions, making the question of coming-to-inhabit particularly complex. Although I have in general chosen to use other conceptual languages, the bioregional approach could provide an equally fruitful language for discussing many of my concerns.

cial—are counterbalanced by their opposite, as useful (and perhaps even essential) psychological tools in making one's way through a complex life and world. In one interesting example, Sebba explores the ways in which the special places of a person's childhood—experienced through the particular developmental capacities, psychological needs, and environmental configurations active at that age—are then selectively interpreted by the adult in the construction of an idealized image of "the landscape of childhood," which may be used to address specifically adult needs and goals, especially in the context of the adult's actual environmental situation. One could complete Sebba's analysis through a study of the *feared* places of childhood, as experienced by the child and remembered by the adult, with special attention to the uses to which these images are put in the context of the developmental, biographical, and environmental needs and patterns both of childhood and of adulthood.

In particular, at each point in an individual's life, an inner representation of and relationship with an appropriately present and positive environment is necessary in order for the person to develop the capacity to be alone. According to Winnicott, the capacity to be alone is rooted in the experiences of infancy but may develop into one of the crucial dimensions of emotional maturity: "The basis of the capacity to be alone is the experience of being alone in the presence of someone. In this way an infant . . . may be alone because of reliable ego-support. . . . Gradually, the ego-supportive environment is introjected and built into the individual's personality, so that there comes about the capacity actually to be alone. Even so, theoretically, there is always someone present, someone who is equated ultimately and unconsciously with the mother" (*Maturational Process*, 36). From an expanded object relations perspective, certain of one's images and experiences of the physical environment are (or at least can be) an element of the "ego-supportive environment" that provides the basis for the capacity to be alone; moreover, those natural or domestic environments in which it is possible to be alone may include or represent a whole range of supportive relationships in addition to the felt presence/absence of one's mother. Other environments, however—"bad" ones—carry a more threatening weight of association and meaning, from which we must somehow feel protected in order to be alone (even if that protection comes only through our own inner strength, courage, or confidence). Thus, in adulthood as well as in childhood, our sense of place identity is grounded both in positive and in negative experiences and images, tied both to our particular present reality and to the inner legacy that shapes our experience of it.

At this point, having discerned an essential ambiguity and tension within our psychological experience of the physical world (natural and built alike), we might begin to ask: Is there a "proper" or "mature" relationship between an adult and her or his nonhuman environment? Of course, the answers vary widely. Discussing the "characteristic *mature* orientation" of the "healthy individual," Searles proposes what he calls "relatedness"—on the one hand, "a sense of intimate kinship, a psychological concomitant to the structural [physiological, evolutionary, ecological] kinship which . . . exists between man and the various ingredients of his nonhuman environment," and on the other hand "a maintenance of our own sense of individuality as a human being." Asserting that "adult living involves an unceasing struggle to maintain, and ever more deeply realize and develop, one's humanity vis-à-vis the surrounding nonhuman world," Searles insists that "however close our kinship, on however multiple levels, to the nonhuman environment, we are not at *one* with it" (101–2). Although a feeling of oneness with the world may be a normal— and even important or essential—experience during adolescence, those who "continue throughout their lives to identify themselves more with Nature than with mankind" are psychologically stunted, having "fail[ed] to carry through to this final differentiation of [one]self as a full-fledged human being" (99).

In contrast, Roszak—reflecting much contemporary popular environmental and spiritual rhetoric—places most value on precisely the feeling of oneness with the world that Searles rejects as adolescent: "Ecopsychology seeks to recover the child's innately animistic quality of experience in functionally 'sane' adults." On the one hand, an oceanic feeling of oneness breaks down many of the constructs of selfhood and patterns of action that alienate humanity from nature (and allow the destruction of the latter); on the other hand, the experience of oneness gives new access to the wisdom stored within us, "awaken[ing] the inherent sense of environmental reciprocity that lies within the ecological unconscious" (320). This sense of reciprocity, the deepest layer of our evolutionary heritage, involves (or requires) "a *transactional* bond with the natural; there must be give and take, courtesy and respect" (79). From this perspective, maturity implies not an "unceasing struggle" to assert our humanity over against the nonhuman (as for Searles) but rather the quest to achieve "a perfect *response* to the environment, one that allows us to grow, move, act within it gracefully" (296).

But can we be so sure that the world will be welcoming of our humanity, whether asserted through struggle or offered in grace? According to Aldous Huxley, "If one would live well, one must live completely, with the whole being—with the body and the instincts, as well as with the conscious mind" (123–24). Although much of twentieth-century psychology (including ecopsychology) claims to honor the body and the instincts, most theorists are not as ready as Huxley to heed the lessons that the body and the instincts teach: "Our direct intuitions of Nature tell us that the world is bottomlessly strange; alien, even when it is kind and beautiful; having innumerable modes of being that are not our modes; always mysteriously not personal, not conscious, not moral; often hostile and sinister; sometimes even unimaginably, because inhumanly, evil" (118). Although I would not go as far as Huxley's rhetoric suggests—the "innumerable modes of being" of the natural world may sometimes include personality or consciousness; the assertion of evil seems to contradict nature's independence from human morality—his insistence upon the concrete differences between humans and the rest of nature is as refreshing now as when it was originally written. The human encounter with the natural world, in adulthood as in childhood, must be understood through as wide a range of categories and responses as emerge in any given person's experience of a given place; rather than imposing normative judgments of morality or maturity, the individual must learn "once more to treat Nature naturally, as he treated it in his youth, to react to it spontaneously, loving where love [is] the appropriate emotion, fearing, hating, fighting whenever Nature present[s] itself to his intuition as being, not merely strange, but hostile" (Huxley, 129).

Interestingly, the one thing that Searles, Roszak, and Huxley all have in common is a belief in the concrete and autonomous reality of the natural world as something "other" to which we can relate in more or less direct and immediate ways—and a presumption that more directness and immediacy is better than less. In Searles's words,

> It is my conviction . . . that the more directly we can relate ourselves to the nonhuman environment *as it exists*—the more our relatedness to it is freed from perceptual distortions in the form of projection, transference, and so on—the more truly meaningful, the more solidly emotionally satisfying, is our experience with this environment. Far from our finding it to be in a state of negativity and deadness, we find in ourselves a sense of kinship toward it which is as alive as it is real. (115)

However, my whole approach is based on the denial of this premise. From the transactional perspective, person and environment are not separate entities that may (or may not) relate but rather constitute an integrated whole in which perceptual, psychological, and cultural patterns— whether "distortions" or not—are essential to the meaning and shape of the reality. Similarly, the object relations approach offers Winnicott's idea of the potential space between person and environment—a space filled with emotion, association, and symbolism, sometimes distorted, sometimes not—as "the place where we live," the matrix out of which the senses of aliveness, of reality, and of kinship are created. To relate to the natural world "as it exists" is *essentially* to relate to and through our own projections, transferences, and other psychological processes; conversely, the only existence and meaning that these psychological processes possess are as forces that shape and infuse our concrete experiences of body, other, and world. It is the forced separation of the two realms that leads to emotional and spiritual deadness; in contrast, aliveness, reality, and kinship arise—or, are created—out of the complex interconnections between person and place, encompassing a whole range of particular and contingent experiences, processes, and realities. This is what it means to say that humans—*all* of us, our psyches and souls as well as our bodies— are *part of* the natural world.

Perhaps, then, assigning a predetermined target for the arc of individual environmental development runs the risk of excluding powerful, important, even essential aspects of human experience; perhaps the multiple intertanglings of psychological, biographical, historical, and geographical factors that constitute each person-culture-environment whole cannot be evaluated according to any single standard of environmental maturity. Rather, in accord with my general Wittgensteinian attitude of *"look and see,"* I propose that we utilize whatever concepts and categories help us to understand how images of and relationships with the physical world actually work in people's lives, what meanings and strengths and textures a powerful relationship with nature can give to a person, what motives and materials provoke a person to construct his or her environment (and, correlatively, identity) in certain ways, with what particular uses and creative contributions. What does a particular orientation towards one's surroundings help one to *do* in the world, or with one's life? What does a particular orientation toward one's surroundings allow the world to do to you? Thus, in exploring Muir's (or anyone's) environmental experiences, my goal is not to impose normative judgments but to strive to understand and describe as sensitively and openly as possible what individuals (and their communities and historical contexts) *make* of those experiences—and what those experiences have made of them.

In this, my approach is similar to that of those scholars in the field of religious studies who analyze religion not according to external standards of theological or philosophical correctness but with respect to the ways in which religious experiences, symbols, actions, and structures actually function in people's lives, to orient them to the world and to help bring them into accord with whatever ideals of health, beauty, strength, and hope they envision (and create) on their own terms. Indeed, along with this general approach, a number of specific insights or models from religious studies can help us in understanding the meanings and dynamics of environmental experience. In particular, we may conceive of symbols of or relationships with the physical world as part of a "centering" or "meaning-making" activity, a form of cultural and personal creativity through which individuals and communities come to some apprehension of depth, meaning, worth, wholeness, reality, power, or whatever else is "highest" or "fundamental" in their lives. Thus, Albanese—understanding religion as "the way or ways that people orient themselves in the world with reference to both ordinary and extraordinary powers" (6)— regards images of and relationships with the natural world (which, I would stress, includes both one's specific surroundings and/or "Nature" as a literal or symbolic whole) as possible ways of orienting oneself in the world and of establishing a center in one's life. Of course, at the fountain- head of modern religious studies, Mircea Eliade stresses the fundamental importance of a particular sort of ritually shaped environmental experi- ence in constituting the world as ordered, as a cosmos, and hence as a world that may be lived in with vitality and purpose. The question then may be asked: Might less structured, more everyday or spontaneous expe- riences of the natural or built worlds similarly serve the human need to be centered? What psychological, symbolic, interpersonal, and environ- mental patterns support the human sense of being welcomed into an or- dered and vital cosmos? Or, do or might our experiences of the world allow or force us to fashion a way of living *without* a center, or with multiple or shifting centers?

Moreover, our particular ways of interacting with our environments— like our religious orientations—help us not only to make sense of the world but also to act within it, to deal with the mundane and extraordi- nary tasks, challenges, and opportunities of our lives. That is, our images of and patterns of relationship with the physical world are part of what Ann Swidler refers to as a cultural "'tool kit' of habits, skills, and styles from which people construct 'strategies of action'" (273). On one level, of course, environmental psychologists for years have been exploring the ways in which our cognitive and behavioral orientations to our environ- ment allow us to function on a pragmatic level; but there are deeper, more meaning-laden dimensions as well. In one instance, as Victor Turner ex- plores, certain configurations of the environment can serve as the ritual sites of liminal experiences, in which an individual's normal culturally constructed identity is temporarily stripped away, allowing a window for symbolic and social creativity—even revolution—before cultural patterns are reimposed (and paradoxically strengthened by the cyclic process). Es- pecially in modern societies, however, we are confronted with crisis and the possibility of transformation not only through formal ritual processes but also in the more unstructured and episodic challenges and perplexities of everyday life. As Robert Orsi argues,

> Religious creativity is provoked by cultural and personal crises, and (especially) by the intersection of the two. The most explosive provocations of this sort come in the most dangerous and serious domains of our material existence—in our efforts to formulate our experiences of our bodies and negotiate our desires (sex), to endure and make sense of physical distress (pain), and to constitute some meaning for ourselves in the face of our finality (death). ("Forum," 3)

I would open up the possibility of an environmental creativity, or creative use and experience of our natural and built surroundings, to parallel religiousness as a means of deeply engaging and addressing these cultural and personal "hot spots." How do our images of and relationships with the natural and built worlds help us to experience our sexuality in more— or less—powerful, satisfying, and/or integrated ways? What patterns of environmental experience help or hinder us in dealing with pain and suffering, practically as well as symbolically? What views and textures of the world make sense of death, or leave it senseless?

In these and other arenas, if the environment—as symbol or as the actual object of an important relationship—can function in any of these ways that religion has been seen to function, it clearly plays an important role in a person's inner life. However, in line with my historicist and biographical perspectives, we must be careful to discern *which* of these (or other) life issues and developmental dynamics are really relevant or vital for a particular person in a concrete historical context—and moreover, the particular ways in which that person and culture construct and experience those issues and dynamics. Thus, it is the sensitive, contextual understanding of the ways in which our patterns of experiencing our environment work *for* us or *against* us—or perhaps merely *on* us—that provides the basis for evaluations of health or maturity, not the imposition of a preconceived standard or ideal.

My proposal here is that the shape, power, and dynamics of these varieties of environmental experience can be more deeply understood through the expanded object relations approach that I have outlined above. However, I must close by stressing again that my whole approach has been developed primarily as a tool to help me explore one particular life, that of John Muir, and secondarily as an occasion for thinking on my own life and experiences (though perhaps those priorities should be reversed, to the extent that my initial attraction to Muir was shaped by questions I was already asking of myself). I am thus left not with conclusions but with more questions. How would this sort of analysis need to be modified, or perhaps entirely refashioned, in understanding the environmental biography of another life, another place, another time? In particular, I am keenly aware that Muir represents yet another in a long line of white men put forward as cultural paradigms and heroes; what different images and dynamics, shapes and styles, narratives and analyses would be necessary to write the environmental biographies of women and of nonwhite persons? On a more personal level, does this way of understanding the emotional and developmental aspects of environmental experience help us to love the natural world and each other more deeply, strongly, and tenderly? Does my approach enrich and enliven your own environmental experience and your life? What further resources of mind and heart—yours, mine, the world's—can help us to a fuller, livelier, and more whole apprehension of the joys and dangers, the powers and limitations of our human embeddedness in the fabric of the physical world?

# Works Cited

## WRITINGS OF JOHN MUIR

Address to the Sierra Club. *Sierra Club Bulletin* 1, no. 7 (January 1896): 271–85.
"The Calypso Borealis: Botanical Enthusiasm." *Boston Recorder* 51, no. 51 (December 21, 1866): 1.
*John of the Mountains: The Unpublished Journals of John Muir.* Ed. Linnie Marsh Wolfe. Madison: Univ. of Wisconsin Press, 1979. Originally published in 1938.
*The Mountains of California.* New York: The Century Co., 1894.
*My First Summer in the Sierra.* Boston: Houghton Mifflin, 1911.
*Our National Parks.* Boston: Houghton Mifflin, 1901.
*The Story of My Boyhood and Youth.* Boston: Houghton Mifflin, 1913.
*A Thousand-Mile Walk to the Gulf.* Boston: Houghton Mifflin, 1916.
"The Treasures of the Yosemite." *Century Magazine* 40, no. 4 (August 1890): 483–500.
"Twenty Hill Hollow." *Overland Monthly* 9, no. 1 (July 1872): 80–86.
"Yosemite Glaciers." *New York Tribune,* December 5, 1871.
"Yosemite Valley in Flood." *Overland Monthly* 8, no. 4 (April 1872): 347–50.

A 51-reel, 53-fiche microfilm edition containing virtually all of the collected papers of John Muir has been edited by Ronald H. Limbaugh and Kirsten E. Lewis and published by Chadwyck-Healey, Inc. (Alexandria, Va., 1986). The collection contains all the Muir materials held at that time by the Holt-Atherton Center for Western Studies of the University of the Pacific (Stockton, Calif.), as well as materials from research archives and private holdings across the country. These materials include Muir's own letters, journals, and manuscripts, along with numerous personal and business letters from family, friends, and associates, as well as unpublished reminiscences of Muir, numerous drawings and photographs, and other memorabilia. I will refer to microfilm material by reference to reel and frame number, e.g., "2:790" would refer to reel 2, frame 790.

## SECONDARY SOURCES

Abbey, Edward. *Desert Solitaire: A Season in the Wilderness.* New York: Ballantine, 1971.

Abrams, Samuel, and Peter B. Neubauer. "Transitional Objects: Animate and Inanimate." In *Between Fantasy and Reality: Transitional Objects and Phenomena,* ed. Simon A. Grolnick and Leonard Barkin, 133–44. New York: Jason Aronson, 1978.

Ahlstrom, Sidney E. *A Religious History of the American People.* 2 vols. New York: Image, 1975.

Albanese, Catherine. *Nature Religion in America: From the Algonkian Indians to the New Age.* Chicago: Univ. of Chicago Press, 1990.

Allen, C. L. "Baconianism and the Bible in the Disciples of Christ." *Church History 55,* no. 1 (1986): 65–80.

Altman, Irwin. "A Transactional Perspective on Transitions to New Environments." *Environment and Behavior 24,* no. 2 (March 1992): 268–80.

Altman, Irwin, and Barbara Rogoff. "World Views in Psychology: Trait, Interactional, Organismic, and Transactional Perspectives." In *Handbook of Environmental Psychology,* ed. Daniel Stokols and Irwin Altman, I:7–40. New York: Wiley, 1987.

Anderson, R. D. *Education and the Scottish People, 1750–1918.* Oxford: Clarendon, 1995.

Anderson, William. *Green Man: The Archetype of Our Oneness with the Earth.* London: HarperCollins, 1990.

Bachelard, Gaston. *The Poetics of Space.* Translated from the French by Maria Jolas. Boston: Beacon, 1969.

Badè, William Frederic. *The Life and Letters of John Muir.* 2 vols. Boston: Houghton Mifflin, 1923.

Barrows, Anita. "The Ecopsychology of Child Development." In *Ecopsychology: Restoring the Earth, Healing the Mind,* ed. Theodore Roszak, Mary E. Gomes, and Allen D. Kanner, 101–10. San Francisco: Sierra Club Books, 1995.

Benfey, Christopher. *The Double Life of Stephen Crane.* New York: Alfred A. Knopf, 1992.

Bentley, D. M. R. "'We in Dreams Behold the Hebrides': Alexander McLachlan's *The Emigrant.*" *British Journal of Canadian Studies 7,* no. 1 (1992): 15–25.

Berry, Thomas. *The Dream of the Earth.* San Francisco: Sierra Club Books, 1988.

Brooks, Walter R. *God in Nature and Life: Selections from the Sermons and Writings of Walter R. Brooks.* New York: Anson D. F. Randolph, 1889.

Buell, Lawrence. *The Environmental Imagination: Thoreau, Nature Writing, and the Formation of American Culture.* Cambridge: Harvard Univ. Press, 1995.

Bunyan, John. *The Pilgrim's Progress.* New York: New American Library, 1981.

Burns, Robert. *Poems and Songs.* New York: Dover, 1991.

Butterfield, C. W. *History of the University of Wisconsin, from Its First Organization to 1879.* Madison: Univ. of Wisconsin Press, 1879.

Calhoun, Craig. "The Problem of Identity in Collective Action." In *Macro-Micro Linkages in Sociology,* ed. Joan Huber, 51–75. Beverly Hills, Calif.: Sage, 1991.

Carr, Ezra S. *The Patrons of Husbandry on the Pacific Coast.* San Francisco: A. L. Bancroft, 1875.

*Catalogue . . . of the Wisconsin State University, for the year . . . 1861.* Madison: Wisconsin State Univ., 1861.

Chandler, Alice. *A Dream of Order: The Medieval Ideal in Nineteenth Century English Literature.* Lincoln: Univ. of Nebraska Press, 1970.

Chandler, Marilyn R. *Dwelling in the Text: Houses in American Fiction.* Berkeley: Univ. of California Press, 1991.

Cobb, Edith. *The Ecology of Imagination in Childhood.* New York: Columbia Univ. Press, 1959.

Coe, Richard N. *When the Grass Was Taller: Autobiography and the Experience of Childhood.* New Haven: Yale Univ. Press, 1984.

Cohen, Michael P. *The Pathless Way: John Muir and American Wilderness.* Madison: Univ. of Wisconsin Press, 1984.

Cronon, William. "The Trouble with Wilderness; or, Getting Back to the Wrong Nature." In *Uncommon Ground: Rethinking the Human Place in Nature,* ed. William Cronon, 69–90. New York: Norton, 1996.

Crunden, Robert. *Ministers of Reform.* New York: Basic Books, 1982.

Curti, Merle, and Vernon Carstensen. *The University of Wisconsin: A History, 1848–1925.* Madison: Univ. of Wisconsin Press, 1949.

Dick, Thomas. *The Christian Philosopher; or, The Connexion of Science and Philosophy with Religion.* 8th ed. Philadelphia: E. C. & J. Biddle, 1850.

Emerson, Ralph Waldo. *Essays & Lectures/Ralph Waldo Emerson.* The Library of America, vol. 15. New York: The Literary Classics of the United States, 1983.

Erikson, Erik. *Identity: Youth and Crisis.* New York: Norton, 1968.

Evernden, Neil. *The Natural Alien: Humankind and Environment.* Toronto: Univ. of Toronto Press, 1985.

Fairbairn, W. Ronald D. *From Instinct to Self: Selected Papers of W. R. D. Fairbairn.* 2 vols. Northvale, N.J.: Jason Aronson, 1994.

Fallows, A. K. *Everybody's Bishop.* New York: J. H. Sears, 1927.

Faulkner, William. *Go Down, Moses.* New York: Vintage, 1990.

Fiske, John. "Following Muir's First Summer Route." *John Muir Newsletter 5,* no. 1 (Winter 1994/95): 1ff.

Fleck, Richard F. "John Muir's Transcendental Imagery." In *John Muir: Life and Work,* ed. Sally M. Miller, 136–51. Albuquerque: Univ. of New Mexico Press, 1993.

Fowler, James W. *Stages of Faith: The Psychology of Human Development and the Quest for Meaning.* San Francisco: Harper and Row, 1981.

Fox, Stephen. *The American Conservation Movement: John Muir and His Legacy.* Madison: Univ. of Wisconsin Press, 1981.

Fredrickson, George M. *The Inner Civil War: Northern Intellectuals and the Crisis of the Union.* New York: Harper and Row, 1965.

Garber, Frederick. "Henry David Thoreau." In *The Columbia Literary History of the United States*, ed. Emory Elliott. New York: Columbia Univ. Press, 1988.

Garber, Frederick. "Pastoral Spaces." *Texas Studies in Literature and Language* 30, no. 3 (Fall 1988): 431–60.

Garber, Frederick. *Thoreau's Fable of Inscribing*. Princeton: Princeton Univ. Press, 1991.

Gittings, Chris. "Canada and Scotland: Conceptualizing 'Postcolonial' Spaces." *Essay on Canadian Writing* 56 (Fall 1995): 135–61.

Goldenberg, Naomi R. *Returning Words to Flesh: Feminism, Psychoanalysis, and the Resurrection of the Body*. Boston: Beacon, 1990.

Goody, Jack. *The Culture of Flowers*. Cambridge: Cambridge Univ. Press, 1993.

Greenberg, Jay R., and Stephen A. Mitchell. *Object Relations in Psychoanalytic Theory*. Cambridge: Harvard Univ. Press, 1983.

Greven, Philip. *The Protestant Temperament: Patterns of Child-Rearing, Religious Experience, and Self in Early America*. Chicago: Univ. of Chicago Press, 1977.

Greven, Philip. *Spare the Child: The Religious Roots of Punishment and the Psychological Impact of Physical Abuse*. New York: Alfred A. Knopf, 1990.

Gridley, A. D. "Laws of Association in Ornamental Gardening." *North American Review* 87, no. 180 (July 1858): 157–70.

Grolnick, Simon A., and Leonard Barkin, eds. *Between Fantasy and Reality: Transitional Objects and Phenomena*. New York: Aronson, 1978.

Guntrip, Harry. *Psychoanalytic Theory, Therapy, and the Self*. New York: Basic Books, 1973.

Hatch, Nathan O. *The Democratization of American Christianity*. New Haven: Yale Univ. Press, 1989.

Hensley, Carl Wayne. "Rhetorical Vision and the Persuasion of a Historical Moment: The Disciples of Christ in Nineteenth-Century American Culture." *Quarterly Journal of Speech* 61 (October 1975): 250–64.

Hobsbawm, Eric, and Terence Ranger, eds. *The Invention of Tradition*. Cambridge: Cambridge Univ. Press, 1984.

Holmes, Steven J. "Place Making, Sacred and Profane: John Muir and a Mountain Meadow." *Soundings: An Interdisciplinary Journal*, forthcoming.

Hovenkamp, Robert. *Science and Religion in America, 1800–1860*. Philadelphia: Univ. of Pennsylvania Press, 1978.

Howe, Henry. *The Diary of a Circuit Rider*. Ed. Jessie Howe Nebelthau. Minneapolis: Voyageur, 1933.

Hoyt, J. G. "Educated Labor." *North American Review* 89, no. 185 (October 1859): 358–83.

Hughes, Judith M. *Reshaping the Psychoanalytic Domain: The Work of Melanie Klein, W. R. D. Fairbairn, and D. W. Winnicott*. Berkeley: Univ. of California Press, 1989.

Hughes, Richard T., and C. Leonard Allen. *Illusions of Innocence: Protestant Primitivism in America, 1630–1875*. Chicago: Univ. of Chicago Press, 1988.

Humboldt, Alexander von. *Personal Narrative of Travels to the Equinoctial*

*Regions of America, During the Years 1799–1804.* Vol. I. Trans. Thomasina Ross. London: Henry G. Bohn, 1852.

Huxley, Aldous. "Wordsworth in the Tropics." In *Do What You Will,* Collected Edition, 113–29. London: Chatto and Windus, 1949.

Hyde, Lewis. *The Gift: Imagination and the Erotic Life of Property.* New York: Vintage, 1983.

Ignatiev, Noel. *How the Irish Became White.* New York: Routledge, 1995.

Jones, Burr. "Reminiscences of Nine Decades." *Wisconsin Magazine of History* 20, no. 2 (December 1936): 143–64.

Jones, James W. *Contemporary Psychoanalysis and Religion: Transference and Transcendence.* New Haven: Yale Univ. Press, 1991.

Jonte-Pace, Diane. "Object Relations Theory, Mothering, and Religion: Towards a Feminist Psychology of Religion." *Horizons* 14, no. 2 (Fall 1987): 310–27.

Kaplan, Rachel, and Steven Kaplan. *The Experience of Nature: A Psychological Perspective.* Cambridge: Cambridge Univ. Press, 1989.

Keeney, Elizabeth B. *The Botanizers: Amateur Scientists in Nineteenth-Century America.* Chapel Hill: Univ. of North Carolina Press, 1992.

Kegan, Robert. *The Evolving Self: Problem and Process in Human Development.* Cambridge: Harvard Univ. Press, 1978.

Kett, Joseph F. *Rites of Passage: Adolescence in America, 1790 to the Present.* New York: Basic Books, 1977.

Kirchhoff, Frederick. *William Morris: The Construction of a Male Self, 1856–1872.* Athens: Ohio Univ. Press, 1990.

Knopf, Richard. "Human Behavior, Cognition, and Affect in the Natural Environment." In *Handbook of Environmental Psychology,* ed. Daniel Stokols and Irwin Altman, I: 783–826. New York: Wiley, 1987.

Kolodny, Annette. *The Lay of the Land: Metaphor as Experience and History in American Life and Letters.* Chapel Hill: Univ. of North Carolina Press, 1975.

Lamartine, A[lphonse] de. *The Stone-Mason of Saint Point: A Village Tale.* Translated from the French. New York: Harper and Brothers, 1851.

Lathrop, John. *Inauguration of Hon. John H. Lathrop, LL.D., Chancellor of the University of Wisconsin, at the Capitol, Madison, January 16, 1850.* Milwaukee: Sentinel and Gazette, 1850.

Lears, T. J. Jackson. *No Place of Grace: Antimodernism and the Transformation of American Culture, 1880–1920.* New York: Pantheon, 1981.

Lebeaux, Richard. *Young Man Thoreau.* Amherst: Univ. of Massachusetts Press, 1977.

LeConte, Joseph. *A Journal of Ramblings through the High Sierra of California by the University Excursion Party.* San Francisco: Sierra Club, 1930.

Levinson, Daniel J., et al. *The Seasons of a Man's Life.* New York: Ballantine, 1978.

Limbaugh, Ronald H. *John Muir's "Stickeen" and the Lessons of Nature.* Fairbanks: Univ. of Alaska Press, 1996.

Lorde, Audre. "Uses of the Erotic: The Erotic as Power." In *Sister Outsider: Essays and Speeches,* 53–59. Freedom, Calif.: Crossing Press, 1984.

Lowenthal, David. "Past Time, Present Place: Landscape and Memory." *Geographical Review* 65, no. 1 (January 1975): 1–36.

Lystra, Karen. *Searching the Heart: Women, Men and Romantic Love in Nineteenth-Century America.* New York: Oxford Univ. Press, 1989.

Manlove, Colin. "Scottish Fantasy." *Extrapolation* 35, no. 1 (1994): 15–32.

Mann, Newton M. "Attraction" and "Repulsion." *The Radical* (Boston) 2, nos. 8 and 9 (April and May 1867): 468–74, 537–42.

Marcus, Clare Cooper. *House as a Mirror of Self: Exploring the Deeper Meaning of Home.* Berkeley, Calif.: Conari, 1995.

McAleer, John J. *Ralph Waldo Emerson: Days of Encounter.* Boston: Little, Brown, 1984.

McDannell, Colleen. *The Christian Home in Victorian America, 1840–1900.* Bloomington: Indiana Univ. Press, 1986.

McDargh, John. *Psychoanalytic Object Relations Theory and the Study of Religion: On Faith and the Imaging of God.* Lanham, Md.: University Press of America, 1983.

Meissner, W. W., S.J. *Psychoanalysis and Religious Experience.* New Haven: Yale Univ. Press, 1984.

Mighetto, Lisa, ed. *Muir among the Animals: The Wildlife Writings of John Muir.* San Francisco: Sierra Club Books, 1986.

Milner, Marion. "D. W. Winnicott and the Two-Way Journey." In *Between Fantasy and Reality: Transitional Objects and Phenomena,* ed. Simon A. Grolnick and Leonard Barkin, 37–42. New York: Jason Aronson, 1978.

Milner, Marion. *The Hands of the Living God: An Account of a Psycho-analytic Treatment.* London: Hogarth, 1969.

Milton, John. *Paradise Lost and Paradise Regained.* Ed. Christopher Ricks. New York: Signet, 1968.

Mitchell, Stephen A. *Relational Concepts in Psychoanalysis: An Integration.* Cambridge: Harvard Univ. Press, 1988.

Morton, Nelle. *The Journey Is Home.* Boston: Beacon, 1985.

Nabhan, Gary Paul, and Stephen Trimble. *The Geography of Childhood: Why Children Need Wild Places.* Boston: Beacon, 1994.

Nash, Roderick. *Wilderness and the American Mind.* 3d ed. New Haven: Yale Univ. Press, 1982.

Norwood, Vera. *Made from This Earth: American Women and Nature.* Chapel Hill: Univ. of North Carolina Press, 1993.

Oelschlaeger, Max. *The Idea of Wilderness.* New Haven: Yale Univ. Press, 1991.

O'Grady, John P. *Pilgrims to the Wild: Everett Ruess, Henry David Thoreau, John Muir, Clarence King, Mary Austin.* Salt Lake City: Univ. of Utah Press, 1993.

Olmsted, Frederick Law. "The Yosemite Valley and the Mariposa Big Trees: A Preliminary Report." With an introductory note by Laura Wood Roper. *Landscape Architecture* 43 (October 1952): 12–25.

Orsi, Robert A. "Forum: The Decade Ahead in Scholarship." *Religion and American Culture* 3, no. 1 (Winter 1993): 1–8.

Orsi, Robert A. *The Madonna of 115th Street: Faith and Community in Italian Harlem, 1880–1950.* New Haven: Yale Univ. Press, 1985.

Park, Mungo. *Travels in the Interior of Africa.* Edinburgh: Adam and Charles Black, 1860.

Parks, Sharon. *The Critical Years: The Young Adult Search for a Faith to Live By.* San Francisco: Harper and Row, 1986.

Piaget, Jean. *Six Psychological Studies.* Ed. David Elkind. Trans. Anita Tenzer. New York: Random House, 1967.

Phillips, Adam. *Winnicott.* Cambridge: Harvard Univ. Press, 1988.

Proshansky, Harold M., and Abbe K. Fabian. "The Development of Place Identity in the Child." In *Spaces for Children: The Built Environment and Child Development,* ed. Carol Simon Weinstein and Thomas G. David, 21–40. New York: Plenum, 1987.

Pyre, J. F. A. *Wisconsin.* American College and University Series. New York: Oxford Univ. Press, 1920.

Reed, Sampson. *Observations on the Growth of the Mind.* Boston: Crosby, Nichols, 1859.

Reid, Harvey. "Diary." *Wisconsin Magazine of History* 1, no. 1 (September 1917): 35–63.

Reid, Harvey. Letter to the editor. *Outlook* (date unknown). Reprinted in *John Muir Newsletter* 4, no. 3 (Summer 1994): 3.

Reser, J. P. "Whither Environmental Psychology? The Transpersonal Ecopsychology Crossroads." *Journal of Environmental Psychology* 15 (1995): 235–57.

Rizzuto, Ana-Maria. *The Birth of the Living God: A Psychoanalytic Study.* Chicago: Univ. of Chicago Press, 1979.

Roberts, Patricia. "Reading the Writing on Nature's Wall." *Reader* (1987): 31–44.

Roszak, Theodore. *The Voice of the Earth: An Exploration of Ecopsychology.* New York: Touchstone, 1993.

Saunders, L. J. *Scottish Democracy, 1815–1840.* Edinburgh: Oliver and Boyd, 1950.

Schofield, Edmund A. "John Muir's Yankee Friends and Mentors: The New England Connection." In "John Muir: Life and Legacy," special issue of *Pacific Historian* 29 (Summer/Fall 1985): 65–89.

Scott, Sir Walter. *The Bride of Lammermoor.* London: Thomas Nelson and Sons, 1905.

Searles, Harold F. *The Nonhuman Environment in Normal Development and in Schizophrenia.* New York: International Universities Press, 1960.

Sebba, Rachel. "The Landscapes of Childhood: The Reflection of Childhood's Environment in Adult Memories and in Children's Memories." *Environment and Behavior* 23, no. 4 (July 1991): 395–422.

Shepperson, Wilbur S. *Emigration and Disenchantment: Portraits of Englishmen Repatriated from the United States.* Norman: Univ. of Oklahoma Press, 1965.

Slotkin, Richard. *Regeneration through Violence: The Mythology of the American Frontier, 1600–1860.* Middletown, Conn.: Wesleyan Univ. Press, 1973.

Smith, Dale C. "Rise and Fall of Typhomalarial Fever: I. Origins." *Journal of the History of Medicine and Allied Sciences* 37, no. 2 (April 1982): 182–200.

Smith, Michael L. *Pacific Visions: California Scientists and the Environment, 1850–1915.* New Haven: Yale Univ. Press, 1987.

Sollors, Werner. *Beyond Ethnicity: Consent and Descent in American Culture.* New York: Oxford Univ. Press, 1986.

Stanley, Millie. *The Heart of John Muir's World: Wisconsin, Family, and Wilderness Discovery.* Madison, Wis.: Prairie Oak, 1995.

Stokols, Daniel, and Irwin Altman. *Handbook of Environmental Psychology.* New York: Wiley, 1987.

Stoll, Mark. "God and John Muir: A Psychological Interpretation of John Muir's Journey from the Campbellites to the 'Range of Light.'" In *John Muir: Life and Work,* ed. Sally M. Miller, 64–81. Albuquerque: Univ. of New Mexico Press, 1993.

Sutherland, Daniel E. *The Expansion of Everyday Life, 1860–1876.* New York: Harper and Row, 1989.

Sutherland, J. D. *Fairbairn's Journey into the Interior.* London: Free Association Books, 1989.

Swidler, Ann. "Culture in Action: Symbols and Strategies." *American Sociological Review* 51 (April 1986): 273–86.

Tallmadge, John. "John Muir and the Poetics of Natural Conversion." *North Dakota Quarterly* 59, no. 2 (Spring 1991): 62–79.

Thoreau, Henry David. *Walden; and, Resistance to Civil Government.* Ed. William Rossi. 2d ed. New York: Norton, 1982.

Thoreau, Henry David. "Walking." In *Great Short Works of Henry David Thoreau,* ed. Wendell Glick, 294–326. New York: Harper and Row, 1982.

Trevor-Roper, Hugh. "The Invention of Tradition: The Highland Tradition in Scotland." In *The Invention of Tradition,* ed. Eric Hobsbawm and Terence Ranger. Cambridge: Cambridge Univ. Press, 1984.

Tuan, Yi-fu. *Topophilia: A Study of Environmental Perception, Attitudes, and Values.* New York: Columbia Univ. Press, 1990.

Turner, Frederick. *Rediscovering America: John Muir in His Time and Ours.* San Francisco: Sierra Club Books, 1985.

Tyson, Phyllis, and Robert L. Tyson. *Psychoanalytic Theories of Development: An Integration.* New Haven: Yale Univ. Press, 1990.

Volkan, Vamik D., and James G. Kavanaugh. "The Cat People." In *Between Fantasy and Reality: Transitional Objects and Phenomena,* ed. Simon A. Grolnick and Leonard Barkin, 289–304. New York: Jason Aronson, 1978.

Walls, Laura Dassow. *Seeing New Worlds: Henry David Thoreau and Nineteenth-Century Natural Science.* Madison: Univ. of Wisconsin Press, 1995.

Wapner, Seymour, Saul B. Cohen, and Bernard Kaplan, eds. *Experiencing the Environment.* New York: Plenum, 1976.

West, Elliott. *Growing Up with the Country: Childhood on the Far Western Frontier.* Albuquerque: Univ. of New Mexico Press, 1989.

Whitman, Walt. *Leaves of Grass.* [Death-Bed edition]. New York: New American Library, 1980.

Wilkins, Thurman. *John Muir: Apostle of Nature.* Oklahoma Western Biographies, vol. 8. Norman: Univ. of Oklahoma Press, 1995.

Williams, Dennis. "John Muir, Christian Mysticism, and the Spiritual Value of Nature." In *John Muir: Life and Work,* ed. Sally M. Miller, 82–99. Albuquerque: Univ. of New Mexico Press, 1993.

Williams, Terry Tempest. "Yellowstone: The Erotics of Place." In *An Unspoken Hunger: Stories from the Field.* New York: Vintage, 1994.

Winnicott, D. W. *Home Is Where We Start From: Essays by a Psychoanalyst.* New York: Norton, 1986.

Winnicott, D. W. *The Maturational Process and the Facilitating Environment.* London: Karnac, 1990. Originally published in 1965.

Winnicott, D. W. *Playing and Reality.* London: Routledge, 1971.

Wolfe, Linnie Marsh. *Son of the Wilderness: The Life of John Muir.* Madison: Univ. of Wisconsin Press, 1978. Originally published in 1945.

Wolfe, Maxine. "Childhood and Privacy." In *Children and the Environment,* ed. Irving Altman and Joachim F. Wohlwill, 175–222. New York: Plenum, 1978.

Wood, Alphonso. *Class-Book of Botany: Being Outlines of the Structure, Physiology, and Classification of Plants; with A Flora of the United States and Canada.* New York: A. S. Barnes and Burr, 1860.

Woodward, Joseph Janvier. *Outlines of the Chief Camp Diseases of the United States Army.* New York: Hafner, 1964. Originally published in 1863.

Wordsworth, William. *Selected Poems and Prefaces.* Ed. Jack Stillinger. Boston: Houghton Mifflin, 1956. [Quotations from *The Prelude* are from the final (1850) version.]

Worster, Donald. "John Muir and the Roots of American Environmentalism." In *The Wealth of Nature: Environmental History and the Ecological Imagination,* 184–202. New York: Oxford Univ. Press, 1993.

Yelverton, Thérèse. *Zanita: A Tale of the Yo-Semite.* Berkeley: Ten Speed, 1991. Originally published in 1872.

# Source Acknowledgments

The State Historical Society of Wisconsin, Madison, Wisconsin, for letters of JM to the Pelton family, 1861, 1862; to Fannie Pelton, 1861; to Frances Pelton, 1861, Mar. 27, 1862, and Sept. 28, 1862; to Emily Pelton, Mar. 1, 1864, May 23, 1865, and Nov. 12, 1865; and to Mrs. James D. Butler, Aug. 1869.

Portions of this book have appeared in slightly different form in "John Muir, Jeanne Carr, and Ralph Waldo Emerson: A Case-Study of the Varieties of Transcendentalist Influence," *Journal of Unitarian Universalist History* 25 (1998): 1–25, © 1998 by The Unitarian Universalist Historical Society and reprinted by permission.

The extract on p. 235 from Rainer Maria Rilke's *Sonnets to Orpheus*, II:14, is from *The Selected Poetry of Rainer Maria Rilke* by Rainer Maria Rilke, edited & translated by Stephen Mitchell. Copyright © 1982 by Stephen Mitchell. Reprinted by permission of Random House, Inc.

# Index